RAEBURN

Sponsored by Elf Exploration UK PLC
in association with Elf Aquitaine

DUNCAN THOMSON
With contributions from John Dick, David Mackie
and Nicholas Phillipson

RAEBURN

The Art of Sir Henry Raeburn
1756–1823

Scottish National Portrait Gallery

Edinburgh · 1997

Published by the Trustees of the National Galleries of Scotland
for the exhibition organised by the Scottish National Portrait Gallery
at the Royal Scottish Academy, Edinburgh, 1 August – 5 October 1997, and
the National Portrait Gallery, London, 24 October 1997 – 1 February 1998
© The Trustees of the National Galleries of Scotland 1997
Documentation section © David Mackie 1997

Paperback ISBN 0903598 69 8   *Hardback* ISBN 0903598 76 0

Typeset in Monotype Bell, based on the types cut by Richard Austin in 1788
Designed by Dalrymple · Printed and bound by BAS Printers Ltd

Contents

6   Preface

7   Foreword and Acknowledgements

9   Sponsor's Foreword

11   Sir Henry Raeburn:
An Introduction to his Art and Life
DUNCAN THOMSON

29   Manners, Morals and Characters:
Henry Raeburn and the Scottish Enlightenment
NICHOLAS PHILLIPSON

39   Raeburn's Methods and Materials
JOHN DICK

47   CATALOGUE
DUNCAN THOMSON

201   Documentation
DAVID MACKIE

214   Frequently Cited Sources

215   Index of Sitters

216   Index of Lenders

Preface

THE LAST MAJOR EXHIBITION of the work of Sir Henry Raeburn was shown at the National Gallery of Scotland over forty years ago, in 1956. Although Raeburn's reputation has fluctuated since his death there has always been a deep undertow of interest in his work, and in recent years the feeling has grown ever stronger that his contribution to the art of painting should be looked at afresh. Such has his popularity become in recent years – and this is only partly due to the great affection in which his most famous painting, '*The Skating Minister*', has come to be held – that faces have always lit up when the prospect of an exhibition has been mentioned. And now that hope has been fulfilled.

The National Galleries of Scotland have been fortunate that, in Duncan Thomson, Keeper of the Scottish National Portrait Gallery since 1982, they have had someone who has taken a dedicated interest in Raeburn over many years, and it is he, with the help of his colleagues, who has brought together the wonderful works in this exhibition and written the major part of the accompanying publication. When he retires later this year, the exhibition will be seen as a fitting culmination of his thirty years of service with the National Galleries.

As was the case with the exhibition of work by Raeburn's great predecessor, Allan Ramsay, which we organised in 1992, the present exhibition will also be seen at the National Portrait Gallery in London. I am delighted that we have been able to continue this kind of cooperation and I am particularly grateful to Charles Saumarez Smith, Director of the National Portrait Gallery, and his colleagues in London for their great interest in the project.

Needless to say, exhibitions of this sort, which draw works from collections worldwide, cost a great deal to mount, and we are all particularly grateful to our sponsors, Elf Exploration UK PLC in association with Elf Aquitaine, who have helped to bring this exhibition to fruition.

TIMOTHY CLIFFORD
Director, National Galleries of Scotland

Foreword and Acknowledgements

ALTHOUGH SIR HENRY RAEBURN, 'Portrait Painter in Edinburgh', as he described himself as early as 1784, will always be associated with a particular society at a particular time – Scotland in the later years of the Enlightenment – his art transcends that limitation and still excites through the sheer freshness of its response to the endless variety of the visible world. The light that he cast on his own place and time elicits a recognition that knows no barriers and has a continuing validity.

Yet, interest in Raeburn has fluctuated in a puzzling way. Contemporaries, like Sir Thomas Lawrence, were clearly aware of his originality and, sometimes in spite of that originality, he fulfilled the needs of the society of which he was part. But he was also over-productive, partly as a result of his success, and was, even in his own lifetime, accused of carelessness. There is little doubt that the sheer size of his output and the quite large proportion of rather pedestrian portraits that he produced damaged his reputation in the second half of the nineteenth century. Thereafter, however, as part of the vogue for British painting – and British sentiment – fostered by dealers like Joseph Duveen, his reputation soared, and many of his greatest paintings (as well as others not quite of the top rank) were exported to the United States, at staggering prices.

However, as the twentieth century proceeded his reputation to some extent declined once more and there has been the spectacle of American museums de-accessioning his paintings. This has been in part a reaction to the enthusiasm for the kind of sentiment that once seemed the primary meaning of his work. A decline in the tradition of portraiture itself also played a part. That phase has now passed and the time is ripe to reassess Raeburn's work, not only his abstract virtues that are perhaps easier to recognise in the light of the painting of our own century, but also his ability to excite the imagination in the same way as the greatest perceptual painters. For this reason the commentaries on the portraits included in this catalogue place a special emphasis on a consideration of how they were made – how the processes of observing and finding painterly equivalents for what was seen cohered in images that seem to have an inevitable truth.

A number of art historians have published persuasive accounts of Raeburn in recent years and I would particularly like to mention David and Francina Irwin and Duncan Macmillan. The Irwins, in their important book, *Scottish Painters at Home and Abroad 1700-1900*, gave Raeburn the extensive and detailed consideration he had long deserved and, although my account of the painter's early years differs in a number of respects, their discussion of his work is an important landmark. Duncan Macmillan has written on Raeburn with deep understanding in a number of places and has introduced the idea of a relationship between Raeburn's painting and the theories of perception of the Scottish philosophers of his time. That I have not felt able to continue discussion of the theme in the present publication does not mean that I am not conscious of the value of this insight.

I must also, of course, mention my fellow contributors, who have worked with me on the exhibition and who have contributed so much to its realisation. John Dick, Keeper of Conservation in the National Galleries of Scotland, has shared my passion for Raeburn over a great many years and his expertise has helped so much in my understanding of the many pictures we have looked at together – in public galleries, in his studio (often in front of serried rows of x-radiographs) and in private collections – sometimes perched precariously at the top of ladders! His help, which has ranged far beyond technical matters, has been invaluable.

I am also grateful to David Mackie whose extensive work on Raeburn culminated three years ago in a thesis which contains a massive catalogue of around a thousand paintings. This has been a useful point of reference during my own work. Besides the records of provenance, exhibitions and literature which accompany the catalogue entries in the present publication, Dr Mackie has compiled the invaluable documentation section which has brought together material and sources for all of the known fixed points in Raeburn's life and career. Finally, it has also been an immense pleasure working with Nicholas Phillipson, who has brought a vivid historical imagination and understanding to bear on Raeburn's Scotland.

A seemingly endless number of practical problems have had to be solved and I could not have been given greater support. I am greatly indebted to Janis Adams, our publications officer, not only for the care she has taken in producing a worthy publication but for the very real interest she has taken in the subject. Susanna Kerr has admirably looked after the greater part of the administration of the exhibition, as well as a whole host of details, scholarly as well as practical. Estelle Barr has worked from my often almost illegible, old-fashioned, manuscripts to produce immaculate typescripts that have amazed me by their accuracy. I am also grateful to Janice Slater for dealing calmly with the complexities of transport matters. Generally, from within the National Galleries of Scotland, I have received help from virtually every quarter and I have been deeply touched by this. I would also like to thank Edward Longbottom for his subtle design of the exhibition, and my former colleague, Robert Dalrymple, for his thoughtful and elegant design of this publication.

I have also been helped in a great variety of ways by a host of people, many of them, I believe, because they felt they were furthering the cause of Raeburn. Their assistance has been profoundly appreciated. Space allows me only to list their names here – and I apologise if I have inadvertently omitted anyone: Lady Airlie; David Alexander; Jean Archibald; William Baillie; Malcolm Baker; Iain Gordon Brown; Moira Brown; Sir John and Lady Clerk of Penicuik; Edna Craig; Aleck Crichton; Lucy Dixon; Sir Philip Dowson; Lavinia Gibbs; Gillian Grant; Jonathan Grant; Ketevan Grant; Martyn Gregory; Christopher Hartley; Leslie Hodgson; Lord Hope of Craighead; Andrew Kerr; Jane Kidd; Richard Kingzett; Bruce Laidlaw; Alastair Laing; David Moore-Gwyn; Andrew McLean; A. V. B. Norman; Geoffrey Parton; Andrew Potter; Jeffrey Regazzoni; Alan Russell; Andrew Shepherd; Jacob Simon; Allen Simpson; Joanna Soden; Kathleen Soriano; Dianne Stein; MaryAnne Stevens; John Watts; Philip Winterbottom; Stephen Wood.

Lastly, but not least, I must mention those without whose help an exhibition of this sort would simply not have been possible – the lenders. Their generosity has been immense and I am deeply conscious of my debt to them. It gives me the greatest pleasure to be able to thank them here, both those who are named in the catalogue and those who have preferred to remain anonymous.

DUNCAN THOMSON
Keeper, Scottish National Portrait Gallery

Sponsor's Foreword

SIR HENRY RAEBURN has long been recognised as one of Scotland's finest painters and a major exhibition of his work is indeed overdue. His work has always been particularly popular in the United States and a number of portraits have been borrowed from collections in that country. Others have been chosen from collections in Australia, Europe and Great Britain, including some that have never been shown in public before.

The exhibition will open at the Royal Scottish Academy, Edinburgh, and will run throughout the period of the Edinburgh International Festival. It will then be shown at the National Portrait Gallery in London. It is bound to be one of the finest exhibitions in the United Kingdom during 1997–98.

We are grateful to Dr Duncan Thomson, Keeper of the Scottish National Portrait Gallery and curator of the exhibition, for his enthusiasm, his meticulous research and his energetic quest to secure the finest examples of Raeburn's work. The exhibition is the culmination of much behind the scenes work and we are also grateful to all those involved. For some visitors this will be their first introduction to Raeburn's work and we have no doubt that they, and all who see the exhibition, will give it a warm reception.

Elf was delighted to be given the chance to play a part in this exhibition and welcomed the sponsorship opportunity. As a significant oil and gas operator in the United Kingdom, Elf takes its role in the communities within which it operates very seriously. Support is given to a wide spectrum of organisations including health and welfare, the environment, education and of course the arts.

Over the last few years Elf has established itself as a major sponsor of the arts in the United Kingdom. In 1992 this included its successful patronage of a new production of Mozart's *Don Giovanni* at the Royal Opera House, Covent Garden, London, and also in that same year the first retrospective exhibition of the work of Alfred Sisley at London's Royal Academy of Arts.

In 1994, Elf supported the National Gallery of Scotland's *Monet to Matisse* exhibition, which brought together a collection of the works of landscape painters active in France during the first forty years of the modern movement (1874–1914). This exhibition took a fresh look at Impressionism, Fauvism, Cubism and Symbolism and was hosted exclusively at the National Gallery of Scotland in Edinburgh, attracting thousands of visitors from all over Europe.

In 1995, Elf continued its patronage of the arts by supporting a new exhibition of drawings from the Prat Collection. After exhibiting at the Louvre in Paris, these one hundred exceptional French drawings from the last three centuries were exhibited at the National Gallery of Scotland in Edinburgh and then at the Ashmolean Museum in Oxford.

The Raeburn exhibition is a milestone in the presentation of the artist's work. It aims to provoke and generate discussion of the artist himself and also his subjects. We hope this exhibition will attract many thousands of visitors in both Edinburgh and London who will be enlightened, inspired and charmed by such wonderful paintings.

PIERRE GODEC
Managing Director, Elf Exploration UK PLC

Sir Henry Raeburn:
An Introduction to his Art and Life

DUNCAN THOMSON

ON 12 May 1810 the young Scottish painter, David Wilkie, who had settled in London five years previously, recorded in his diary: 'Had a call from Raeburn (the painter), who told me he had come to London to look out for a house, and to see if there was any prospect of establishing himself.'[1] Raeburn, who by this time was well established as the leading portrait painter in Scotland, was reacting from what he believed was economic necessity, having experienced such severe financial difficulties two years previously that he envisaged the remainder of his career as one of unremitting effort in order to pay his creditors and to maintain the standard of living he had already achieved. He may also have sensed that his work readily merited the awards that were available to painters whom he considered in no way his superior.

In the event he decided against taking the road which had brought so many of his predecessors, like Allan Ramsay and David Martin, as well as his contemporaries, like Wilkie, to London. By taking that decision he preserved an important moment in Scottish history intact, for so much of our understanding of the society and life of Scotland from the 1780s to the early 1820s is illuminated by his unique vision. In a sense, if he had gone, part of our past would have been lost. For he made not simply a record of the times in which he moved, but because of his gifts of observation and image-making, he was able to give a society which was burgeoning with intellectual and artistic creativity, as well as reaping, at last, the economic benefits of the Union of 1707, a rare substance and credibility. The freshness and honesty of his response, the unique visual acuity he possessed and his imaginative ability to translate what he saw, and sensed, into something that remains always new and vivid, have become an integral part of the history of that time. This part of Scotland's past, the latest years of its Enlightenment, would not have looked the same, indeed, would not have been the same, had he gone south. His return to Edinburgh enabled his country, somehow, to fulfil itself.

Henry Raeburn was born on 4 March 1756, the younger son of Robert Raeburn, a yarn-boiler, and his wife, Anne Elder. Their dwelling house and the buildings in which Robert Raeburn carried on his business were situated on the east bank of the Water of Leith where it ran north through the village of Stockbridge. The village in which the future painter would grow up was situated a little more than half a mile north by north-west of Edinburgh Castle, poised on the crag that marked the western limit of the increasingly congested Old Town of Edinburgh. Beneath the Castle, in the open fields to the west, was the presbyterian church of St Cuthbert's (or West Kirk) where Henry Raeburn was baptised a few days after his birth.

As the century progressed the fields that separated Stockbridge from Edinburgh began to fill up with the regularly laid out terraces, squares and circuses of the classical New Town. These developments, intended to relieve the over-crowding of the Old Town, were initiated with a plan of 1766 drawn up by the architect James Craig. In due course the rectilinear first phase of the New Town was built in the fields that rose to the north of the valley beneath the Castle walls – Princes Street facing the Castle, George Street on the central spine and Queen Street to the north, looking towards the distant River Forth. This area, which would be central to Raeburn's professional life, was completed by the end of the eighteenth century.

It was not until much later that housing appeared on the Moray estate, the high ground above the steep slopes that ran along the eastern side of the Water of Leith, near the Raeburn home. The development of this land was only begun in 1822, the year before the painter's death, so that throughout his childhood he was a mere stone's throw from a place of great natural beauty, rich in trees and their associated undergrowth. There can be little doubt that this kind of natural world lodged itself in the painter's imagination, for the settings of many of his outdoor portraits are rife with foreground growth – a variety of grasses, dock and thistle – and their geometry is often supported by tree trunks, in every state of decay and supple growth, foliage shimmering with light in spring and turning russet and gold in autumn. Such settings were common enough currency in eighteenth-century British portraiture but with Raeburn they often seem less conventional, more experienced, than, for example, in the outdoor portraits of Reynolds, and this may well be due to the virtually rural setting in which the Scottish painter spent his childhood.

The Water of Leith, its ever-present sound varying with the seasons, provided the power for the industries carried on along its banks, including Robert Raeburn's yarn-boiling mill. The waters were controlled within a mill-lade (or lead), which ran more or less parallel to the river, confined in a wooden trough in places, before turning to within a few yards of the Raeburn property and then flowing eastwards to the eponymous Silver Mills and Canon Mills.[2] Robert Raeburn's yarn-boiling business appears to have been reasonably successful but its progress must have been thrown into disarray by the death both of himself and his wife at some time before 1765. On 15 April of that year Henry Raeburn is described as an orphan when he was entered as a pupil in George Heriot's Hospital, a school that had been founded in the seventeenth century from the bequest of George Heriot, the Scottish banker and jeweller of James VI and I, for the education of the sons of indigent burgesses. The school was (and is) situated on the southern edge of the medieval town on a platform of land above the Grassmarket, its main, northern entrance facing towards the Castle. Built between 1628 and the end of the century in a Scots Renaissance style, the four-storey building with a large central courtyard, the 'fantastic four-square prodigy',[3] must have overwhelmed any new entrant (fig.1). It lay rather more than a mile from the Raeburn home, a distance which the schoolboy must have walked by tracks crossing the fields where the New Town was planned to rise, skirting St Cuthbert's where he had been baptised and climbing the 'Vennel' from the west end of the Grassmarket.

fig.1 Heriot's Hospital today

He must at this time have been in the care of his elder brother William, twelve years his senior, who continued to run the family yarn-boiling business – and who would do so until his death in 1810. It is likely that Henry Raeburn's manual skills were noticed during his years at Heriot's Hospital, for, in 1772, at the age of sixteen, he was indentured as apprentice to a jeweller and goldsmith, James Gilliland. The jewellers of Edinburgh were at this time congregated in the luckenbooths (literally, locked-up shops) in Parliament Close, clustered around the medieval church of St Giles which is situated about a quarter of a mile east of the Castle, on the long spine of the Old Town, which leads down to Holyroodhouse. Raeburn may well have moved in with Gilliland's family, for that was the custom. The work of Edinburgh's jewellers was of a very high standard and in the course of the five or six years Raeburn spent with Gilliland he must have developed into a considerable craftsman, even if at some stage he began to contemplate a career as a portrait painter. It is a remarkable feature of the portraits that he would paint throughout a career of virtually forty years that, even in those which are painted in his broadest manner, there are often passages of intricate, carefully crafted detail – buttons (in enormous variety), laces on shoes, buckles, spectacles, books of a specific type, ink-wells, epaulettes, swords, shot-belts – which, miraculously, without any kind of straining for effect, are integrated into their broader context.

Little is known of Raeburn's personal life at this time, just as little is known of his aspirations as a painter and how he fulfilled them. The one major painter with whom he might have made contact was Alexander Runciman who acted as master of the Trustees' Academy from 1772 to 1785. The Academy was initially housed in Raeburn's old school, Heriot's Hospital, and later, when he was with Gilliland, in the decaying, original Old College building, less than a quarter of a mile away. Could someone with Raeburn's propensities have been oblivious to what was going on there? The aims of the Academy were concerned with drawing for industrial design, but it is clear that Runciman allowed the students to veer in a fine art direction. It is known, for example, that antique drawing from plaster casts was practised. In a slightly different context there is more certain evidence of contact between Raeburn and Runciman in these years – a record that, in 1782, Raeburn, the miniature painter Archibald Robertson, the portrait painter George Watson and the genre painter Walter Weir formed a life-drawing evening class in the Theatre Royal with Runciman as some kind of instructor. How long the class lasted is not known, nor what Raeburn got out of it. What the class did not entail, of course, was drawing from the nude figure, a discipline which, if it had been available at the time, would have helped Raeburn to a greater understanding of the articulation of the body beneath the clothes, something that is lacking in a number of his portraits.

The Academy, run by the Board of Trustees for Improving Fisheries and Manufactures, had been founded in 1760 at the instigation of the Select Society of Edinburgh which had itself been founded by Raeburn's great predecessor, Allan Ramsay. It is a tenuous link, if a link at all, between the two artists who were ultimately of different traditions, Raeburn a spontaneous observer of unparalleled responsiveness, Ramsay a premeditated designer. Some kind of contact is usually posited with Ramsay's former pupil David Martin. There is no evidence that Raeburn had any kind of training from Martin, and Allan Cunningham's story about Martin giving the young painter portraits to copy may simply stem from the fact that such portraits clearly exist – the portrait of *Thomas Tod*,[4] for example, or the brilliant *Robert Cunninghame Graham* (fig.2), quintessential Raeburn in most respects, except for the head, which is virtually pure Martin. Such a painting may lie behind Cunningham's story of a quarrel between the two painters over Raeburn passing off one of his copies as his own work.

At some time during 1779 or, more probably, during 1780, the painter married Ann Edgar, a widow of about thirty-five, and thus some eleven years his senior. Daughter of Anne Hay (whose father had been minister at Peebles) and Peter Edgar of Bridgelands, who had been factor to the Earl of Selkirk, she had married a James Leslie in 1772. Little is known of Leslie, but he was clearly a man of considerable means. He died in 1778 – there is an unsubstantiated rumour of suicide – having purchased Deanhaugh House in Stockbridge for his family the previous year. The house was of three storeys and quite substantial, and lay, more or less, opposite the Raeburn home on the other side of the Water of Leith. Raeburn now crossed the river and also crossed a not entirely invisible social barrier. Besides her considerable means, his wife also brought him two step-daughters, Jacobina and Ann. Within the first four years of their marriage Raeburn and Ann Edgar had two sons, Peter born on 18 May 1781 (he was to die at the age of sixteen) and Henry, born on 24 October 1783.

Adjacent to Deanhaugh House was an even grander building, St Bernard's House, which belonged to Raeburn's lawyer, Walter Ross. Ross died in 1789 and Raeburn seems to have moved with his family into St Bernard's a year or two after this, perhaps in 1792, although he did not complete the purchase until 1798.[5] His step-daughter Ann and her husband James Philip Inglis remained as sole occupants of Deanhaugh House, along with their two sons, one of whom, Henry Raeburn Inglis, would be the subject of *'Boy and Rabbit'* (cat.no.57), presented by Raeburn to the Royal Academy in 1816 to mark his election as an Academician the previous year.

St Bernard's was also a three-storeyed building, with two square, castellated projections on the façade, with the entrance between. On each of these projections was a large Gothic window but, curiously, one was only an imitation painted on the stonework. An engraving of the time shows the building in marked contrast to the much humbler buildings on the opposite side of the river, of the type, if not the actual ones, in which Raeburn had spent his childhood (fig.3). Between them, and just a little upstream is the Roman temple, St Bernard's Well, which the painter, and friend of Raeburn, Alexander Nasmyth, had designed in 1788. Raeburn would continue to reside at St Bernard's House for the rest of his life, which was a not inconsiderable distance from his second studio, in York Place. By 1804 the painter owned about ten acres of land around St Bernard's and Deanhaugh, as well as a stretch of land on the other side of the river between St Bernard's Well and his parents' old house and mill. On the land to the west of St Bernard's he planned three streets of elegant housing, and by 1814 the erection of Ann Street, named after his wife, had begun. When complete, with its surprising, long front gardens, it would be of exceptional beauty. The development of the area was continued by his family after his death.

At the beginning of July 1784 Walter Ross, from whose family Raeburn would later acquire St Bernard's House, wrote from London about a number of financial matters to Sir James Hunter Blair, banker and Lord Provost of Edinburgh. Part of his letter began: 'Mr Raeburn the Painter, my neighbour is here and intends setting off for Rome.' He then goes on to discuss credit for the journey, to be provided by Raeburn's

fig.2 *Robert Cunninghame Graham* by Henry Raeburn
Scottish National Portrait Gallery

fig.3 Engraving of Stockbridge showing St Bernard's House, *c.*1794
Edinburgh University Library

brother William.[6] Nothing is known of Raeburn's motives in making this journey but the imperative must have been strong for his second son, Henry, had been born only a few months before the decision was likely to have been made. He was, of course, only following in the footsteps of most of his predecessors of note – Ramsay made the first of four visits to Italy in 1736, Alexander and John Runciman had gone out to Italy in 1767 and Alexander Nasmyth, two years his junior, had travelled there as recently as 1782. Nasmyth did not return until 1785, so that their visits overlapped.

Little is known of Raeburn's activities in Rome, nor indeed of how long he stayed. There is some evidence that he began his return journey in the spring of 1786, perhaps by way of Paris. He presumably made a second stay in London on his way to Edinburgh, with opportunities to view the works of painters like Reynolds, if not to make actual contact with them. His experience, by one means or another, must have widened enormously during his period of absence from Edinburgh but it must be significant that even at the beginning of this episode Ross describes him as 'the Painter'.

Although there are still many unanswered questions about Raeburn's acquisition of the wonderfully original skills that he demonstrated so soon after his return from Rome, it is now possible to trace the outlines of his early career with a good deal of precision. This view involves discarding certain traditions and accepting others. There is also a necessary element of speculation in what is proposed. The first step in what follows is a consideration of the miniature of the *2nd Earl Spencer* (cat.no.4), a relatively recent discovery, which Raeburn copied in Rome in the latter part of 1785 or early in 1786 from a pastel portrait by Hugh Douglas Hamilton. This copy was commissioned on behalf of the sitter by James Byres, the Scottish *cicerone* (or guide), then resident in Rome, a man who probably had a profound influence on Raeburn at the time and whom he ever after admired. What exactly does the style of this miniature, even allowing for its being a copy, say about the painter's development at this particular point in time? Of even greater significance for an understanding of Raeburn's early work, however, has been the emergence of the full-scale portrait of the young nephew of James Byres, *Patrick Moir* (cat.no.3), also painted in Rome at some date during the years 1784 to 1786.

What the miniature of Lord Spencer demonstrates is that, by the time of his sojourn in Rome, Raeburn had acquired, by some means, a fully developed, sophisticated British miniature technique. In this sense it is a world away from the miniature portrait of *David Deuchar* (cat.no.1) for which there is an entirely reasonable tradition that it was painted by Raeburn in 1773, a year after he had begun his apprenticeship with the jeweller, James Gilliland. Though lively, the miniature of Deuchar is a naïve, laboured work when compared to the suave, fluid miniature of Spencer, painted more than ten years later. The implication is that Raeburn, perhaps by the example of works that passed through Gilliland's workshop, had acquired a mainstream miniature technique and practised independently as a miniaturist, at least after 1778 when his apprenticeship to Gilliland officially ended. Byres after all is hardly likely to have offered a commission of this sort to someone who had no reputation for such things. It is, therefore, likely that other miniatures by Raeburn exist, although none are presently recognised with any degree of certainty.

However, one strong candidate has only recently come to light, a portrait said to be of Sir John Clerk of Penicuik (fig.4). Unlike the *Spencer*, which is painted in oil on ivory, this is a watercolour drawing on paper, but in the traditional format of a miniature. The watercolour is washed on to the paper with the greatest delicacy and there are passages of the finest cross-hatching on the side of the nose and in the lower background areas. A number of features seem to connect with Raeburn's known work, not least the sense of breadth that persists within the intricacies of the technique. The sharply outlined dark coat, for example, is given its inner shape by the addition of deft, perfectly pitched, even darker shadows. The upper part of the face is washed with a lilac-grey cast shadow, a feature of a number of Raeburn's mature portraits, and the contours of the hat brim, which has thrown the shadow, have been subtly modified a number of times in a way that speaks clearly of portraits like the *David Hunter of Blackness* (cat.no.8) and the *Revd Robert Walker* (cat.no.19). Equally telling is the careful articulation of a range of tones within the dark shadow at the end of the nose, something that connects with Raeburn's highly original lighting experiments of the early 1790s.

fig.4 *Sir John Clerk of Penicuik*
attributed to Henry Raeburn
Martyn Gregory

Although the miniature, therefore, might be as late as this, it is unlikely to be an isolated example, but is almost certainly part of a continuum that had already begun before Raeburn travelled to Rome.

The life-size portrait of *Patrick Moir*, a work of calm, meditative beauty, has, especially in the flesh areas, a rather tentative, smoothly finished manner, and a degree of awkwardness in the drawing of the figure. Only in certain details, like the crisp frills on the shirt front and the deftly contrived cuffs at the wrists, are there hints of the swift handling, so responsive to appearances, that was to come. Although the portrait could have been painted at any time during the Roman visit, it does not suggest that Raeburn had only turned to full-scale portraits during these two to three years, but rather that he had already started on such a career before setting off for Rome. The visit was presumably to further the aims of such a career and it is highly significant that, in the document he signed in the spring of 1784 giving his wife Ann Edgar authority to manage his affairs during his absence (and to draw on an annuity from the estate of her late father-in-law, George Leslie), he describes himself as 'Portrait Painter in Edinburgh'. The description has obviously been carefully chosen, and, of course, accords with Walter Ross's description shortly afterwards. What he might have accomplished in the field of full-scale portraiture up until his departure is discussed below.

There is very little information on what Raeburn did in Italy although, being intimate with James Byres, he must have had quite wide-ranging contacts and would not have lacked information on what he should see, and help in seeing it. Clearly the whole world of contemporary Roman painting was within immediate reach, as was the Baroque painting of the previous century, the vigour and dramatic lighting of which must have had considerable impact on him. The work of the elderly Pompeo Batoni, for whom Byres would be one of two executors on his death in 1787,[7] was probably somewhere in his mind when he worked on the portrait of Moir, although it is also strangely reminiscent of the American painter, John Singleton Copley's portraits of Henry Pelham (see fig.54), painted in 1765.

Two other paintings by Raeburn survive from this time, tiny copies, one of which is particularly significant. The first, of a *Woman Descending Steps* (fig.5), may be after a Roman wall-painting and has no obvious connection with his later work. The second, a *David with the Head of Goliath* (fig.6), is a quite accurate copy of a painting by Giovanni Francesco Romanelli (1610–1662).[8] The painting by Romanelli contains a plinth and a space-filling tree that seem to be echoed in a number of Raeburn's much later full-lengths, but what must have interested him most was the fall of bright light across the body of the youthful figure of David. The intermingling of almost equal areas of strong illumination and dark shadow, defining shapes in a sometimes quite surprising way, the light also flaming briefly on the drapery around the boy's body, certainly presages Raeburn's interests in the early 1790s, when he devised lighting schemes of great originality. This distinctive interplay of suffused light and deep shadow actually finds its way into a small area of the portrait of Moir, the fingers of his left hand where it is cupped against his forehead. From such modest beginnings would come some of Raeburn's most distinctive work.

The portrait of Moir also makes it abundantly clear that a number of paintings, which in the past have been posited as works done in the years before the journey to Rome, cannot possibly have been painted at that time. These are, primarily, the skating portrait of the *Revd Robert Walker* (cat.no.19), a unique – and now uniquely famous – work, which long bore a traditional date of 1784 but which is likely to be as much as ten years later, the portrait of the geologist *James Hutton* (cat.no.10) and the full-length seated portrait of the Dunfermline merchant, *George Chalmers* (fig.7), which has long been dated 1776, on the simple grounds that such a date is inscribed on the frame. The portrait of Hutton is awkwardly constructed but has a fluidity of handling, especially in the wonderful still-life of books and geological specimens (see p.69), that is well in advance of the portrait of *Moir*. It seems likely, therefore, that it was painted in the year or two following Raeburn's return from Italy. The *Chalmers* is obviously later still: its pattern appears to derive from Reynolds's portrait of *Dr John Ash* of 1788 but its rather dry quality suggests a date of a few years later. It remains something of a mystery why it should for so long have been accepted as Raeburn's earliest full-scale portrait.

LEFT fig.5 *Woman Descending Steps* by Henry Raeburn

RIGHT fig.6 *David with the Head of Goliath* by Henry Raeburn after Romanelli
Locations unknown

fig.7 *George Chalmers* by Henry Raeburn
Dunfermline City Chambers

fig.8
John Clerk by Henry Raeburn
Destroyed

What then did Raeburn paint in the years immediately prior to his journey to Rome (by which time he was twenty-eight) and which would have allowed him to describe himself as 'Portrait Painter in Edinburgh'? Whatever is postulated clearly must bear a stylistically coherent relationship to the one fixed point in these years, the portrait of *Patrick Moir*. Despite the fact that there should probably be a number of paintings from the early 1780s, there are only two candidates, and one of them is a borderline case as far as its relationship to the visit to Rome is concerned. These are the so-called *Lady in a Lace Cap* (cat.no.2), with a traditional attribution to Raeburn that has long been ignored, and the portrait of the young *John Clerk* (later Lord Eldin), which virtually disappeared from view in the 1930s and is now believed to have been destroyed (fig.8). The case for the portrait of the *Lady in a Lace Cap* being Raeburn's earliest work, painted about 1780, is made in the catalogue entry. What has to be emphasised about the nature of that portrait is its concern with questions of how to fashion the surface of a painting. While the face is carefully and meticulously painted, to the point of smoothness, there is a rough, often not entirely resolved, quality about the handling of areas of the costume, especially the darks. Within the whites, especially, there is also what is virtually a decorative handling of the pigment, which is often spun out in a series of waves and ripples. This is something found in a rather subtler form in parts of the flesh areas of the *Patrick Moir*. Two other points of convergence between these two portraits are worth noting. The first is a staccato element in the handling: in the portrait of the woman, a series of repeated blobs forming the shadow on the third finger of her left hand and the repetitious nature of the painting of the brass studs on the back of her chair; while in the portrait of *Moir* there is a similar grouping of red marks on the turned-back edge of his coat lapel. The second point of agreement is a very careful recording of areas of nuanced shadow: in the woman, the small, repeated shadows cast on the side of her face by the folds in her translucent cap, in the *Moir*, the shadows formed within the undulating pages of the printed book over which the sitter pores. By comparison, the problems of direct observation are more subtly tackled in the *Moir*, but with the same underlying vision, so that it is possible to argue that one portrait is a step in the direction of the other.

The problem of fitting the lost portrait of the young John Clerk into this picture of Raeburn's earliest years is compounded by the fact that it has not been seen by any recent writer on Raeburn and is only known from old reproductions. On the evidence available, however, it is clearly of the greatest importance in tracing the trajectory of Raeburn's early development. Like the *Lady in a Lace Cap*, it has long borne an attribution to Raeburn; in addition, it has a Clerk of Penicuik provenance. It is in many ways an awkward, rather raw portrait, although it presages many of Raeburn's later concerns. The face is linear and not greatly modulated by light and shade, unlike the *Moir*, and this would tend to suggest an earlier date – as does the rather boneless structure of the foreshortened left hand when it is compared to the delicate subtlety of Moir's left hand, pressing on his open book. On the other hand, the still-life elements of books, papers, bust and marble-topped table, including the small, carefully observed cast shadows, seem of greater accomplishment than similar features in the *Moir*. And although the Turkey rug on the near table has a clotted, disproportionate feeling, Clerk's satin coat and waistcoat seem to be painted with a plasticity and freedom that is not very far away from the portrait of *Lord Arniston* (cat.no.5), painted during 1787, shortly after the return from Rome. If the portrait of Clerk is post-Rome, it would, nevertheless, because of the degree of naïvety that it demonstrates, have to predate the *Arniston* by a few months, and this is quite possible. However, its very naïvety, including its flatness and rather ungainly construction, relate it more readily to the *Lady in a Lace Cap*, although it is a more ambitious painting. Further, Clerk's apparent youthfulness (he was born in 1757) suggests a date of about 1783. This, then, would make the portrait one of those which entitled Raeburn to describe himself as a portrait painter before he set off for Rome and the foundation on which he would build his rapidly expanding reputation immediately after his return.

The portraits painted in the years immediately after his return from Rome, when he set up his studio in a building on the south side of George Street, are marked both by a plasticity that is lively and direct and by an uncertainty in matters of composition and balance. The *Lord Arniston* of 1787, which is certainly one of the earliest paintings of this third phase in his career (if pre-Rome and Rome are taken as separate stages), has not only delicious harmonies of colour and a richness of tone which are confidently contrived but also a certain stiffness in its attempts to translate the Baroque into a local language. Nevertheless, its firm assurance and its credibility must have deflected attention from its degree of awkwardness and a grandeur not entirely attained, for the floodgates which led to Raeburn's dominance seem to have opened almost immediately.

A similar kind of uncertainty of purpose marks what may be the earliest of Raeburn's full-length portraits, that of *Margaret Hepburn, Mrs Downey* (fig.9), which is likely to have been painted about the same time as the *Arniston*, perhaps even earlier. Its rather bland pastoral poetry has a distinct English feeling, derived, perhaps, from some source that lacked, though it imitated, the magic of Gainsborough. Despite its apparent gentleness of subject, the surface of the painting has a restless, over wrought quality which gives equal weight to every area of the canvas. The brushstrokes both fail to summarise form and never quite become an adequate equivalent of what is depicted, so that, for example, the lower areas of the dress are never more than obsessionally worked paint, and the birch trees and foliage, traced in virtually the same way, become a more or less independent fragment of landscape. The portrait does, of course, contain felicities that look forward to the assured work of his prime, like the sheer panache of the brim of the hat and the soft shadow that envelops the upper part of the sitter's face, the latter a motif that fascinated Raeburn and which he explored in a number of paintings, some as late as the end of the first decade of the nineteenth century.

This slight uncertainty is also found in the hunting portrait of *Robert Ferguson* (cat.no.11), which again echoes English pastoral portraiture, but the landscape setting is in this instance distinctly topographical and gains in credibility as a result.

fig.9 *Mrs Downey* by Henry Raeburn
Tate Gallery, London

This, of course, would not be the ultimate direction Raeburn would take as far as outdoor settings were concerned. Although there is quite often a topographical reference, they tended more and more towards a vaguely allusive abstraction, in accordance with his belief as recorded, paradoxically, by a topographical draughtsman, John Morrison: 'Landscape in the background of a portrait ought to be nothing more than the shadow of a landscape: effect is all that is wanted'.[9] The portrait of *Ferguson* is also far more felicitous in its handling than the *Mrs Downey*. Certain areas such as the pointer, the young man's boots and the earth around them are swept by a fresh wind of pure observation, the lesson that, according to Cunningham, James Byres (whose understanding of the art of painting Raeburn held in high regard) had taught the artist in Rome – 'never to copy any object from memory, but, from the principal figure to the minutest accessory, to have it placed before him'.[10] This principle, whatever the precise accuracy of Cunningham's report, is of the profoundest significance in the understanding of Raeburn's originality. Whatever kind of contrivance, abstraction or sentiment may imbue any particular painting – and he could not step completely outside his own time and the conditions that prevailed – the essential truth of each is the transformation of what his eye has observed and his consciousness filtered, into assemblies of tone, colour and shape that have an essential relevance to the world of objects.

LEFT fig.10 *Sir William Forbes of Craigievar*
by Henry Raeburn
Craigievar Castle, National Trust for Scotland

CENTRE fig.11 *Lady Forbes*
by Henry Raeburn
Craigievar Castle, National Trust for Scotland

RIGHT fig.12 *John Smith of Craigend*
by Henry Raeburn
National Gallery of Scotland

The portrait of *Ferguson* is also characterised by an increase in the expressive plasticity of paint and this is found in a number of portraits on either side of the year 1790. They include the *Sir William Forbes of Craigievar* (fig.10) and the companion portrait of *Lady Forbes* (fig.11) which are documented as having been painted in 1788,[11] the *Lieut-Colonel Lyon* (cat.no.6) which has a palpable creaminess, the portrait of *John Smith of Craigend* (fig.12) and the *James Hutton* (cat.no.10) where the flow of loaded pigment is a feature of the hands and the 'still-life' of books and geological specimens. The high-keyed, painterly quality of these portraits may contain a memory of the work of Batoni which Raeburn must have been struck by in Rome, and there may also be echoes of the work of Reynolds, but they have a fresh, exploratory quality which comes from a kind of innocence of seeing: there is, it seems, no worry in the painter's mind about making quite radical changes as the portrait grows empirically – there appears to have been little in the way of pre-planning of the composition, no under-drawing other than quite cursory, brush-drawn indications of placing – and there is a good deal of 'wet-in-wet' technique used, which is done with an assurance that avoided the dangers of muddy colour and formlessness. This method also involved a good deal of 'scoring', the drawing of shapes or outlines into undried paint with a sharp object, probably the handle end of the brush. As in Smith of Craigend's cravat, this scoring of contours could work simply by the ridge of displaced paint casting a shadow, by revealing a different colour or tone at the bottom of the trench, or by the later infilling of the trench with a different pigment when the paint had dried. It is a method employed at its subtlest in the scores in the ice in the foreground of '*The Skating Minister*' (cat.no.19).

The freshness and vibrancy of these portraits, and Raeburn's evident sympathy for the individuals portrayed, must have set him on the fair road to success, indeed to the near-monopoly that would lead to over-production and a quality that was more variable than it need have been. One feature, however, may have been more difficult for conservative clients to accept and that was his urge to experiment with lighting effects, and particularly the expressive possibilities of shadow on salient parts of the face. This had already been tried out in the *Mrs Downey*. It was used to far greater effect in the *David Hunter of Blackness* (cat.no.8) and in the *Lady Forbes*, where, in the latter picture, the great confection of the bonnet cuts out the downward light to a point just beneath her nose before flaring brightly on the near side of her mouth and chin. The light that forms the chin is reflected back towards its source so that this secondary light plays around the left nostril, defining its particular form, and it is this kind of interplay that looks forward to a group of astonishingly original portraits of the early 1790s.

While there are precedents in Reynolds for the casting of soft shadows across quite substantial areas of the sitter's face, most notably, perhaps, in his *Catherine Moore* (fig.13), and, nearer home, in John Runciman's *Self-portrait* (fig.14), there is no obvious source for the group of portraits of which the most remarkable examples are the *Sir John and Lady Clerk of Penicuik* (cat.no.13), the *William Glendonwyn* (cat.no.15) and the *Captain David Birrell* (cat.no.16). In each of these the subjects are placed against

the light source, so that they are largely in shadow. The shadows, however, are softly illuminated by light that is reflected from within the figures and, most remarkably, their outer edges are almost incandescent with a direct light that flares there, but hardly penetrates the forms that it has defined. Although these effects must ultimately have been devised in the studio and have a certain degree of contrivance, they are observable in nature and their possibilities must have seized Raeburn's imagination, which was always attuned to such things. It is a method for which the nearest precedent is the painting of Adam Elsheimer, active in Rome from 1600 and an important influence on Rembrandt, although his light source is usually artificial, lunar, or supernal. The method also recalls the painting of the French seventeenth-century master, Georges de La Tour, who took the same kind of delight in illuminated edges, and the passage of light through fingers and sheets of paper, but his source, a candle, was always included within the picture rather than placed outside it. Raeburn could not, in any case, have known his work, and while there may be some kind of common source in Caravaggio and the tenebrists – and Raeburn's interest in this kind of painting is evident from his Roman copy after Romanelli (fig.6) – there is nothing quite like these portraits in the history of painting.

Raeburn did not pursue this kind of painting in its purest form, for it is likely that his sitters were not very keen on what they believed – mistakenly – to be the salient points of their 'likenesses' being made subordinate to these startling lighting effects. Variations, however, and some of them almost as startling in their originality, did occur in the later 1790s, among them the seated portrait of *Professor William Richardson* (fig.15) and the full-length of the haughty entrepreneur, *William Forbes of Callendar*

(cat.no.31). In each of these the lambent light retains almost the same intensity but spreads further into the forms. Indeed it will occur again, as late as 1811, in the portrait of the Highland chieftain, *Colonel Macdonell of Glengarry* (cat.no.47).

On the question of taste for such things, Henry Mackenzie, 'the man of feeling', expressed what may have been the prevalent view of Raeburn's experiments at this time: 'After Skirvine [Archibald Skirving], but much superior as an artist, and more estimable as a man, was Raeburn, who painted some admirable portraits, very little inferior … to Sir Thomas Lawrence's. He studied some time in Italy, and on his return got into the first business in Edinburgh. At first he indulged in a sort of trick of the art, a violent contrast of light and shade, which afterwards he ceased to practise, warned of its inferiority and bad taste by some good judges, tho' it had surprised and pleased the million of the unskillful. The best specimen of it is a portrait of Sir John and Lady Clerk at Pennycuik House, which, in that *falsetto* style (if the expression may be allowed me) is striking, as well as in point of resemblance.'[12] Despite pleasing the uninformed, Mackenzie's view prevailed and the most original aspects of these lighting methods were replaced by something broader and more generalised.

Having viewed his subject against a strong light source and become keenly sensitive to outline, it is not surprising that Raeburn's eye alighted on the potential of pure profile. The head of Robert Ferguson in *'The Archers'* (cat.no.12) may be one of the earliest examples of this interest, and the purest expression his self-portrait, modelled in low relief and cast in James Tassie's distinctive glass paste (cat.no.16). There may have been some classical precedent for this, remembered from Italy, but Tassie himself is an obvious inspiration. No doubt by moving this three-dimensional object around and observing the interplay of shadow, Raeburn was able to explore its expressive possibilities and the type recurs in the figure of Miss Wedderburn in the *John*

Johnstone of Alva conversation piece (cat.no.23) and, most memorably, in *'The Skating Minister'* (cat. no.19). In the latter, the head of Walker has a subtle delicacy of modelling, both in its outline and in its inner forms, that is remarkably close to the medallion portrait. In the *'The Skating Minister'*, of course, the notion of profile is carried into the whole figure and this palpable outline gives the man an exquisite clarity and conveys a remarkable sense of his relationship, not only to the light of sky and ice, but to the very air around him.

Again, this form must have been of limited acceptability to sitters, and the remainder of the decade is marked by portraits of a more conventional pattern, but with a number of features that can be isolated as an expression of Raeburn's need to continually explore the possibilities of visual expression, even while satisfying his clients. This gives rise to a sometimes bewildering variety of 'styles', some a reversion to types and manners practised at an earlier stage in his career, something which makes the dating of so many of his pictures extremely difficult purely on grounds of style. Disconcertingly, this can give the impression that Raeburn is, in a sense, really more than one painter – which raises the question of studio assistance, a subject on which there is virtually no information and which is unresolved. On balance, there does not seem to have been any of a significant nature, and the explanation of this variety would seem to be Raeburn's personality itself – his urge to respond directly to the visible, his need to experiment, his need, ultimately, to keep his creative fire bright, despite the exigencies of the demands made upon him by society and by economics.

Portraits of the middle part of the decade tend to be marked by a sparer use of paint, which often seems intended to exploit the texture of the canvas, nearly always a twill weave. A number of portraits, often of women, are predominantly roseate in hue, where the handling of paint has a rough, 'squarish' quality and the backgrounds of foliage, tree-trunks, distant fields and hills are abstractions of shape and colour almost as much as an attempt at any kind of descriptive realism. An example is the portrait of *Jacobina Copland* (fig.16). Among male portraits of a similar type are the *Robert Brown of Newhall*[13] and the *Douglas, 8th Duke of Hamilton*.[14] There is then a change to a more angular, geometric form of handling in which the shapes are slotted, or interwoven into each other – the hands, for example in the portrait of the *Revd Hugh Blair* (cat.no.25), the *Lady Mackenzie of Coul* (cat.no.24) and two full-lengths, a world away in their breadth from the early *Mrs Downey* (fig.9), a portrait of *Lady Carnegie* (fig.17) and the double portrait of the *Countess of Dumfries and her Daughter* (fig.18).

A number of portraits of this period and the later 1790s are also distinguished by a wide range of intense colour, of which none is more remarkable in this respect than the full-length *Sir John Sinclair* (cat.no.28), the first in Raeburn's great series of Highland chieftains – each astonishingly different in style from the other – whose exoticism must have astonished London audiences. Other portraits of this period with rich harmonies of colour are the gay and finger-snapping group portrait of *'The Macdonald Children'*

fig.16 *Jacobina Copland* by Henry Raeburn
National Gallery of Canada, Ottawa

LEFT fig.17 *Lady Carnegie* by Henry Raeburn
Private collection

RIGHT fig.18 *Countess of Dumfries and her Daughter* by Henry Raeburn
Private collection

(cat.no.34), which must have been painted at the turn of the century, and the *Niel Gow* (cat.no.27), where the tartan trews are flashing squares of pink and bluey-green.

Almost as a reaction to these colouristic developments and complex compositional arrangements, as well as the rich surface vagaries that went hand in hand with them, Raeburn produced a number of portraits severe in their outlines, austere in their colour schemes, and undemonstrative in their handling. These tendencies perhaps first appear in the portrait of *Mrs James Gregory* (cat.no.30), which must have been painted about 1798. It is simple in colour and outline, in a neo-classical way, yet there are the subtlest variations in the contours that suggest breath and movement. A purer expression of the neo-classical spirit is the remarkable portrait of *Sir Patrick Inglis* (cat.no.32) which dates from about 1800. Raeburn had painted him a few years earlier in a landscape setting but what he produced now had an almost rigid clarity of design, sharply defined contours and a colour scheme of greys, lit by the sudden flare of his yellow glove.

These developments, which imparted elements of clarity and control to Raeburn's work in the first decade of the new century, coincided with the presence in Edinburgh from September 1796 to February 1798 of the French émigré painter, Henri-Pierre Danloux. Danloux had fled to London from the French Revolution in 1792, the same year he had seen, and been impressed by, Raeburn's *Clerks of Penicuik* (cat.no.13). He had come north to paint the heir to the French throne, the Comte d'Artois, who had been given sanctuary in Holyroodhouse, and while in Edinburgh had been patronised by the Duke of Buccleuch. It would be surprising if Raeburn had not been conscious of the presence of this one-time friend of the French academician, Jacques-Louis David, and made efforts to see his work – Raeburn was, after all, always deeply conscious of his distance from the major art of his time.

There are traces of this neo-classical spirit in two of the finest portraits that Raeburn painted during the first decade of the nineteenth century, indeed two of the finest pictures he would paint at any time during his forty-year career – the pair of three-quarter length, seated portraits of *James Cruikshank*, who had made a fortune in the West Indies, and his wife, *Margaret Gerard* (figs.19 and 20). The figure of Cruikshank is carved with angular lines against a completely plain background, and he is both grandly and casually linked to the back of the simple chair in which he sits. Mrs Cruikshank faces him from a more exotic chair, but placed against an equally plain wall. Both figures are seen from below eye-level, the foreshortening slightly more emphasised in her case. The strange intricacies of Mrs Cruickshank's costume have allowed Raeburn to indulge in a range of marks denied him by the plainer costume of the husband. These marks have their own remarkable life, but they are always responsive to what has been seen, and all are related within a perfectly balanced tonal scheme. In terms of that vital aspect of portraiture, likeness, we are persuaded that Raeburn has succeeded, so convincingly honest is his response to these individuals who may not have been remarkable in any way and of whom we know very little.

It is this immediacy of response to the world observed, and his ability to translate his reaction into the terms of the object he is creating, that makes Raeburn a painter endlessly engrossing to modern eyes; and, although he employed a variety of styles and was not immune to how other painters made their works, there were always these constants: first, a reliance on Byres's dictum always to have the object before him; and secondly, an unpremeditated view of the outcome, which meant a minimum of planning and little preliminary 'drawing' on the canvas in the sense that Lawrence would have understood the term. (Almost the closest we can come to drawing in Raeburn is a long, quite casual vertical line running down the sky in the portrait of *Forbes of Callendar* (cat.no.31), where at one stage he had evidently thought of placing the outer limit of the room.) A major aspect of Raeburn's ability to grasp the essence of what, by its nature, was always changing, was his seemingly intuitive control of tonal relationships. A shadow, for example, would always be correctly modulated against a different dark, or against a white. No contemporary could do this with such certainty, and, taking a wider perspective, it places Raeburn in some ways in the company of painters like Velázquez and Manet.

It was this truthfulness of observation that allowed him to seize the particular essence of those he painted, so that their humanity and individuality speaks directly across time. This sense of the very breath of life and the complexity of the personality within the mere lineaments of the image, relates him, again, to the most perceptive of portrait painters. That he was able to step outside the confines of his particular place and time is evident from the fact that many of his most profound and affecting portraits are of individuals of no great social or intellectual note – *Mrs Campbell of Park* (cat.no.36), or *Mrs James Campbell* (cat.no.40), with its Rembrandtesque resonance.

By 1799 Raeburn had moved his studio from George Street to a terraced house on the north side of York Place, virtually a prolongation of Queen Street into the eastern extension of the original New Town. According to the diarist Farington, who called (in Raeburn's absence) in 1801, the house had been 'built by Himself' but it was in fact a house which he adapted for his own use, to include reception areas, a gallery for the display of portraits and a studio. He enlarged the north-facing rear windows at first floor level (out of all proportion to the normal Edinburgh scale) and installed a complex series of shutters which enabled him to control the flow of light into the room. Such was his desire to maximise the light that fell on his sitters that the ceiling of the great room was actually chamfered into the floor above and the stone lintel outside the window similarly chamfered (figs.21 and 22). It is not known precisely when he moved to York Place, and some of the paintings which might seem to be the result of the effects he could produce in the new studio, which faced the vast sky above the River Forth, such as the *Forbes of Callendar* of 1798 (cat.no.31), may have been begun, if not completed, in George Street. Many portraits, however, do bear the imprint of this light, particularly a number of portraits of military figures, who must have been placed on a high platform near the window. The outstanding example is probably the *Sir Duncan Campbell of Barcaldine* (cat.no.41). There is little doubt that this new studio played a significant role in many of the great full-lengths of the latter years of Raeburn's career, such as the *'The MacNab'* (cat.no.46) and the *Macdonell of Glengarry* (cat.no.47), or in the complex, yet almost playful lighting of the group portrait of the Drummond children (cat.no.37). It was also a vital element in more modest portraits, where the need for drama might have been deemed to be less, such as the *Mrs James Hamilton of Kames* (cat.no.45) or the late, unfinished, *Sir John Maxwell of Pollok* (cat.no.63).

It is difficult to characterise the style of Raeburn's portraiture during the last two decades of his life, because the bewildering variation in manner persists. Paintings close in date, and clearly the product of his imagination alone, often demonstrate an opposition of breadth to refinement, for which there is no obvious explanation. The portraits of the two Highland chieftains, *MacNab* and *Macdonell*, are examples, the former open and planar in treatment, the latter precise, polished, minutely descriptive. It is a contrast that persists to the end, in, for example, the full-lengths of the *Marquess of Bute* (cat.no.60) and *Major James Lee Harvey* (cat.no.62), both of which must have been painted about 1820. The former is broad, four-square, its romanticism wrapped in a near-cubic geometry, while the latter is finely honed and descriptive in the manner of Lawrence. Again, this kind of contrast is startling if portraits like the *Lord Newton* (cat.no.44) and *Professor John Playfair* (cat.no.43), both painted close to each other at the end of the first decade of the century, are placed together. The *Newton* has a breadth of gesture that is almost violent, the paint thick and liquid, the contrasts of colour and tone held in a clamorous equilibrium, whereas the Playfair is quiet, subtle and nuanced, the paint intricately woven into a pulsing web of flesh and material. Or again, the rapid, reactive painterliness of the *Mrs James Campbell* (cat.no.40) seems in sharp contrast to the delicately handled, porcelain-like effects of the *Mrs William Urquhart* (cat.no.53), painted perhaps a year later.

fig.21   Rear elevation of Raeburn's studio at 32 York Place

fig.22   Interior of Raeburn's studio today

Another shift of emphasis takes place around 1810–12, which may be the result of a particular kind of demand from Raeburn's clients, for a number of paintings are swamped with an informational quality which seems concerned with the recording of property. There is a group of female portraits where costume and the contents of rooms are described with a meticulousness that seems almost at variance with their emerging romanticism. They include paintings like the later portrait of *Lady Carnegie* (fig.23) – Raeburn had already painted her at full-length in 1798 – and the remarkable *Miss Cumming*, spectral within her setting of a grand, pillared room and almost overpowered by the elaboration of her clothes (fig.24). Curiously, the male counterparts of these portraits are painted in a much lusher fashion, the paint rich and fluid, like the full-length of *Neil Primrose, 3rd Earl of Rosebery* (fig.25) in the robes of the Order of the Thistle, painted about 1811, dominating an even grander room than Miss Cumming's. Of the same type is the seated portrait of the *5th Duke of Roxburghe* (cat.no.49), the furnishings of the room both descriptively and lusciously painted, the urn, carved tables and draperies flowing seamlessly into a romantically charged outdoor setting.

TOP fig.23 *Lady Carnegie*
by Henry Raeburn
Location unknown

ABOVE fig.24 *Miss Cumming*
by Henry Raeburn
Private collection

RIGHT fig.25 *3rd Earl of Rosebery*
by Henry Raeburn
Earl of Rosebery, Dalmeny House

There is little doubt that the near-monopoly situation that Raeburn found himself in after the turn of the century – George Willison had died in 1797, David Martin in 1798 – affected the quality of his work, and contemporary references to carelessness were not always ill founded, although, when a subject seized his imagination, his response remained fresh and original until the end of his life. The other factor that led to over-production was his bankruptcy in 1808, with debts of over £30,000 – a 'wreck' of the kind that would in due course befall Walter Scott, whom he painted in the same year. The causes of his bankruptcy are not clear, but were probably the result of failures in his mercantile activities and through his involvement in insurance underwriting. This seems more likely than the failure of clients to pay on time, although such things happened, as a letter to Sir Duncan Campbell of Barcaldine (see cat.no.41) in 1812 makes clear. The letter gives a rare glimpse of the personality of Raeburn, and hints at a literary style that might have matched the verve and wit of his painting: 'Painters and poets and these sort of people, you know, are always poor, and as I am no exception to this general description, and have considerable sums to pay about this term, I have taken the liberty to remind you of your portrait, and to say it would be doing me a particular favour if you would send me an order for the amount: the sum is 50 gns. I would not have taken this liberty but that I know it is a trifle to you, and may have escaped you.'

Most of his debts were paid in part by the end of the year and the sequestration was lifted. For those that were not, his representative vowed that Raeburn would commit 'the remaining years of his life' to the task of restitution, although he (that is, Raeburn), 'could not promise himself a long period of successful exertion; for it [his profession] is one which the trembling hand of age is unfit to execute long before the faculties decay …' Again, it was the same task that Scott would set himself in 1826, and it was, of course, the situation that Scott remarked on when he said of Raeburn as late as 1819 that he 'works just now chiefly for cash poor fellow as he can but have a few years to make money …'[15] Among the work that he undertook was the production of copies of other artists' work – a task he usually accomplished brilliantly, although it was a strange one for an artist of his eminence.

The house in York Place had to be sold as a result of the catastrophe, although Raeburn was able to remain as a tenant. He was not, however, forced to dispose of St Bernard's, which remained the family home for the remainder of his life. His position now seems to have made him sensitive, perhaps unduly, about the rivalry that did exist and there is evidence of a certain jealousy of George Watson, eleven years his junior. In 1812 he resigned from the recently founded Associated Society of Artists, who exhibited in his own rooms, because he believed that Watson, who seems to have been in charge of the hanging, had usurped space that he believed he should have had. No doubt with his parlous financial situation in mind, he wrote to the committee that he could not 'prevail upon himself to act a second part in the eye of the public to any man in [my] own line'. The committee could not afford to lose Raeburn, and the solution was to dispense with Watson, who was President, and elect Raeburn in his place.

In the same year Raeburn was elected an associate of the Royal Academy of Arts in London, and a full academician in 1815. His relationship with London had always been an ambivalent one, and had been marked by confusions and misunderstandings. He spent, perhaps, only five periods of time in the metropolis: two during his journeys to and from Rome, his visit in 1810 when he contemplated taking up residence, in 1812, when he signed the candidate list at the Academy and in 1813 when he received his associate's diploma.[16] Although he had exhibited two portraits there as early as 1792, that year was notable for the failure of the double portrait of *Sir John and Lady Clerk* (cat.no.13) to arrive at the Academy on time. He then exhibited only sporadically – a total of five paintings – until his election in 1812, when his portrait of *Macdonell of Glengarry* (cat.no.47) was given pride of place. Thereafter he exhibited a handful of pictures each year until his death. Understandably, he was concerned that he saw so little of the work being produced by the London painters and had little idea how his works would look hanging next to theirs. His visit to London in 1810 lasted at least from the middle of March until the beginning of June and he went the rounds with David Wilkie. It is likely that Wilkie enabled him to see a number of Old Masters in private collections (although it should never be forgotten that Raeburn's friend in Edinburgh, John Clerk,

Lord Eldin (see cat.no.54), had a substantial collection with which Raeburn must have been intimate, including a nearly complete set of Rembrandt etchings). Wilkie also introduced him to a number of contemporary painters, and on 4 June they dined at the Crown and Anchor with a group of academicians, including Flaxman, Beechey and the president, Benjamin West. In Wilkie's words, 'great attention was paid to him'.[17]

The principal outcome of his visit of 1810 was his decision not to settle in London. In 1815 came the confusion over his diploma picture, when he sent a self-portrait without realising that such things were inadmissible. This must have been particularly frustrating, for he had taken great pains (indeed he had tried too hard) to make this self-portrait a worthy representation, not simply of his appearance, but of his high seriousness (see cat.no.56). The confusions and his feelings of remoteness, however, are expressed most clearly in a letter he wrote to Wilkie four years later, on 12 September 1819. He begins by informing Wilkie that he is still alive and asks him to write at least once a year on what the artists in London are doing, for, in a memorable *cri de coeur*, he writes '[I have] as little communication with any of them and know almost as little about them as if I were living at the Cape of Good Hope.' The pictures that he sends to the Academy each year are, he remarks, 'merely … an advertisement that I am still in the land of the living, but in other respects it does me no good, for I get no notice from anyone, nor have I the least conception how they look beside others.' He then goes on to ask about how the London portrait painters are faring – Beechey, Phillips, Owen and, especially, Sir Thomas Lawrence, the latter clearly much on his mind. The letter, like the one to Sir Duncan Campbell, is one of the very few of those that survive where there is a clear sound of Raeburn's voice and a distinct sense of his personality.

LEFT fig.26 *Lady Gordon Cumming* by Henry Raeburn
Location unknown

RIGHT fig.27 *Mrs Jens Wolff* by Thomas Lawrence
The Art Institute of Chicago
(Mr and Mrs W. W. Kimball Collection)

His remoteness from the mainstream, while it had let his great originality flourish in his early days, may latterly have meant that he did not always remember where his own strengths lay, and his evident interest in Lawrence was not necessarily to his ultimate advantage. The influence is benign in portraits like the *Mrs Urquhart* (cat.no.53) or in the acceptable sentimentality of the *'Boy and Rabbit'* (cat.no.57), with which he replaced his self-portrait in the Academy's collection, or even in the great military portrait of *Major James Lee Harvey* (cat.no.62). It is perhaps just acceptable in the decorous ecstasy of *Mrs Scott Moncrieff* (cat.no.52) but it becomes faintly ludicrous in the portrait, now lost, of *Lady Gordon Cumming* (fig.26). Partly in form, and certainly very much in feeling, it derives from Lawrence's highly mannered portrait of his intimate friend, Mrs Jens Wolff, in the guise of the Erythraean sibyl, completed in 1815 and kept for many years in his studio (fig.27). Raeburn believed that his portrait of Lady Gordon Cumming, exhibited at the Royal Academy in 1817, was 'by much the best and handsomest female picture I have yet painted …'[18]

His art, of course, was never free of artifice, but its fresh, direct response to the visible world remained its greatest attribute. Nor did his powers wane towards the end of his life, as he had once suggested to his creditors they might. The full-length of the

NOTES AND REFERENCES

1. Allan Cunningham, *The Life of Sir David Wilkie*, London, 1843, vol.1, p.296.

   Generally, in what follows, when precise dates are mentioned, or can easily be inferred, the source will be found in the documentation section by David Mackie. Sources of information concerning portraits included in the exhibition will be found under the appropriate catalogue entry.

2. Much information on the houses in which Raeburn lived, their immediate surroundings and the lands he possessed can be found in Andrew Kerr, *A History of Ann Street*, privately published, 1982. The mills at Canon Mills (now Canonmills) were set up in the fifteenth century by the canons of Holyrood Abbey.

3. John Gifford, Colin McWilliam and David Walker, *Edinburgh*, The Buildings of Scotland series, Harmondsworth, 1984, p.66.

4. Edinburgh, Scottish National Portrait Gallery, PGL353, on permanent loan from the Dean Orphanage and Cauvin's Trust. The original, which has a different colour scheme and a port scene in place of the view of the orphanage, passed through Sotheby's, 20 November 1985 (57).

5. Andrew Kerr, *A History of Ann Street*, privately published, 1982, p.3.

6. Irwin, p.240.

7. Anthony M. Clark, *Pompeo Batoni*, Oxford, 1985, p.47.

8. I am grateful to my colleague, Aidan Weston-Lewis, for pointing out this source to me. The painting by Romanelli is in the Capitoline Gallery, Rome, inv. 230.

9. Quoted in Greig, p.xxxii.

10. Allan Cunningham, *The Life of Sir David Wilkie*, London, 1843, vol.1, p.214.

11. Irwin, p.243.

12. *The Anecdotes and Egotisms of Henry Mackenzie*, ed. Harold William Thompson, London, 1927, pp.213–14.

13. Chicago, The Art Institute of Chicago.

14. Collection of The Duke of Hamilton.

15. *The Letters of Sir Walter Scott*, ed. H. J. C. Grierson, vol.v, London, 1933, p.349.

16. William T. Whitley, *Art in England*, vol.1, 1800–1820, New York, 1973, p.209.

17. Allan Cunningham, *The Life of Sir David Wilkie*, London, 1843, vol.1, p.299.

18. Transcript in Scottish National Portrait Gallery, Library, Greig Archive.

19. Andrew, pp.76–7.

2nd Marquess of Bute (cat.no.60) is a startling new invention, painted as late as 1820. The unfinished portrait of *Sir John Maxwell* (cat.no.63), if not the last, certainly one of the latest of his works, although it contains some of the 'ecstatic' mannerism of the late paintings, still shows the same eagerness for the visible that had marked his art from the beginning. This too is the case with the portrait of *Sir Walter Scott* (cat.no.64), which he completed for his own gallery shortly before his death – a portrait that had brought together the two greatest men of the age in a new harmony.

That he had become a significant figure of his age was recognised by a number of honours that came near the end of his life. In 1820 he was elected a member of the prestigious Royal Society of Edinburgh. Two years later, on 29 August 1822, the final day of the week-long visit by George IV to Edinburgh, Raeburn was knighted at Hopetoun House, some ten miles to the west of Edinburgh, along with Scott's friend, Captain Adam Ferguson. Scott, who had orchestrated the king's visit as a kind of expression of re-awakening nationhood, no doubt had a hand in Ferguson's knighthood. Raeburn's honour, as he soon discovered, was due to the influence of the MP, John Maxwell of Pollok, whose portrait (cat.no.63) was begun about this time, although he had initially believed that either William Adam, Lord Chief Commissioner of the Scottish Jury Court, or Viscount Melville, had been responsible. While the preparations for the ceremony were underway, Raeburn found himself in conversation with a young man of 'great affability and politeness' whom he failed to recognise and who was not formally introduced to him. This gentleman, Raeburn soon discovered to his dismay, was the secretary of state, Robert Peel, who had intimated the king's intention; all he could now do was to beg John Maxwell to convey his apologies for the oversight. The incident was, in its small way, a continuation of the theme of a never entirely satisfactory relationship with the southern kingdom.

The following day Raeburn celebrated his knighthood at St Bernard's House, in the company of Sir Adam Ferguson, David Wilkie, William Collins and other friends. In Wilkie's words, they 'had a most royal jollification … and the ceremony, as it happened, was told us over and over, with new jokes every time'. After toasts 'Sir Henry made a very modest reply' and Sir Adam sang 'The Laird of Cockpen'. Lady Raeburn, according to Wilkie, 'would not allow herself to be called *My Lady* on any account …'[19]

The following year, on 10 May, Raeburn heard from Peel that he had recommended him for appointment to the office of Painter to his Majesty in Scotland. Often referred to as 'His (or Her) Majesty's Painter and Limner for Scotland', the office had been created by Queen Anne in 1703. It quickly became a sinecure and Raeburn was the first professional painter to hold it for over a hundred years. He did not, however, enjoy the honour for long.

Towards the end of June 1823 he set off on an excursion into Fife with a group of friends – Scott, Sir Samuel Shepherd, Lord Chief Baron of the Scottish Exchequer, Sir Adam Ferguson, Lord Chief Commissioner Adam, and Maria Edgeworth, the novelist, who happened to be visiting Scott at the time. The excursion, 'a very merry party' in Scott's words, was of an antiquarian sort and they visited sites at Ravensheugh (Ravenscraig) Castle, which had featured in Scott's *Lay of the Last Minstrel*, Pittenweem and St Andrews. Raeburn, it is said, walked with his hat in his hand, with the diminutive Miss Edgeworth clinging to his other arm. On the day after his return to Edinburgh, he attempted to resume work in his studio, but became unwell. After a few days confined to bed, he died on 8 July, of 'water in the head', according to Scott though his doctor spoke of 'a total failure of the system'.

For some reason Raeburn was not buried at St Cuthbert's, where he had erected a monument against the east wall of the churchyard as long ago as 1792, but in the dormitory of the episcopalian church of St John's that had recently been erected at the west end of Princes Street. Scott, perhaps surprisingly, because he had to return to Abbotsford, was unable to attend the funeral and sent his regrets to the family that he would not be present, at 'the last obsequies of a friend whom he esteemd and respected so entirely as the late Sir Henry Raeburn'.

Manners, Morals and Characters:
Henry Raeburn & the Scottish Enlightenment

NICHOLAS PHILLIPSON

fig.28 *Henry Raeburn* by David Deuchar
National Gallery of Scotland

fig.29 *The arrival of the Royal Party at Hopetoun House, 1822* by Denis Dighton
Hopetoun House

HENRY Raeburn is the most 'Scottish' of painters. He was born in Edinburgh in 1756. His parents both came from Edinburgh. His father was a somewhat shadowy, not to say shady, figure who was involved in the textile business and owned land and a quarry in Stockbridge, on the outskirts of the city; his mother, Anne Elder was probably the kinswoman of an influential local politician. He was educated at George Heriot's Hospital and apprenticed to a local silversmith in 1772. He soon found his way into local artistic circles – his first known portrait is a miniature of a well-known local etcher and satirist, David Deuchar. Around 1781, he married young, married well and married happily, and it was his wife Ann Edgar's fortune that allowed him to spend two seminal years in Rome between 1784 and 1786, the longest period he was to spend outside his native city. For apart from a couple of curiously desultory and conspicuously unsuccessful attempts to establish himself in London, he was to spend the rest of his life in Edinburgh.

Raeburn's clientele was also overwhelmingly Scottish. Most of his enormous output of perhaps 1,000 canvases portrays the landed, literary, professional and mercantile classes of Scotland at the turn of the eighteenth and nineteenth century. It is an output that forms an extraordinary visual biography of élite Scottish society in the later years of the Scottish Enlightenment, when Edinburgh basked in its reputation as the Athens of the North and feared, as Henry Cockburn memorably but misleadingly put it, that the country had entered its 'last purely Scotch age'.[1] In a fitting climax to a remarkable Scottish career Raeburn was knighted by George IV in 1822 at Hopetoun House (fig.29), one of the two first Scots to have been so honoured in his native country by his sovereign since the Union.[2]

Whether or not Raeburn's skills as a painter have distinctively Scottish characteristics is for others to decide; the matter is contentious. What a historian of the Scottish Enlightenment may suggest is that one of his best-known and most endearing characteristics, his sensitivity to the character and manners of his sitters and his equally striking ability to suggest that his sitters all belong to the same social and cultural world and to the same nation, does indeed have a peculiarly Scottish provenance. For it reflects Raeburn's sensitivity to the culture of a class which had a distinctive sense of its place and importance in Scottish society. It also reflects his sensitivity to philosophical questions that lay at the heart of the Scottish Enlightenment, questions about the processes by which our characters are formed in everyday life, and about the things we can do to cultivate and refine our personalities. It is his disciplined, visual sensitivity to such questions that makes it possible to think of him as the visual philosopher and moralist of the Scottish Enlightenment.

RAEBURN'S EDINBURGH: IMPROVEMENT AND ENLIGHTENMENT

Raeburn lived and worked in an extraordinary city. It was during the 1760s that Edinburgh became known as a centre of Enlightenment of international importance, the city of David Hume and William Robertson, Allan Ramsay and the Adam brothers; the city whose university was setting new standards of academic excellence; the city whose myriad intellectual clubs and societies seemed to harness learning and letters to the public life of Scotland's capital city. It was a city, Allan Ramsay thought, which deserved to be known as the Athens of Britain.[3]

Contemporaries saw these remarkable developments as connected, wholly or in part, to recent changes in the city's constitution and character which were nothing short of revolutionary and were certainly unparalleled in the Anglo-Saxon world. Before the Act of Union of 1707, Edinburgh had been the capital city of an independent kingdom, linked to England by dynastic ties; as such it had been the seat of the Scots Parliament, Privy Council, the Courts of Session and Justiciary, the General Assembly of the

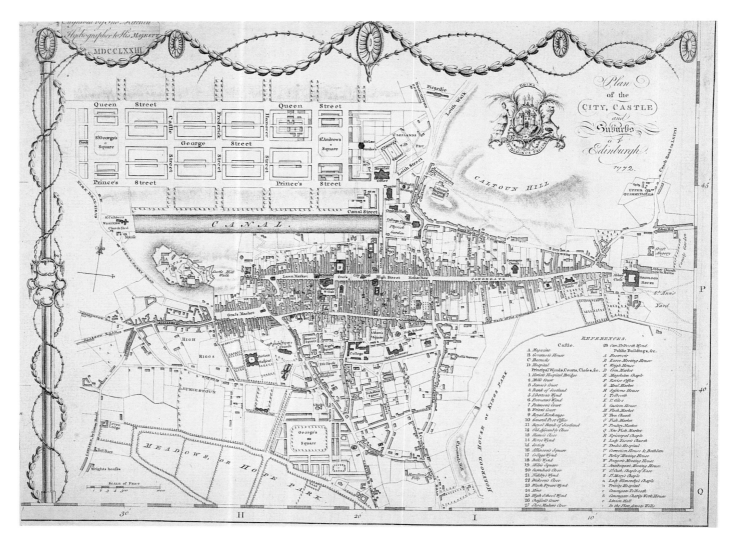

fig.30 *Plan of Edinburgh*, 1772,
engraved by Thomas Kitchin
Scottish National Portrait Gallery

Church of Scotland and the newly established Bank of Scotland; as such it had accommodated a highly aristocratic society of noblemen and country gentlemen and their dependants, who kept houses or rented apartments in and around the city during the winter months in order to attend to their political, legal and social business. The immediate effects of the Union on Edinburgh were catastrophic. With the loss of its political institutions, its noblest, wealthiest and most ambitious residents took the high road to London, leaving the city, as Robert Mudie remarked, a 'widowed metropolis' whose loss of status was symbolised by the derelict state into which the Canongate, its aristocratic suburb, soon fell.[4] As Allan Ramsay, the painter's father, and the city's self-appointed bard, wrote in 1717 in classically nostalgic verse:

> O Cannigate! Poor elritch hole!
> What loss, what crosses does thou thole!
> London and Death gars thee look drole,
> An hing thy head;
> Wow, but thou has e'en cauld coal
> To blaw indeed.

For all that, Edinburgh recovered from the shock of the Union rather well. The city continued to accommodate the courts, the General Assembly, the banks and the new tax offices set up after the Union to deal with the country's fiscal administration; as such it remained an important centre of professional life. And although the centre of political power had shifted decisively to London, the city soon recovered something of its former political importance. By the 1720s the ministry, its Scottish 'manager', the Earl of Islay, later 3rd Duke of Argyll, and his *sous-ministres* were doing much of the ordinary political business of the country in Edinburgh rather than in London. Like Dublin, Philadelphia or Charleston, in other words, the city had emerged as the capital of one of the great provinces of the British Crown.

This somewhat unexpected development owed much to English reluctance to burden themselves unduly with Scottish business; it was much easier to offload it on to the shoulders of trusted natives. Even so, turning the Duke of Argyll into the 'uncrowned king of Scotland' and watching the Duke hold court every year at Holyrood, waited on by the judges, bailies, professors and ministers in their robes, offended many Unionists who looked forward to the day when the Union would be 'compleat' and the different functions of Scottish government would be handled by the appropriate ministers in London. But Edinburgh's re-emergence as a capital city, albeit a provincial capital, owed as much to brute facts of Scottish social life as to English political indifference. For while the greater nobility and the most ambitious politicians had naturally taken the high road to London after the Union, their less wealthy and ambitious brethren, the minor nobility and gentry, continued to treat Edinburgh as the focal point of their collective lives for much of the century. The political importance of this class to post-Union Scotland was enormous. It provided the country with most of its MPs, judges and county sheriffs. After the restoration of lay patronage in the Kirk in 1712, it played an increasingly influential part in shaping the ecclesiastical and religious life of the counties. In other words, the minor nobility, the gentry and the professional classes – the so-called 'middling ranks' of Scottish society – formed a class on which the routines of ordinary government and much of the political business of the country depended. It was a class which no political manager could afford to ignore, a class whose political needs would have to be serviced in Edinburgh rather than in London. It was also the class from which Raeburn drew most of his sitters.

From the 1720s until the turn of the century, the middling ranks dominated the political, social and cultural life of Edinburgh. Their politics, their estate business, their notorious litigiousness monopolised the attention of political managers, the courts and the legal profession. They sent their sons to the College for professional education and to prepare them for public life. Their social and cultural life revolved around the assembly rooms in the old town and later in the new, and in the clubs that flourished in the inns and coffee-houses of the old town. And when proposals were published in 1752 for improving the old town and building a new suburb to the north of the old city, it was to provide the city with new public buildings and new, elegant housing appropriate to the rank of the city's dominant élite.

Soon all that was to change, for Raeburn grew up in a city whose élite was at last financially and culturally ready to sample the social and cultural delights of London. James Boswell's early Journals suggest that regular social contact with London began in the 1760s and 1770s and generally took the form of short summer jaunts to supplement the social routines of the long winter Edinburgh Season. By the end of Raeburn's life the position was reversed and visits to Edinburgh were being regarded as a means of supplementing the London Season. Edinburgh had become a largely professional city in which social leadership was provided by the judges, advocates and professors and by well-born dowagers, spinsters and remittance men. As Robert Mudie put it in 1825:

> Wherever the executive and legislative powers of the state are allocated, it is there that the gay and the rich will throng; and notwithstanding all the boasted elegance and taste [of Edinburgh], no Scottish nobleman, or even squire, spends his winter there, if he can afford to spend it in London. Hence, [Edinburgh] is not only destitute of the source whence fashion flows, but she is also left without the means by which it could be supported: she is second-rate in her very nature, and also in those who form her leading society.[5]

As Ramsay's 'Ode to the Canongate' and Mudie's tart comments about the decay of good society in Edinburgh suggest, the fear of provincialism was endemic in post-Union Edinburgh. Nevertheless it was a fear that Edinburgh's élite learned to express in a highly distinctive way. Their understanding of what the future held in store for their country and class had its roots in the important and strangely neglected debate about the Union which took place in the Scots Parliament and in the Edinburgh press in the early years of the century. Then both pro- and anti-Unionists had seen Scotland as a 'failing nation' whose political and religious divisions, underdeveloped economy and appalling relations with England were threatening the country's 'independence' and prosperity. Predictably, pessimists had seen the Union as the first step on the road to the complete assimilation of the two countries and the destruction of an ancient and honourable nation. Optimists, on the other hand, saw the Union as a deal which offered patriots the chance to modernise, or 'improve', Scotland's economy and to launch a movement for national regeneration which would restore Scotland's 'independence' within the framework of a modern British state. As Alexander Wedderburn, an advocate and future Lord Chancellor – the first Scottish advocate to hold that office – wrote in the introduction to the *Edinburgh Review* of 1755–6:

> *The memory of our ancient state is not so much obliterated, but that, by comparing the past with the present, we may see the superior advantages we now enjoy, and readily discover from what sources they flow …*
>
> *If countries have their ages with respect to improvement* North Britain *may be considered as in a state of early youth, guided and supported by the more mature strength of her kindred country.*[6]

Wedderburn's voice was that of the Edinburgh élite and he addressed the middling ranks as the natural leaders of modern Scottish society. The language he spoke was that of Cicero and the Roman stoics who believed that the future of liberty lay in the hands of an educated élite which was willing and able to pursue wealth, power and wisdom with an eye on the public good. The culture of the middling ranks in enlightened Edinburgh was deeply influenced by these stoic ideals. They can be seen at work in the early years of the Union in the activities of the tiny Easy Club (1712–14) whose members hoped that discussing Addison and Steele's *Tatler* and *Spectator* essays, would turn them into polite patriots. They animated the activities of the larger, grander and more aristocratic Honourable Society for Improvement in the Knowledge of Agriculture (1723–*c*.1746) which set out to encourage the improvement of the fisheries and the linen industry as well as agriculture and turned itself into an influential and effective watchdog of Scottish economic interests. The failure of the '45 and tangible evidence of economic recovery gave fresh impetus to this cult of improvement and this ambition to see the middling ranks as new and enlightened patriots. The celebrated Select Society (1759–*c*.1763), whose members included David Hume and Adam Smith, the painter Allan Ramsay and Robert Adam, encouraged debate about the problems of creating and maintaining the liberties of a free commercial polity, and founded satellite societies to encourage practical improvements in the arts and sciences and, famously, the correct use of spoken English. Raeburn grew up at a time when this club culture was at its liveliest. Societies like the Belles Lettres Society (1759–*c*.1765) and the Speculative Society (founded in 1764 and still thriving) met regularly to encourage young men destined for the Kirk and the legal profession to practise the arts of public speaking. Smaller, more rumbustious clubs like the Cape Club (1764–87) acted as a forum for the city's poets, painters and musicians as well as a host of tradesmen and artisans. The small but influential Mirror Club (fl.1778–81), to which we shall return, set out to engineer a sophisticated and influential campaign to encourage the improvement of manners.

The University was of incalculable importance in developing and propagating this culture among the middling ranks in the second half of the century. In the late seventeenth century it had been little more than a small seminary for training boys for the ministry and for preparing others for further education in Holland. By 1760, it had become a large and sophisticated university with faculties of law and medicine as well as a faculty of divinity. Its chief glory, however, was the philosophy curriculum and the course in moral philosophy which was regarded as the hinge on which the entire academic system hung. Formidable professors like Adam Ferguson (cat.no.26) and Dugald Stewart (fig.31) taught their students to reflect on the organisation and operation of the mind and the working of the passions and affections. They discussed the principles of justice, morality, politics, religion and taste. They showed how it was possible to live virtuously and sociably by learning the principles of prudence and self-command and by cultivating the benevolent affections. In so doing they laid the foundations of an enlightened philosophical culture of liberty which emphasised the importance of education and active citizenship in maintaining a free society. It was an intellectual culture brilliantly epitomised in Raeburn's portraits of the formidable academic élite who presided over the University's fortunes in the latter decades of the century. His portraits of *Professor Adam Ferguson* and of *Dr William Robertson*

fig.31 *Dugald Stewart* by Henry Raeburn
Scottish National Portrait Gallery

(cat.no.22), one of the greatest historians of the Enlightenment, present intellectuals who belong to the public world as well as to the world of learning and who are as renowned for their prudence and sagacity as for their erudition and scholarly judgement.

Two sophisticated and influential periodicals, the *Mirror* (1779–80) and the *Lounger* (1785–86), popularised this philosophy and showed Edinburgh's élite how it could be applied to the improvement of manners. These periodicals were the work of the Mirror Club, a small society of literary lawyers led by Henry Mackenzie (fig.32), a novelist of some distinction. The periodicals took the form of essays – twice-weekly in the case of the *Mirror*, and weekly in the case of the *Lounger* – on manners and morals. They were written in the style and manner of Joseph Addison's celebrated *Spectator* essays; indeed, Mackenzie was known as 'The Scottish Addison'. It was sophisticated moral journalism written for Edinburgh's élite by some of the city's leading *literati* and it was published at precisely the moment Raeburn's career as a portrait painter began to take shape. It is moral journalism written by a group of men, most of whom Raeburn painted.[7] It throws light on the moral culture of his sitters and on his own conceptions of how they should be characterised.[8]

fig.32 *Henry Mackenzie* by Henry Raeburn
National Portrait Gallery, London

PORTRAITURE AND PROPRIETY

Like Addison, Mackenzie and his friends wrote for readers who were sensitive to the complexities and uncertainties of modern life and wondered whether it would ever be possible to live sociably, at ease with themselves, with others and with the world the Deity had created. They wrote, too, for an Edinburgh public which was troubled by the revolution in manners which had taken place in the previous generation and by the increasing provincialism of this 'mimic-metropolis'. 'I found myself in almost every sense of the word an utter stranger', says one of the *Mirror*'s elderly characters, returning to the city after a life abroad; 'everywhere a new race, new manners and new modes of living'.[9] What made the problem more acute, William Craig observed, was that Scotland now had no court to set standards of taste and manners.[10] In a city in which culture was now king, it was up to moralists like the professors and essayists of the *Mirror* and *Lounger* to fill the moral vacuum.

At their most philosophical, the essayists saw themselves as philosophers practising the 'science of manners'.[11] Their subject was the study of the *petites morales* which shaped social intercourse in a modern society and the sort of behaviour which met with the approval and disapproval of candid and virtuous men and women. Their moral 'language' (the term was Mackenzie's) was derived from Addison's *Spectator*. The anxious and alienated citizen could become reconciled to the world by learning how to behave with 'moderation'. This was a form of stoic self-command that involved learning how to defer to the opinions of others without a loss of dignity or self-respect. This was a complicated skill which could be recommended for prudential reasons; after all it was absolutely necessary for getting on in life in a polite commercial society. But once mastered, the moralists argued that their disciples would soon acquire the sort of social self-confidence that encouraged the benevolent, sociable instincts. In other words, like the stoics, the Edinburgh moralists thought that prudence and self-command were the keys to living sociably and virtuously as nature and the Deity had intended. As Mackenzie put it: 'To think well of, and have respect for ourselves and the world around us, is one step to virtue and benevolence'.[12]

The moralists developed this language of manners in a distinctive way. They had a sharp Calvinist eye for fantasy and self-deception and were determined to keep their readers' feet firmly on the ground. They constantly preached up the dangers of overly relying on the Epicurean attractions of rank and natural genius rather than industry and application for getting on in life; in one of the *Lounger*'s little stories, it was Clodius who got on in politics, in spite of having 'little knowledge, no finesse of genius, and a taste altogether uncultivated' and not the cleverer and more eloquent Cornelius and Lelius. For Clodius had a quick, practical, unflashy mind and a greater capacity for the ordinary business of politics and was all the more respected for it.[13] The essayists also deplored the cynical aristocratic bravura Lord Chesterfield had peddled in his celebrated *Letters to his Son* on the grounds that it encouraged arrogance and insincerity instead of the more sociable and amiable qualities of sincerity, candour and humanity.

What brought their views into focus was their distinctive view of 'moderation'. They drew on Adam Smith's great treatise on moral philosophy, the *Theory of Moral Sentiments* (1759) and his remarkable discussion of the way in which the constraints of modern society teach us to see ourselves as others see us, and encourage us to harmonise our behaviour with those around us, by 'tuning up' and 'tuning down' our sentiments.[14] This was what Smith and the moralists called acquiring a sense of 'propriety'. It was a sense which signified a respect for the common values of class and culture, the values which had to be respected if one was to lead a useful, happy and virtuous life. In Victorian hands, propriety would be seen as a stifling form of social control which discouraged the expression of individual talent and character. But that was not the view of the moralists. In a developing society such as Scotland, they argued, the sense of propriety of a modern patriot élite would never be offended by those who indulged their peculiar talents provided they did so in a way which was useful to society. After all, in a commercial society there was a need for a much greater variety of talents than there had been in simpler ages. In a modern society, in other words, propriety was a means of liberating neglected talents, not stifling them.

To see the sense of propriety of enlightened people as a means of unlocking talent led them to see women in a strikingly new way. They criticised Chesterfield for dismissing women as 'children of a larger growth' instead of seeing them as a sex with as many natural talents as men.[15] No doubt some of these talents were different from mens' – it was a question which interested them greatly; no doubt the sphere in which women were destined to excel was domestic. But domesticity was a value which mattered to the moralists. They knew that the home had always been the place in which fathers taught their children – usually their sons – the traditional manly virtues of industry and application. But in the enlightened home there were new social skills to be learned. None was more important than 'complaisance', that art of behaving pleasantly to others according to their age, rank and station. It was a skill which was essential to the smooth working of society, a skill which was essential to an enlightened sense of propriety. No doubt it had peculiarly feminine attributes, but it was one men needed to acquire as well as women, one which wives and mothers were uniquely well qualified to teach. Indeed Mackenzie looked forward to the day in which the male and female virtues complemented each other. 'Were the men to derive from the society of the women gentleness, complacence, sensibility,' he wrote, 'were the women to borrow from that of the men steadiness, deliberation, and fortitude; characters might be formed not less amiable than useful, not less engaging than enlightened.'[16] Even though these views were anathema to radical feminists like Mary Wollstonecraft, they reflected a liberalisation of thinking about women and the relation between the sexes that was characteristic of the Scottish Enlightenment and they were views to which Raeburn was to be particularly sensitive.

But the moralists were not simply moral scientists. They also saw themselves as moral painters who were required to portray the virtues and vices in short stories and fables. This was far from easy. Modern novelists, Craig complained, often wasted time on narrative which ought to be spent on characters '[painting] all their shades and attitudes, and making us, as it were, intimately acquainted with them, deeply [engaging] our hearts in every circumstance which can affect them'.[17] Moreover, as Mackenzie complained, novelists were too much attracted by characters who were torn by conflicting loyalties to parents, lovers, friends and countries, when all moral science taught that even the most discordant passions and affections could be managed and mastered when men and women listened to the voice of propriety.[18] What they wanted were stories in which characters were drawn with precision, using 'those middle tints which it requires a nice pencil to hit' rather than the 'stronger colouring' and 'deeper shades' beloved of contemporary moralists.[19] On the other hand it was obviously important that characterisation was not allowed to become too particularised so that the subject lost any sense of '[belonging] to human kind'.[20] Robert Cullen, the moralists' chief authority on painting, favoured private rather than public portraits for the classic reason that public behaviour is more inscrutable than private: 'In the more trifling circumstances of manner and behaviour, and in the more ordinary occurrences of life, which tend to no particular object, and in which therefore men are less upon their guard, the disguise is forgot to be assumed, and we give way to the natural cast of our mind and disposition. It is there we are apt to betray those peculiar features of character, and those often nice shades of distinction, that difference and discriminate us from one another.'[21]

These were the views of moralists whose natural genre was philosophy and fiction, but they embody an attitude to portraiture and character to which Raeburn responded as a man who was sensitive to the moral culture of his world and as a painter who chose to supply his sitters with characteristics and virtues which were admired in contemporary Edinburgh and could be recognised as the moral attributes of a patriotic and enlightened élite. Raeburn's portraits display 'character' and 'virtue' in the sense that the Edinburgh moralists understood it. They are studies of spirited men and women who have mastered the art of self-command and are in control of their infinitely various and idiosyncratic affections and appetites. Above all, they are studies of virtuous people who understand the meaning of propriety in the sophisticated sense in which the moralists used that term, who are sociable, prudent and benevolent, and are at ease with themselves, with the world and with the Deity.

'Character', 'self-command', 'propriety' and 'serenity' then are the moral qualities that are explored and celebrated in Raeburn's portraits. 'Character' or natural talent and personal idiosyncrasy is generally explored in the treatment of the eyes, 'self-command' and 'serenity' in the set of the face, 'propriety' in the treatment of dress, pose and *mise-en-scène*, and the moral structure of the portrait is to be found in the often complex interplay of these three elements. But it is the all important spirit of self-command which assures us that individual talents have been socialised, and that the sitter has acquired: 'that serenity which disposes the mind to friendship, love, gratitude, and every other social affection; they make us contented with ourselves, our friends, and our situation, and expand the heart to all the interests of humanity'.[22]

It comes as no surprise, then, to discover that, for all his sensitivity to natural characteristics, Raeburn shared the moralists' distrust of genius and high rank. The great portraits of the professoriate of Edinburgh University and of the judges of the Court of Session, mostly painted before 1800, suggest that self-command and serenity are the product of hard work and public spirit as much as natural talent. In his portraits of sportsmen he manages to suggest that sporting skill relies on practice and self-command as much as natural flair. What is more, the portraits of *Dr Nathaniel Spens* (cat.no.17) and the young *Robert Ferguson* (cat.no.11) suggest that the skills of these practised and accomplished sportsmen can be transferred from the private to the public world and used for the benefit of the public. The *Revd Robert Walker* (cat.no.19) makes the same sort of point with more humour and subtlety. It is a portrait of a celebrated and learned divine who has mastered a somewhat perilous, amusing and graceful skill with the same assurance he has brought to the most abstract philosophy. It is amusing to suggest that there is a natural affinity between the skill of the skater and the philosopher but the philosopher's face suggests that if there is, he has discovered it. It is an eighteenth-century Scottish moralist's gentle joke.

Raeburn's treatment of that great metaphor of propriety, dress, is fascinating. One of the recurrent complaints of the essayists was that Edinburgh ladies and gentlemen lacked the 'ton' to carry off the fashions of London and they periodically reflected ruefully on the difficulty of acquiring this most subtle of arts. But none of this is apparent in Raeburn's portraits. His sitters are invariably dressed with consummate but unassuming propriety in fashionable but unflashy clothes appropriate to their rank, age and profession and their appearance reminds one of the *Lounger*'s comment: 'Dress is only an accessory, that should seem to belong to the wearer, and not the wearer to it'.[23] In the case of the men, orders and decorations are at a discount and even the most gorgeous robes and uniforms appear as sometimes well-worn work-clothes which are worn out of a sense of propriety to allow the wearer to get on with his public duties. This striking lack of swagger and extroversion is also evident in his treatment of women. The sensuous fashions of the period are worn in a manner becoming to girls who are destined for early marriage or to wives whose place is in the enlightened home. Nevertheless, the problem of dealing with swagger and sexuality was one which continually teased Raeburn. It is hard to imagine two more breathtakingly sensual portraits than those of *Isabella Macleod, Mrs Gregory* (cat.no.30) and *Mrs Scott Moncrieff* (cat.no.52). But theirs is the sensuality of young wives who have scarcely acquired the propriety and self-command that is expected of them and that they expect of themselves, and in any case, they are too lost in romance to have been able to experience the joys of serenity. It must have been difficult for Raeburn, painting in the age of swagger and fantasy and idiosyncrasy, to have come to terms with some of the greatest fantasists of all, the highland ladies and gentlemen who had taken to the cult of pseudo-clanship and were determined to strut on Raeburn's canvases in full and fanciful highland costume. Here his masterpiece is the portrait of *Francis MacNab* (cat.no.46). At one level, the MacNab is a ridiculous old man who offends every canon of propriety by parading in a young man's swagger costume. But he is also a defiant old man who is just about master of himself and the role he has chosen to play. His clothes are not mere fashion statements; they are used and lived in and worn in such a way that they appear as servants, not masters, of a grim, dogged fantasist who is to be judged by his character and his power of self-command, not by his costume; his lack of serenity hints at the moral price he has had to pay for his performance. It is a portrait which contrasts strikingly with *John, 2nd Marquess of Bute* (cat.no.60) who is the embodiment of modern stoicism. He is decently dressed in business costume, and the hint of swagger suggested by the plaid is fully controlled by the Marquess's self-command and somewhat austere serenity. It makes one regret that Raeburn died before he could tackle the greatest fantasist of all,

fig.33 *George IV in Highland Dress* by David Wilkie
The Royal Collection © Her Majesty The Queen

George IV, who swaggered into Edinburgh in 1822 in a kilt and pink tights and would have been painted by the newly knighted Limner Royal for Scotland, had he lived, in full highland dress.

Raeburn's views of women and marriage also seem consonant with those of the moralists. Although his female portraits have always been admired for capturing personal idiosyncrasies, here again idiosyncrasy is moderated by propriety, self-command and serenity, qualities which are to be valued in women as much as in men. In other words, in suggesting that men and women should aspire to the same social virtues, Raeburn follows the lead of the moralists in closing the gender gap. His portrait of *John Johnstone of Alva* (cat.no.23) is remarkable for being a family conversation piece dominated by a characterful young woman to whose conversation her elders are listening politely. Even more striking, her uncle and aunt both possess the new, feminine quality of complaisance that the moralists believed to be so necessary for the improvement of manners. His even more celebrated portrait of *Sir John and Lady Clerk of Penicuik* (cat.no.13) likewise celebrates a marriage of two people of character, self-possession and serenity, who behave with perfect propriety and are at ease with themselves and each other. It is not, to be sure, a marriage of equals; that notion lay ouside the reach of the idiom in which Raeburn and the moralists were working. But it is a marriage based on friendship as well as love and it helps, in reading the portrait, to remember that Lady Clerk was a well-known heiress in her own right. For Sir John is surely pointing to *their* property, not just his. In this genre, the anomalous portrait is one of the greatest. In *General Francis Dundas and Mrs Francis Dundas* (cat.no.50), husband and wife are playing a demanding game of chess and the meticulous attention Raeburn pays to the chess-board suggests the seriousness with which the couple treated the game. The state of the game suggests equality of talents, equality of skill and also equality within marriage. But the game has upset the natural balance of marital relations; Mrs Dundas seems to be winning; the General is faced with disaster. General Dundas's total concentration seems to typify respect for the male capacity for industry and application. But he has been routed by his wife whose expression suggests not merely amusement but also a capacity for complaisance which will shortly be tested when she has to console her husband in defeat. As with the great portraits of the *Revd Robert Walker*, and the *'The MacNab'*, it is a portrait that hints at the possibility of gentle satire that was always possible and always permissible within the 'science of manners'.

Raeburn's treatment of children provides a fascinating counterpoint to the moral themes that are being worked out in the portraits of adults. Children could not reasonably be expected to show much self-mastery, or respect for propriety and serenity – unless they were grossly sentimentalised paragons of virtue such as the cloyingly sentimental *'Boy and Rabbit'* (cat.no.57) and *Sir George Sinclair* (cat.no.29). His treatment of *'The Allen Brothers'* (cat.no.20) is more interesting. The boys are playing an obscure, slightly sinister game that demands physicality as well as the skill which neither seems to have mastered. The boys are dressed *en Jacobin* and the stick-wielding brother's face is treated with an Epicurean expressionism that does not at all suggest self-mastery, let alone a capacity for mastering the stoic skills of his class and culture. In the same way, *Robert and Ronald Ferguson* (cat.no.12), two brothers Raeburn knew well and painted on several occasions, suggest a striking contrast. The archer is practising skills and exercising the self-command that will fit him for a useful life. But these do not interest his brother. Like the unruly Allen brother, the expressionistic treatment of his eyes and dress hints at Jacobinism, and a capacity for prudence and self-command that may very well not conform with the canons of propriety.

David Mackie suggests that Raeburn's sensitivity to the expressionistic possibilities of portraiture was acquired in Rome and Edinburgh, from Fuseli and Alexander Runciman.[24] However, as he points out, this Epicurean expressionism lay at the peripheries of his moral vision of his sitters. But it is because it is there and visible in the eyes of his sitters that he is often able to invest his best portraits with a powerful moral and social tension. For these are portraits of people with strong, individual characters and talents who have cheerfully submitted to the sophisticated and demanding stoic disciplines that the Edinburgh moralists and the middling ranks extolled and associated with the education of a cultured patriot élite. No one was more sensitive to these

NOTES AND REFERENCES

1. H. Cockburn, *Life of Lord Jeffrey ...*, Edinburgh, 1852, vol.i, p.157.

2. I am grateful for the help of the Lyon Clerk, Mrs Elizabeth Roads, on this point.

3. *Curiosities of a Scots Charter Chest 1600–1800*, ed. Mrs. A. Forbes, Edinburgh, 1897, p.198.

4. [Robert Mudie], *The Modern Athens: A dissection and demonstration of men and things in the Scotch Capital*, London, 1825, p.162.

5. *Ibid*, p.163.

6. *Edinburgh Review*, 1755–6, preface.

7. He painted Henry Mackenzie and William Craig more than once, Alexander Abercromby and William McLeod Bannatyne once (see Mackie, nos.171, 501 and 512).

8. It was also journalism which circulated widely. The *Mirror* went through 11 editions before 1802, the *Lounger* went through 6 editions by 1812. Moreover, no fewer than 23 of the essays and one poem were reprinted in Edinburgh in the *Calendonian Mercury*, *The Scots Magazine* and *The Bee*. It is likely that the pattern was repeated in other Scottish towns (John Dwyer, *Virtuous Discourse; Sensibility and Community in late Eighteenth Century Scotland*, Edinburgh, 1987). I am much indebted to this book for what follows.

9. *Mirror*, nos.83–4 and 94.

10. *Mirror*, no.83.

11. *Lounger*, no.49.

12. *Lounger*, no.57.

13. *Lounger*, no.39.

14. *Mirror*, no.27. Mackenzie, who knew Smith well, tried unsuccessfully to get the philosopher to contribute to the *Mirror*. Smith sketched a paper but abandoned it, saying, 'My manner of writing ... will not do for a work of that sort; it runs too much into deduction and inference' (I. S. Ross, *The Life of Adam Smith*, Oxford, 1995, p.343).

15. *Lounger*, no.23.

16. *Lounger*, no.24.

17. *Mirror*, no.29.

18. *Lounger*, no.20.

19. *Lounger*, no.2.

20. *Lounger*, no.49.

21. *Lounger*, no 12.

22. *Mirror*, no.39.

23. *Lounger*, no.4.

24. Mackie, vol.1, p.35.

25. *The Letters of Sir Walter Scott*, ed. H. J. C. Grierson, vol.v, London, 1933, vol.v, p.349.

pressures than Sir Walter Scott, the Great Unknown, whose poetic romances and historical novels were a self-conscious attempt to rebuild the moral and historical culture of modern Scotland and to place it within the framework of an always problematical, sometimes infuriating, Anglo–British union. Raeburn owed his appointment as Limner Royal for Scotland and his knighthood to Scott and he owed him the commission to paint the monarch he was never able to carry out. In return, Raeburn painted Scott on three occasions. The earliest portrait (cat.no.38), painted in 1808 when Scott was at the height of his reputation as a poet and before he had published any fiction, is the portrait of a man whose natural genius is unmoderated by any of the conventional signs of hard work and propriety. It is the portrait of a poet who lives for his imagination and owes little if anything to others. It is in this sense the only great romantic portrait Raeburn ever painted and it is interesting that Scott did not much like it; Raeburn had, he said, made 'a very chowderheaded person of me'.[25] He preferred the later more modestly-conceived portrait (cat.no.64), painted in 1823, in which he appears in one of Raeburn's favourite poses. Here the proprieties of dress can be quickly recognised and registered so as to allow the portrait to develop as a classic study of serenity and genius shaped by prudence and self-command, the extraordinary serpentine treatment of his watch-chain reminding us of Scott's wisdom and imaginative power. It is surely characteristic of Scott that he chose to be represented, not in the language of poetic genius, but in the sophisticated, sentimental, stoic idiom which had done so much to shape the culture of his class and the moral vision of the Scottish Enlightenment.

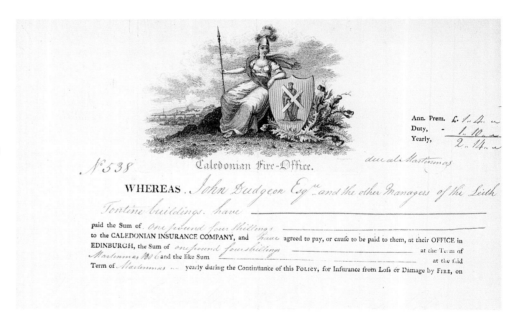

fig.34 *Heading of Caledonian Insurance Company policy engraved by James Kirkwood after Henry Raeburn*
Guardian Royal Exchange Assurance plc

Raeburn's Methods and Materials

JOHN DICK

O VER the past few years the National Galleries of Scotland have been collecting and investigating hitherto unpublished basic data on Raeburn's methods and materials. What is presented here represents 'work in progress' in the hope that it may go some way to help in clarifying his development as a painter. This information is, of necessity, partial and is constrained both by the incidence of works passing through the conservation department and by the means of investigation at our disposal. It is based on low-power microscopy, x-radiography and cross-sections of paint samples. The Galleries are uniquely well placed to carry this out with some sixty portraits in the combined collections of the Portrait Gallery and the National Gallery.[1]

On the few occasions when Raeburn's technique has been discussed, attention has focused on his so-called 'square touch', and on his habitual use of twill canvas.[2] Comment has also centred on his well-known shortcomings in drawing and perspective, often found, for instance, in the arms of chairs.[3] A particularly acute example is to be seen in the portrait of John Stirling of Kippendavie at Fyvie although the many, and sometimes extensive, compositional adjustments which appear throughout his career suggest he was at least aware of these.

Raeburn's initial reputation, as a miniaturist, depends on very few existing examples, ranging from the rather stilted *David Deuchar* (cat.no.1) to the accomplished *2nd Earl Spencer* (cat.no.4), documented as having been painted in Rome, which, while probably somewhat compromised due to its being a copy of a full-scale work by another painter, displays a complete mastery of the miniaturist's technique, albeit in the rather unusual medium of oil paint on ivory.[4] But even on this scale there is a robust quality in the stippled modelling of the face and a notable breadth of handling in the painting of the coat which may be seen as a sign of what was to come (fig.35).

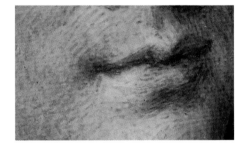

fig.35 Detail from *2nd Earl Spencer* (cat.no.4)

Although never lacking in skill or craftsmanship, Raeburn displays a confusing variety of paint handling and technique in the early part of his career which is difficult to place in a chronological sequence, and it is possible that this simply represents a period when he was engaged in a great deal of experimentation. The sparsity of documentary evidence related to Raeburn's portraits has encouraged several attempts at a chronology in this period. One of the obstacles to this is the apparent non-existence of paintings prior to the years 1784-6 which he spent in Rome, and consequently there are various proposals, none entirely convincing or universally accepted, which have been put forward to fill this perceived void.[5] This gives the impression that he springs from almost complete obscurity to become the painter of the restrained and sensitively handled *Patrick Moir* (cat.no.3), documented as having been painted in Rome, and, on his return to Scotland, to the comparatively more assured, almost flamboyant handling of *Lord Arniston* (cat.no.5), which displays a greater strength in modelling and use of colour.

The latest candidate to be suggested as a pre-Rome work is the *Lady in a Lace Cap* (cat.no.2). Attributed to Raeburn since its acquisition by the National Gallery of Scotland from the Raeburn family it bears a more than superficial resemblance to Raeburn's style and is deemed to be this early partly because of the rather atypical nervous, decorative brushwork which has a notable, persistent zigzag characteristic throughout, including the background, which makes it difficult to place in any later period (fig.36). However, there are several changes in composition: in the hat and in the painting out of the fragment of the chair by the sitter's left shoulder, which are similar to those seen in many paintings by Raeburn. The materials used, the twill canvas and the restricted palette are also consistent with his usual practice.

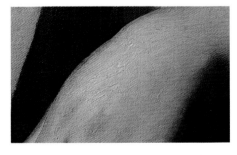

fig.36 Detail from *Lady in a Lace Cap* (cat.no.2)

The anecdotal evidence of a brief period of study with Alexander Runciman in 1782 or a spell spent with David Martin, who would at least have had a solid technical grounding in the studio of Allan Ramsay to pass on, does not explain adequately

Raeburn's impressively sound, early technical ability. There are several treatises on painting technique which it would be reasonable to suppose would have been in Raeburn's possession but these could only have assisted with very basic information.[6] It is tempting therefore to accept the reported influence of a visit to Reynolds's studio in London either before or after his stay in Rome.[7] Typical of the work being produced by Reynolds in this decade are the portraits of the young *Alexander, Duke of Hamilton* of 1781 and *The Ladies Waldegrave* of 1782, with their fluid paint and dashing brushwork. These in no way prepare us for the very different handling of *Patrick Moir* (cat.no.3), a painting which appears to look back in time to the example of Batoni, who was still working in Rome, in its refinement of brushwork and modelling, while at the same time anticipating Raeburn's later work in the simplification of the details of the coat and the precise observation of the softbound book.[8] Certainly, there is no sign of any of the esoteric materials pressed into use by Reynolds in his attempt to recreate the methods of the Old Masters nor the resulting damage wreaked with time on the paintings thus produced.[9] It is more logical to suppose that Raeburn, if influenced at all by Reynolds, saw his work on his return from Rome and, arguably, this can be discerned in the paintings he produced on his return to Edinburgh.

fig.37 Detail from *Niel Gow* (cat.no.27)

The recent reappearance of the *Patrick Moir* demands a reconsideration of the early paintings. A logical technical progression might be to the thinly painted works with translucent brown-toned backgrounds, such as the *Robert Ferguson of Raith* (cat.no.11) and the *6th Marquis of Lothian* (cat.no.9), which sit uncomfortably elsewhere in the chronology.[10] These would be followed by the group of works with medium-rich paint and a fluid, creamy appearance: *Lord Arniston* (cat.no.5), with its inscription convincingly dating it to 1787, *James Hutton* (cat.no.10), perhaps the earliest of the group by virtue of its relatively naïve quality, *Lieut-Colonel Lyon* (cat.no.6), dated 1788 by his uniform, and *Rear-Admiral Inglis* (cat.no.7) – all showing an increasing fluency of handling and ease of modelling in the face. We are then on more secure ground with *Dr Nathaniel Spens* (cat.no.17), commissioned in 1791 and completed in 1793, and the very similar *Niel Gow* (cat.no.27), most tellingly in the apparently effortless treatment of the modelling of the face which is arrived at by a series of overlapping thin scumbles fully exploiting the characteristics of the canvas weave (fig.37). *William Forbes of Callendar* (cat.no.31), commissioned in 1798, has so many points of similarity to *William Ferguson of Kilrie* (cat.no.18) – the oblique lighting, the brilliantly rendered shirt fronts and the bright blue coats with the highlights modified by a scumble of mauve paint – that they must be very close in date.

Raeburn's technique then shades into the more restrained and neatly modelled features of *Lady Raeburn* (cat.no.21) and *The Revd Hugh Blair* (cat.no.25). Up to this point the medium used is almost certainly a traditionally sound drying oil such as linseed, which helps to explain the generally well preserved condition of these earlier works. Work carried out by the National Gallery of Art in Washington DC, investigating the binding media used in *John Johnstone of Alva* (cat.no.23), suggests that, while linseed is the main oil there is a possibility that walnut or poppyseed oil was used in the lighter colours because it yellows less with age. If this is so, it is further evidence of the relatively sophisticated practice of which Raeburn was aware.[11] The more softly modelled works such as *William Hunt of Pittencrieff* (cat.no.39) and *Professor John Playfair* (cat.no.43), dating from the end of the first decade of the nineteenth century, represent a clear change in handling and use of materials. This is apparently achieved with a greater admixture of resinous material, possibly megilp, which would increase the ease of handling and the range of effects available to the painter.[12] This resinous material, while extremely beautiful in the translucency and transitions of the modelling of the heads, is much more susceptible to the action of the restorer's solvent than the materials used in the earlier paintings and may go some way to explain the relatively large number of paintings of this period which are damaged, not only by deterioration through ageing, but also by poor or careless cleaning.[13] The later paintings are more seriously affected by severe traction cracking, particularly in the darkest passages, notably the *Self-portrait* (cat.no.56) and *Mrs Scott Moncrieff* (cat.no.52). This may be due to the use of a bituminous pigment, such as asphaltum, which, if used in excess, could produce these results. Raeburn is also reputed to have used gumption, a form of megilp, as a painting medium. This was an apparently attractive material for many painters of the period, but it was also capable of such drastic damage if used rashly.[14] However, the head-size portrait of *Sir Walter Scott* (cat.no.64), one of Raeburn's last completed paintings, shows him painting once again in a more straightforward manner, although there is a suspicion that the head is completed in a possibly tinted glaze.

Alterations in Raeburn's paintings are common from his earliest works on. They range from minor adjustments to profiles or outlines, such as the position of the *Revd Robert Walker*'s hat or the hands of *James Hutton*, to more radical compositional changes such as the pose of *William Hunt* or the stance of *Forbes of Callendar* which are now visible to the naked eye, due to the tendency of oil paint to become translucent with time. In those portraits which have been examined by x-radiography, a pattern emerges which tends to corroborate the proposed chronology of the visual evidence. The *Lady in a Lace Cap* shows peculiar characteristics – the use of narrow brushes and a swift execution. There may be difficulty in seeing this lead into the more careful painting, almost amounting to a filling-in of outlines, with very little alteration, in *Patrick Moir*, with its fastidious, fine impasto. The medium-rich group contains a relatively high proportion of white lead in the flesh paint. As this pigment is opaque to x-rays it shows as dense white in the radiographs. Below the seemingly smooth appearance of these portraits we find careful, yet restive, dabbing strokes in liquid paint in *James Hutton*, more solid, searching brushwork in *Lieut-Colonel Lyon*. In contrast, *Niel Gow* records poorly in the radiograph, probably because of the low white lead content in the flesh colour. The ruddy hue is apparently composed mainly of earth colours which are relatively transparent to x-rays. Economy of means with a dextrous use of impasto is the most notable feature of the *Lord Eldin* (cat.no.54) and the *Self-portrait* which belies its slightly troubled visual appearance due in the main to condition (figs.38–41).

Other information which is confirmed by x-radiography is the weave of the canvas. The canvas most commonly used by Raeburn is a prepared twill weave which remains remarkably consistent throughout his career.[15] All the available evidence points to the canvas being bought prepared and stretched on lightweight wooden strainers by the artist's colourman.[16] It might be expected that the direction of the twill would be utilised consistently to catch the paint applied by the natural stroke of the right-handed painter. 'S' twill, with a weave angle of about 60°, is the type most often used and this is almost certainly as it came off the loom. 'Z' twill is produced (with a consequential weave angle of 30°) when the cloth is turned through 90°, probably to cut it in the most

fig.42 Macro detail of paint on twill from *Lieut-Colonel Lyon* (cat.no.6)

fig.43 Detail of *Sir John Sinclair* during cleaning (cat.no.28)

economical way. This is used sufficiently often to suggest that the weave direction was not all that important for the painter. Indeed the pair of portraits of Mr and Mrs Kinnear are on different weaves.[17] However, there are numerous instances of the painter using the weave to produce flickering highlights and transitions in the modelling of a face by dragging a stiff paint over the tops of the weave (fig.42).

Twill weave canvas has a long history of use. It was widely used in sixteenth-century Venice, notably by Veronese and to a lesser extent by Titian and Tintoretto.[18] Raeburn would obviously have noted the use of twill by the Old Masters when in Rome, more particularly as he moved in the circle of James Byres who is known to have dealt in the works of many of these painters. Twill was also used widely by many late eighteenth- and early nineteenth-century British painters, probably due to the influence of Reynolds with his well documented interest in the materials and methods of the Old Masters. As the weave persists through the finished paint surface, it is likely that this somewhat decorative and unifying effect is one of the reasons for its use. Unfortunately this effect is often compromised by the effects of relining and the build up of varnish coatings. It is worth remarking that the recovery of this surface texture is one of the less widely recognised benefits of the successful removal of an old varnish (fig.43).

It is, therefore, a matter for speculation why relatively few paintings are on normal weave canvas, among them *Patrick Moir* (cat.no.3), the portrait painted in Rome. It would be tempting to see the use of normal weave canvas as typical of his early years,

as other examples are *Robert Ferguson of Raith* (cat.no.11) and the *6th Marquis of Lothian* (cat.no.9). However, other paintings appear on normal weave: the *Revd Robert Walker* (cat.no.19), *'The Allen Brothers'* (cat.no.20), *Rear-Admiral Inglis* (cat.no.7), *William Hunt of Pittencrieff* (cat.no.39) and *Lady Montgomery* (cat.no.58). There is no obvious technical reason for this.[19]

Paint sample cross-sections allow an examination of the layer structure of the paintings from the ground to the final varnish. The grounds are almost always of a single white layer comprising an oil-bound white lead pigment with a high proportion of chalk as an extender.[20] The *Lady in a Lace Cap* has a notably more intense white ground than usual, probably due to a higher white lead content, and the ground of *Patrick Moir* is considerably more granular and discoloured. The ground of the unfinished *Sir John Maxwell of Pollok* (cat.no.63), which was originally white, has yellowed, probably due to its exposure to light. It also demonstrates how much of the cracking visible in the finished paintings actually originates in this layer.

No known preparatory drawing exists by Raeburn, but in the unfinished portrait of *Lord Braxfield*[21] there is evidence of a preliminary, linear brushed, dark brown lay-in. A similar technique is used by Reynolds in several unfinished compositions – for example *Mrs John Spencer and her Daughter*.[22] Further examples of this are now visible through the thinly brushed upper paint layers in the early paintings of *Robert Ferguson of Raith* and the *6th Marquis of Lothian*. The use of this lay-in may continue in the later paintings but is probably too well covered by the comparatively denser superimposed paint layers to be visible.

Raeburn's palette, which is preserved in the Royal Scottish Academy, sadly, has been thoroughly cleaned and now gives no indication of his colour range. Very little is known of Raeburn's workshop practice. A very restricted range of pigments supposed to have been used by Raeburn has been reported but recent discoveries from the paint samples in cross-section and dispersion show this to be too exclusive.[23] This compares well with a record of the pigments used by Romney which gives an interesting parallel. There is a notable lack of ultramarine in both cases and this can possibly be accounted for on grounds of the cost of this relatively expensive pigment.[24] This can be seen as further evidence of Raeburn's place in the mainstream of British painting of the period.

Nineteenth-century materials were increasingly mass-produced commercially and might be thought to be somewhat predictable. But the cross-sections reveal a surprising range in pigment particle size compared with the uniformity of those of the present day, considering they were almost certainly bought from commercial suppliers. It was known since early times that the coarser the particle size the more vibrant the colour produced. It is a matter for speculation whether they were produced thus naturally or whether this characteristic was specified by Raeburn and possibly paid for accordingly. Although there is ample evidence of adulteration of pigments made by unscrupulous producers, those seen in samples from Raeburn's paintings are generally of high quality. It is interesting to see in the *Sir John Sinclair* (cat.no.28) the use of a very coarsely ground pigment in the detail of the tartan which may be a deliberate attempt by the painter to enliven further the surface texture of his painting. Cross-sections also confirm the subtle mixtures of pigments used by Raeburn and the methodical build up of the layers as well as much evidence of 'wet-in-wet' handling (fig.44).

The samples from *Niel Gow* show clearly how subtly Raeburn chose and mixed his colours, such as the pinks, greens and blues of the tartan which appear to be underpainted in a dull red (figs.45 and 46). The analysis overleaf is gleaned from the examination of minute samples of paint mounted in polyester resin in such a way as to allow microscopic inspection of the layer structure in both reflected and ultraviolet light. Samples have also been examined in dispersion, where a tiny sample of paint is ground in a solvent to disperse the component parts which can then be examined under the microscope in transmitted and polarised light. This allows a reasonable opportunity to identify the pigments present.

An investigation of Raeburn's materials and practice point to a painter working in the mainstream of early nineteenth-century British art with a sound grasp of technique. There appears to be no ill-effect from the painter's own estimation of his remoteness from his peers in the south. The source of his often brilliant perception and execution still awaits a rational explanation.

fig.44 Macro detail from *Lieut-Colonel Lyon* (cat.no.6) showing 'wet-in-wet' handling of the epaulette

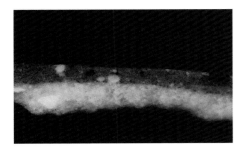

fig.45 Cross-section of paint sample (400 × magnification) from the pink in the tartan trews in *Niel Gow* (cat.no.27)

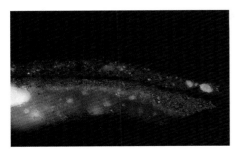

fig.46 Cross-section of paint sample (400 × magnification) from the green in the tartan trews in *Niel Gow*

Paint Analysis

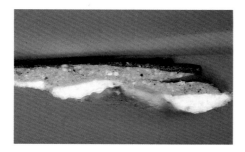

fig.47 Cross-section of paint sample (400 × magnification) from the green tartan, showing vermilion pigment particles, in *Sir John Sinclair* (cat.no.28)

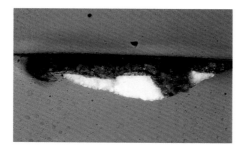

fig.48 Cross-section of paint sample (200 × magnification) from the sky in *Lieut-Colonel Lyon* (cat.no.6)

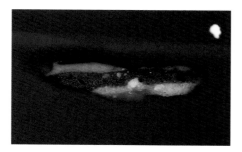

fig.49 Cross-section of paint sample (200 × magnification) from the green tablecloth in *Peter Wood*

ABOVE fig.50 Cross-section of paint sample (200 × magnification) from the hat feathers in *Sir John Sinclair*

RIGHT fig.51 Cross-section of paint sample (400 × magnification) from the trews in *Niel Gow* (cat.no.27)

FAR RIGHT fig.52 Cross-section of paint sample (400 × magnification) from the coat in *Patrick Moir* (cat.no.3)

RED

Raeburn rarely used red pigments pure, apart from the occasions when vermilion was called for, for instance, in military tunics such as those in *Sir John Sinclair* (cat.no.28) and *Sir Duncan Campbell* (cat.no.41). The vermilion in the leather sitter's chair in *Professor Adam Ferguson* (cat.no.26) is modified by an organic red glaze. Intriguingly, vermilion pigment particles appear in virtually every layer examined (fig.47). Organic red (Lake) is often mixed with vermilion, as in the legal robes of *Lord Newton* (cat.no.44) and *Lord Arniston* (cat.no.5) to produce a subtle and distinctive pink. A particularly intense and distinctive organic red used in the very similar pink-red in *Niel Gow* (cat.no.27) is possibly precipitated on chalk, judging by the discovery of a coccolith in the dispersion.

BLUE

The rich blue-green often seen in table coverings and other drapery, in the thin, broadly brushed backgrounds in *Niel Gow* and *Sir John Sinclair* and in the sky of *Lieut-Colonel Lyon* (fig.48) is Prussian blue. A strikingly powerful example of this pigment also appears in the uniform of *Lieut-Col Lyon* (cat.no.6) and in the coat of *William Forbes of Callendar* (cat.no.31). The rather unusual pigment, blue verditer, was identified in the portrait of *Peter Wood* (fig.49).[25] As the evidence of Raeburn's reported pigment range suggests, no ultramarine has been found.

YELLOW

Yellow ochre was found in a green mixture in *Niel Gow*. A fibrous-appearing yellow pigment in the green tablecloth in *Patrick Moir* (cat.no.3) is also a form of yellow ochre. A possible organic yellow occurs in this sample. Very finely ground yellow ochre is present in the feathers of Sinclair's hat (fig.50). An unusual, pale yellow, crystalline pigment, in the anklets of the trews in the same painting, is possibly Turner's, or Patent yellow. The same pigment appears in the orange of the shawl in the *Duchess of Roxburghe* (cat.no.48).

GREEN

As no reliable green pigment was available at this time, apart from the poorly colouring Terre-Verte, most of the greens examined are mixtures of Prussian blue and probably yellow ochre. The green in *Niel Gow's* tartan trews was confirmed as being of this mixture (fig.51).

BROWN

Terracotta-like red earths are used in the shawls of *Mrs Hamilton of Kames* (cat.no.45) and *Mrs James Campbell* (cat.no.40). An unusually muddy mixture, contrasting with Raeburn's normal simple practice, of brown and red ochres, along with the ubiquitous vermilion particles, appears in *Patrick Moir's* coat (fig.52).

BLACK

In the samples examined the black pigment used is mainly charcoal black. It is seldom used pure but appears mostly in the subtle range of grey, green and mauve in the coats of *The Revd Hugh Blair* (cat.no.25), *Sir Walter Scott* (cat.no.64) and *Niel Gow* respectively. The dense shadows, such as those in *Niel Gow* and *Lord Newton* (cat.no.44), are tinted by the addition of red. Bone black was identified by SEM examination in a sample from the green tablecloth in *Patrick Moir*.

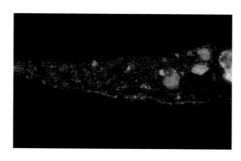

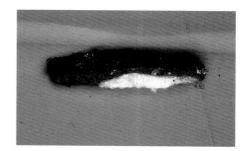

1. The most convenient list appears in
D. Thomson, *Sir Henry Raeburn*, Scottish Masters 21,
Edinburgh, 1994, p.32.

2. The first mention of the 'square touch' appears to
come in a letter from Sir David Wilkie to Thomas
Phillips, listed in Allan Cunningham, *The Life of Sir
David Wilkie*, London, 1843, vol.2, pp.502–6.

3. This same criticism was levelled at Reynolds by
Nicholas Penny in the Reynolds exhibition catalogue,
Royal Academy, London, 1986, p.19.

4. It has been suggested that the date on the label on
the reverse of the *David Deuchar* has been added by a
later hand. Recent examination suggests that the date
has simply been strengthened.

5. Caw; Irwin and Irwin; and Macmillan.

6. Thomas Bardwell, *The Practice of Painting and
Perspective Made Easy*, London, 1756; *The Artist's
Repository*, London, 1784–6; and James Northcote,
The Life of Sir Joshua Reynolds, London, 1819.

7. Perhap co-incidentally, Raeburn is reputed to have
fallen out with his supposed teacher, David Martin, in
much the same way as Reynolds fell out with his
teacher Hudson.

8. A portrait with a more than passing echo of Moir is
the portrait of *Henry Pelham* by J. S. Copley, dated
1765, in the Museum of Fine Arts, Boston (fig.54).
This, intriguingly, shows the same hairstyle almost
twenty years earlier! I am grateful to Michael Cassin
for drawing my attention to this work.

9. Kirby Talley, 'All good pictures crack': Sir Joshua
Reynolds's practice and studio. Reynolds catalogue,
op.cit.

10. There is a remarkable similarity in the pose and
handling of the *6th Marquis of Lothian* (cat.no.9) and
the portrait of *Charles Gordon of Buthlaw* (National
Trust for Scotland, Fyvie Castle). I would include in
this group *George Chalmers of Pittencrieff* (Dunfermline City Chambers) and *Mrs Ferguson and her
Children* (Private collection).

11. Medium analysis was carried out by Suzanne
Lomax of the Scientific Research Department in the
National Gallery of Art in Washington DC. I am
grateful to her for permission to report these findings.

12. Megilp is a gelled painting medium consisting of
sugar of lead, mastic varnish and linseed oil.
Gumption is a variety of this (Alexander Fraser RSA
in *The Portfolio* quoted in Grieg, p.xxxvii).

13. The Edinburgh University version of *Professor
John Playfair* has suffered possibly from both actions,
particularly in the face.

14. See note 12; also John Gage, 'Magilphs and
Mysteries', *Apollo*, vol.80, no.29, pp.38–41.

15. Twill: a woven fabric showing diagonal lines, the
weft yarns having been worked over one and under
two or more warp yarns (*Chambers Dictionary*). The
direction of the twill weave is described convention-
ally by referring to the slopes of the letters S and Z.

16. Several canvases have been noted as bearing
excise and colourman's stamps on the reverse. All are
of the established London firm, John Middleton. The
dates of the portraits thus marked range from 1805–
12. While it has often been suspected that these
stamps may include a date none until now has been
legible. The stamp on the reverse of *Lord Newton*
appears to be dated 1810. The finding of this evidence
depends on canvases being unlined – a relatively rare
occurrence so that while other colourmen's stamps
may exist they may simply have not been seen
(William T. Whitley, *Artists and their Friends in
England, 1700–1799*, London, 1928, vol.2, pp.333–4).
A letter in the British Museum, from Raeburn to John

Morrison referring to his dealing with Middleton
is reproduced in Grieg, p.xxxvii.

Further information found on the reverse of
paintings consists of inscriptions vouching for the
authenticity of the painting by Raeburn's
grandson, Logan White Raeburn, who also signs
the reverse of the canvas. This is accompanied by
a seal with a crest, devised posthumously for
Raeburn and referred to by Greig, p.xiii. These
are presumably the paintings sold by the family at
Christie's on 7 May 1877 and include the portraits
of *Lady Raeburn* (cat.no.21), the *Self-portrait*
(cat.no.56) and *Sir Walter Scott* (cat.no.64).

17. The portraits of Mr and Mrs Kinnear are in
the collection of the National Gallery of Scotland,
Edinburgh (NG 1222 and 1223).

18. A more complicated diaper weave has also
been used by several painters down through the
years. Other painters frequently using twill
canvases are Velázquez, Claude and Poussin. An
early occurrence is to be found in Mantegna's, *The
Virgin and Child with the Magdalen and S. John the
Baptist* of *c.*1500 (National Gallery, London,
no.274).

19. The portrait of *Henry Mackenzie* (Burrell
Collection, Glasgow) is painted on a herringbone
or chevron weave canvas.

20. Coccoliths, microscopic fossil marine
organisms, indicative of chalk, were found in all
the grounds examined.

21. The portrait of *Lord Braxfield* is in the
collection of the Scottish National Portrait
Gallery.

22. The painting of *Mrs John Spencer and her
Daughter* is in the collection of the Duke of
Devonshire at Chatsworth.

23. Alexander Fraser RSA in *The Portfolio*, quoted
in Grieg, p.xxxvii.

24. Hermann W. Williams, 'Romney's Palette',
Technical Studies in the Field of the Fine Arts,
Fogg Art Museum, Harvard University, July
1937, vol.VI, pp.19–23.
  Middleton's list of artists' materials published in
1785 states: 'Ultramarine of a sort could be had at
three guineas an ounce but for his best quality
[he] asked ten guineas. This compared with
Prussian blue which cost sixpence a bladder'
(Whitley, *op.cit.* p.334).

25. The portrait of *Peter Wood* is in Trinity
House, Edinburgh.

ACKNOWLEDGEMENTS

I am greatly indebted to my colleagues in the
Conservation Department for many fruitful
discussions on Raeburn, particularly Donald
Forbes who cleaned the portrait of *Niel Gow*
(cat.no.27) and Nicola Christie whose work in
producing and analysing the cross-sections and
dispersions, and for many helpful insights at
manuscript stage, was invaluable. Thanks are also
due to Keith Morrison and William Fernie for
their work on the frames. Lesley Stevenson,
Culpeper Paintings Conservation Fellow at the
National Gallery of Art in Washington DC, kindly
shared the findings from investigation during her
cleaning, and the result of the medium analysis by
the Scientific Department in Washington DC of
the portrait of *John Johnstone of Alva* (cat.no.23).
My thanks are also due to Paul Wilthew of the
National Museums of Scotland who, yet again,
kindly carried out SEM based energy dispersive
microanalysis of several pigments.

Catalogue

1   *David Deuchar 1743 – 1808*

Watercolour on ivory 2⅜ × 1⅞in (6 × 4.8cm)

National Gallery of Scotland, Edinburgh

PROVENANCE

By descent in the sitter's family; the Revd J. Seton Deuchar, from whom purchased by the National Gallery of Scotland, 1931

EXHIBITIONS

Edinburgh, Royal Scottish Academy, 1863 (376); Edinburgh, Royal Scottish Academy, *Exhibition of the Works of Sir Henry Raeburn*, 1876 (305); London, Royal Academy, *Scottish Art*, 1939 (109); Edinburgh, National Gallery of Scotland, *Ramsay, Raeburn and Wilkie*, 1951 (51); Edinburgh, National Gallery of Scotland, *Raeburn*, 1956 (2)

LITERATURE

Andrew, p.113; *Caledonian Jottings ...4*, Caledonian Insurance Company, January 1900, pp.5–9; Armstrong, pp.36–7, 49, 88, 99; Pinnington, pp.60, 63, 69, 70, 254; Greig, pp.xv, 43; Cursiter, p.58; Dibdin, pp.24, 25, 27, 110, 133; George S. Draffen, *Pour La Foi*, Dundee, 1949, pp.8–84; Daphne Foskett, *A Dictionary of British Miniature Painters*, 2 vols, London, 1972, vol.2, p.460; Irwin, p.243; Irwin and Irwin, p.152; Macmillan, 1986, p.74; Charles C. Smith, 'The Man Who Discovered Raeburn', *The Scots Magazine*, July 1987, pp.434–6; Macmillan, 1990, p.151; Mackie, vol.1, pp.33–4 and no.778

NOTES

1. Scottish National Portrait Gallery, PGL 75. This is one of a large series of such drawings. Brown also portrayed him in a highly classicised 'miniature' drawing which is dated 1787 (Scottish National Portrait Gallery, PG 980).

This miniature appears to be Raeburn's earliest surviving work. The attribution and date derive from an old inscription on the paper-backing on the reverse of the frame – supported, of course, by the traditional contact between the sitter and Raeburn at a very early stage in his career, and by the miniature's provenance. The inscription reads: 'David Deuchar, Esq., of Morningside, by Sir Henry Raeburn, being the second portrait done by him, during the time he was an apprentice with Mr. Gilland [Gilliland], Jeweller, Parliament Square, Edinburgh.' Beneath this, in what may be a later hand, is written: 'Painted about 1773'. The date has been strengthened, or perhaps even altered.

Whatever the origin and status of these inscriptions, the information they contain appears credible. The miniature itself, although accomplished in some respects, generally has a formal naïveté which would not be surprising if the date is correct. This is most evident in the emphasis given to contours, where, for example, one element of the costume is separated from another. Again, the collar of the coat and the stock have little sense of continuing behind the forms that they should enfold. This rather too meticulous linearity is clearest in the dark lines that define the curls at the right ear, the eyebrows and the upper eyelids. On the other hand the bluish shadows on the pale face are sensitively integrated and the shadows around the mouth and down the left side of the sitter's face show a certain mastery. A surprising detail that might be taken to look forward to the mature painter is the careful description of the woven pattern of the buttons on the coat.

David Deuchar was a goldsmith, seal engraver and amateur etcher. He was born in Kinnell in Forfarshire, the son of a farmer, Alexander Deuchar, who had become a lapidary after the 1745 Rising, setting up a lapidary mill at Croft an Righ near Holyroodhouse. A member of the Society of Antiquaries (and portrayed as such by John Brown),[1] David Deuchar was also a member of the Royal Company of

Archers and their 'recorder of medals'. His etchings after the Dutch little masters, which he published in 1803, were an important source of imagery for Sir David Wilkie. Deuchar is also credited with having encouraged Raeburn in his move from jeweller to painter. This is merely a traditional belief, first formulated in Raeburn's obituary, and there is no other firm evidence for it.

2 *Lady in a Lace Cap*

Oil on canvas 36¼ × 28in (92 × 71cm)

National Gallery of Scotland, Edinburgh

PROVENANCE
Bequeathed by Miss Alice Leslie Inglis to the National Gallery of Scotland, 1934

EXHIBITIONS
London, Royal Academy, *Scottish Art*, 1939 (117)

NOTES
1. National Gallery of Scotland accession files, NG 1816.
2. Collection of Sir James Hunter Blair.
3. I am grateful to my colleague, Rosalind Marshall, for this analysis of the costume.
4. Cunningham, vol.v, p.211.
5. I am grateful to Lindsay Errington for her suggestion that Cunningham's story could refer to this portrait.

fig.53 *Sarah Ballantine* by David Martin
Private collection

This undocumented portrait is at first sight no more self-evidently by Raeburn than his documented portrait of *Patrick Moir* (cat.no.3), painted in Rome at some time between 1784 and 1786. It appears, however, to have always borne an attribution to Raeburn within the family of Miss Alice Leslie Inglis, a descendant of Raeburn's step-daughter Ann Leslie, who bequeathed it to the National Gallery of Scotland in 1934. At the time, it was received enthusiastically by the Gallery's trustees who had 'no hesitation' in accepting it as the work of Raeburn. The Director, Stanley Cursiter, was convinced that it was 'in every way characteristic of his early work and a very good example', although he clearly had grave reservations about the quality of the hands, as he soon arranged to have the rectangular painting reframed as an oval, so that they were no longer visible.[1] His phrase, 'characteristic of his early work', is slightly puzzling, since it is difficult to know with which full-scale works he was comparing it. At this time the portrait of Moir was completely unknown and even if he had in mind the portrait of *George Chalmers of Pittencrieff*, which was long – and mistakenly – believed to have been painted in 1776, it is difficult to comprehend what similarities he saw between them. This also applies if he happened to be comparing it with the portrait of *Lord Arniston* (cat.no.5) which was certainly painted in 1787, the year following Raeburn's return from Rome, and which bears a number of the hallmarks of the mature painter. It is also worth noting that Cursiter frequently refers to the subject as 'an old lady' (and it was so exhibited at the Royal Academy in 1939), whereas it is quite obvious that she is scarcely even middle-aged. In the event, the work soon disappeared from view and lost any credence as being an early work of Raeburn. Nevertheless, Cursiter's connoisseurship was of a kind that should not easily be discounted and he may well have been conscious of some quality in the picture that pointed to Raeburn and that, taken with the picture's provenance, did indeed support such an attribution.

That this portrait is, in fact, very likely to be Raeburn's earliest known full-scale work is given some support, as far as the date is concerned, by the nature of the costume. On her head the lady wears a *dormeuse* or French 'nightcap'. The side wings, or 'cheek wrappers' are muslin (rather than the 'lace' of the traditional title). This style of cap was popular from about 1750 to 1790. A very similar cap, seen from the side, is included in a portrait dated 1787 of *Sarah Ballantine* by David Martin (fig.53).[2]

The kerchief worn round the neck and shoulders is tucked into the breast knots, or bows, on the bodice of the dress. This style is known as early as 1750 and it continued for several decades. By the 1780s the kerchief was large and was usually called a neckerchief. Of particular significance is the shawl, since these did not come into fashion until the 1780s. There is thus good evidence for dating the portrait to the early 1780s.[3]

In stylistic terms the portrait also seems to relate to other works that are certainly by Raeburn. The hands and the areas of visible arm (which are certainly not those of an elderly person) have a smoothness and clarity of outline that recall the hands in the portrait of Patrick Moir, although the fingers are not articulated with the same sophistication. But within these apparently rather simple fleshy areas are agitated, zigzag brushstrokes that relate to the treatment of flesh areas in mature works. The gradation of the pink that describes the shadow under the subject's left arm is again close to the method used in the shadows on the undersides of Moir's hands and on the bottom edge of the lobe of his left ear. There is also a crispness in the muslin at her cheeks and round her arms that is similar to the cuffs on Moir's shirtsleeves, painted in both cases in that deft and attentive manner that Raeburn used in so many of his later pictures. It is also noteworthy that the box-like folds of the cheek wrappers break the even light

that passes across the face, casting a series of small, horizontal shadows that run in ladder-like fashion from the hairline down almost to the sitter's right jaw. This interest in the flow of light and the formation of cast shadows is something that, in stylistic terms, would become of paramount importance to Raeburn in the early 1790s.

In contrast to such subtlety is the broad application of the thick highlights that are worked into all the locally black areas of the dress. The shawl is also painted with a particularly impasted vigour, especially in the valleys of the crumpled left arm and in the long descending inner fold of the shawl, from the left shoulder down to just above the sitter's left wrist. It is the kind of 'attack' on the material of dress that is so evident in a portrait like the *Mrs James Campbell* painted about 1811 (cat.no.40).

The portrait, of course, has a somewhat bland frontality and a plainness of approach which are perhaps closer to the work of David Allan than to that of David Martin, Raeburn's more obvious predecessor. There are elements which verge on the naïve, including the four-square nature of the chair, the top line of which should continue beyond the sitter's left shoulder – and a ridge of paint indicates that it once did so, but the thick, darkish yellow ochre of the empty background has obliterated it. The studs on this chair also have a staccato peremptoriness, regular blobs of yellow ochre each with an identical lemon yellow highlight.

The portrait thus seems to contain sufficient evidence to place it very near the beginning of Raeburn's career, later than the miniature of David Deuchar, which he seems to have painted in 1773, but earlier than the portrait of Patrick Moir – and thus, perhaps, the only oil painting that Raeburn had produced before he set off for Rome.

Finally, it is interesting to note that Cursiter briefly toyed with the notion that the sitter might be Ann Edgar, the widow of James Leslie whom Raeburn would marry, probably in the summer of 1780.

Cursiter did not pursue the idea, and it hardly seemed to make sense because of his references to her as an 'old lady'. However, given both the painting's provenance and the fact that the degree of black in the lady's costume seems to indicate a widowhood of a year or two (her first husband, James Leslie, had died in early 1778) the idea may not be entirely ridiculous. Further, Allan Cunningham in his brief biography of the artist recounts how 'a young lady' appeared at his studio at the time he was switching from miniature to easel painting and sat for her portrait. The lady was Ann Edgar, daughter of Peter Edgar of Bridgelands and 'within a month or so after the adventure of the studio she gave him her hand in marriage …'[4] While there is nothing to corroborate Cunningham's story, when taken with the picture's descent in the family of Raeburn's elder step-daughter Ann Leslie (who married a James Philip Inglis), it is just possible that Cursiter's rather ill-thought-out speculation was actually correct.[5]

A test that can be applied is, of course, a comparison with Raeburn's later portrait of his wife, painted in the early 1790s (cat.no.21). There is a great gulf in the degree of sophistication of the two portraits which, inevitably, makes a comparison of the physiognomic information difficult. The lady in the earlier portrait seems to have a much narrower face but this is perhaps the result of the tent-like cheek wrappers from which the sitter looks out. There is certainly some similarity in expression, and the feature of bare forearms is something that is common to both portraits – in this case a sexual response, rather than a mere record of circumstance or a reaction to the dictates of an employer.

3 *Patrick Moir 1769–1810*

Oil on canvas 29 × 24in (73.8 × 61cm)

Private collection, Western Australia

PROVENANCE
By descent in the sitter's family

LITERATURE
J. Mitchell Gill, *The Families of Moir and Byres*, Edinburgh, 1885, pp.31–2; Brinsley Ford, 'James Byres, Principal Antiquarian for the English Visitor to Rome', *Apollo*, June 1974, pp.456, 461; Mackie, vol.1, pp.41–2 and no.540

NOTES
1. The equation of the references with a photograph of the painting in the Witt Library was first made by David Mackie in a public lecture at the University of Edinburgh in 1985: see Mackie, vol.1, pp.41–2 and no.540.
2. National Library of Scotland, Dep. 184 Moir/Byres papers.
3. The 'lost' painting was traced to its present owner by Helen Smailes.
4. See Introduction.
5. Basil Skinner, *Scots in Italy in the 18th Century*, Edinburgh (National Galleries of Scotland), 1966, p.17.
6. J. Mitchell Gill, *The Families of Moir and Byres*, Edinburgh, 1885, p.67, quoting a transcription from an *Aberdeen Journal* of 1812 of the epitaph on his tomb in Calcutta.

fig.54 *Henry Pelham (Boy with a Squirrel)* by John Singleton Copley
Museum of Fine Arts, Boston

Patrick Moir was the nephew of James Byres, the famous antiquarian and *cicerone* (guide) to British visitors to Rome. It is not known when Moir joined his uncle in Rome to assist him in his various financial and antiquarian activities, but it cannot have been later than the period 1784–6 when the present portrait must have been painted – that is, the time that Raeburn is known to have been in the city. The portrait, until recently virtually unknown,[1] and unseen by any writer on Raeburn, is listed in an inventory of Byres's possessions prepared, apparently by Byres himself, in May 1790.[2] Among the furnishings, a wide range of paintings is mentioned, including works by Franciszek Smuglevicz, Jacob More, Gavin Hamilton, David Allan, Pompeo Batoni and Angelica Kauffman. The inventory is subdivided by room and, 'In what was my Mothers Room', is listed 'a portrait of Patrick Moir by Mr Raeburn'. That the present portrait, which has a continuous provenance and traditional identification in the sitter's family,[3] is the same as the portrait mentioned in this inventory is virtually certain. It is also extremely likely that the portrait had been painted in Rome rather than taken out from Scotland and represents, therefore, the only known outcome (apart from two tiny subject pictures of single figures and a miniature copied for Lord Spencer (cat.no.4))[4] of this early watershed in Raeburn's life.

There is, as a consequence, little in Raeburn's earliest works with which it can readily be compared and if the evidence had not been so conclusive it is doubtful if it would have been easily recognised as his work. It was only natural, of course, that Raeburn should establish contact with his fellow-countryman, Byres, and move in the same circles, so that the conjunction of Raeburn and Moir is not surprising.

The pose of the young man – Moir was only about fifteen or sixteen at the time – is languorous, the long right arm crooked to support the down-turned head, part of the long-established tradition of portraits of melancholic subjects. This sense of languor is emphasised by the heavily lidded, downcast eyes. The fleshy areas have a refined smoothness of modelling that was not to be typical of Raeburn and this, taken with the general disposition of the elements of the figure within the picture space, is far more suggestive of someone like the young Copley than Raeburn. Nevertheless, the reds on the brighter folds of the coat as well as the intense shadows in the valleys of these folds do appear to link, although they are rather awkwardly merged, with Raeburn's later, characteristic works. Even more suggestive of the mature painter are the carefully observed pages of the book, the area of grey type subtly indicated, and the sharp precision of the sitter's cuffs and shirt-frills. The profiles of these white areas where they lie against darks are close in quality to the same features in the *Lady in a Lace Cap* (cat.no.2). A rather awkward immaturity is always present, perhaps no more so than in the lack of foreshortening in the drawing of the rear of the head, which greatly exaggerates the distance from the tip of the chin to the base of the skull.

Patrick Moir was the son of the Revd George Moir of Peterhead and his wife Martha Byres, sister of James Byres. After the French invasion of Rome in 1797 and Byres's removal to Britain, Moir took responsibility for his uncle's effects, including this portrait, and ultimately arranged their return home. Moir was sometimes referred to as 'the English [*sic*] Banker in Rome' and in 1800 was involved in conveying funds from England to Prince Henry Benedict, Cardinal York, brother of the late Pretender.[5] By 1807 he was in Bengal as secretary to Lord Minto, president of the board of commissioners for the affairs of India. In the same year he was appointed Commissioner of the Court of Requests at Calcutta, 'a trust which he discharged with integrity, assiduity, and ability to the time of his decease'. He died, still in Calcutta, on 5 February 1810.

4   *George John Spencer, 2nd Earl Spencer 1758–1834*

Oil on ivory miniature 2⅝ × 2⅛in (6.7 × 5.5cm)

Althorp Park

PROVENANCE
By descent in the sitter's family

LITERATURE
Daphne Foskett, *A Dictionary of British Miniature Painters*, London, 1972, vol.1, pp.460–1; Brinsley Ford, 'James Byres, Principal Antiquarian for the English Visitors to Rome', *Apollo*, June 1974, p.453; Irwin and Irwin, p.151; Macmillan, 1986, p.76; Macmillan, 1990, p.151; Mackie, vol.1, p.41 and no.779

NOTES
1. The miniature and documents were first mentioned in Daphne Foskett, *A Dictionary of British Miniature Painters*, London, 1972, vol.1, p.460. They are fully published in Irwin, pp.239–44.

Of the four known works that Raeburn painted in Rome, this miniature copy is the most fully documented, James Byres, the resident Scottish antiquary in Rome, noting in a letter of 26 January 1786 to Lord Spencer, subject of the portrait, that it had been completed the day before.[1] It was copied from a pastel drawing by the Irish artist, Hugh Douglas Hamilton (*c*.1739–1808), who was resident in Italy from 1778 to 1791, and was intended for Lady Spencer. Why Byres should have arranged for his untried countryman to have the commission, and how he persuaded Lord Spencer that he was an appropriate choice is unclear, but it may well be that he was able to show him examples of Raeburn's work that demonstrated his prowess as a miniature painter and he may also have shown him the full-size portrait of *Patrick Moir* (cat.no.3), if it had been completed by the beginning of 1786.

Byres, in Rome, writes to Lord Spencer, in Paris: 'I have the honour of forwarding the miniature copy of your Lordship's portrait for Lady Spencer … Her Ladyship desired me to have it sett here but if I had (as it was only finished yesterday) I am afraid it would not have reached you at Paris and was sure Lady Spencer would prefer having it soon to having it sett. I think Mr Raeburn has succeeded remarkably in the likeness; I do not like the very high collar of the coat, but it is a good miniature and I hope will meet with your Lordship's and Lady Spencer's appreciation …'

On 14 June of the same year, Byres writes hoping 'that Lady Spencer received the miniature copy of your portrait by Mr Raeburn from Mr Hamilton's crayon picture …' Although there are pastel portraits by Hugh Douglas Hamilton in the Spencer collection, the original portrait which Raeburn copied does not appear to have survived. However, Byres's remark on its being a good likeness can readily be believed, given Raeburn's immense skill as a copyist of other artists' work much later in his career.

While the miniature, therefore, can tell us little about Raeburn's life-size work at this period in his life, it does show an immense increase in skill and sophistication in the ten or more years that had elapsed since his miniature portrait of *David Deuchar* (cat.no.1). Also, its unhesitant, mature handling of the forms of mainline British portraiture of the period presages the otherwise surprising accomplishment of portraits like the *Lord Arniston* (cat.no.5) and the *Lieut-Colonel Lyon* (cat.no.6), painted in the year or two immediately after his return to Scotland.

Lord Spencer was on the Grand Tour from 1778 to 1780. In 1781 he married Lavinia Bingham, daughter of the 1st Baron Lucan, for whom the miniature was copied. From 1780 to 1782 he was MP for Northampton, and, from 1781 until his father's death in 1783, MP for Surrey. In the Lords he supported Charles James Fox until 1794, when he transferred his allegiance to William Pitt. He was well known as a book collector and became president of the Roxburghe Club in 1812. He was also a trustee of the British Museum.

5   *Robert Dundas, Lord Arniston 1713–87*

Oil on canvas 47⅞ × 40⅜in (121.5 × 102.5cm)
Inscribed bottom left: This Picture Was in Aug.ᵗ 1787 Drawn/For JOHN DAVIDSON Writer
to the Signet/And Was in Dec.ʳ Thereafter Presented by/him to [?the] LORD ADVOCATE

Mrs Althea Dundas-Bekker, Arniston House

PROVENANCE

John Davidson of Stewartfield and Haltree;
Robert Dundas of Arniston; thence by descent

EXHIBITIONS

London, South Kensington Museum, *Second
Special Exhibition of National Portraits*, 1867
(790); Edinburgh, Royal Scottish Academy,
Exhibition of the Works of Sir Henry Raeburn,
1876 (151)

LITERATURE

Brown, p.88; Chaloner Smith, vol.2, p.748;
Andrew, p.116; Armstrong, pp.89, 100;
Stevenson, p.411; Pinnington, pp.89, 131, 226;
Caw, 1908, pp.73, 78; Caw, *Masterpieces*, p.58;
Greig, pp.xxiii, xxx, 44; Dibdin, p.131; Sander-
son, pp.133, 139; Collins Baker, p.162; Irwin and
Irwin, p.152; Macmillan, 1986, pp.75, 76;
Macmillan, 1990, pp.152, 153; Mackie, vol.I,
pp.44, 45–7, 54, 58, 77 and no.241

NOTES

1. London, National Portrait Gallery.
2. Edinburgh, Scottish National Portrait Gallery.
3. Collection of Viscount Cowdray.

This is the first painting known to have
been painted by Raeburn after his return
from Rome. It must almost immediately
have become a demonstration of what this
largely untried painter was capable, and its
seriousness and solid accomplishment
were the foundation of the long and
successful career that was to follow.

The painting, other than in perfect
lighting conditions, seems to have a rather
forbidding darkness, but this is not so.
Properly lit, it has a unified chromatic
richness that Raeburn worked hard to
attain. The portrait, in fact, has no easy
graces, and the handling of paint, even in
areas that might be read as broadly

brushed, such as the wonderful effulgence
of pink ribbons lying on the subject's
thighs, has a tentative, hesitant quality, so
that even broad areas of colour are com-
prised of short dabs of paint. The slightly
deceptive air of darkness is largely due to
the ochre-coloured drapery behind the
sitter. This drapery was originally green,
not dissimilar to the green of the tablecloth on the right, and minute traces of the
original colour are still widely visible. This
inevitably affects the chromatic balance of
the whole.

There is other evidence of a change of
mind at a quite late stage in the production
of the portrait, particularly in the area

fig.55 *Warren Hastings* by Joshua Reynolds
National Portrait Gallery, London

around the sitter's right cuff which has been substantially redrawn, and in parts of the stock and cloak near the throat. These changes in themselves do not indicate inexperience, for quite dramatic alterations at a relatively late stage were to remain a feature of Raeburn's work throughout his life. Inexperience does show, however, in Raeburn's failure to define exactly where the sitter's right knee is – it remains unclear if the blackish area with a rather 'smeared' grey high-light towards the bottom right corner of the picture represents a misplaced part of the seat of the chair, or the top of the knee in question. If it is the knee, as seems most likely, it is unconvincingly related to the left thigh and knee immediately above it.

There are other indications of a certain immaturity, including the pains-taking, carefully descriptive manner in which the chair is depicted (the studs, the smooth highlight of the horsehair back and the moulding of the front upright), the tentative nature of the fluted pilaster on the right and the ponderous, over-solemn quality of the drapery in the rear. This drapery may carry a reference to the Baroque portraits Raeburn must have seen in Rome, but a closer source would be Reynolds, in portraits like the *Warren Hastings* (1766–8, fig.55),[1] *William Robertson* (1772)[2] or the *Joshua Sharpe* (probably 1785).[3] The influence of David Martin may be evident in the cream and pink linearity, a kind of 'streakiness', of the hands and face. The left hand is beautifully drawn in paint and with an anatomical force which is astonishing for a painter whose career had scarcely begun and who had very few academic credentials. The face has a yellowish base with an overall chalky quality, broken on the right cheek by a series of parallel, pure pink brushstrokes, while the fore-head is composed of a grouping of seemingly haphazard, zigzag strokes, something which would become a feature of Raeburn's treatment of that particular area.

The sitter died on 13 December 1787, only a few months after the portrait was completed, if the inscription is wholly credible. It is so specific that this seems probable, although it appears to be rather later than the painting. The 'Lord Advo-cate', to whom the commissioner, John Davidson of Stewartfield and Haltree, gave the painting, was presumably Dundas's son, Robert, who did not attain that office until 1789. A line engraving of the portrait by William Sharp was published in 1790.

Dundas was the son of Robert Dundas of Arniston (Lord President from 1748 to 1753) and his first wife, Elizabeth Watson. He studied at the universities of Edin-burgh and Utrecht and was admitted advocate in 1738. Appointed Solicitor General in 1742, he entered parliament for Midlothian in April 1754 and became Lord Advocate a few months later. He was appointed Lord President of the Court of Session in 1760, a position he held until his death. He was publicly mobbed in March 1769 when the House of Lords overturned the decision against Archibald Stewart in the Douglas peerage case which had resulted from Dundas's casting vote. His eyesight failed towards the end of his life.

He married, first, Henrietta Baillie (1741), and second, Jean Grant, daughter of Lord Prestongrange (1756). By the latter he had four sons, including Robert, who became Lord Advocate and Chief Baron of the Exchequer, and Francis who became a general and was the subject of a double portrait by Raeburn (cat.no.50).

6   *Lieut-Colonel George Lyon (fl.1788 – 1801)*

Oil on canvas 35½ × 27in (90.1 × 68.5cm)

National Gallery of Scotland, Edinburgh

PROVENANCE
David Smith, 1876; by descent to Lord Kinnear, 1895; bequeathed by Miss Kinnear to the National Gallery of Scotland, 1919

EXHIBITIONS
Edinburgh, Royal Scottish Academy, *Exhibition of the Works of Sir Henry Raeburn*, 1876 (248); London, Grafton Galleries, *Scottish Old Masters*, 1895 (49); Edinburgh, National Gallery of Scotland, *Ramsay, Raeburn and Wilkie*, 1951 (55); Edinburgh, National Gallery of Scotland, *Raeburn*, 1956 (10)

LITERATURE
Andrew, p.135; Armstrong, p.107; Pinnington, p.425; Stevenson, p.407; Greig, p.51; *Raeburn*, exhibition catalogue, National Gallery of Scotland, 1956, p.17; Irwin, p.240; Irwin and Irwin, p.152; Macmillan, 1986, p.77; Mackie, vol.I, pp.48–9 and no.474

NOTES
1. National Gallery of Scotland accession files, NG 1224.
2. He is last referred to in the Army List of 1801. On his career and for a discussion of the uniform, see the note by L. E. Buckell in the above file.

The overwhelming impression of this portrait is of a luscious creaminess of pigment and a striking contraposto pose – body to the front, head to the right – the face imbued with a strong sense of concentration prior to imminent action. The actual substance of paint is constantly asserted, from the concoction of white, whitish ochre and grey that makes up the lapels of Lyon's coat and cravat to the 'loops' of foliage to the right of his head. Much of this light area at his breast seems to have been painted 'wet-in-wet', an indication of the confidence with which Raeburn was moving his brush at this relatively early stage in his career. Even the lighter blues in the breast area of the Prussian blue coat appear to have been worked in this way. In contrast, although thick white is used on the starred epaulettes and their fringes, it is a leaner pigment and dragged over the diagonal weave of the canvas to create the texture of the fringes (tails).

The tension of the pose owes much to the upthrust of Lyon's left leg, his boot presumably planted on something raised above ground level, on which he rests his portfolio. This portfolio, bearing in its turn a sheet of paper pinned down by the pressure of his left thumb and the *porte crayon* in his right hand, is foreshortened in a masterly way and with a sense of the tangibility of paper and board that would become a hallmark of Raeburn's treatment of still-life elements. The keen eye for foreshortened form extends to the buttons positioned on the folds of Lyon's coat.

Although the handling is different, the high key (brightness) of the picture and the fixing of a moment of significant action are reminiscent of the work of Batoni, which is very likely to have impressed Raeburn in Rome. The evidence of the costume indicates that the portrait was painted in 1788, which places it close to the start of Raeburn's career: Lyon became a cornet in the 11th Light Dragoons in that year and the coat he wears had been replaced by a different type in 1789.[1]

If this date is correct, then Raeburn has developed considerably in ease and suppleness in the two or three years that separate this portrait from that of *Patrick Moir* (cat.no.3). The carefully modulated drawing of the hands, especially the foreshortening of the left one, is reminiscent of the *Moir*, but the handling is far freer and considerably more confident. The painting also has a vigour – even panache – that distances it from the stiff, restrained manner of the portrait of *Lord Arniston* (cat.no.5) which can have been painted little more than a year earlier. It does, however, share with that portrait the carefully worked, yellowish highlights of the face.

The identification of the sitter as Colonel Lyon is derived from the information on an old label formerly on the reverse of the picture. It read: 'Colonel Lyon/Father of Capt Lyon/who went to the North/Pole. Painted by/Sir H. Raeburn'. The explorer was George Francis Lyon, born in Chichester in 1795 to George Lyon and his wife Louisa Hart. George, who rose to the rank of captain in the Navy, made two voyages to the Arctic, the first with William Parry in 1821–3, the second in command of the *Griper* in 1824. He published accounts of both expeditions. His father, subject of Raeburn's portrait, although much promoted, seems to have had a less notable career. He was promoted to lieutenant in 1792, captain in 1793, major in 1795 and lieutenant-colonel in 1798. Little else is known.[2] Nor is there any record of how he acquired the scar which Raeburn so carefully depicts on his right cheek.

7 *Rear-Admiral Charles Inglis c.1731–91*

Oil on canvas 49½ × 41in (125.7 × 104.1cm)
Inscribed (later) lower left: Admiral Charles Inglis/5th son of Sir J. Inglis & Anne
Cockburn.; and (later) lower right: Sir H. Raeburn, pinx!

Scottish National Portrait Gallery, Edinburgh

PROVENANCE
The sitter's son, by his mistress Nelly Finlayson;
by descent in the Inglis and Wauchope families to
Sir John Don-Wauchope, by whom bequeathed to
the Scottish National Portrait Gallery, 1951

EXHIBITIONS
Edinburgh, Royal Scottish Academy, *Exhibition
of the Works of Sir Henry Raeburn*, 1876 (99);
Edinburgh, National Gallery of Scotland,
Raeburn, 1956 (7)

LITERATURE
Andrew, p.131; Armstrong p.105; Pinnington,
pp.137, 236; Greig, p.49; Macmillan, 1986, p.77;
Mackie, no.419

NOTES
1. London, National Gallery.
2. Letter in Scottish National Portrait Gallery
accession files, PG 1567, from G. P. B. Naish of the
National Maritime Museum, 17 February 1955.

fig.56 *Lord Heathfield* by Joshua Reynolds
National Gallery, London

Although this portrait in its original state
must be close in date to the *Lord Arniston*
(cat.no.5) it has an ease and stylishness
that suggest rather greater experience and
therefore a slightly later date. The portrait
has undergone considerable alteration by
Raeburn himself after it was completed,
but it is clear that Inglis was originally
depicted in the uniform of a captain of the
Royal Navy, a rank he held from 1761 to
1790, when he was promoted to rear-
admiral. It must, therefore, have been
painted between 1787 and 1790, and,
given its gain in sophistication over the
Lord Arniston, most likely in 1788 or 1789.

This gain in sophistication may indicate a debt to Reynolds, for the portrait
recalls in a number of respects the English
painter's *Lord Heathfield* (fig.56),[1] exhibited at the Royal Academy in 1788 and
therefore perhaps available for Raeburn to
see in London on his return journey from
Rome. The poses and general disposition
of the figures within the picture spaces are
similar – the legs, for example, are trun-
cated at precisely the same point. Also
similar are the turbulent, shifting skies, an
atmospheric extension, as it were, of the
fire of battle. The sky in *Inglis*, in fact, has
a rather highly wrought, descriptive,
almost meteorological quality that is quite
rare in Raeburn's work, a narrative
element which might have been dictated
by the circumstances of the commission
rather than by purely painterly reasons.
Finally, like the *Heathfield*, the swing of
the subject's body, and even the more
passive hands, imply action, a particular
involvement in a specific moment of time.
This sense of a personality at a juncture of
great events is, again, common to both
pictures, though the face of the younger
Inglis, nearly profile and very carefully
built up, is more inwardly contemplative.

Inglis was the youngest son of Sir John
Inglis of Cramond and Anne Cockburn,
daughter of Adam Cockburn of Ormiston.
He first saw action as a midshipman under
Rear-Admiral Hawke in 1747. On promo-
tion to captain he commanded the frigate
Lizard in 1770 and the *Salisbury* in 1778.

In the latter he brilliantly captured the
large Spanish privateer, *San Carlos*, in the
Bay of Honduras. He subsequently commanded the 64-gun *St Albans* and took
part in the relief of Gibraltar in 1781. In
the following few years he was involved in
the victories of Hood and Rodney. It is
impossible to relate the action of the
vessels in the sea behind Inglis's figure to
any specific event, although the three-
masted ship on the extreme left which is
carefully detailed may well have some
special significance.

Inglis was not actively employed in the
Navy after 1783. Having been made rear-
admiral in 1790 he died towards the end of
the following year at his brother's house of
Craigs. Both the surface of the picture and
the evidence of x-radiographs make it
clear that the uniform worn by Inglis was
then altered to take account of his late
promotion and to memorialise his achievement. The cannon on which his right
forearm initially rested was also altered, to
be replaced by a heavy ship's rail draped
with a hawser, and a signals manual was
inserted in his hand.

The 'first' uniform was that of a full-
dress captain, with lacing on the lapels and
down the front of the coat. There was also
a lace edging round a pocket on the left
side of the coat and a slashed sleeve.
Raeburn obliterated all of this detail in an
attempt to show the sitter in the undress
uniform of a rear-admiral, presumably at
the request of some member of Inglis's
family. The plain coat, the sleeve buttons
and lace and the epaulettes are all correct
features of an undress uniform that was
introduced in 1795; however, the number
of buttons down each side of the front of
the coat should be nine, and Raeburn
shows only five.[2] There was, therefore,
either some flexibility in such matters, or
whoever commissioned the alterations was
sufficiently happy with the general effect
as to accept what Raeburn gave them. The
picture is thus mainly of the late 1780s but
with an unquantifiable degree of reworking of 1795 or later.

8   *David Hunter of Blackness 1743 – 1809*

Oil on canvas 29⅞ × 24¼in (76 × 61.5cm)

National Gallery of Scotland, Edinburgh

PROVENANCE
H. H. Russell, Glendouglas, Jedburgh; Mrs
Elizabeth Adeline Powell (neé Russell), by whom
bequeathed to the National Gallery of Scotland,
1977

EXHIBITIONS
Dundee, Art Gallery, 1867 (139)

LITERATURE
Mackie, vol.I, p.49 and no.414

NOTES
1. Edinburgh, Scottish National Portrait Gallery.
2. National Gallery of Scotland accession files, NG
2394: a letter of 16 July 1992 from Iain Flett,
Archivist of the City of Dundee District Council,
quoting entries from the Mormon Church's
International Genealogical Index.
3. *Catalogue of Paintings by the Old Masters, in the
Gallery at Blackness …*, Dundee, 1867, p.17. The
collection contained pictures attributed to a
variety of very eminent Old Masters, including
Duccio, van Dyck, Rubens, Claude and
Rembrandt. It also contained pictures that had
been bought at the sale of the collection of Lord
Eldin (see cat.no.54) in 1833, including works
attributed to Correggio, Adrian van Ostade and
Jan Steen. See correspondence from Charles
Sebag-Montefiore in the National Gallery of
Scotland accession file quoted in note 2.

There is a long-standing tradition that this portrait was painted in 1788. If correct, it must therefore stand in close proximity to the portrait of *Lieut-Colonel Lyon* (cat.no.6), and both paintings certainly share the fluid handling of thickish pigment. This is most evident in the working of the lighter areas into the rather dark, warm grey of Hunter's coat (note also the precise perspective of the pewter buttons, so close to those in the *Lyon*) and in the 'rolling' forms of the bright, though cloudy, sky. On the other hand, the portrait shows an engagement with themes that seem to have been a concern of the early 1790s: the casting of very carefully observed shadows and the drawing of profile forms so endlessly modified and corrected that the final outline acquires a wire-like tension. The sub-themes of the present portrait are both the placing of shadows, not only the dramatic one across the forehead but also that cast on the creamy inside of his right collar and on the upper part of the cravat, and the continuous contours of the black, broad-brimmed hat. These are themes that are picked up in the double portrait of the *Clerks of Penicuik* (cat.no.13), the portrait of *William Glendonwyn* (cat.no.14) and the unique portrait of the *Revd Robert Walker* (cat.no.19). With the Clerk and Glendonwyn portraits the present picture also shares a wide expanse of sky resting on a very low horizon, the landscape itself rather scuffed and peremptory, with a hint of gleaming water.

The most compelling feature of the portrait is, of course, the frank acknowledgement of the painter's presence, that is, our presence, by the engagement of eyes from the two different realms, the actual and the imagined. The source of the device of one eye glowing from the dark shadow, the other brightly illuminated, may have been John Runciman's *Self-portrait* of 1767 (see fig.14),[1] which Raeburn is likely to have known – and which he appears to have had in mind when he painted his own, much later, *Self-portrait* (cat.no.56). Even more auda-

ciously, in the portrait of *Mrs Colin Campbell* of about 1808 or 1809 (cat.no.36), the engagement takes place with the cast shadow being allowed to cover both eyes.

Not a great deal is known of David Hunter of Blackness. He appears to have been the son of Alexander Hunter and Amelia (or Emilia) Garden who had been married in the parish of Kirkden in Angus on 31 December 1741. Hunter married an Elizabeth Gibson in Dundee on 3 December 1770. Among their children was Alexander Gibson Hunter of Blackness, who became a Writer to the Signet in 1797. He married in 1800 Ann Gibson Wright of Clifton Hall in Midlothian.[2] Although it is not clear who collected them, it is known that Blackness House had a picture gallery containing Old Masters as well as ancestral portraits, for a catalogue of them was published in 1867. It is there that it is unequivocally stated that the portrait of David Hunter was 'painted in 1788'.[3] When the portrait was exhibited in the Volunteer Hall in Dundee in the same year, 1867, to mark the visit of the British Association, the catalogue rather carefully repeats the same detail. It is therefore worthy of a good deal of credence.

9 *William Kerr, 6th Marquis of Lothian 1763—1824*

Oil on canvas 35⅛ × 27⅛in (89.2 × 68.9cm)

The Marquis of Lothian

PROVENANCE
Professor Dugald Stewart, by whom bequeathed to the sitter's family and thereafter by descent[1]

EXHIBITIONS
Edinburgh, Royal Scottish Academy, *Exhibition of the Works of Sir Henry Raeburn*, 1876 (193)

LITERATURE
Andrew, p.134; Armstrong, p.107; Pinnington, p.238; Greig, p.51; Mackie, no.449

NOTES
1. The canvas is inscribed with the number '252' bottom left, which refers to the Newbattle Abbey (former seat of the Marquises of Lothian) inventory of pictures.

There is no external evidence to date this portrait but stylistically it is early. William Kerr, Lord Ancram (as he was styled until he succeeded his father in 1815), married his first wife, Henrietta Hobart, on 14 April 1793, but that this event might have been the occasion for the portrait is unlikely, although it remains a possibility. The russet colours of Kerr's setting and the stylised loops of the dark foliage tend to be associated with the early 1790s, but the thick, creamy paint, 'wet-in-wet', of the coat lapels, shoulders and cravat are more readily related to the style of the *Lieut-Colonel Lyon* of 1788 (cat.no.6). In addition there are certain gaucheries in the structure of the young man's body which suggest inexperience – there is no clear relationship between the sitter's right arm and the side of his body, the shoulders are not very convincingly placed and the hand holding the hat (which in itself is not easily read) is not very felicitous – although this latter feature in itself need not indicate an early date when the beautifully drawn right hand of Lord Arniston is recalled, a portrait of 1787 (cat.no.5).

Kerr's left arm has also undergone a massive shift, the elbow having been moved a number of inches towards the body. This is one of the most dramatic pentimenti from a large number in Raeburn's work and the question remains unanswered as to whether it was carelessly left visible or whether overcleaning in the bottom corner of the picture has made it more readily detectable. These strictures aside, the sitter's head is painted simply and with careful sensitivity, its generally smooth, delicate finish recalling the portrait of *Patrick Moir*, painted in Rome (cat.no.3). The dark accents of the full lips and the tiny lines of lustre on the lower rims of the eyes create a powerful image of youthful sentience, a mind conscious of itself and the possibilities of time. This luminous head is surrounded by a particularly rich, dark halo of pigment which seems to remain as much part of the initial definition of the head shape (as we see it in

the late *Maxwell of Pollok* (cat.no.63)) as the powerfully brushed foliage of the tree. The double, V-shaped trunk of this tree is described with similar rough markings which merge in character with the strokes that suggest the hair powder on Kerr's shoulders. The green coat, of a bluish, yet earthy, green is much more 'placid' in treatment, the pigment almost watery in character and largely unbroken by accents, other than by the shadows beneath the outsize buttons. The final chromatic element is the wedge of yellow waistcoat revealed by the open coat.

Lord Ancram was Lord-Lieutenant of Midlothian and Roxburghshire and a colonel of the Edinburgh militia. By his first wife he had three sons and one daughter and by his second wife, Harriet Montagu, daughter of the third Duke of Buccleuch, whom he married in 1806, he had three sons and five daughters. Otherwise little is known of his life and personality. Curiously, the portrait appears to have been bequeathed to the sitter's family by the philosopher and teacher, Dugald Stewart, four years after the sitter's death. Although Ancram was only ten years younger than the philosopher, he may have been his pupil.

10 *James Hutton 1726–97*

Oil on canvas 49¼ × 41¼in (125.1 × 104.8cm)

Scottish National Portrait Gallery, Edinburgh

PROVENANCE
John Davidson of Stewartfield and Haltree; Hugh
Warrender, ws; his nephew, Sir George
Warrender, 4th baronet of Lochend; by descent
to the 8th baronet, later Lord Bruntisfield of
Boroughmuir; Christie's, 18 April 1986 (129B);
bought by the Scottish National Portrait Gallery

EXHIBITIONS
Edinburgh, Royal Scottish Academy, *Exhibition
of the Works of Sir Henry Raeburn*, 1876 (160);
Edinburgh, University of Edinburgh, *James
Hutton and Some of His Friends*, 1976; Edinburgh,
University of Edinburgh, *Masterpieces of Scottish
Portrait Painting*, 1981 (17)

LITERATURE
Andrew, p.130; Armstrong, pp.9, 89, 105; James
L. Caw, *Scottish Portraits with an Historical and
Critical Introduction and Notes*, Edinburgh, 1903,
vol.2, pp.54–5; Pinnington, p.235; Stevenson,
p.411; Caw, 1908, p.73; Greig, p.49; *Raeburns and
Eighteenth-Century Silver*, exhibition catalogue,
National Trust for Scotland, Edinburgh, 1951,
p.5; Macmillan, 1986, pp.75, 79; National Art
Collections Fund, *Review*, London, 1987, p.141;
Macmillan, 1990, p.151; Mackie, vol.1, pp.47–8
and no.418

NOTES
1. I am grateful to Professor Gordon Craig for
the nomenclature of these specimens and for an
explanation of their significance.
2. Dennis R. Dean, *James Hutton and the History
of Geology*, Ithaca and London, 1992.
3. Letter to James Lind: quoted in *A Scottish
Postbag: Eight Centuries of Scottish Letters*, eds
George Bruce and Paul H. Scott, Edinburgh,
1986, p.56.
4. *A Series of Original Portraits and Caricature
Etchings, by the late John Kay, Miniature Painter,
Edinburgh*, Edinburgh, 1838, plates xxiv, xxc and
xcix.

This is likely to be one of the earliest of Raeburn's portraits, but its precise relationship to the other more plausibly dated portraits from the beginning of his career, like the *Patrick Moir* (cat.no.3), painted in Rome, and the *Lord Arniston* (cat.no.5), painted in August 1787, shortly after his return, is difficult to establish. It has none of the studied smoothness of finish of the former, though in a number of ways the drawing, especially the relationship of the figure to the chair, is more awkward; but it is, of course, a more ambitious composition. On the other hand, in terms of the handling of pigment, it has a loose, rather creamy quality, and an overall painterliness, that is not so far away from the *Arniston*. This fluid pigment is most evident in the hands, which are composed of rivulets of dark pink, running over a dark base (presumably areas of shadow on the coat which were later discarded), and in the white stock circling the throat and bulging from the open waistcoat. These areas seem to place the portrait in the same context as the *Lieut-Colonel Lyon* (cat.no.6), which dates from 1788. The latter is markedly creamy, even juicy, in the way in which the brush throws up liquid ridges of paint (with attendant shadows in the troughs) to delineate the high-keyed forms. The creaminess and density of the pigment in the face of Hutton (not unlike the treatment of the same area in the *Arniston*) is also close to another portrait which is certainly early, that of *Admiral Inglis* (cat.no.7) which seems to have been complete (though altered in detail later) by 1788. Comparisons should also be drawn with the lost portrait of *John Clerk* (fig.8) for which a date as early as 1783 (that is, immediately before the journey to Rome and considerably earlier than the *Arniston)* is postulated (see Introduction). It has some, but fewer of the gaucheries of that picture and indeed has a unified painterliness that the portrait of Clerk appears not to have achieved, which is closer to the stiffer, more formalised qualities of the *Moir*. There is also, again by comparison, a

certain element of the kind of carelessness that can be the obverse side of confidence, most noticeably in the summary treatment of the chair, which has none of the descriptive precision of the chair in the *Arniston* and where the perspective of the back is not very well judged, so that Hutton's left shoulder seems to be impaled by the upright rather than positioned in front of it. Taking all of these comparisons into account a date of 1789 or 1790 seems most likely.

The portrait has an unassertive plainness of statement that is in keeping with a man who was both a farmer and a scientist who revolutionised our understanding of the history of the earth. It is based on a simple colour harmony of reddish brown and green: these colours permeate the entire picture. Even the pale background in the area around the head, which is made up from quite small brushstrokes, mainly light green, has a fleeting admixture of brown, which darkens into Hutton's cast shadow and the even darker corner of the room on the right. The material which is massed on the green tablecloth is predominantly grey and white but with a stroke of pale pink on the corner of the portfolio by Hutton's left elbow, which is repeated in the paper to the left of the shell. These papers, paper-bound books (with his quill of authorship) and geological specimens are a wonderfully fresh *tour de force* of observation, with a life that virtually echoes that of Hutton himself – in effect they make up a still-life of a modernity that it is difficult to see equalled anywhere at this time. The geological specimens consist of a chalk fossil (shell), two examples of mineral veins, a druse, a septarian nodule and a breccia.[1]

Hutton was born in Edinburgh on 3 June 1726, the son of a merchant, William Hutton, and Sarah Balfour. He was educated at the High School and the universities of Edinburgh, Paris and Leiden. He then took up farming near Duns in Berwickshire before returning to Edinburgh about 1765 where he lived at St John's Hill in the Pleasance. He had

business interests which included property, a salammoniac plant (using soot collected by chimney sweeps) and membership of the Forth and Clyde Canal committee. His intellectual interests ranged across chemistry, philosophy, phonetics, meteorology and tillage, but it was his work in geology, pursued initially while farming, that gained him fame. In his fundamental paper, 'Theory of the Earth', which he delivered to the Royal Society of Edinburgh in 1785, he showed that continents are gradually being worn away to form new continents on the sea floor, that the interior of the earth is hot and that the processes that shape the earth operate extremely slowly over a very long period of time. The result of his enquiry he summarised in the famous phrase: 'we find no vestige of a beginning, no prospect of an end'.[2] Each of the specimens in Raeburn's portrait, which must have been from Hutton's collection, relate specifically to these theories: the fossil shell as evidence that the land has been raised from the sea floor; the nodule as evidence of the power of heat and fusion on rocks; and the veined rocks as evidence of the intrusive power of molten rock. More obliquely, and more generally, the prominent bulging pocket at Hutton's right thigh seems to proclaim his statement of a life-long interest – 'a bag of gravel is a history to me' – which he had made to a correspondent as early as 1772.[3]

Hutton was portrayed by one other major artist, James Tassie, and one minor one, John Kay. Tassie's Romanised profile medallion was made in 1792 and shows a man of surprisingly youthful appearance for someone of sixty-six which agrees well enough with Raeburn's portrait, except that the latter, even allowing for the three-quarter view, seems to have reduced the large aquiline nose of the former to less dramatic proportions. That Tassie was probably more truthful in this respect seems borne out by the three etched portraits by John Kay,[4] whose works, although naïve and virtually caricatures, often have an uncompromising truthfulness in the matter of likeness.

11 *Robert Ferguson of Raith 1770–1840*

Oil on canvas 94½ × 59⅞in (240 × 152cm)

Private collection

PROVENANCE
By descent in the sitter's family

EXHIBITIONS
London, Grafton Gallery, *Scottish Old Masters*, 1895; London, Royal Academy, *Scottish Art*, 1939 (84)

LITERATURE
Armstrong, pp.61, 62, 64, 101; Pinnington, pp.134, 135, 229; McKay, p.38; Greig, pp.xxxi, 45; Brotchie, p.64; Irwin, p.244; Irwin and Irwin, p.153; Mackie, vol.I, p.50 and no.277

NOTES
1. Irwin and Irwin, p.153.
2. University of Edinburgh. See *The University Portraits, Second Series*, compiled by John H. Burnett, David Howarth and Sheila D. Fletcher, Edinburgh, 1986, pp.199–200, pl. 2; and also Mackie, no.277.
3. London, National Gallery.
4. Althorp, Earl Spencer. The portrait was painted for the sitter's sister, Georgiana (died 1814), mother of Raeburn's patron who succeeded as Earl Spencer in 1783 (see cat.no.4).

fig.57 *William Poyntz*
by Thomas Gainsborough
Althorp Park

This portrait has traditionally been identified as Sir Ronald Ferguson (1773–1841), who pursued a long and distinguished career in the army and only succeeded to the estate of Raith on the death of his elder brother Robert in 1840. This, however, may be incorrect. The assumption has already been made that, in the double portrait popularly known as '*The Archers*' (cat.no.12), which has the same continuous provenance, the dominant figure on the left who pulls the bow represents Robert, while the figure standing behind him in shadow is his brother Ronald, three years younger.[1] If this is correct, then the subject of the present portrait must be Robert, for he bears a strong physical resemblance to the bowman and little resembles the young man who stands in the shade.

This identification is borne out by the nature of the landscape which stretches behind the young huntsman. It is quite remarkably specific, to a degree unusual for Raeburn and has every appearance of being a record of a real place. Indeed, the sitter seems to draw himself well to the left of the picture space so that the woods and low hills remain visible. This semi-proprietorial arrangement would be in keeping with the expectations of an eldest son who would in due course inherit the lands, in this case of Raith, as Robert did on the death of his father in 1810. Although it has not been possible to pin this landscape down in a topographical sense, it does bear a marked resemblance to the quality of the land between the Auchtertool Road and Raith Park. Looking forward almost thirty years to the full-length portrait of the *Marquess of Bute* (cat.no.60), one finds Raeburn perfectly willing to provide an actual setting if requested, based in that case (as perhaps in the Ferguson portrait) on a sketch provided by a third party.

The problem of this portrait is compounded by the fact that the sitter appears to be a little older than he is shown in '*The Archers*', while stylistically the painting seems a little earlier. There is a rather bright, unmodulated use of pink pigment in the face and a sharpness about the upper areas of the coat – the shadows on and around the right arm, for example, or the brown belt which simply 'stops' at the top of the shoulder rather than continuing around that form – that lack something of the subtlety of '*The Archers*' and certainly the finely nuanced lighting of the portrait of *Sir John and Lady Clerk* (cat.no.13). The right hand clasping the butt of the gun has the same slightly mechanical quality and is over-scaled. On the other hand there is a wonderful fluency in the way the sitter's boots are painted, their inner shadows and the shadows cast on the ground all swept into one eddying form of light and shade. The liver and white setter that turns in the same direction as the lowered gun partakes of this same vivid handling, where each brushstroke of the whole can virtually be accounted for, something that conveys an impression of the warmth and movement of the animal.

Is it possible that the discrepancies can be accounted for by the picture being completed over an extended period of time? This might mean that the more formalised areas of the figure were completed first, possibly about 1789 and before '*The Archers*', while the freer, 'impressionistic' areas brought the picture to completion about 1792, the likeness being revised or completed at the same time.

Raeburn's idea for the portrait, if it was solely his, seems to lie in another full-length of a huntsman, David Martin's portrait of Robert Trotter which is signed and dated 1782.[1] It features a languid, awkwardly drawn man at full-length with a gun before a hilly landscape, a small retriever (after a Stubbs engraving) scuttering in the distance. It is a faintly ridiculous portrait and, although it may have provided a starting point for Raeburn, shows the immense gulf in modernity and naturalness that Raeburn had opened up between himself and his predecessors. For a forerunner of this *à la chasse* type that can compare in bucolic ease – man, gun, dog and land in a simple intimacy – one has to look back to Gainsborough, in an early portrait, like the *Mr and Mrs Andrews* (about 1748),[3] or the later *William Poyntz* (1762, fig.57).[4] The latter was in the collection of Raeburn's Roman patron, Lord Spencer, but there is no reason to believe that he had ever seen it.

12   *Robert Ferguson of Raith 1770–1840 and Lieut-General Sir Ronald Ferguson 1773–1841: 'The Archers'*

Oil on canvas 39½ × 48⅝in (100.5 × 123.6cm)

Private collection

PROVENANCE
By descent in the sitter's family

EXHIBITIONS
London, Grafton Galleries, *Scottish Old Masters*, 1895 (71); Edinburgh, Loan Exhibition, 1901 (164); London, Royal Academy, *Scottish Art*, 1939 (93); Edinburgh, National Gallery of Scotland, *Ramsay, Raeburn and Wilkie*, 1951 (62); Edinburgh, National Gallery of Scotland, *Raeburn*, 1956 (25); Madrid, Prado, *British Painting from Hogarth to Turner*, 1988–9 (38)

LITERATURE
Armstrong, pp.61, 101; Pinnington, p.229; McKay, pp.38, 41; Greig, p.xxxi, plate 13; Cursiter, p.58; Dibdin, p.135; Irwin, p.244; Irwin and Irwin, p.153; Mackie, no.275

NOTES
1. Collection of The Trustees of the Tetton Heirlooms Settlement.
2. Nicholas Penny (ed.), *Reynolds*, exhibition catalogue, Royal Academy, 1986 (74).
3. *Journal of Henry Cockburn being a continuation of the Memorials of his Time 1831–1854*, Edinburgh, 1874, vol.1, p.274.
4. *Ibid.*, pp.274–6.

This double portrait, though not as profoundly assured, must be very close in date to the portrait of *Sir John and Lady Clerk* (cat.no.13), some of whose themes it presages. It is likely to date, therefore, from about 1790. The control of light, the wonderfully outlined profile of Robert (on the left) and the ease and simplicity of the handling and colour scheme seem quite distant from the creamy substantiality of a portrait like the *Lieut-Colonel Lyon* (cat.no.6) or the Reynolds-like *gravitas* of the *Rear-Admiral Inglis* (cat.no.7), and suggest that, since only a year or two must separate them, Raeburn's manner was changing rapidly at this stage in his development.

The painting has a pronounced geometry, both actual and emotional, and a number of oppositions and contrasts of an almost heraldic nature. Robert, on the left, in a yellowish-grey coat is brightly illuminated from a high light source to the left which strikes across the turned-back brim of his hat, itself holding some of that light in its chalky pigment, while his younger brother Ronald, in a plummy brown coat, stands entirely within a pale shadow – not so greatly different in measurable tone from his brother, but very different in effect, such is Raeburn's subtlety. Ronald also holds the viewer in a concentrated gaze, while his brother's attention lies, almost abstractedly, at the end of the flight of the, still to be released, arrow. This horizontal arrow bisects the picture precisely, the archer's gloved hand tensing the gathered diagonals of the string, painted in at a late stage with the help of a rule. The horizontality is carried on in Robert's right forearm and the long left arm which curves the bow just beyond his brother, whose arms play no part in the composition. These formal relationships may speak in some way, planned or unconscious, of the particular family relationship of an elder and younger brother.

Between the brothers is a hill of a fairly peremptory sort, like the foliage that flickers a little aimlessly along the top of the picture. The rather fractured nature of the shaded tree-trunks on the left, which silhouette Robert's right elbow, are in character close to those in that other archery portrait, *Dr Nathaniel Spens* (cat.no.17), which was commissioned in 1791 and completed by 1793. It seems that the Ferguson portrait must be rather earlier than this, perhaps as early as 1789. (Its relationship to another Ferguson portrait, the full-length hunting picture which is assumed here also to represent Robert, the elder of the two, is complicated by the fact that it seems to show him at a slightly greater age, although the picture's style might suggest an earlier date (see cat.no.11).)

The portrait inevitably recalls Reynolds's double portrait of the two young archers, the *Thomas Townshend and Colonel Acland*, exhibited at the Royal Academy in 1770.[1] It is highly unlikely that Raeburn could ever have seen that painting and it appears never to have been engraved.[2] Probably both artists were simply reacting independently to a social phenomenon, the recent revival of archery as a fashionable sport. While the Reynolds has a Rubensian tension and fire, the actors overcharged to an almost ridiculous extent, the Raeburn has a solemn stillness that is entirely rational.

Robert and Ronald Ferguson were the sons of William Ferguson of Raith in Fife and Jean Craufurd, daughter of Ronald Craufurd of Restalrig. Both would become members of the Royal Company of Archers, Robert in 1792, and Ronald in 1801.

Lord Cockburn described the brothers as 'two admirable Scotch Whigs'.[3] Robert entered parliament as MP for Fife in 1806, the year of the brief Whig ascendancy. He succeeded his father in the estate of Raith in 1810 and the house attracted a cultivated society. He was a dedicated collector of books and pictures. He sat again in parliament for Kirkcaldy in 1831–2 and 1837–40, and latterly for Haddingtonshire from 1835 to 1837.

Ronald joined the Army as an ensign in

the 53rd regiment on 3 April 1790 (a fact which may suggest that the portrait is earlier than that date). He had a distinguished and varied career, serving in the Low Countries, India, the Cape and the Iberian peninsula, where he was highly praised by the future Duke of Wellington. Promoted lieutenant-general in 1813, his military career virtually ended the following year, although he became general in 1830. He had made an advantageous marriage to Jean, the natural daughter of Sir Hector Munro of Novar in 1798.

Given his prominence in the military establishment, he expressed astonishingly liberal views on political and religious matters. He sat in parliament for Kirkcaldy from 1806 to 1830 and for Nottingham from 1830 to 1841. Of the liberal, enlightened views of both men Cockburn wrote that they 'showed what good may be affected by mere steadiness of principle and its honest exhibition ... at a time when political independence had few attractions either for military officers or for country gentlemen ... Nothing could be more beautiful than the mutual affection of these handsome, gentlemanlike, and popular brothers ...'[4]

13   *Sir John Clerk (d.1798) and Lady Clerk (b.1745) of Penicuik*

Oil on canvas 57 × 80½in (144.8 × 204.5cm)

National Gallery of Ireland, Dublin

PROVENANCE

By descent to Sir George Clerk, 8th baronet of Penicuik; purchased from him by Sir Otto Beit in 1911; by descent to Sir Alfred Lane Beit by whom bequeathed to the National Gallery of Ireland, 1987

EXHIBITIONS

London, Shakespeare Gallery, 1792; Edinburgh, 1850 (38); Edinburgh, Royal Scottish Academy, *Exhibition of the Works of Sir Henry Raeburn*, 1876 (211); Edinburgh, 1908 (349); London, Royal Academy, *Winter Exhibition*, 1910 (154); Amsterdam, Stedelijk Museum, *Twee Eeuwen Engelsche [sic] Kunst*, 1936 (112); Paris, Louvre, *English [sic] Painting*, 1938 (100); London, Royal Academy, *Exhibition of Scottish Art*, 1939 (lll); Cape Town, National Gallery of Art, *Old Master Paintings from the Beit Collection*, 1949 (44); Edinburgh, National Gallery of Scotland, *Raeburn*, 1956 (8); Leningrad and Moscow (British School), *British Painting*, 1960 (40); Glasgow, Art Gallery and Museum, *Scottish Painters*, 1961 (59); Detroit, Detroit Institute of Art, *Romantic Art in Britain, Paintings and Drawings, 1760–1860*, 1968 (90); Paris, Petit Palais, 1972 (211); Edinburgh, Talbot Rice Art Centre, and London, Tate Gallery, *Painting in Scotland, the Golden Age*, 1986–7 (105)

LITERATURE

Obituary, p.12; Cunningham, pp.219–20; Andrew, pp.109–10; Armstrong, pp.9, 11, 61, 62, 90, 98; Pinnington, p.223; Caw, 1908, pp.73, 77; Caw, *Masterpieces*, p.61; Greig, pp.xxx, lii, 41; *Catalogue of the Beit Collection*, 1913, no.94; Brotchie, pp.63, 64; Dibdin, p.130; William T. Whitley, *Artists and Their Friends in England, 1700–1799*, London, 1928, vol.2, pp.168, 169, 170; Collins Baker, p.162; Kenneth Garlick, 'Sir Henry Raeburn', *Encyclopaedia of World Art*; Harris, p.4; Irwin, pp.240, 244; Irwin and Irwin, pp.152, 153, 154; Macmillan, 1986, pp.77, 195; Macmillan, 1990, p.153; Mackie, vol.I, pp.50–1, 66 and no.158

fig.58 *Sir Rowland Winn and Lady Winn* by an unknown artist
Nostell Priory, National Trust

Sir John Clerk and his wife are wrapped in the light that flows across the bare, hilly landscape which Sir John's raised right arm indicates. To a quite exceptional degree the couple owe their being to this light which articulates their every gesture, binding them together as much as their interlinked arms. The source of this light is a summer's morning sky, brightest above the dried-out grasses of the yellow hills, scumbled bluish greys higher up. Yet despite its luminosity, which is perfectly pitched to define Clerk's hat, sweeping round and on to the edge of its rim and breaking momentarily into its crown, it seems hardly bright enough to account for the whiteness of Clerk's shirt cuff or the dart of the cravat where it turns behind his neck, or, especially, for the highlights that mould the right side of Lady Clerk's face and spill across the loose folds of the upper part of her dress. This pure illumination is therefore not fully accounted for by the fictions of the picture space, but its contrivance allows Raeburn to create some of the loveliest equivalences between light and form in any of his paintings and to probe aspects of the human predicament – love, dependence, time and its effects – with the profoundest understanding, transcending the temporal and contingent in a way that only the greatest of artists can accomplish. This degree of accomplishment is the more astonishing when it is recalled that Raeburn's career had been underway for only a mere handful of years at the time he painted this portrait.

Contre-jour portraits, where the principal forms are placed against a strong light source so that they are essentially dark by contrast, their outlines clearly defined and their inner forms verifiable mainly by the ambient light that travels back by weakened reflection, were clearly something of great interest to Raeburn in the early 1790s – for example, the *Hunter of Blackness* (cat.no.8), 'The Archers' (cat.no.12), *William Glendonwyn* (cat.no.14) and the *Revd Robert Walker* (cat.no.19). An important feature of these portraits is that in addition to the defining role of subdued, reflected light, rays of direct light are allowed to pick up the outer edges of forms, flaring briefly before dying into the general darkness of the shape. This is the method used to describe the profiled forms in the head of William Glendonwyn and it is seen here on the right side of Lady Clerk's face, strong light carving out the contour of her forehead, touching the bridge and top of her nose, flowing down her right cheek and defining the curve of her chin. Most tellingly, this brightness plays around the forms of her upper lip (which remains dark in tone) and falls sharply on the far side of the lower lip, not only giving the face a remarkable sculptural effect but also, in conjunction with the dark parting line of the lips, contributing something vital to the contemplative serenity of the woman's expression.

More mundanely, but essentially in the same way, a yellowish light catches the chamois lining of Clerk's collar, flickers along the upper edge of his outstretched arm and marks the folds and pocket flap of the right side of his coat. At the same time this light loses its yellowness as it passes through the butterfly shape of his linen cuff before alighting on the upper edges of his hand and fingers.

Clerk's features are almost wholly in shade, although within that darkness there are wide tonal variations, so that the features are fully defined, but without drama. Much of the light that does reach his face, for example, the muted pink on the line of his nose, a brighter pink round his right nostril, has its source in his wife's dress.

Raeburn evidently hoped to set down a marker in London with the present portrait, intending to exhibit it at the Royal Academy in the spring of 1792. However, its arrival in London was delayed and it was exhibited at Boydell's Shakespeare Gallery instead.[1] It was noticed by an anonymous writer in the *Public Advertiser* who was clearly greatly struck by it: 'In this last class [pictures that arrived too late for inclusion in the

Academy exhibition] was a large picture by Mr Raeburn of Edinburgh. It exhibits the portraits of Sir John Clark [sic] and his Lady, and is painted in a most forcible and singular style; figures in shadow though in the open air. In this painting there is a boldness of touch and strength of effect which have seldom been equalled. The shadows are given with the confidence of a man who knows his ground, and not fearful of making a false step, and the lights are peculiarly brilliant – so much so that the whole has at first sight the hue of moonlight. The landscape is properly subordinate but the size of the tree, which in part shadows the figures, ill accords with the gooseberry bushes, (for such they appear) on the other side of the picture. The artist has evidently considered the figures as the leading objects and properly made them principal, but a little more attention to the foliage of his trees, and a little more verdure to their colouring as well as to the colouring of his landscape, would have improved the picture which, with all its trivial errors, gives great promise of the painter's future excellence.'[2]

Henry Mackenzie, 'the man of feeling', also remarked on the portrait, with rather less understanding when he spoke of Raeburn's 'trick of the art, a violent contrast of light and shade, which afterwards he ceased to practise …'[3]

The portrait was also noticed by the French émigré painter, Henri-Pierre Danloux, who viewed it with his friend, the Abbé Luchet. He described it (in translation) thus: 'Monsieur de Luchet, who is no connoisseur, was greatly pleased by the subtle beauty ['la grâce'] of some of the pictures. The one which made the greatest impression on him represents a man and a woman painted by an artist from Edinburgh. The total effect is indeed rather striking. The sun, which is concealed behind the head of the husband, illuminates the head of the woman and the blue dress ['habillements bleus', probably a mis-reading of 'habillements blancs'] which she is wearing.'[4] This is a rare instance of

a painting by Raeburn being judged by a critic he might have respected.

The theme of a couple at ease in their estate is not unusual in British art – Gainsborough's lovely portrait of Mr and Mrs Andrews[5] in equal balance with their rolling fields comes readily to mind, although it is not a close precedent. A double portrait that does, however, have clear echoes of the placement of the figures, though not in a landscape, is the painting *Sir Rowland and Lady Winn in the Library at Nostell Priory* (fig.58), which has been dated about 1770. The easy intimacy of the two figures and the relationship of heads, hands and gestures is surprisingly close to Raeburn's portrait. It remains an open question how he might have had knowledge of the portrait and there may, of course, have been a common source rather than direct influence.[6]

Sir John Clerk had succeeded his father in the baronetcy of Penicuik in 1784. Of considerable wealth, he carried on a distinguished family tradition of involvement with the arts, literature and history. He played host to many of the great figures of his day – Anna Seward, poet and friend of Scott, who attended one of his evening parties was much impressed by the 'constellation of Scottish talents' she found there.[7] Clerk was nephew of John Clerk of Eldin, naval tactician and amateur etcher, and cousin of the judge, Lord Eldin (see cat.no.54). He married Rosemary Appleby D'Acre of Kirklington in Cumbria, granddaughter of Sir George Fleming, bishop of Carlisle. She has left an interesting account of the circumstances surrounding her birth on 15 November 1745 at Rose Castle near Carlisle, while her father, who was a member of the king's militia, was held prisoner by Prince Charles. When the Jacobite forces who intended to plunder Rose Castle heard that her mother was about to give birth, they withdrew, giving her a white cockade to pin on the child's cap at her baptism as a means of protection.[8]

Referred to by her friends as Mary, or Molly, she lived for many years as a

widow, surviving until at least 1832. She had a town house in Edinburgh at 100 Princes Street in the later years of her life. Here this 'able and peripatetic lady' displayed a fierce temperament by leading a successful campaign to stop the erection of buildings on the green slope to the east of the Castle; she also protested to the police about attempts by the Edinburgh Lighting Committee to remove her own lamp-posts when gas-lighting was being installed on Princes Street.[9] The Clerks had no children.

NOTES
1. *Morning Chronicle,* 31 May 1792.
2. *Public Advertiser,* 2 June 1792, 'A Picture Painted in Scotland'.
3. *The Anecdotes and Egotisms of Henry Mackenzie,* ed. Harold William Thompson, London, 1927, pp.213–14.
4. Baron Roger Portalis, *Henri-Pierre Danloux: Peintre de Portraits et son Journal durant l'Emigration (1753–1809),* Paris, 1910, p.94. I am grateful to my colleague Helen Smailes for drawing this to my attention.
5. London, National Gallery, c.1748–9.
6. National Trust, Nostell Priory. I am grateful to my colleague Stephen Lloyd for pointing out this resemblance to me.
7. *Letters of Anna Seward written between the years 1784 and 1807,* Edinburgh, 1811, vol.iii, pp.261–2. In the same letter (from Buxton, 15 June 1793, to a Mr Saville) she describes Sir John Clerk as speaking 'with a broad Scottish brogue, and a high feminine tone of voice, makes odd cadences in speaking'. Her picture continues:
'… but his smile is festive, and arch; shrewd comic humour streams from his little laughing eyes; and he is genuinely good-natured … He dotes upon his lovely lady; and when narrating circumstances, with which she must be familiar, his eyes involuntarily fix on her face, as he were informing her rather than the company.'
8. Mary, Lady Clerk, communicated this story to *Blackwood's Magazine* on 21 April 1817. It was reprinted in *Blackwood's Magazine,* vol.311, January 1972, p.45.
9. Lord Cockburn, who describes her thus, relates the story of the building campaign (*Journal of Henry Cockburn, 1831–1854,* Edinburgh, 1874, vol.ii, p.322). The remaining information here is derived from Clerk of Penicuik family papers shown to me by Andrew Kerr.

14 *William Glendonwyn of Parton (fl.1781)*

Oil on canvas 49⅛ × 40in (124.8 × 101.6cm)

The Syndics of the Fitzwilliam Museum, Cambridge

PROVENANCE

H. O. Collins; Christie's, 22 February 1890 (78); Lesser; William Holden, London, from whom purchased by the Fitzwilliam Museum, 1892

LITERATURE

C. Winter, *The Fitzwilliam Museum*, Cambridge (University Press), 1958, p.383; J. W. Goodison, *Catalogue of Paintings*, Cambridge (University Press), 1975, vol.3, p.197; Mackie, no.327

NOTES

1. Also sold at Christie's on 22 February 1890 (79). Now in a private collection in New Haven, Connecticut.
2. Francis J. Grant (ed.), *Register of Marriages of the City of Edinburgh, 1751–1800*, Edinburgh (Scottish Record Society), 1922, p.286.
3. Francis H. Groome, *Ordnance Gazetteer of Scotland…*, Edinburgh, 1884, vol.v, p.159.

In the early 1790s Raeburn developed a particular interest in *contre-jour* effects – the device of lighting the subject from behind – and produced a number of portraits that are breathtakingly original and with no obvious precedent. The outstanding examples are the double portrait of *Sir John and Lady Clerk* (cat.no.13) and the present portrait. These are also among the purest examples of the type, with the figures placed against a bright, luminous sky, their near sides largely in shadow and their salient features described by an intense light that plays around their edges. Between the deepest darks of those parts furthest from the source of light and the near dazzling whiteness of the lit contours is a subtly modulated variety of tones whose source is the secondary light that is reflected back and forth within the principal forms. The method is, of course, never used with complete purity – the incidence of the light is not always entirely logical – and there are variations in degree. Other portraits that clearly fall within the group are those of *David Hunter of Blackness* (cat.no.8) and *Captain David Birrell* (cat.no.15). The latter is very like the Glendonwyn portrait in many respects, but the lighting is generally much more diffused. Also related is the companion portrait of Mrs Glendonwyn and her daughter.[1] Strangely, while it aims at the same kind of effects, it is far less successful, lacking the sharp, clear depiction of form of the male portrait.

The portrait of Glendonwyn also relates to a parallel interest of these years – the expressive potential of profile. This might seem to derive from the self-portrait modelled in the manner of James Tassie in 1792 (cat.no.16) but it is found rather earlier in a portrait like '*The Archers*' (cat.no.12). Nor is it simply a matter of the human profile, for the notion is also concerned with dark shape made palpable by means of its interplay with the strong light behind, like the emotive clarity of the dark figure of the skating minister, the Revd Robert Walker.

Glendonwyn stands above a wooded valley that rises in the distance to sketchily indicated hills. The tree-trunks on the left and the landscape that rolls away from him have a golden, russet glow, some of which colour permeates the large expanse of bright sky. Glendonwyn's head, small in relation to the great bulk of his body, is outlined in a process of constant refinement, dark against light at its rear, which is a continuation of the same tone that fills much of his right cheek and neck, and virtually pure white on his forehead, the bridge of his nose, the area around his right eye and the surface of his lower lip. These immensely subtle light areas, which play over the front of his face, are, in effect, more intense in places than the actual source of light. This light also breaks free from these areas into the darker tones on the side of the head to record with dry, licked paint the texture of his hair by his temple. Subtlest of all is the pin-prick of pure white on the pupil of the eye, with a trace element breaking into the iris, so that the whole eye has a wonderful luminosity.

This same light, perceived as entering the picture space at the angle defined by the shadows of the trees in the valley beneath, breaks in near pure white across the front of his frilled shirt, the turned-out lapels and front of his waistcoat. Similar themes of intense light, subtle mid-tones and intense darks are played out in the secondary focus of his left hand grasping his stick, hat and kerchief. The man's girth is encased in a yellowish coat, largely in shadow, and, in the illuminated side, perhaps less high keyed than the other bright areas of the costume might imply it should be.

Little is known of Glendonwyn. He was married on 28 February 1781 in the College Kirk parish of Edinburgh to Agnes Gordon, daughter of Alexander Gordon of Craigie.[2] Their eldest daughter, and Glendonwyn's co-heir, Mary, married James Gordon of Letterfourie in Banff in 1801 (Gordon assumed the baronetcy of Letterfourie in 1806). The Glendonwyn family had held the barony of Parton in Kirkcudbrightshire since the fifteenth century. Parton House stood on rising ground above a wide stretch of the River Dee[3] and it is highly likely that the landscape setting of the portrait is some kind of representation of the estate.

15 *Captain David Birrell 1757/8 — 1800*

Oil on canvas 50 × 40in (127 × 101.6cm)

The University of North Carolina at Chapel Hill

PROVENANCE

The sitter's brother; Mrs M. I. McLeod, grand-niece of the sitter; J. A. Holms, 1911; Vicars, 1923; Knoedler, 1925; Marshall Field; Knoedler, New York; Mr and Mrs John M. Morehead, 1950, by whom given to the University of North Carolina

EXHIBITIONS

Agnew's, 1903 (11); Edinburgh, French Gallery, 1909 (4); Glasgow, *Scottish Exhibition*, 1911 (170); London, French Gallery, *Pictures by Sir Henry Raeburn R.A.*, 1911 (3); New York, Knoedler, 1925 (1); Glasgow, *Empire Exhibition*, 1938 (25); London, Royal Academy, *Exhibition of Scottish Art*, 1939 (90)

LITERATURE

Greig, pp.xxxiv, 40; V. C. P. Hodson, *List of the Officers of the Bengal Army, 1758–1834*, vol.I, London, 1927, p.150; Mackie, no.49

NOTES

1. See Mackie, no.49.
2. *The Gentleman's Magazine and Historical Chronicle for the year MDCCCI*, vol.LXXI, part 1, London, 1801, p.83.

This painting belongs to the innovative group of portraits which Raeburn painted in the early 1790s, in which the sitters are placed against a luminous sky, so that much of their bodies are in deep shadow, but where the light that does infiltrate the mass of the figure is highly selective in defining the forms. Within the darks there are also the subtlest of modulations caused by reflected secondary light. The supreme example is the double portrait of *Sir John and Lady Clerk* (cat.no.13). Another is the single portrait of *William Glendonwyn* (cat.no.14) with which the present portrait has a great deal in common and can be presumed to be of a closely similar date. In both portraits the heads are painted with the subtlest refinement, with the rest of the picture very broadly, even sketchily, brushed in.

Although Birrell's head is turned towards the viewer, as opposed to the virtually pure profile of Glendonwyn, the salient features are suffused with intense, defining light in the same way. This light, in effect direct sunlight, enters from high on the left and floods across much of the top of the head and face, forming deep shadows on the underside and left side of the facial features. There are subtle transitions by means of half tones and light is reflected upwards from the brightly lit areas of the costume on to, for example, the underside of the jaw and around the nostrils.

In a broader fashion this light also defines the front of the body – the pure white of the cravat, the strong grey of the coat lapels, the vigorously brushed slope of the vermilion coat, where Birrell folds his arms, and the front of the crimson sash at his waist and the buff breeches. At the same time it picks out the left-facing edge of the sword and buckle at its belt. The large black tricorne hat is formed, not only as a silhouette against the sky but from a half tone that breaks across its near rim, the consequence of light reflected from the front of his waistcoat. The landscape, yellowish with distant blue hills, and the creeper-garlanded tree on the right, are

virtually autonomous abstractions, a foil to Birrell's towering, compacted red figure.

It has been noted that Birrell was on leave from the East India Company between 16 January 1789 and 27 September 1793 and it was presumably in this window of opportunity that the portrait was painted.[1] Although so close to the *Glendonwyn*, the face is fractionally more painterly, more nuanced in handling, which suggests that it was painted rather later. Birrell had joined the East India Company as a cadet in 1778 at about the age of twenty. In the same year he progressed to cornet, then lieutenant. After his return to India he was promoted captain in 1796 in the East India Company's Bengal Cavalry, and major in June 1799. The portrait has traditionally been called *'Captain' David Birrell*, in the belief that it was painted after 1796 and before his ultimate promotion. This is stylistically impossible and also fails to take account of his return to India in 1796. Little else is known of Birrell's life. His death was recorded in *The Gentleman's Magazine*, under 'Marriages and Deaths of remarkable Persons', as follows: '1800. June 15 At Futty Ghur, in the East Indies, Major Davis Birrell, of the East India Company's service'.[2] The name 'Davis' is presumably a misprint. Futty Ghur (now Fatehgarh) was a major town in the state of Uttar Pradesh.

16 *Sir Henry Raeburn 1756–1823: self-portrait*

Paste medallion, height 3in (7.6cm)
Cursive inscription on truncation: *H. Raeburn/1792*

Scottish National Portrait Gallery, Edinburgh

PROVENANCE
W. Carlisle Baillie; purchased by the Scottish
National Portrait Gallery, 1922

LITERATURE
John M. Gray, *James and William Tassie*,
Edinburgh, 1894, pp.44–5, 138 (317); Armstrong,
p.51; Greig, p.57; Brotchie, p.53; Irwin and Irwin,
p.151

NOTES
1. 'Sir Henry Raeburn', *The Annual Biography*,
1823, pp.15–16.
2. City of Glasgow Archive, Mitchell Library, TD
68/1,'Letters from James Tassie to the late Alex^r
Wilson Esq Glasgow', dated, at London, 14
February 1792 (transcription in Scottish National
Portrait Gallery, Library, letter no.55).
3. *Ibid.*, dated, at London, 12 April 1792.

Everything points to this exceptional work being a self-portrait of Raeburn, modelled by him in wax or other malleable material and cast in the distinctive vitreous paste of James Tassie, the Scottish gem and portrait modeller resident in London. The style of modelling is quite unlike that of Tassie, which was meticulously descriptive, and the inscription on the truncation is not composed of impressed capital letters, which was typical of a Tassie portrait, but appears to have been freely drawn into the soft material of the original model in a form not unlike Raeburn's own written signature.

That Raeburn had an interest in sculptural art and had produced such a medallion is stated in the obituary of 1823: 'Sculpture was also an object of his peculiar study; and so great was his taste for it, that at Rome, he, at one time, entertained the idea of devoting himself to that noble art as a profession in preference to painting. A medallion of himself, which he afterwards executed, satisfied all men of taste who saw it, that he would have attained to equal excellence in this art, had he made it the object of his choice.'[1]

The style of the medallion portrait is entirely in keeping with Raeburn's work as a painter, the forms deftly described and not overburdened with detail. The hair, including the ribbon that ties the pigtail, and the cravat, have a lively plastic quality suggestive of texture and movement, and the gathering of the two sides of the coat by the button on the near side is particularly felicitous. The profile face, so much in accordance with the painted self-portrait of more than twenty years later (cat.no.56), is also significantly like a group of portraits of the early 1790s when Raeburn had a particular interest in the expressive properties of pure profile: for example, the *William Glendonwyn* (cat.no.14) and, especially, the *Revd Robert Walker* (cat.no.19), which it resembles to a remarkable degree.

There is no evidence of a link between Raeburn and Tassie, but the painter must have known and admired the modeller's work. Tassie was, after all, defining Scottish society in a way similar to Raeburn, albeit on a more modest scale and from the distance of London. Tassie maintained close contacts with Scotland and was in Edinburgh in January or February 1792, as a letter to his long-standing correspondent in Glasgow, the stationer Alexander Wilson, shows: 'Hurry prevented me from writing you a few lines from Edinburgh, I modelled there in addition to those in Glasgow 20 Portraits. The whole will take me a long time to finish.'[2] By 'finish' he meant preparing moulds and casting them in his distinctive vitreous material, a time-consuming task. Writing in April of portraits of Wilson's wife and the geologist James Hutton which he intended exhibiting at the Royal Academy, he says that it 'will take me all the summer before I get through with the Scotch Models'.[3] They were still incomplete by July. Whether or not Raeburn's model was one of those cast during the year, through some special arrangement between the two artists, is not recorded but it is highly likely. It is difficult to estimate how many casts Tassie produced of any particular portrait: two of the Raeburn portraits are known, but presumably many more were cast.

17 *Dr Nathaniel Spens 1728–1815*

Oil on canvas 93¼ × 58¾in (236.9 × 149.2cm)

Queen's Bodyguard for Scotland (Royal Company of Archers)

PROVENANCE
Queen's Bodyguard for Scotland (Royal
Company of Archers)

EXHIBITIONS
Edinburgh, 1850 (37); Edinburgh, Royal
Scottish Academy, 1863 (193); Edinburgh,
Royal Scottish Academy, *Exhibition of the
Works of Sir Henry Raeburn*, 1876 (157);
London, Royal Academy, 1877 (268);
Edinburgh, 1884 (220); London, Grafton
Galleries, *Scottish Old Masters*, 1895 (52);
Edinburgh, *Loan Exhibition*, 1901 (147);
Edinburgh, 1926 (133); London, Royal
Academy, *Exhibition of British Art*, 1934
(280); London, Royal Academy, *Exhibition of
Scottish Art*, 1939 (118); London, Royal
Academy, 1954–5 (49); Edinburgh, National
Gallery of Scotland, *Raeburn*, 1956 (14);
Edinburgh, Talbot Rice Arts Centre, and
London, Tate Gallery, *Painting in Scotland,
the Golden Age*, 1986–7 (104)

LITERATURE
Brown, pp.5, 7, 93; Andrew, p.151;
Armstrong, pp.63, 73, 76, 90, 112;
Pinnington, pp.141, 142, 195, 196, 208, 248;
McKay, p.43; Stevenson, p.407; Caw,
Masterpieces, p.63; Caw, 1908, pp.73, 74;
Greig, pp.xxxi, xxxiii, xlvii, 60; Brotchie,
pp.62–3, 64, 73–4, 91; Dibdin, pp.135, 136;
Sanderson, pp.131, 132, 152; Collins Baker,
p.163; Harris, pp.4–5, 7; Irwin, p.144; Irwin
and Irwin, pp.152, 153–4; Macmillan, 1986,
pp.77, 195; Macmillan, 1990, p.153; Mackie,
no.661

fig.59 *Sir James Pringle of Stitchell*
by David Martin

*Queen's Bodyguard for Scotland
(Royal Company of Archers)*

The commission for this portrait was
linked to one given to David Martin to
paint the president of the Royal Company
of Archers, Sir James Pringle of Stitchell
(fig.59). The decision to commission
portraits of Pringle and the colourful
surgeon, Spens, was taken by the Company in April 1791 and the two artists
were chosen from its own membership.
Pringle, as president, was given first

choice and decided on Martin, the better established – and much more conservative – of the two. Thus Spens, by chance, was to be memorialised in one of the most original of all archery portraits.

It is not known when Raeburn commenced the portrait but he had completed it by 24 October 1793 when he submitted his account for 50 guineas.[1] In date the painting is therefore only a year or two after the full-length hunting portrait of *Robert Ferguson* (cat.no.11), but the hesitancy and slight awkwardness of that portrait has been overtaken by a far greater certainty of aim and by vigorous, endlessly inventive variations of colour and surface texture. Curiously, given the nature of the sport, Spens is not shown in an open space but in a distinctly wooded setting, with luscious undergrowth encircling the place where he stands.

Spens is solidly rooted between a tilted rock and a clump of dangerous thistle leaves (chalky green, with pure black shadows), his feet forming a precise right angle and his muscular body tilted slightly backwards and to the left, reiterating the backward tension of the pulling right arm and counterbalancing the thrust of the left arm. Crossing this slight diagonal movement is the much stronger one of the thick tree-trunk that lies behind Spens. This tree, and indeed the whole triangle of boscage on the left hand side of the picture, is thickly painted using virtually the whole of the warm range of Raeburn's palette, the brushstrokes ceaselessly shattered, splintered and interpenetrating (in a way strangely reminiscent of Magnasco) for reasons that are not entirely clear. These colouristic effects continue in the clusters of dock leaves and the rock in the bottom left.

This use of surprisingly thick pigment continues in Spens's white waistcoat and trousers (but not fractured in the same way) and in a number of other areas of the costume, notably the clotted and pulled coruscations of pure white that make up the froggings on the silvery green tartan of the coat and in the feathers of the

bonnet where Raeburn has scored in their texture with the wrong end of his brush. (This latter technique he used not infrequently at this time – in, for example the portrait of *John Smith of Craigend* (fig.12) of about 1790.)[2] In contrast is the remarkably thin application of the warm hues that constitute the face, the expression and structure stated with such economy that the weave of the canvas is far more visible than in most other areas of the picture. Of immense subtlety are the tiny flecks of white on the left of each eyeball that help to direct Spens's glance beyond the tightened fingers of his left hand and the cast shadow of the upper half of the bow string that follows (that is, defines) the contours of the right side of Spens's face. Of an equal subtlety are the three support strings bound at the wrist and taken round the fingers of Spens's right glove, described with something of the virtuosity of the lacings of the skates in the *Revd Robert Walker* (cat.no.19).

The forerunners, if any, of this strikingly original portrait are difficult to suggest. The geometry of the converging strings and arrow and the way they frame and even subdue the face has an audacious realism that must have raised eyebrows, at least at first. Nevertheless, its remarkable originality certainly seems to have been accepted by members of the Company, for they had an engraving produced by subscription and a number of the 150 prints were given as prizes. The engraving (at least equal in quality to what would have been produced in London at the same time) was commissioned from John Beugo on 10 June 1794 and published during 1796.[3] The painting itself was hung in Archers' Hall in May 1795. One particularly interesting feature of Beugo's engraving is the way he has given rather more form to the hills in the distance than Raeburn's free and suggestive handling suggests, perhaps an unconscious response by the engraver to the problem felt by many about the lack of definition in certain areas of Raeburn's paintings.

Nathaniel Spens was the son of Thomas

Spens of Lathallan in Fife and Janet Douglas. While the portrait was underway he purchased Craigsanquhar, an estate near Cupar in Fife, which, centuries before, had been a family property. From 1794 to 1796 he was president of the Royal College of Physicians of Edinburgh. He married Mary Millikan of a Renfrewshire family. Two of their sons also became members of the Royal Company.

Spens appears to have been a remarkable archer and was active in the Company from 1750, when he was elected, until near his death. He served on the Company's council for many years, became vice-president in 1792 and succeeded Sir James Pringle as president in 1809.

NOTES
1. Payment was delayed. He received £30 on account on 28 March 1800, but there is no record of payment having been completed. The information quoted here is taken from annotations added by Sir James Ferguson, Keeper of the Records of Scotland, to his text in the Raeburn exhibition catalogue of 1956 (Scottish National Portrait Gallery, Library). The documents from which he quoted were catalogued by the National Register of Archives (0180, Royal Company of Archers, Box N 467).
2. Edinburgh, National Gallery of Scotland, NG 1027.
3. Beugo's drawing from the portrait is preserved in the Royal Scottish Academy. Beugo's correspondence about the engraving was also catalogued by the National Register of Archives: Case G, Bundle 131, item 25; 26 1–7; Box K, no.360; Box N 466 1–6 and 487.

18 *William Ferguson of Kilrie* c.1779–1838

Oil on canvas 30½ × 25½in (77.5 × 64.7cm)

Private collection

PROVENANCE
By descent

EXHIBITIONS
Edinburgh, Royal Scottish Academy, *Exhibition of the Works of Sir Henry Raeburn*, 1876 (53); London, Grafton Gallery, *Scottish Old Masters*, 1895 (39); Glasgow, *International Exhibition*, 1901 (17); London, Royal Academy, *Exhibition of British Art*, 1934 (428); London, Royal Academy, *Exhibition of Scottish Art*, 1939 (85); Edinburgh, National Gallery of Scotland, *Ramsay, Raeburn and Wilkie*, 1951 (47); Edinburgh, National Gallery of Scotland, *Raeburn*, 1956 (19)

LITERATURE
Andrew, p.109; Armstrong, pp.61, 70, 90, 102; Pinnington, pp.136, 229; McKay, pp.38, 40, 45; Caw, 1908, p.73; Caw, *Masterpieces*, p.61; Greig, pp.xxx, 45; Cursiter, p.63; Brotchie, p.64; Dibdin, p.134; Collins Baker, p.163; Irwin, p.244; Mackie, no.279

NOTES
1. Edinburgh, National Gallery of Scotland, NG 2183.
2. *Raeburn*, exhibition catalogue, National Gallery of Scotland, 1956 (19).

Raeburn has focused the viewer's gaze on his sitter by framing him within the old-fashioned device of a simulated oval, traditionally an opening in a wall that reveals the subject's 'real' space (rather than a painted picture frame), but used here rather like a lens that sharpens the focus of what lies behind it. This notion, in turn, is continued in the young boy's gaze which is fixed steadily on something in that world in which the painting was created, Raeburn's own painting room. Flooding into that room from the left is the white light which glances softly on the pinks of the forehead, cheek, nose, line of jaw and throat, deepens into luminescent shadows on the other side of the face and fractures brightly on the almost crystalline cascade of the open shirt.

Within the idea that the boy moves in a dimension beyond the wall lies, of course, a contradiction – the casting of shadows from other less potent light sources, behind his right arm and beyond his left shoulder, onto whatever this chalky brown background represents. These purely painterly, abstract rather than perceptual, markings, are perhaps a memory from the art of the miniature painter.

The fragile sentience of the portrait, in which the directional light plays such an important role, both by warming flesh and suggesting texture, also owes much to the sense of exhaled breath that hovers around the half-open, faintly smiling mouth – hence, also, the feeling of a passing moment which seems so much part of the picture's intention. It is not impossible that Raeburn derived such an intention from Reynolds (for example, from a portrait like that of the young future Duke of Hamilton, painted in 1782 for William Beckford (fig.60).[1] Reynolds's painterly, excited manner at this time owed much to Rubens, whose work he had recently seen in the Low Countries, but that does not carry over into Raeburn's handling. Indeed, the sharp impression of the shirt is surprisingly reminiscent of the work of Frans Hals, though that is likely to be nothing more than mere coincidence.

The sitter's date of birth is not known which makes the dating of the portrait difficult. However, from the fact that he must have been at least twenty-one when the lands of North Kilrie and South Kilrie in the parish of Kinghorn were settled on him by his father, William Ferguson of Raith, in 1800, it has been surmised that he must have been born about 1779.[2] Given his apparent age, perhaps about twelve, this places the portrait in the early 1790s which is broadly acceptable.

William Ferguson married Elizabeth Crichton Baillie, daughter of Major James Baillie, in 1811. They lived at Balsusney House in Kirkcaldy. Their eldest son, James, a lieutenant in the 79th Regiment of Foot, sold the lands of Kilrie in 1839, his mother having renounced her liferent.

fig.60 *8th Duke of Hamilton* by Joshua Reynolds
National Gallery of Scotland

19 The Revd Robert Walker 1755–1808: 'The Skating Minister'

Oil on canvas 30 × 25in (76.2 × 63.5cm)

National Gallery of Scotland, Edinburgh

PROVENANCE

The sitter's eldest daughter, Magdalene Walker; Margaret Scougall, daughter of Magdalene Walker and Richard Scougall; Beatrix Scott, granddaughter of Margaret Scougall and James Bairnsfather Scott; Christie's, 6 March 1914 (89); bought in and sold privately to Lucy Hume, Bournemouth, 1926; Christie's, 25 February 1949 (80), when purchased by the National Gallery of Scotland

EXHIBITIONS

Edinburgh, National Gallery of Scotland, *Ramsay, Raeburn and Wilkie*, 1951 (50); Edinburgh, National Gallery of Scotland, *Raeburn*, 1956 (3); Madrid, Prado, *British Painting from Hogarth to Turner*, 1988–9 (37)

LITERATURE

Macmillan, 1990, p.152; Mackie, vol.i, pp.50–3 and no.731

NOTES

1. The minutes of the Club record: 'January, 1780: Rev Mr Walker of Crammond'. See Margaret Elliot, 'The Edinburgh Skating Club 1778–1966', *The Book of the Old Edinburgh Club*, vol.xxxiii, part 2, Edinburgh, 1971, pp.96–136.
2. General Register Office (Scotland), Monkton and Prestwick Parish Register, OPR 606: 'Robert Walker son to Mr William Walker min[iste]r here was born upon the 30th of April 1755 & baptized by Mr Lesley min[iste]r of Kilmarnock upon the 11th of May thereafter'.
3. Colin Thompson and Hugh Brigstocke, *Shorter Catalogue*, Edinburgh (National Gallery of Scotland), 1978, p.81
4. A skating portrait of 1813 by Andrew Geddes provides some tangential support for the idea that Walker is shown on Duddingston Loch. It shows the subject, an Edinburgh lawyer called Charles Knowles Robinson, against a background that includes Arthur's Seat and Duddingston Church. At the time, Robinson was secretary to the Edinburgh Skating Club and wears the badge and red ribbon of the Club's insignia. It is not unlikely that this portrait was done with Raeburn's in mind, although it is very different in many respects. Duddingston Church contained the safety equipment of the Club, which implies that this was their natural resort. However, they also skated at Lochend Loch, a little more than half a mile to the north.
5. It is arguable that the two levels of this crag are simply the result of a pentimento – that is, that the upper part was simply added on later for aesthetic reasons. But even if that were originally the case, Raeburn could well have then realised that he had 'accidentally' created the roadway or track that runs below the area called the 'Lion's Haunch'. There is certainly no other stretch of water in the vicinity of Edinburgh that has anything remotely resembling the craggy formation shown in Walker's portrait.

In character quite unlike any other surviving painting by Raeburn, this portrait has been the object of a great deal of speculation since it became widely known in 1949, after a history of almost total obscurity, when it was bought by the National Gallery of Scotland. This speculation has concerned its date, the identity of the sitter and even the authorship of Raeburn himself. Partly this has been due to the family traditions which the picture brought with it when it entered the public domain. Some of these traditions flow quite naturally from the painting itself and from its subject. It was, for example, believed to have been painted in 1784, the year in which Walker was said (mistakenly) to have joined the Edinburgh Skating Club, or Society.[1] It would, therefore, in this view, have been painted before Raeburn set off for Rome. Walker, however, was born in 1755,[2] which would have meant that he was depicted at the age of twenty-nine, which was patently wrong. To take account of this discrepancy, the notion emerged that Raeburn had changed the head at a later date to take account of Walker's appearance immediately prior to his death in 1808, when the artist presented his friend's portrait to Mrs Walker. It is highly likely that this idea owes a good deal to the now very visible signs of alterations around the hat. There is, in fact, no technical evidence at all that the face itself has been altered. On the other hand those who accepted that the head had not been updated, but continued to believe that this was one of Raeburn's earliest works, simply suggested that the portrait could not represent Walker. At the same time a belief gained currency that, despite the traditional attribution and the picture's reliable provenance, it was not the work of Raeburn at all, because its scale, handling, and canvas were completely untypical.[3] This belief, however, failed to supply any remotely reasonable suggestion as to who the alternative artist might be.

Many of the problems, however, fall away if the painting is removed from any consideration of Raeburn's earliest works

and is instead related to his work of the 1790s – as can be done very easily, despite its seemingly unique characteristics. Those who sought to place it at the very beginning of his career presumably discounted the *Lady in a Lace Cap* (cat.no.2) and knew nothing of the documented portrait of *Patrick Moir*, painted in Rome in 1784–6 (cat.no.3). It is in every respect a very sophisticated work compared to these portraits. If, for a moment, it is possible to overlook the singular form of the painting, certain essentials can be seen to relate quite closely to works of the early 1790s: the facial profile, with its purity and precision, for example, is remarkably close to the medallion *Self-portrait* of 1792 (cat.no.16), despite the very different medium. The whole notion of profile seemed to obsess Raeburn at this time as well as the related idea of what in only a few years would be termed a silhouette – dark forms containing the essence of a subject, although defined by the light that lay behind. The dark clothes of the presbyterian minister, against the icy vastness of wherever it is he skates, allowed Raeburn to test the full expressiveness of the form and it is his extraordinary success in doing so which gives the painting its unique power over the imagination. This particular interest in profile is also found in the portrait of *William Glendonwyn* (cat.no.14), although there the outline of the head is a line of white light within a darker form rather than, as here, a more diffused, lighter tone against the slightly darker sky. Closer in 'morphology', or the reading of shapes and tones as abstractions, is the portrait of *David Hunter of Blackness* (cat.no.8). By divorcing the upper halves of both pictures a remarkable congruity becomes evident – the same treatment of dark shape against light background, the black line searching always for a precise definition and abutting in a refined, continuously corrected way against paint that describes distance.

Within the painting is a contrast that is so naturally managed that it hardly

registers as such – the free, open handling of the sky, the crags on the left and the distant hills, all spreading in a pink greyness down more than half the picture surface, as opposed to the refinement of detail within the figure and the lower third of the picture. The filigree within the buckle on the strap at the skater's right knee and the taut complexities of the arrangement of the pink ribbons that bind the skates to his shoes are a reminder of the manipulative skills that Raeburn must have developed during his apprenticeship as a jeweller and in his early assays into miniature painting. And perhaps the *tour de force* of observation and the finding of equivalent forms are the marks that the skater (or those who have circled with him) has made on the ice: the curving grooves incised with some appropriate tool (a technique not unusual for Raeburn) in a liquid, greyish white which has been spread over a darker grey that has been allowed to dry and the edges of these tiny furrows, more pronounced towards the bottom of the picture, tipped in with a purer white to simulate the froth of ice thrown aside by the cutting blade.

If, therefore, the painting is dated in the period 1792–4, the traditional identification of the sitter is more easily accommodated, for Walker would be aged between thirty-seven and thirty-nine, still a trifle young for his appearance, but acceptable. Another part of the tradition attached to the portrait that can probably also be accepted is that Walker is skating on Duddingston Loch, a stretch of water at the foot of the volcanic mass of Arthur's Seat, which lies just to the east of Edinburgh city centre.[4] The base of this hill abuts hard against the loch, exactly as it does on the left of the painting; the crag is also encircled by a narrow road, which may just be discerned rather more than half-way up the darkish mass.[5] The low, distant hills would thus represent the high land that rolls to the south of Edinburgh, which, with a little artistic licence have been brought round slightly towards the east.

There is no obvious source for Raeburn's image. Somewhere, perhaps, lurk memories of Dutch seventeenth-century winter landscapes with skaters – did Walker, given his links with Holland, own such a picture? Or did the type filter through to Raeburn via the etchings of David Deuchar after such pictures? One picture, however, does relate more closely than any other, but the chances of Raeburn

having seen it seem fairly remote. This is a life-size portrait of a skater, the Scot William Grant of Congalton, by the American artist Gilbert Stuart, painted and exhibited in London in 1782 (fig.61). Stuart's painting is on a quite different scale, with other figures disporting themselves on wooded banks in the background, and the figure turned almost fully towards the spectator. Yet there is still a certain correspondence between the two pictures: a hatted gentleman in black (his very blackness dominating the picture space), arms tightly folded to his breast, his skates cutting a carefully delineated pattern on the ice. Stuart's painting caused a sensation when it was shown at the Royal Academy and it is possible that, somehow, Raeburn got wind of it.[6]

Robert Walker was the third son of William Walker, a Scottish minister who had been translated to Rotterdam in 1760, and his wife Susanna Sturment,[7] whom he had married in 1749. Robert was born on 30 April 1755 in Monkton in Ayrshire, where his father was minister. He was thus five when he was taken to Holland, where he spent the formative years of his life. He was subsequently licensed by the presbytery of Edinburgh in 1770, when he was fifteen (an early, but not impossible age) and presented to the church of Cramond, near Edinburgh, by Willielma, Lady Glenorchy. On 19 August 1784 he was translated to the church of the Canongate in Edinburgh – the same year in which he is mentioned in the minute book of the Wagering Club. (It is perhaps more than a coincidence that this, the crucial date in the latter part of his life, is the one that was traditionally attached to the painting.) Walker had married Jean Fraser, daughter of a solicitor, John Fraser, in 1778; they had five children. He became a member of the Royal Company of Archers in 1779 and their chaplain in 1798.

He published a number of books: *Sermons* (1791), *Observations on the National Character of the Dutch, and the Family Character of the House of Orange* (1794) and *The Psalms of David Methodized* (1794).[8]

The history and reputation of this painting have become a part of its meaning in a way that is highly unusual, and are worthy of mention here. It passed through a number of the sitter's descendants, until offered for sale by Christie's in 1914. Perhaps not surprisingly it failed to sell; later, it was sold privately to a Miss Lucy Hume, of Bournemouth, who ultimately

put it up for sale at Christie's in 1949. Throughout this period the picture was virtually unknown and had played no part whatsoever in Raeburn's reputation. After its acquisition by the National Gallery of Scotland, however, it started to intrigue and fascinate, so that eventually it supplanted famous pictures like the *Mrs Scott Moncrieff* (cat.no.52) as the archetypal Raeburn, which in many ways it is not. It has since become – a curiosity in the history of taste – one of the most famous paintings in the world.

6. National Gallery of Art, Washington DC, 1950.18.1. (1051). See Ellen G. Miles, *American Paintings of the Eighteenth Century*, Washington (National Gallery of Art), 1995, pp.162–9. The author draws attention to Robert Jones's *Treatise on Skating* (London, 1772) which illustrates a skater with the same crossed-arm pose as Grant and Walker, which was said to be 'a proper attitude for genteel rolling'. The portrait of Grant is also discussed by Richard McLomathan, *Gilbert Stuart*, New York, 1986, pp.37, 45–6, 47.
See also Andrea G. Pearson, 'Gilbert Stuart's *The Skater (Portrait of William Grant)* and Henry Raeburn's *The Reverend Robert Walker, D.D., Skating on Duddingston Loch*: A Study of Sources', *Rutgers Art Review*, VIII, 1987, pp.55–70. She argues that there is no essential connection between the two portraits.
7. Hew Scott, *Fasti Ecclesiae Scoticanae*, vol.III, Edinburgh, 1920, p.57.
8. Walker is also often credited with a publication called *Kolf, a Dutch Game*. This, in fact, was an extensive footnote 'communicated by the Rev. Mr Walker, one of the ministers of the Canongate, whose former residence in Holland has enabled him to give a very satisfactory description of that game', to Sir John Sinclair's *Statistical Account*. It was included under the parish of Inveresk. Although it begins by saying that the word 'golf' is derived from 'kolf', the game Walker describes is a curious indoor game very unlike modern golf.

fig.61 *The Skater (Portrait of William Grant)* by Gilbert Stuart
National Gallery of Art, Washington DC
(Andrew W. Mellon Collection)

20 *John Lee Allen (b.1781) and James Allen (b.1783): 'The Allen Brothers of Errol'*

Oil on canvas 60 × 45½in (152.4 × 115.6cm)

Private collection

PROVENANCE
Leopold Hirsch, 1901; Henry Hirsch; Christie's, 11 May 1934 (142); bought by Allinson for J. A. Dewar; Viscountess Ward of Witley; thence by descent; on long term loan to the Tate Gallery, 1981 to 1994

EXHIBITIONS
Paris, British Pavilion, *International Exhibition*, 1902; London, Guildhall, 1902; Birmingham, City Art Gallery, *Loan Exhibition of Portraits*, 1903 (67); Vienna, *British Exhibition*, 1927

LITERATURE
Armstrong, p.95; Pinnington, p.218; Greig, p.37; Mackie, no.20

NOTES
1. See, for example, the painting *A Young Female Artist* (Dunrobin Castle), which Watson exhibited at the British Institution in 1813 and which was bought by the Marquis of Stafford. In this form of lighting the deepest shadows tend to run down the central axis of the face, with one side of the face strongly lit, the other in half shadow. Another example, surely by Watson, is the portrait called *Master Hay* in the Auckland City Art Gallery which has always been attributed to Raeburn.
2. This information is taken from a transcript of a letter from a firm of Edinburgh solicitors, W. & F. Anderson of 48 Castle Street, to Sir James Caw, director of the National Galleries of Scotland, dated 16 March 1934, Scottish National Portrait Gallery, Library, Greig Archive.

Although the elements of this double portrait are firmly and intricately composed (in such a way that raises the question of how Raeburn set about paintings of this degree of complexity) the actions of the two boys create the kind of instability always present when children play unpredictably, and virtually out of control. Yet, not only do they play with, and for, each other, but they also play in collusion, even coyly, with the artist. What actions he asked them to perform and virtually impossible poses he asked them to hold can only be guessed at. It is difficult to believe that in such a composition, where there are no obvious precedents, preparatory drawings were not made, but evidence of that kind is still totally lacking. The intellectual basis for the composition is another intriguing area of speculation: what did Raeburn aim to convey of childhood aping manhood and how did he accommodate whatever wishes – and there must have been some – the boy's parents expressed? An important imposition here must have been the virtually identical dressing of the two boys, presumably the parents' idea. Did their views also colour the actions, or did Raeburn arrive at these through his interaction with the boys and through his own view of childhood and the times in which they lived – revolution and the potential for war? Although there is what can only be termed charm in the relationship of the two heads, there is also an element of complicitous precocity in the glance of the younger boy and a single-minded, underlying ferocity in the severe profile of the elder boy that is unsettling. And, despite the fact that the children seem to clasp each other lovingly (of the two hidden arms, only the fingers of the older boy are visible at his brother's waist), there is a lingering unease in the gesture made with the stick – what, in the context of the game, does it represent; into what target, more than the mere lining of a hat, is it thrust with such lust for action?

This action is contained not only in the older boy's left arm (which shows signs of substantial alteration as the painting proceeded) but in the tension of his leaning body, that movement held in equilibrium by the countering curve of his brother's body, supported unsteadily against the back of the rustic seat and pivoted by his bent right leg. The singularity of what is happening is aided by the near mirror effect of the boys' costumes. Each is dressed in a short, dark green coat with large buttons, a foam of white linen at the breast bursting from square-cut waist-coats. The waistcoats have a fine pattern of parallel, horizontal lines, pink on a lighter base, the lighter base darkening into grey shadow on each boy's left side. Their knee breeches are a brightish yellow ochre, cut just below the knee, half in shadow and thrown into bright relief by the light that cuts across them from upper left. This almost heraldic mirroring has a tiny variation in the shoes, the younger boy's silver-buckled, the elder boy's bound instead by wide laces.

The form the lighting takes, the loose vigour of the handling of pigment and the flake-like fracturings of paint that make up the two vaguely defined tree-trunks on the right, all suggest a date in the early 1790s – close in some respects to the *Clerks of Penicuik* (cat.no.13), although the emotional charge of the picture is so different. Such a date is borne out by the apparent ages of the sitters (if they are correctly identified). Of particular interest, because rather unlike any other painting by Raeburn of this period, is the 'double' lighting of the younger boy's face. Not only are shadows cast on to the left sides of the forms, in varied degrees of darkness, by light falling from high on the left of the picture, but shadows and highlights are also thrown upwards from the brightness of the shirt. This means that the lower lip is, atypically, darker than the upper one; in addition, light finds its way to the under-sides of the nostrils where one would normally expect only shadow. This form of double (even multiple) lighting seems to have intrigued Raeburn's contemporaries in Edinburgh, notably George Watson,

who took its effects to extreme lengths in a number of paintings, some of which have been mistakenly attributed to Raeburn.[1]

The sitters were the sons of John Allen of Inchmartine and his wife Flavel, whose family name is not known. Inchmartine is in the Carse of Gowrie on the north bank of the River Tay, a few miles from the estate and mansion house of Errol, which John Allen purchased in 1786. A deed of settlement of 1794 makes it clear that the eldest son, John Lee Allen, was to inherit the estate of Errol and that his second son, James Allen, was to succeed to Inchmartine. Near to Errol is Port Allen, now completely silted up but a thriving port in the early nineteenth century, which presumably took its name from the family.

John Allen also owned a house in St Andrew Square in Edinburgh and the boys may have been born there. The boys' father was dead by 1795 when the elder boy was granted sasine of Errol. He remained proprietor of Errol until 1846 when he was succeeded by his own eldest son, John James Allen.[2]

21   *Ann Edgar, Lady Raeburn 1744–1832*

Oil on canvas 58 × 44in (147.3 × 111.8cm)

Private collection

PROVENANCE

By descent in the sitter's family; Christie's, 7 May 1877 (31); John Heugh; Christie's, 10 May 1878 (226); Agnew's; Sir William Andrew, 1884; Christie's, 9 July 1887 (143); Agnew's; Lord Tweedmouth, 1888; Christie's, 3 June 1905 (33); C. Davis; Sir Ernest Cassel, 1906; by descent to Countess Mountbatten

EXHIBITIONS

Edinburgh, Royal Scottish Academy, 1863 (211); Edinburgh, Royal Scottish Academy, *Exhibition of the Works of Sir Henry Raeburn*, 1876 (23); London, Royal Academy, 1877 (47); Edinburgh, *Exhibition of Scottish National Portraits*, 1884 (229); London, Royal Academy, 1888 (13); Berlin, Königliche Akademie der Kunste, *Aelterer Englischer Kunst*, 1908 (74); Copenhagen, 1908 (20); Vienna, *British Exhibition*, 1927; Edinburgh, National Gallery of Scotland, *Raeburn*, 1956 (28)

LITERATURE

Andrew, p.145; Henley, no.2; Armstrong, pp.47, 110; Pinnington, pp.83, 161, 162, 207, 245; Greig, pp.xxiv, xliv, xlvii, lii, 57; Brotchie, p.91; Dibdin, p.32; Harris, p.5; Macmillan, 1990, p.154; Mackie, no.599

NOTES

1. I am grateful to my colleague Rosalind Marshall for discussing details of the costume with me.
2. Hew Scott, *Fasti Ecclesiae Scoticanae*, vol.1, Edinburgh, 1915, p.287.
3. William Raeburn Andrew, *Life of Sir Henry Raeburn, R.A.*, London, 1886, pp.75–7. Wilkie's letter is dated 15 September 1822.

Raeburn's *second* portrait of his wife (second, if it is accepted that the early portrait of a *Lady in a Lace Cap* (cat.no.2) is the same person, and the work of the artist) appears to date from the early 1790s. Although the lighting is carefully controlled, there is a certain evenness in the dispersal of bright areas and shadows throughout the picture which is less adventurous than the meticulously contrived and profoundly expressive lighting of the *Clerks of Penicuik* (cat.no.13), which must date no later than 1792. This suggests that the portrait is earlier, perhaps of 1790, when the sitter would have reached the age of about forty-six.

What is certainly profound in the present picture is the chord of intimacy struck between the artist and the mature woman whose gaze meets his. Painted a year or two after Raeburn's return from Rome, it is possible to interpret the portrait as an act of reaffirmation, each of the beautifully painted, entwined arms comforting the other – benignly domestic as well as uxorious and sensual. A similar insistence on the fleshiness of the forearms is something that has already been noted in the *Lady in a Lace Cap.*

The subject is perhaps imagined as seated against a wall at the family home of Deanhaugh House, a deeply toned landscape in the distance, the hills vaguely reminiscent of the Pentlands, to the south of Edinburgh. However, in fact, she had no doubt walked up the hill from Stockbridge to the studio in George Street, wearing the loose, voluminous coat, greyish chocolate brown in colour and perhaps of a fine woollen material, which is such a notable feature of the portrait. Did Raeburn suggest that she continue to wear it so that its deep folds and dark colour disguise the matronly figure? Or at a simpler level of meaning, was there some degree of pride in the fur-trimmed garment itself, in fashion again from the 1780s – or, simpler still, was the requirement purely an aesthetic one?

Beneath the coat is a closed robe of layered white muslin, its considerable length caught up in the subject's right foot at the left edge of the picture. On her head is a turban, popular from the 1760s to the 1790s, which seems to consist of a scarf twisted informally around the head, the ends left dangling on both sides, the loose fringes suggested with broken wisps of white pigment which, as in some other paintings, exploit the diagonal lines of the twill canvas. At the front, the material virtually merges with the hair which is pushed informally to each side of the forehead. The casual nature of turbans had begun to be replaced by a more premeditated shape by the 1790s, and to some degree Mrs Raeburn's may have tended to the old fashioned.[1]

The young Raeburn, his career scarcely begun, may or may not have met Ann Edgar, the widow of James Leslie, in the circumstances that Allan Cunningham describes (see cat.no.2). At any rate, they were probably married at an unknown date during 1780, rather more than two years after she had been widowed. She was born at Marchfield in the parish of Cramond, daughter to Peter Edgar of Bridgelands, factor to the Earl of Selkirk, and Ann Hay, daughter of the minister at Peebles.[2] Her first husband, Leslie, was a man of considerable wealth and she brought this, including the property of Deanhaugh, to her marriage with Raeburn. She also brought two daughters and a son. She and Raeburn subsequently had two sons, Peter, born on 18 May 1781 and Henry, born on 24 October 1783. One can only speculate as to why neither of these children was included in the present portrait.

In 1794, some fourteen years after their marriage, the Raeburns acquired land adjacent to Deanhaugh House and started to develop it as modest, but elegant housing. The earliest street, Ann Street, one of the loveliest streets in any neo-classical city, was named after Raeburn's wife. Apart from her portrait there is little information on her personality. There was, however, a revealing moment at the dinner party which Raeburn and his wife

gave at St Bernard's House (a property close to Deanhaugh House to which they later moved) on 30 August 1822, the day after receiving his knighthood. David Wilkie describes the occasion in a letter to his sister. Among those present was the soldier, and friend of Scott, Adam Ferguson, who had received a knighthood at the same time as Raeburn. The ceremony at Hopetoun House was gone over endlessly, 'with new jokes every time'. Ferguson blushed a great deal and sang songs, including 'The Laird of Cockpen', and Raeburn made a modest speech.

Wilkie continues: 'Lady Raeburn would not allow herself to be called *My Lady* on any account, but was exceedingly hospitable to her guests, and pressed them to eat in the good old-fashioned Scottish style.'[3]

22 *Dr William Robertson 1721–93*

Oil on canvas 50 × 40in (127 × 101.6cm)

University of Edinburgh, Edinburgh

PROVENANCE
University of Edinburgh

EXHIBITIONS
London, South Kensington Museum, *Third and Concluding Exhibition of National Portraits*, 1868 (888); Edinburgh, Royal Scottish Academy, *Exhibition of the Works of Sir Henry Raeburn*, 1876 (83); Edinburgh, National Gallery of Scotland, *Look Alike*, 1982 (19)

LITERATURE
Dugald Stewart, *Biographical Memoirs of Adam Smith, of William Robertson, and of Thomas Reid*, Edinburgh, 1811, pp.308–9; Duncan, p.16; Andrew, pp.146–7; Armstrong, pp.60, 110; James L. Caw, *Scottish Portraits with an Historical and Critical Introduction*, Edinburgh, 1903, vol.2, pp.35–7; Pinnington, pp.131, 132, 246; McKay, p.42; Stevenson, p.406; Greig, p.58; Brotchie, pp.62, 88; James L. Caw, *University of Edinburgh Journal*, summer 1929; *The University Portraits*, eds D. Talbot Rice [and] Peter McIntyre, Edinburgh (University Press), 1957, pp.183–6; Macmillan, 1986, p.79; Macmillan, 1990, p.153; Mackie, no.618

NOTES
1. These books have been identified as follows: Geronimo de Blancas, *Ad Regum Aragonum Veterumque Comitum*, Zaragoza, 1587; Geronimo Zurita, *Anales de la Corona de Aragon* (6 volumes), Zaragoza, 1562–80; Ludovico Antonio Muratori, *Antiquitates Italicae Medii Aevii* (6 volumes), Milan, 1738–42. I am grateful to Iain Gordon Brown for these identifications.
2. According to Caw (1903) Raeburn actually made a copy of Reynolds's portrait for a member of Robertson's family. Caw does not say whether this was done before or after the University commissioned the present portrait. There is no other record of such a portrait.

fig.62 *William Robertson* by Joshua Reynolds
Scottish National Portrait Gallery

The circumstances of the creation of this portrait are known in considerable detail, and the painting also bears, uniquely, what can be accepted as Raeburn's signature. On 31 March 1792, thirty years after Robertson had become Principal of 'the College of Edinburgh', Andrew Dalzel, Professor of Greek and correspondent of Heine, and Dugald Stewart, mathematician, Professor of moral philosophy and sympathiser with the early stages of the French revolution, proposed, at a meeting of the General Convention of the College, that he should be requested 'to sit to Mr Raeburn for his portrait, to be hung up in the Library'. The portrait was intended to mark his long period of office as well as his immense, and international, reputation as an historian, but was particularly linked to the library of the college because of Robertson's assiduous attention to its growth. The minute of the meeting also notes the historian's absence, 'occasioned by want of health', and it is not difficult to read the portrait as an image of a sick man, his head sunk with a suggestion of fatigue into his shoulders and the light of the face perhaps fading. He was to die in the year following the portrait's completion.

Raeburn was paid 30 guineas for the portrait and charged 7 guineas for the frame, which still contains it. The total cost was met by a contribution of £1 9s from each of twenty-seven professors, the remaining 6s being paid to a janitor who collected the money from the contributors.

Leaning against Robertson's chair in the bottom left hand corner of the painting are four books, piled haphazardly, their rather battered condition depicted with a good deal of attention to detail. Perhaps surprisingly, even in portraits painted with characteristic breadth, Raeburn rarely treated books cursorily, but tended always to carefully describe the quality of their bindings and paper. Three of these books bear titles or fragments of titles on their spines, not purely visual in treatment but painted so that their identity is unmistakable – the message being allowed to transcend the medium. The horizontal one is lettered 'HIER:/BLANCA/COM:'; while the two others are lettered 'ZORIT:/ANAL:/DE ARAG:' and 'MURAT/ANTIQ/ITAL:'.[1]

On the back cover of the former of these two books is an inscription in italic capitals with rather blunt serifs, which runs horizontally and with no perspectival relationship to the book; it reads: 'H: RAEBURN:/PINXIT.EDIN:GI·/A.D. 1792.'. This 'inscription' seems to be part and parcel of the facture of the whole picture and can therefore be assumed to have been put there by Raeburn himself. The reasons for its inclusion, either at the College's behest or from some decision taken by the painter, remain unclear.

Although Robertson's gown, breeches and leggings are locally black, they are so modulated in greys that the picture as a whole is quite light toned, with focal highlights on the head and the hands. The paint that composes the elderly face is quite thick and almost 'clotted' in character, while in the hands it runs fluidly, especially in the left one, which relates in an entirely painterly way to the highly significant university mace shining among quills, inkwell and books on the table-top. One of these books is lettered 'TACITUS', while the neatly propped ten volumes behind, in the shadow cast by the reddish, conventional drape in the background, are lettered 'ROB/SCOT.', along with volume numbers. These are a reference, and a tribute, to Robertson's widely acclaimed, though now forgotten, *History of Scotland*, written while he was minister of the parish of Gladsmuir and published in 1759.

Apart from the highlights, the one area of positive colour in the painting is the crimson chair, covered with damask. The most intensely coloured part is the small area of visible seat, which probably contains an organic red. To describe the nature of the wood of the chair upright, as well as the quality of light that shines on it, Raeburn has dragged some of this red diagonally across it which meets the more carefully placed highlights on the carved grooves.

Robertson was educated at the primary

school in Borthwick and later at Dalkeith, before entering the University of Edinburgh at the age of twelve in 1733. He subsequently had charge of the churches of Gladsmuir, and Lady Yester's and Old Greyfriars, both in Edinburgh. Famous for his eloquence, Dr Johnson declined to attend one of Robertson's sermons in 1773 because of his presbyterianism, which Johnson could not stomach. An active moderator of the Church of Scotland from 1763, Robertson dedicated his life to study and to writing his three great histories: the above mentioned *History of Scotland*, *The History of the Reign of Charles V* (1769), and *The History of America* (1777).

Liberal in a perhaps understated way, Robertson, while still at Gladsmuir, had defended his friend and fellow minister, John Home, from the attacks of the

presbyterian establishment for having written and produced a stage play. He was also a founding member of the painter Allan Ramsay's Speculative Society (1754), which included figures of the stature of Adam Smith, David Hume, Adam Ferguson and Lord Kames. His eloquence was a feature of the Society, and in its written form a cause of astonishment to Horace Walpole who pronounced the *History of Scotland* 'the best modern history' and 'written by a man whose dialect I scare understood … in the purest English'. The initiation of the rebuilding of the University in Edinburgh was also one of his many achievements, retaining the services of Robert Adam for the design of the new college (now known as Old College), the foundation stone of which was laid in November 1789.

Robertson was portrayed by a number of other artists, including James Tassie (1791) and, most notably, Sir Joshua Reynolds (1772). In its general disposition of figure, chair and book-strewn table, as well as the gestures of the hands, Reynolds's portrait seems to presage the same features in Raeburn's portrait of twenty years later, though the subjects are reversed (fig.62). This could suggest Raeburn's knowledge of the earlier portrait through Dixon's mezzotint engraving of 1773.[2] In many important respects, however, the two portraits are quite different – that of Reynolds having a rather severe, intellectualised structure and a deliberate, rather stiff surface, while Raeburn's portrait has a natural fluidity of effect and a responsiveness to actual appearances that is vigorous and immediate.

23 *John Johnstone of Alva 1734—95, Betty Johnstone and Miss Wedderburn*

Oil on canvas 40 × 47¼ (101.5 × 120cm)

National Gallery of Art, Washington DC

PROVENANCE

By descent to Johnstone's great-grandson, Major James Johnstone; Christie's, 26 May 1906 (92); Wood; Mrs P. Nelke; Christie's, 9 July 1926 (131); Samuel; Lewis and Simmons, Paris, July 1928; Mr and Mrs Robert W. Schuette; given by Mrs Schuette to the National Gallery of Art, Washington DC, 1945

EXHIBITIONS

Chicago, The Art Institute of Chicago, *Century of Progress*, 1933 (201); Pittsburgh, Carnegie Institute, *Survey of British Painting*, 1938 (37); New York, World's Fair, *Masterpieces of Art: European and American Paintings 1500–1900*, 1940 (146)

LITERATURE

Armstrong, p.106; Pinnington, p.237; Greig, p.50; Mackie, vol.I, pp.50, 53 and no.437

NOTES

1. Thomas Babington Macaulay, *Lord Clive*, London, 1851, p.70.

Miss Wedderburn, her head in delicate, pure profile, speaks words of sufficient consequence to catch the full attention of her aged aunt and uncle. As they focus their minds on whatever that utterance might have been, so they focus their eyes on her young face. Although she holds a blue, paper-bound book in the valley between her thighs, the front cover turned carelessly back on itself, there is no indication that she reads from the book or even that its contents are the subject of discussion, though that may be the case. And not only are words being spoken, but there is also a strong suggestion that the other two will in a moment make reply. The picture is in this way more literally a 'conversation piece' than many pictures that are so classified.

The sense of casual ease that implies a further stage in this domestic narrative is condensed in a highly distinctive way in the figure of John Johnstone on the right. He is painted with such a lack of contrivance on Raeburn's part and with such a degree of naturalness, rare in the painting of the time, that the kind of similitude it represents is photographic in essence. This degree of naturalness gives some credence to Joseph Farington's remark, usually dismissed as a misunderstanding, that Raeburn had 'looked very much at Nature' as reflected in a camera obscura. If such a device were used, then it is para-doxically not a lack of contrivance that characterises Johnstone's face but in fact a very high degree of contrivance. To take the idea one step further, the figure is in many ways close in its naturalness to the photographic imagery of D. O. Hill and Robert Adamson of the mid-1840s: it represents the kind of visual truth that they sought. That the picture may have been 'compiled' in such a way is given added weight by the slight but clearly detectable discrepancy in the scale of Betty Johnstone, giving her the air of a certain physical detachment from the other two figures. Despite this, it remains one of the most remarkable of Raeburn's early paintings.

The painting must date from before December 1795, when Johnstone died. It seems likely to be quite close to that date since it shares little of the agenda of that other landscape-shaped group portrait, the *Clerks of Penicuik* (cat.no.13) which could not be later than the beginning of 1792. Essentially, the present portrait is more emphatically 'painterly' than the Clerk portrait, the impasto thicker, rougher, more abstract in quality. Nowhere in the Clerk portrait, for example, is there an area that reads so independently as Betty Johnstone's bonnet: broken planes of white, grey and pale blue with dark accents untidily – but with exact tonal correctness – dashed in as a last act of observation in that particular area. Indeed the sense of 'working' the surface of the picture as a continuum of brushed pigment is perhaps more obvious in this painting than in any other by Raeburn. This virtually autonomous nature of the paint is most marked, not in areas with their own textural logic, but in Johnstone's head, which is a mass of tight, linear brushstrokes of varying weight, the impasto thickest – and most contorted – above his eyebrows and in the whorls that turn within his high forehead. In textural contrast to this creamy flow is the series of dry highlights, drawn by the canvas from the tips of a broad, stiffly loaded brush, on the clump of greyish hair on the left side of his head.

The profile of Miss Wedderburn's head is close in quality to the profile head of the *Revd Robert Walker* (cat.no.19), a portrait probably of about 1794. Profile was evidently much in Raeburn's mind at the time – perhaps because of his modelled self-portrait in the manner of James Tassie of 1792 (cat.no.16). Here the contour of the evenly lit face is helped by a slight intensification of the sky, taking some of the blue from the ribbons in Miss Johnstone's bonnet. Like many other areas of the picture, the hair, not naturally grey, but powdered, and tied at the back in a chignon and bound by a white bandeau, is painted with a swift roughness. Her dress,

held at the waist by a black band, is also evenly lit, in gleaming white. Her neck and breast are revealed by a turned-back, frilled collar, gathered at the front, and, by juxtaposition with the dress of her aunt, a commentary on youth and age. Betty Johnstone is wrapped in a black satin stole, her bare left hand crossed over a buff gloved one. Johnstone is the most colour-fully dressed of the three. He wears a warm brown coat, with large pewter buttons, and cream waistcoat with a long row of smaller, brass buttons, their perspectival relationship to the horizontal folds within which they lie very carefully calculated.

Johnstone, who presumably commis-sioned the portrait, does not appear to

have been a very pleasant man. He was the fourth son of Sir James Johnstone of Westerhall in Dunfermline and as such obviously had to make his way in the world. He made a career in the East India Company and was on the Council of Bengal from 1761 to 1765. A not very complimentary impression of his behav-iour is given by Lord Macaulay in a description of a meeting of the Council in the latter year, at which the Governor General, Lord Clive, signalled his inten-tion of stamping out the bribery and corruption which were rife among serv-ants of the Company: 'The Council met, and Clive stated to them his full determi-nation to make a thorough reform, and to use for that purpose the whole of the

ample authority, civil and military, which had been confided to him. Johnstone, one of the boldest and worst men in the assembly, made some show of opposition. Clive interrupted him, and haughtily demanded whether he meant to question the power of the new government. Johnstone was cowed, and disclaimed any such intention. All the faces round the board grew long and pale; and not another syllable of dissent was uttered.'[1] Johnstone returned to Scotland a very wealthy man and purchased Alva in Clackmannanshire and other estates; he also sat as MP for Dysart from 1774 to 1780. He employed the architect Robert Adam to alter Alva House and to provide him with a mauso-leum, which still exists.

24 *Katherine Ramsay, Lady Mackenzie of Coul (fl.1778–96)*

Oil on canvas 34½ × 26 (87.6 × 66.1cm)

Professor Philip Rieff

PROVENANCE
By descent to Sir Robert Mackenzie of Coul; Christie's, 20 November 1970 (205); private collection, on loan to Philadelphia Museum of Art

EXHIBITIONS
Edinburgh, Royal Scottish Academy, *Exhibition of the Works of Sir Henry Raeburn*, 1876 (315); London, Grafton Gallery, *Scottish Old Masters*, 1895 (16); Edinburgh, National Gallery of Scotland, *Raeburn*, 1956 (21)

LITERATURE
Andrew, p.137; Armstrong, p.108; Pinnington, p.239; Greig, p.52; Mackie, no.499

NOTES
1. See Mackie, nos 500a and 500b. The later portrait was exhibited at the Royal Academy in 1813 (52). More recently (1997) it was with Lane Fine Art.

The inward, contemplative mode of this portrait is so finely judged that it is not overpowered by its chromatic richness and 'sculptural' variety. Lady Mackenzie's face, its gaze profoundly focused, is carved, as it were, in simple lines and from a subtle material – as are the angled fingers of her left hand. This planar quality then expands in a kind of loose crescendo into the circling rhythms of the muslin dress and the nearly endless turns of the entangling shawl. Although these movements are circular in effect, they are, paradoxically, largely composed of forms that are rectilinear and angular – the crisp white highlights around the breast, for example, the long, defining shadows within the shawl where it crosses the sitter's right arm, and the darker contours in the lower right of the picture.

The voluminous shawl, which was presumably a symbol of considerable significance, is a curious lime green not found, certainly in this quantity, elsewhere in Raeburn's work. It appears to be a mixture of white, black and a yellow. Its visual contours are broken and undefined, although in actuality it has a fine border embroidered in red and dark blue. At her waist is an encrustation of gold and black shadow, also consistently linear in handling, that represents a broad belt or sash. The rhythms of her hair, powdered grey – a fashion that was soon to end – are more truly circular, in a series of interwoven whorls, held loosely by a wide, pale pink ribbon. In terms of colour harmony this pink seems an almost too sweet complement to the green of the shawl.

The portrait is likely to have been painted between 1792 and 1796 – and more likely towards the end of this period. Katherine Ramsay, a daughter of Robert Ramsay of Camno, married Alexander Mackenzie, son and heir of Sir Alexander Mackenzie of Coul, in 1778. He served with the East India Company, becoming major-general and provincial commander-in-chief in Bengal in the years 1790–2. He succeeded to the baronetcy of Coul in 1792, but enjoyed the title for only four years, dying on 14 September 1796. As Lady Mackenzie is clearly not wearing any vestige of mourning in the portrait it follows that it was painted before that date. While the portrait might have been a consequence of Alexander Mackenzie's succession to the baronetcy in 1792, it does not seem quite as early as that date, what has been defined as its 'sculptural' qualities placing it after the experiments with lambent lighting of the earlier 1790s. A date of about 1793–5 seems most likely.

The sitter's son, George Steuart Mackenzie (1780–1848), who succeeded to the baronetcy in 1796, became a renowned scientist, notable for proving that diamonds are composed of carbon. He is said to have destroyed his mother's jewels in the course of his early experiments. He was painted by Raeburn when a boy, about the same time as his mother, and also when grown up, in about 1811–13.[1] In 1820 he was one of Raeburn's three sponsors (with Sir David Brewster and William Adam of Blairadam), when the painter was elected to the Royal Society of Edinburgh.

25 *The Revd Hugh Blair 1718–1800*

Oil on canvas 36 × 28in (91.5 × 71.1cm)

Kirk of the Canongate, Edinburgh

PROVENANCE

Henry Temple Blair of Avontoun; Charles
Cornelius Maconochie (died 1930); by descent to
Sir Robert Maconochie; presented by Charles
John Maconochie to the Canongate Kirk,
Edinburgh

EXHIBITIONS

Edinburgh, 32 York Place, *Portraits by the late Sir
Henry Raeburn*, 1824 (25): this may, however,
have been a different portrait as another Raeburn
type is known, showing the sitter in gown and
bands and wearing a wig (Christie's, April 1986
(128)); Edinburgh, Royal Scottish Academy,
Exhibition of the Works of Sir Henry Raeburn, 1876
(37); Glasgow, Palace of Arts, *Empire Exhibition*,
1938 (39b); Edinburgh, Scottish National Portrait
Gallery, *Scottish Literary Personalities*, 1951;
Edinburgh, National Gallery of Scotland,
Raeburn, 1956 (26)

LITERATURE

Mackie, no.526

NOTES

1. James Mackay, *A Biography of Robert Burns*,
Edinburgh, 1992, pp.175–6.
2. *Ibid.*, p.268.
3. *Ibid.*, p.269.
4. *Ibid.*, p.336.
5. J. De Lancey Ferguson, *The Letters of Robert
Burns* (second edition), ed. G. Ross Roy, Oxford,
1985, vol.I, pp.110–11.

This portrait, on stylistic evidence, must date from a year or two before the sitter's death. It has a gentle, rather casual air, its impact quite unrhetorical, despite the figure being brought unusually close to the picture plane. Nevertheless, there is a strong sense of the subject and the painter being in close communion, although the soft grey eyes, their dark irises marked with a fleck of pink, may focus just to the side of the observer. The canvas is generally painted thinly, and in that sense also the portrait is understated, but the paint, in the hands and face, does flicker constantly round the vagaries of form in a search for the nuances of the skin and the substances pulsing beneath. In the same way, the folded-under edge of the hat is as much concerned with suggesting the string or stiff lining that lies within the fold as it is with defining the contact between it and the forehead and right side of the face. It is a technique that is often loosely termed 'impressionistic' and it is not entirely inappropriate here. There is also a lack of definite contour, as in the beautifully lit clasped hands, and an introduction of mere traces of contrasting colour that contribute so much to the portrait's liveliness, such as the fleck of bluish grey on the upper right lip that hints at shaved hair or the dry scuffs of whitish pigment that suggest the fronds on the tassel on the rear of Blair's hat. There are two exceptions to this lightness of touch: a few strokes of bold, dark red impasto in the drape to the right of the sitter's head and the precise, crisp contours of the sheets of manuscript that lie on the table-top against Blair's right elbow.

This seemingly relaxed method does not, of course, preclude both careful calculation and flexibility. The pyramidal shapes of the great buttons on Blair's coat are noted for their quiddity and a number of quite radical changes have occurred as the portrait has progressed. These include a lowering by two or three inches of the position of the hands (their original position has become visible again under the dark grey of the waist-coat) and the painting of the green tablecloth over an area of reddish pink that was presumably once part of the chair.

Blair graduated from the University of Edinburgh in 1739. Licensed to preach by the presbytery of Edinburgh in 1741 he was ordained minister of Collessie in Fife the following year. There then followed in fairly quick succession three charges in Edinburgh: second minister of the Canongate in 1743, Lady Yester's church in 1754, and the high church of St Giles in 1758 (having been succeeded at Lady Yester's church by William Robertson (cat.no.22)). He remained in that charge for the rest of his life.

In August 1760 the council of Edinburgh appointed him Professor of rhetoric and two years later created a regius chair of rhetoric and belles lettres for him. This reflected the reputation he had gained as both a preacher and a literary figure. His published sermons were enormously popular and were translated into many languages. He would count among his closest circle David Hume, Adam Smith and William Robertson and he was an enthusiastic, if misguided, supporter of James Macpherson's 'Ossianic' verse.

Blair was also one of the 'literati' who encouraged the poet Robert Burns on his first visit to Edinburgh in 1786. Burns evidently liked the man but he had no great respect for his Augustan good taste. Nevertheless he seems to have been persuaded by Blair to exclude his vivid, raucous and slightly bawdy cantata, 'The Jolly Beggars', from the Edinburgh edition of his poems (1787).[1] While referring to his 'liking' for the man 'when he descends from his pinnacle and meets me on equal ground', Burns sums him up rather wickedly: 'In my opinion Dr Blair is merely an astonishing proof of what industry and application can do … his vanity is proverbially known among his acquaintances'.[2] Although Burns had inadvertently insulted him at a dinner

party by stating a preference for the preaching of his associate minister at St Giles, William Greenfield,[3] Blair did not allow it to affect their friendship and he went on helping the poet in such matters as, for example, providing him with an introduction to the Duke of Atholl's family. Burns marked his gratitude to Blair by presenting him with an impression of Beugo's famous engraved portrait of himself.[5] Raeburn's portrait of Blair was engraved by Bartolozzi in 1802 and by Bertland in 1822.

26 *Professor Adam Ferguson 1723—1816*

Oil on canvas 50 × 40in (127 × 101.6cm)

University of Edinburgh, Edinburgh

PROVENANCE

Sir John Macpherson, by whom bequeathed to the
University of Edinburgh in 1821

EXHIBITIONS

London, South Kensington Museum, *Second
Special Exhibition of National Portraits*, 1867
(842); Edinburgh, University of Edinburgh, *James
Hutton and Some of his Friends*, 1976

LITERATURE

Andrew, p.120; Armstrong, pp.60, 101;
Pinnington, pp.131, 132, 229; Greig, p.44;
Brotchie, pp.62, 63; Dibdin, p.39; *The University
Portraits*, eds D. Talbot Rice [and] Peter
McIntyre, Edinburgh (University Press), 1957,
pp.69–71; Macmillan, 1986, p.76; Mackie, no.271

NOTES

1. It was lent to the Raeburn exhibition of 1876
by Mrs Admiral Ferguson (173) and to the
Exhibition of Scottish National Portraits, 1884
(276). It was last recorded at Sotheby's, New
York, 15 October 1987 (128).
2. Henry Cockburn, *Memorials of his Time*,
ed. Harry A. Cockburn, Edinburgh and London,
1909, p.45.
3. *Ibid.*, p.44.

In composition, though reversed,
Ferguson's portrait has much in common
with the portrait of his friend, Dr William
Robertson, painted in 1792 (cat.no.22).
Ferguson is seated in a reddish chair, a
table with a pile of books hard against it,
the background closed up with a rather
featureless, claret-coloured drapery.
However, in Ferguson's case the gestural
hand, his right, clasps the arm of the chair
and his gaze is concentrated on some point
within the room rather than on the
painter. Another significant difference is
that Ferguson's chair (clearly the *same*
sitter's chair, a property of Raeburn's
studio) has been widened so as to accommodate a slightly more frontal view of the
sitter. This widening is not entirely
convincing and the orthogonals of the
arms diverge rather than converge on the
chair-back. This carelessness over the
perspectival relationship of sitter and chair
is not all that unusual for Raeburn –
though it is surprising given his natural
feel for the diminution of other objects in
space – books, papers and even heads (see,
for example, the portrait of *William
Forbes* (cat.no.31)).

Although the painting is generally
'drier' than that of Ferguson – that is, the
ratio of medium to pigment is less – the
handling, particularly in the face, is
broader, which seems to indicate a date in
the later 1790s. There is no event in
Ferguson's life to which it can certainly be
linked, unless it was the publication in
1792 of his *Principles of Moral and Political Science, being chiefly a Retrospect of
Lectures delivered in the College of Edinburgh*, in two volumes. The two vellum-
covered volumes (which may contain
manuscripts rather than printed text) by
his right hand are conceivably a reference
to this: they are lettered on the spines
'LEC:/ON/MOR:PHIL/VOL. 1 [and] VOL.2'.
The horizontal book lying on top of these
is inscribed 'INSTIT:/OF/MOR:[?]', a
reference to his *Institutes of Moral Philosophy* which had been published in 1772,
while the upright volumes are inscribed
'ROM:HIST', presumably intended to indi-

cate his *History of the Progress and Termi-
nation of the Roman Republic*, published in
1782, with a dedication to the king. A
revised edition of this, in five volumes,
came out in 1799, and the portrait could be
as late as that date.

The portrait was bequeathed to the
university in 1821, five years after
Ferguson's death, by Sir John
Macpherson, governor-general of India
and a devoted student of Ferguson's in the
1760s. They had a Gaelic inheritance in
common and both were supporters of the
authenticity of James Macpherson's
'Ossianic' poems. Macpherson (during his
brief and controversial tenure of the
governor-generalship in 1785–6) had been
of financial help to Ferguson concerning a
farm near Currie which he took on shortly
after his marriage and it may well be that
Macpherson actually commissioned the
portrait. This supposition, however, is
complicated by the fact that another
version was with Ferguson's descendants
until late in the nineteenth century.[1] It
does not appear to have been of quite the
same quality but questions of which came
first and whether Macpherson commissioned the first or second version are
unresolved. However, it is worth noting
that it was the present picture which was
engraved by J. B. Lane in 1815.

Ferguson was born at Logierait in
Perthshire and educated at the Academy
in Perth, at the University of St Andrews
and subsequently at the University of
Edinburgh. After a spell as private secretary to Lord Milton he joined the Black
Watch regiment as deputy-chaplain,
subsequently chaplain, and was present at
the battle of Fontenoy. The following
year, 1746, he published in London his
own translation of 'A Sermon preached in
the Erse Language' to his regiment, which
was commanded by Lord John Murray.
This was a timely attack on the young
Pretender and was intended to gain him
preferment from the Duke of Atholl's
family, but when this failed to transpire he
gave up the clerical profession in 1754.

After a brief period as David Hume's

successor as librarian of the Advocates'
Library, he was appointed to the Edinburgh chair of natural philosophy,
acquiring enough physics during the
summer of 1759 to carry out the duties. In
1764 he was appointed to the chair of
'pneumatics' (mental philosophy) and
moral philosophy, his lectures gaining
him considerable fame. Two years later
he published his *Essay on Civil Society*, the
first of his major publications which were
widely translated and went into many
editions.

An odd episode in his life, indicative of
his versatility, was his journey to Philadelphia in 1778 with the British commissioners to treat with the colonists. As

secretary to the group, his progress was
thwarted by George Washington and he
returned home later in the year, having
achieved nothing.

By middle age good living had obviously affected his health. He was treated
by his kinsman, the chemist Joseph Black,
who wrote a paper on the subject, and he
became a vegetarian and total abstainer.
Cockburn records a description by
Ferguson's son of 'the two philosophers
rioting over a boiled turnip', his natural
conviviality sadly curbed by his treatment.[2] In 1785 he resigned the chair of
moral philosophy and was given the
sinecure of the chair of mathematics. It
was in his house, The Sciennes, just to the

south of Edinburgh, during the following
winter, that the famous meeting took
place between the poet Burns and the
young Walter Scott. It must also have
been to this time that Cockburn's picture
of the man applies: 'His hair was silky; his
eyes animated and light blue; his cheeks
sprinkled with broken red, like autumnal
apples, but fresh and healthy; his lips thin,
and the under one curled.'[3]

After his wife's death in 1795,
Ferguson spent an uncomfortable winter
in Neidpath Castle, perceived as a kind of
ivory tower. He subsequently lived at
Hallyards, near Peebles, and latterly in
St Andrews. Scott composed an elaborate
epitaph for his gravestone.

27 *Niel Gow 1727–1807*

Oil on canvas 48½ × 38½in (123.2 × 97.8cm)

Scottish National Portrait Gallery, Edinburgh

PROVENANCE

By descent to Raeburn's son Henry; given by him to Robert Salmond, of Glasgow, in 1861; Dowell's, Edinburgh, 13 April 1886 (219), when purchased by the Scottish National Portrait Gallery

EXHIBITIONS

Manchester, *Art Treasures*, 1857 (616); Glasgow, *Portrait Exhibition*, 1868 (355A); Edinburgh, Royal Scottish Academy, *Exhibition of the Works of Sir Henry Raeburn*, 1876 (237); Edinburgh, Scottish National Portrait Gallery, *Scottish Literary Personalities*, 1951; Edinburgh, University of Edinburgh, *Masterpieces of Scottish Portraiture*, 1981 (19); Edinburgh, Talbot Rice Art Centre, and London, Tate Gallery, *Painting in Scotland: the Golden Age*, 1986–7 (102); Edinburgh, Talbot Rice Gallery, and New York, Fashion Institute of Technology, *Tartan*, 1988–9; Edinburgh, Royal Museum of Scotland, and Kilmarnock, Dick Institute, *Pride and Passion*, 1996–7

LITERATURE

Brown, pp.7, 79–80; Andrew, p.124; Armstrong, p.103; Pinnington, p.231; Stevenson, pp.407, 411; Caw, *Masterpieces*, p.59; Caw, 1908, p.73; Greig, pp.46–7; Brotchie, p.88; Dibdin, p.142; Sanderson, pp.139, 151; Irwin and Irwin, pp.157, 223; Macmillan, 1986, pp.74–7, 79, 171, 195; Macmillan, 1990, 152; Mackie, no.333

NOTES

1. The appearance of the portrait has been dramatically changed by recent cleaning.
2. This date was suggested by James L. Caw in his 'Catalogue of Pictures' in Sir Walter Armstrong, *Sir Henry Raeburn*, London and New York, 1901, p.103.
3. *The Scots Magazine*, January 1809, p.4. Gow appears to be uttering his 'sudden shout' from parted lips in David Allan's *The Highland Dance* of 1780 (Dunimarle collection, now at Duff House). The painting shows a younger Gow accompanied by his brother Donald on the violoncello. The pose is similar to that in Raeburn's portrait, but this may be no more than a common reaction to the contingencies of the action.
4. J. C. Ewing, *Journal of a Tour in the Highlands in the year 1787 by Robert Burns*, London and Glasgow, 1927, p.13.
5. T. Garnett, *Observations on a Tour through the Highlands and part of the Western Isles of Scotland*, London, 1811, p.73 (first published in 1800). The entry is dated 3 August 1798.
6. See Mackie, no.333.
7. Scottish Record Office, Minutes of the Board of Manufactures, vol.48, p.295 (letter dated 28 January 1861).

Gow, popular composer of reels and strathspeys, is so inwardly absorbed in the intricacies of his music that his warm features have assumed a kind of heaviness that somehow, paradoxically, suggests silence. On the other hand, the liveliness of the music that had made him famous sings out in the wonderful chromatic invention of the rest of the portrait and the audacious handling of these strongly coloured areas.[1] His coat and waistcoat are a uniform purplish slate colour. The paint of the waistcoat blends, as a result of the 'wet-in-wet' technique that Raeburn has employed so widely in this portrait, at its lower edges with the predominant pinks of his trousers. In the same way, the coat, where it turns under his right thigh, is infused with the rich browns of the background. The tartan trews are a spectacular *tour de force* of rapidly manipulated colour – vermilion with some organic crimson, slaty blues and greens mixed from Prussian blue and yellow (the same yellow that is audaciously twisted into buttons on the outside of Gow's right thigh). The greenish diagonal criss-cross of the stockings is, if anything, more daring, the broad brush simply turned one way and then the other in a continuous movement. The spontaneity here is such that, while the glimpse of leg visible between trews and stockings on the left leg has been touched in with flesh colour, the same opening on the right leg is carelessly left untouched. Articulating the fall of the material of his trews between his legs is a series of strong, angular strokes of liquid brown.

Dark shadows swarm behind Gow in the lower half of the painting, the dark hem to the 'curtain' of much lighter colour, brown in essence but with dilute reds and greeny blues flowing within it, in the upper part of the picture. On the left edge of the painting, below Gow's right elbow, the darks make it difficult to identify the shapes that lurk there – a thick stick perhaps, with a strip of tartan material twisted round it, or perhaps Gow's tam o'shanter.

The traditional date of 1787[2] is clearly wrong, the result perhaps of nothing more than a romantic wish to see Gow as he was in the year he met the poet, Robert Burns – or perhaps a guess that he was about sixty years of age. The thin, rather dry treatment of the face has much in common with the portrait of *Dr Spens* (cat.no.17), which would tend to place it about 1793, while the angular vigour of the trews suggests a date of 1796 or even later. Such a date, which seems inescapable, has, however, to be reconciled with the sitter's apparent age. If the picture was painted in, say, 1797, Gow, born in 1727, has been depicted as a man of seventy. The colour of his hair and the vigour of his face pose a problem here, but in the end it seems necessary to accept that either Raeburn indulged in a degree of flattery or, simply, that Gow was in old age remarkably well preserved.

Niel (the usual unusual spelling) Gow was the son of a weaver from Inver in Perthshire. He was a noted fiddler from an early age, becoming a part of that interest in folk music that burgeoned in Scotland (and in London) in the 1770s. His patrons included the Duke of Atholl and the Duchess of Gordon and he moved freely in the aristocratic society of the time: his reels, hornpipes, jigs and strathspeys were in great demand. He achieved considerable fame, although doubts remain about the originality of his compositions. He published a *Collection of Strathspey Reels* in Edinburgh in 1784, as well as a number of other collections during his lifetime, which had enormous sales.

Gow's style of musicianship is described in a biographical account written shortly after his death at the age of eighty: 'There is perhaps no species whatever of music executed on the violin, in which the characteristic expression depends more on the power of the bow, particularly in what is called the upward or returning stroke, than the Highland reel. Here accordingly was Gow's forte. His bow hand, as a suitable instrument of his genius, was uncommonly powerful; and when the note

produced by the up-bow was often feeble and indistinct in other hands, it was struck, in his playing, with a strength and certainty, which never failed to surprize and delight ...' The same account goes on to describe another element in the liveliness of his performance: 'the effect of the sudden shout, with which he frequently accompanied his playing ... and which seemed instantly to electrify the dancers ...',[3] an effect which has to be read into the inevitable stillness of the portrait.

The poet Burns visited Gow and his wife on 31 August 1787 during his Highland tour and recorded the musician's appearance: '... a short, stout-built, honest highland figure, with his grayish hair shed on his honest social brow – an interesting face, marking strong sense, kind open heartedness mixed with unmistrusting simplicity'.[4] Thus, at a time well before the portrait was painted, it is the greyness of his hair that is noted, something which once more is difficult to reconcile with the portrait – unless dye or flattery provide an explanation. Yet the unabated vigour of the man was described by another visitor to Dunkeld more than ten years later, in 1798. Thomas Garnett (who refers in passing to Raeburn's portrait), heard Gow play twice in the same day: '... he plays the Scotch airs with a spirit and enthusiasm peculiar to himself. He is now in his seventy-second year, and has played publicly at assemblies ... for more than half a century'.[5]

There are a number of versions of the portrait, probably as many as eight,[6] a further testimony to Gow's fame. The present portrait remained in Raeburn's own collection, strong evidence that it was the primary version, something that was further attested to by the artist's son Henry in 1861, who wrote that it was 'the original portrait painted by the late Sir Henry Raeburn, my father'.[7] Two engravings of the portrait appeared after Gow's death: a stipple engraving by R. Scott in 1809 and a large mezzotint by William Say in 1816.

28 *Sir John Sinclair of Ulbster 1754–1835*

Oil on canvas 93½ × 60½in (237.5 × 153.7cm)
Inscribed, later, bottom right: RT HON BLE SIR JOHN SINCLAIR BART/AS COLONAL [*sic*]
of ROTHSAY [*sic*] & CAITHNESS FENCIBLES/BY RAEBURN.

National Gallery of Scotland, Edinburgh

PROVENANCE
By descent to Sir John Tollemache Sinclair;
Christie's, 16 July 1909 (139); Colnaghi's;
Archibald Sinclair; Viscount Thurso; the Hon.
Robin Sinclair; purchased by the National Gallery
of Scotland, 1967

EXHIBITIONS
Edinburgh, Royal Scottish Academy, 1863 (138);
Edinburgh, Royal Scottish Academy, *Exhibition
of the Works of Sir Henry Raeburn*, 1876 (172);
Glasgow, 1901 (128); London, Royal Academy,
1910 (109); Brussels, 1929; London, Royal
Academy, *Exhibition of Scottish Art*, 1939 (88);
Edinburgh, National Gallery of Scotland, *Ramsay,
Raeburn and Wilkie*, 1951 (45); London, Royal
Academy, 1954–5 (53); Edinburgh, National
Gallery of Scotland, *Raeburn*, 1956 (11); Paris,
Petit-Palais, *British Romantic Painting*, 1972;
London, Tate Gallery, *The Swagger Portrait*,
1992–3 (46)

LITERATURE
Andrew, p.150; Armstrong, pp.18, 64, 73, 74, 76,
85–6, 90, 91, 111; Pinnington, pp.90, 163, 166,
195, 196, 205, 208, 247; McKay, 43, 44–5; Caw,
Masterpieces, p.64; Caw, 1908, pp.73–4; Greig,
pp.xxxi, xxxii, xxxiii, xlvii, lii, lv, 59; Cursiter,
p.62; Brotchie, pp.62–3, 77–78; Dibdin, pp.130,
136; Collins Baker, p.163; Harris, pp.5, 7; John
Telfer Dunbar, *History of Highland Dress*,
London, 1979, pp.185–6; Raymond Lister, *British
Romantic Painting*, 1980, no.25; Macmillan, 1986,
pp.77, 132; Macmillan, 1990, p.156; Mackie, vol.I,
p.54 and no.646

NOTES
1. *The Girlhood of Maria Josepha Holroyd (Lady
Stanley of Alderley) recorded in letters of a hundred
years ago from 1776 to 1796*, ed. J. H. Adeane,
London, 1896, p.293. The letter is dated 24 July
1794, from Sheffield Place, and is addressed to
Miss Ann Firth.
2. *Literary Correspondence of John Pinkerton, Esq.*,
London, 1830, vol.I, p.405.
3. *Ibid.*, pp.409–10.
4. Wick Town Hall, Caithness. There is a
preliminary drawing in the British Museum.
5. See Helmut von Erffa and Allen Staley, *The
Paintings of Benjamin West*, New Haven and
London, 1986, pp.552–4.

Sinclair is shown in the elaborate and richly coloured uniform of the Rothesay and Caithness Fencibles, a regiment of six hundred men which he raised at the invitation of the prime minister, William Pitt, in 1794. The portrait was presumably painted shortly after that date, and before 1799 when the regiment was disbanded (but see below). It is the earliest, and most flamboyant, of a series of Highland chieftains which Raeburn would paint at full-length during the next three decades, all imbued with varying degrees of family and national pride (see cat. nos 46 and 47).

Although the poses are quite different, the tonality, colouristic effects and fractured handling of the painting have a good deal in common with the slightly earlier portrait of *Dr Nathaniel Spens* (cat.no.17). As in the *Spens*, the broken, 'splintered' handling is a particular feature of the near-theatrical prop material of plant, piled rocks and tree-trunk. There is something essentially romantic about these areas of the picture, a hint of natural forces in perpetual action in a way quite strongly reminiscent of the landscapes of the seventeenth-century Roman painter Salvator Rosa. In their sense of mineral embedded in organic material – creeper tightening around the rock and circling the darkly shimmering tree-trunk – is there some potent memory of Rosa's fiery landscapes seen during the visit to Italy?

The colour range is, if anything, wider than in the *Spens*. At one end of the spectrum are the near whites of the sporran, tunic and belt, then ranging through the vivid yellow of the upper part of the sporran, the vermilion of the coat and the crimson sash to the whole series of greyish blues, silvery greens and deep greens of the trews and plaid. Beneath these orchestrations of colour, however, and unlike the *Spens*, the anatomical structure of the figure is not entirely convincing, as if the wealth of detail in the uniform had distracted Raeburn from the need to imagine the body beneath the clothes.

Sinclair was a man of enormous energy

who dedicated his life to the improvement of the human lot, yet at the same time was possessed of an overweening self-esteem that seemed ridiculous to many. Having inherited his father's estates in Caithness in 1770, when he was sixteen, he subsequently trained as a lawyer, though he never practised. He entered parliament as member for Caithness in 1780 and sat for that constituency until 1811, subsequently representing Lostwithiel and Petersfield. A proponent of peace with France and America he suggested surrendering Gibraltar in a pamphlet published in 1783, *Propriety of retaining Gibraltar considered*. In the course of his life he would publish more than three hundred tracts and pamphlets on a whole variety of topics, ranging from the political to military, agricultural, medical and educational. Cockburn remarks that 'in spite of his almost weekly deliveries, [he] was always pregnant of pamphlets'.

Outside parliament he dedicated himself to improving the tillage, livestock and fisheries of his estates in Caithness, and founded the British Wool Society. He rebuilt the town of Thurso and founded the herring-fishery at Wick. He is, however, now best remembered for the multi-volume *Statistical Account of Scotland* which he conceived, edited, and published between 1791 and 1799. This was based on information supplied by parish ministers throughout Scotland on the history, customs, population and manufactures of the country. Though uneven, it is a unique record for its time of a single country.

One of his more esoteric interests was in the origins of Highland dress. He designed the uniform for his Fencibles and concocted a dress edition for the officers, which he wore at court – and wears in the portrait. He was seen, with some amazement, by Maria Josepha Holroyd: 'One day he treated us with a sight of him in the Uniform of his Rothesay and Caithness Regiment, and a more curious figure I never saw. The Coat was the only part of his Dress not perfectly outlandish. Scarlet turned up with yellow, a large silk Plaid,

partaking of the Nature of a Spanish Cloak crossed before and was flung over one shoulder. Trousers of the same Silk halfway down the leg and checked Red and White Stockings. He was not quite compleat, as he had not his Scotch bonnet, which would have added a foot or so to his Stature.'[1] In the portrait, in fact, he carries such a bonnet in his right hand.

Sinclair, typically, had produced a pamphlet on the subject of Highland dress which he sent to the antiquarian, John Pinkerton. His main concern was the question of trews (trousers) as opposed to the philibeg (kilt). He had little doubt that his men should wear trews, the philibeg being a recent invention, and was supported in this view, perhaps rather judiciously, by Pinkerton, who wrote to him on 23 February 1795: 'When I first saw in the papers that you had appeared at court in a new Highland dress, substituting trousers, or pantaloons, for the philibeg, I was highly pleased with the improvement. The Highland dress is, in fact, quite modern; and any improvement may be made without violating antiquity. Nay, the trousers are far more ancient than the philibeg.'[2] He then continues, slightly ambiguously (and without much foresight): 'Nothing can reconcile the tasteless regularity and vulgar glow of tartan to the eye of fashion; and every attempt to introduce it has failed. But in your uniform, by using only two tints of a colour proverbially mild, and without glare, all such objections are avoided, and the general effect rendered very pleasing.'[3]

By 1799 the government had decided to disband those fencible regiments whose services were limited to Britain (in the meantime Sinclair had raised a second battalion which served in Ireland) and the dissolution took place in the same year at Bruntsfield Links, to the south of Edinburgh. Shortly before this Sinclair, in the same uniform, had been painted at full-length by another major painter, the American Benjamin West, by this time president of the Royal Academy (fig.63). The relationship of the two portraits raises intriguing questions, both about the date of Raeburn's portrait, and the direction in which influence might have flowed.

West's portrait is signed, and dated 1798.[4] The subject stands within a room in a pose remarkably similar to that in Raeburn's portrait, his left arm crooked against his hip, his right arm extended by his side holding the feathered bonnet (with the addition of a letter signed by George Washington, with whom Sinclair had corresponded, particularly on agricultural matters). To his right is a table littered with inkwells, books, a model plough and harrow, and the charter of the Board of Agriculture, which he had been instrumental in founding. Beyond the curtained opening to the room is a landscape with sheep, far more particularised than Raeburn's landscape but with the same distinctive mountain (apparently Morven on the Berriedale estates, the highest hill in Caithness). There is no record of why the portrait by West was painted and it seems to have remained with the painter.[5] Given the respective status of the two artists in the 1790s it might be expected that, if one was to base his painting on the example of the other, Raeburn would be the more likely to be derivative. This would mean, however, that Raeburn's portrait was painted in 1798, or later, but, especially given its relationship to the *Spens* (cat.no.17), this does not seem very likely. If West, then, was influenced by Raeburn, which seems to be the case, how did he gain knowledge of the picture? Did the egotistical subject, perhaps, provide some kind of pattern of Raeburn's painting to West, with instructions that the portrait should sum up his achievements to date? The West does seem to attempt such a summing up (a paper protruding from the book at the bottom right refers to the *Statistical Account*) but the end result is a rather stiff and stilted painting compared to the fresh and vivid image that Raeburn had created.

fig.63 *Sir John Sinclair* by Benjamin West
Wick Town Hall

29 *Sir George Sinclair of Ulbster, as a child 1790–1868*

Oil on canvas 57 × 42½in (144.8 × 108cm)

English Heritage, the Iveagh Bequest, Kenwood

PROVENANCE
The sitter's brother, Alexander, 1876; Sir John
Tollemache Sinclair; Colnaghi's; Agnew's;
Edward Cecil Guinness, 1st Earl of Iveagh; his
bequest to Kenwood House, London

EXHIBITIONS
Edinburgh, Royal Scottish Academy, 1863 (280);
Edinburgh, Royal Scottish Academy, *Exhibition
of the Works of Sir Henry Raeburn*, 1876 (24)

LITERATURE
Andrew, p.149; Armstrong, p.111; Pinnington,
p.247; Greig, p.59; Harris, pp.5–7; Mackie, no.646

George Sinclair, eldest son of Sir John Sinclair of Ulbster (see cat.no.28) and Diana Macleod, seems to inhabit a kind of Elysium, a green Highland landscape of swift-flowing streams and hazy hills beneath a vast expanse of sky. So predominant is this landscape that there is a temptation to link it with the narrative of the boy's life and to see it as standing for some kind of 'land of lost content' which the child soon must leave, as his father, the Highland chieftain, prepares to send him off to boarding school in England. The boy in fact entered Harrow in 1800, at the age of ten. His precocity earned him the soubriquet, 'the Harrow prodigy'. He seems younger in the portrait, which should perhaps, therefore, be dated about 1796 or 1797, but this does not discount the possibility, which the pictorial and narrative elements reinforce, that it was intended to mark a momentous stage in the child's life.

The sitter is dressed in the comfortable 'skeleton' suit of the time, with the trousers buttoned on to the matching short jacket, both lemon yellow in colour. Such a garment would be worn until the child was about eleven, when he would graduate to more adult clothes. This suit is worn with a gleaming white, open frilled collar and a short, dense vermilion jacket. In his right hand is clutched some form of soft black velvet cap.

Sinclair left Harrow, where his intimates had included (Sir) Robert Peel and Lord Byron, in 1806. He travelled to Göttingen where he was mistakenly arrested as a spy and had the experience of being interrogated by Napoleon himself. Rather like his father, he was inclined to publication and issued a narrative of this, to him, momentous event, in 1826.

In 1811 he succeeded his father as Whig MP for Caithness, which he represented intermittently for many years, retiring from parliament in 1841. He supported Catholic emancipation and the freeing of the West Indian slaves and opposed patronage within the Church of Scotland. Rather prigishly, he refused, on one occasion, to dine with William IV on a Sunday, which gained him much public notice. He married Lady Catherine Tollemache in 1816 and had three sons and three daughters.

Sinclair's many publications include *A Letter on the Church Question* (1843), *Comme Charles X* (1848), the record of one of many interviews with the exile at Holyroodhouse, and *Miscellaneous Thoughts on Popery, Prelacy, and Presbyterianism* (1853).

30 *Isabella Macleod, Mrs James Gregory 1770–1847*

Oil on canvas 49½ × 40¼in (125.7 × 102.2cm)

Fyvie Castle, the Forbes-Leith Collection, National Trust for Scotland

PROVENANCE

By descent to a Miss Gregory, 1876; bequeathed in 1881 to the sitter's grand-niece, Margaret Forbes, wife of Rear-Admiral John Leith; bequeathed by her to her daughter, Mrs Patrick Stirling of Kippendavie; sold by Mrs Stirling's son John to his uncle, Alexander Forbes-Leith, later Lord Leith of Fyvie; by descent, until acquired by the National Trust for Scotland, 1984

EXHIBITIONS

London, Royal Academy, 1871 (54); Edinburgh, Royal Scottish Academy, *Exhibition of the Works of Sir Henry Raeburn*, 1876 (132); London, Royal Academy, 1877 (91); London, Grafton Galleries, *Scottish Old Masters*, 1895 (53); Paris, British Pavilion, 1900; Glasgow, *Empire Exhibition*, 1938 (17); London, Royal Academy, *Exhibition of Scottish Art*, 1939 (116); Edinburgh, National Gallery of Scotland, *Raeburn*, 1956 (9); Aberdeen, Art Gallery, *Artist and Patron in the North East 1700–1860*, 1975 (25); Edinburgh, Scottish National Portrait Gallery, *Treasures of Fyvie*, 1985 (37); Edinburgh, Talbot Rice Art Centre, and London, Tate Gallery, *Painting in Scotland, the Golden Age*, 1986–7 (106)

LITERATURE

Brown, p.7; Andrew, p.125; Armstrong, pp.90, 91, 103; Pinnington, p.232; Greig, pp.xlvii, 47; *Treasures of Fyvie*, exhibition catalogue, Edinburgh (Scottish National Portrait Gallery), 1985, pp.58–9; Macmillan, 1986, pp.80, 129, 195; Macmillan, 1990, pp.154, 157, 158–60; Mackie, vol.1, p.57 and no.353

NOTES

1. Fyvie Castle, National Trust for Scotland
2. Irwin and Irwin, p.158.

This portrait of Isabella Macleod appears to have been painted as a 'companion' to Raeburn's portrait of her husband, Professor James Gregory, a member of a remarkable medical and scientific family who was appointed to his father's old chair of medicine in Edinburgh in 1790, in succession to the great physician, William Cullen. The portrait of Gregory seems to have been painted about 1798,[1] which suggests a similar date for the portrait of his wife, although the two are not strictly a pair, there being a difference of scale in the figures. The couple had been married in 1796 and it is therefore not improbable that the portrait is connected with that event.

It is one of the loveliest and most compelling of Raeburn's portraits, its simplicity of placement and outline containing breathtaking felicities of handling and nuances of tone. Nowhere in his work are there such delicious concoctions as the whorls of pale brown, dashes of grey and strokes of creamy white that constitute the hair and turban-style bandeau folded across her head; and even within the clean, classical outline of the figure there are almost imperceptible variations, such as the imbrications of both shoulders that imply warmth and movement. But this simplicity, within an overall colour scheme of green and white, was not arrived at simply. There is evidence that the plain, silver green background, that now plays such an important role in the painting, once contained foliage. Raeburn's decision to eliminate it was resoundingly well judged.

It has been suggested that, if the portrait is as late as 1798, its neo-classical simplicity of pose and colour may owe something to the French émigré painter, Henri-Pierre Danloux, who was in Scotland at the time and was working for the Duke of Buccleuch.[2] This may well be true but there is no evidence for it, other than the appearance of the portrait itself.

The sitter was the daughter of Donald Macleod of Geanies, sheriff of Ross, and his first wife Margaret Crawford. She married Gregory, as his second wife, on 28 October 1796, in the parish of Canongate. Gregory was an acquaintance of Robert Burns and it is possible, therefore, that Isabella could have come within the ken of the poet before her marriage. However, she should not be confused with someone of the same name, a kinswoman of the Raasay branch of the family, who was the recipient of admiring lines from the poet.

31 *William Forbes of Callendar 1743–1815*

Oil on canvas 93¼ × 59¼in (236.8 × 150.5cm)

Scottish National Portrait Gallery, Edinburgh: on loan from Captain W. F. E. Forbes

PROVENANCE
By descent in the sitter's family

LITERATURE
Mackie, no.407

NOTES
1. Scottish Record Office, GD 171/70/39 (photocopy in Scottish National Portrait Gallery accession file).
2. *Ibid.*, GD 171/26/35.
3. His origins were not to be forgotten. When Sir Stuart Threipland reports the purchase of his own forfeited estate at the same auction, he also refers to the Callendar and Linlithgow estates as having been bought at double the upset price 'by a coppersmith who sheaths ships; his name is Forbes, an Aberdeenshire man …': see *The House of Forbes*, eds Alistair and Henrietta Tayler, Aberdeen (Third Spalding Club), 1937, p.391.

Raeburn acknowledged receipt of 60 guineas for this portrait on 19 May 1798.[1] From what can be surmised of Forbes's character it seems quite likely that payment was reasonably prompt and that the portrait had been painted in the early months of the same year. Its casual power and degree of hauteur are also in keeping with the facts of the man's life.

Shortly after receiving the portrait Forbes sought advice through an intermediary on how best to hang it in Callendar House. The 'different situations' of the house were described to Raeburn and he decided that the best place was a room described as 'the Little Drawing Room'. It was evidently not especially little, for 21 or 22 feet were reckoned to be 'a sufficient distance for it [the portrait] to be view'd at' and, crucially, 'it should be placed 5 feet from the floor'.[2] This last measurement must almost certainly have referred to the distance from the floor to the underside of the picture frame. When viewed at that height the foreshortening of the figure, and particularly of the head, is certainly wholly credible and is an extremely important element in the total meaning of the picture, particularly in the bright emphasis thrown on the upper part of the white waistcoat and the cravat. The subdued drama of the portrait, including the casual placement of the left hand, half tucked into the waistcoat pocket, and the relaxed disposition of the legs, is activated by the high light source – which is not the drifting clouds and patches of sky of the landscape beyond but rather the upper parts of the window in Raeburn's studio. This light is an important aspect of both the foreshortening and the sentience of the man's head – though here in the darkening of the left side of the sitter's face there are suggestions of the kind of *contre-jour* effects that interested Raeburn so much in the earlier 1790s. To this extent the light imagined to flow from the landscape also plays a part. The strongest focus of the light, however, is on the white waistcoat from where it passes in both directions through the paper which Forbes clasps in his right hand. Elsewhere, light flickers almost flamelike at the edge of forms – the tassel and its cord, the mass of loose papers and quill on the table and both the fore-edge and the sloping boundary of the Turkey carpet which lies on the table.

The portrait contains a rare indication of how Raeburn composed on the canvas. A long, vertical brushstroke running down through the area of the sky, which has become visible once more with the increasing transparency of the paint, marks what he must have originally considered to be the outer limit of the room in which Forbes stands.

William Forbes was a self-made man. He and his elder brother George ran a coppersmith business in Aberdeen, inherited from their father in 1762. William was then contracted to the government to sheathe the hulls of ships with copper and made a fortune in the process. His rapid rise in the world was marked by his purchase in 1783 of the estates of Callendar and Linlithgow near Falkirk which had been forfeited by the Earl of Linlithgow after the 1715 Rising. At the auction he is said to have produced a banknote for £100,000, which he had had specially printed for the purpose.[3] Whatever legend may have attached to the transaction, the story seems indicative of the kind of man he was.

The date of the portrait does not appear to relate to any specific event in Forbes's life. He married a Miss Macadam of Craigengillan and, in 1808, at a considerable age, Agnes Chalmers of Westfield. His elder son by the latter was in due course MP for Stirlingshire and married a daughter of Francis, 8th Earl of Wemyss.

32 Sir Patrick Inglis (d.1817)

Oil on canvas 49 × 39in (124.5 × 99cm)[1]

The Minneapolis Institute of Arts, Minneapolis:
the William Hood Dunwoody Fund and Gift of Dorothy Record Baumann, Mrs John
Washburn, Mrs Philip Little, junior, and Mrs Keith Merrill by exchange

PROVENANCE

Blakeslee Gallery, New York, 1898; Mrs James
M. Johnston, Washington, 1924; John Levy
Gallery, New York, 17 January 1986 (143);
Colnaghi's, New York

EXHIBITIONS

Jacques Seligmann, New York, *Portraits by Sir
Henry Raeburn*, 1938 (15)

LITERATURE

Mackie, vol.I, p.57 and no.423b

NOTES

1. The portrait formerly bore a later inscription,
'Sir Patrick Inglis Bart./by Raeburn', which was
removed after January 1986.
2. The house, renamed Kingston Grange, still
exists in what is now the Edinburgh suburb of
Gilmerton. Now a golf clubhouse, it was
'Jacobeanised' in the 1840s.
3. National Gallery of Scotland, Edinburgh
(NG 2151 and NG 2152). A copy of the portrait of
Lady Inglis, traditionally by Raeburn, is recorded
in 1925.

fig.64 *Sir Patrick Inglis* by Henry Raeburn
National Gallery of Scotland

Although the underlying structure of this portrait accords with many seated male portraits which Raeburn painted in the latter years of the eighteenth century and the first decade of the nineteenth, so many variations are played on that theme as to make it one of the most remarkable. In so far as these variations are compositional, they are based on the interplay of the rich complexity of the figure – his costume and his accessories – and the severity of the space he inhabits, undifferentiated apart from the suggestion of his cast shadow, which gives some idea of recession, and defined in the flat by the upper and outer edges of the canvas and the stark horizontality of the back of the chair. That this classically austere shape had a particular pictorial significance for Raeburn, and was not a mere by-product of his usual spontaneity of observation, is attested by the way, at its lower perimeter, he has attempted to define it even more clearly by drawing a narrow dark line, a concentrated form of the background colour, along the upper side of Inglis's left forearm.

These themes of complexity and simplification are intended, ultimately, to fix attention on the compelling head of Inglis, the classical echo being at once imperious and stoical. The classical echo is also found in the facts of Inglis's life: he had employed the architect Robert Adam, in the years 1785–8, to build a Roman Doric mansion, Sunnyside, which lies to the south of Edinburgh.[2] Inglis's weather-beaten face, beneath his own grey hair, is toughly and honestly painted, with few felicities of handling, although the crescent of subdued light reflected on to the underside of his chin from the white cravat is a memory of Raeburn's obsession with such effects in the works he painted in the early and mid–1790s, a few years before this portrait. From this eagle-like face flow naturally the psychological projections of its strength: the thrust of the gloved left hand, its thumb pinned in the upturned hat, the empty yellow glove of the right hand talon-like, escaping from its grip; and the gnarled, arthritic right hand planting

the elaborate stick firmly into an imagined territory.

The portrait is likely to have been painted close to 1800 and demonstrates the easy mastery Raeburn had reached a dozen years after his return from Rome. His ability to paint with a breadth which never denies the act of painting, and is yet a convincing translation of the forms and materials observed, and to integrate descriptive but always painterly detail into the fabric of his work, is hardly anywhere better exemplified than in this portrait. The qualities of the head have already been noted. The faintly plum-grey coat, which somehow seems an essential part of Inglis's being, is painted with the same balance of means and observed substance, the brass buttons all lying at precisely the correct angle within the folds of the thick material, their edges gleaming neither more nor less than they must have done in reality – yet on the canvas surface, only rapid flashes of yellow pigment. The right hand is a similarly convincing storm of flesh from flickering paint, and little in Raeburn can surpass the 'actuality' of the empty glove, the yellow brushstrokes virtually countable, yet the soft contours and inner textures of kid leather and the hardness of the seams seemingly all accounted for.

Patrick Inglis, a merchant in Edinburgh, was the fourth son of Sir John Inglis of Cramond and his wife, Anne Cockburn (daughter of Adam Cockburn of Ormiston). These two had been painted by Allan Ramsay in the late 1740s.[3] Patrick succeeded his brother John (who had succeeded *his* brother, Adam, in 1772) in 1799 and it is tempting to assume that the present portrait is associated with that event. Raeburn had painted his younger brother Charles (Admiral Inglis) in the late 1780s (see cat.no.7). Patrick Inglis never married and the baronetcy became extinct on his death. There is an earlier portrait of Inglis by Raeburn in the National Gallery of Scotland. The pose is similar but the background is opened up into a landscape. It has none of the classical gravity of the present portrait (fig.64).

33 *Professor John Robison 1739–1805*

Oil on canvas 50 × 40in (127 × 101.6cm)

University of Edinburgh, Edinburgh

PROVENANCE

The sitter's widow; given by her to the University of Edinburgh, 1850

EXHIBITIONS

London, South Kensington Museum, *Second Special Exhibition of National Portraits*, 1867 (734); Leeds, 1868 (1025); Edinburgh, Royal Scottish Academy, *Exhibition of the Works of Sir Henry Raeburn*, 1876 (174); Edinburgh, *Loan Exhibition*, 1901 (155); Edinburgh, *Scottish National Exhibition*, 1908 (24); London, Royal Academy, *British Art*, 1934 (476); Venice, 1934; Glasgow, *Empire Exhibition*, 1938 (476); London, Royal Academy, *Exhibition of Scottish Art*, 1939 (86); Edinburgh, National Gallery of Scotland, *Raeburn*, 1956 (36); London, Royal Academy, 1962 (311); Edinburgh, University of Edinburgh, *James Hutton and Some of his Friends*, 1976

LITERATURE

Brown, pp.5, 7, 40–1; Andrew, p.147; Armstrong, pp.68, 70, 71, 73, 111; Pinnington, pp.132, 201, 202, 246; Stevenson, p.411; Caw, *Masterpieces*, pp.39, 63, 73; Caw, 1908, pp.73–4; Greig pp.xxxiv, xxxv, xxxviii, 58; Dibdin, pp.131–2; Sanderson, pp.138, 139, 141; University of Edinburgh, *Journal*, summer 1929; *The University Portraits*, eds D. Talbot Rice [and] Peter McIntyre, Edinburgh (University Press), 1957, pp.186–9; Irwin and Irwin, p.157; Macmillan, 1986, p.131; Macmillan, 1990, p.160; Mackie, no.621

NOTES

1. Henry Cockburn, *Memorials of his Time*, ed. Harry A. Cockburn, Edinburgh and London, 1909, p.51.
2. In the collection of the Royal Society of Edinburgh: see Mackie no.621b.

Among the many offices that Robison held in a life of astonishing variety and accomplishment was the general-secretaryship of the Royal Society of Edinburgh, a post which he relinquished in 1798, after fifteen years' service. Raeburn's portrait has traditionally been dated in that year, and the two circumstances may be related, but the emphatic breadth of the handling seems to point to a date within the first decade of the new century, though not necessarily as late as 1805, the year in which the portrait was engraved in mezzotint by Charles Turner – and also the year in which the sitter died.

The great splendour of Robison's costume, a dressing gown over a waistcoat of the same striped material, has given Raeburn an opportunity to indulge in a virtuoso performance of vigorous brushwork in the orchestration of an area of a single colour, a rather orange vermilion, which must account for about a third of the picture's surface. Both the longitudinal stripes on the waistcoat and main body of the gown, and the transverse ones on the sleeves that articulate the vermilion, are greyish and two toned, the darker stripe verging on green and outlined with a narrow white border. This green is intensified in the two long strokes on the edges of the dressing gown lapels, particularly the one on Robison's left side which has a brilliance verging on viridian. At the throat, the complex and thickly painted arrangement of collar and drawstring is broken into with a pattern of remarkably fine criss-cross lines of dull pink and some of the white at the lower border of the collar has been teased out to describe a frayed edge. The overall white of this area is subtly reflected upwards on to the underside of Robison's throat and chin.

Above this the squarish head and the wrapped nightcap tower as a unified focus of the portrait, the gaze fixed imperturbably from darkly shaded eyes on the universe that is implied beyond, and certainly beyond the open book that lies

at Robison's left elbow. But within this dramatic statement a faint flicker of amusement plays around the mouth.

The figure of the sitter is fixed within the picture space with a clarity that is in essence neo-classical, the dark background severely empty, except for the implement of vision, the telescope. The pose, the composition and the informality of the man's dress are all part of the tradition of the portrait of the natural philosopher, but the decision, be it of Raeburn or Robison, to show the subject in night attire may have been a simple consequence of the fact that astronomical studies, with which the portrait is primarily concerned, are a night-time activity.

Robison's interests and accomplishments, however, ranged far beyond astronomy. He was the son of a Glasgow merchant and was educated at the university in that city. As a young man he spent time in Canada and was in the company of General Wolfe on the night before his death. He subsequently went on a voyage to Jamaica in charge of John Harrison's chronometer.

Among his closest associates were the engineer, James Watt, and the chemist, Joseph Black. He was of great help to Watt in defending his engineering patents and he prepared and published Black's lectures on his chemical discoveries. Black had supported his election to a lectureship in chemistry at Glasgow in 1766. This was followed by a spell in St Petersburg, before he accepted the chair of natural philosophy in Edinburgh in 1773, a post which he retained until his death. His lectures there were principally on hydrodynamics, astronomy, optics, electricity and magnetism; his paper on 'The Motion of Light as affected by refracting and reflecting substances' is of fundamental importance.

Dress appears to have had some special significance for Robison, as it is the aspect of his character that Henry Cockburn dwells on. He refers to the professor's 'pigtail so long and so thin that it curled far down his back, and a pair

of huge blue worsted hose without soles, and covering the limbs from the heel to the top of the thigh, in which he both walked and lectured, [that] seemed rather to improve his wise elephantine head and majestic person.'[1]

There is another portrait of Robison by Raeburn which is compositionally very close to this portrait but where the subject is dressed in sober, everyday clothes. It is not of the same quality and may be posthumous.[2] Robison's wife, Rachel Wright, whom he married in 1777, long outlived him. She presented the present portrait to the university in 1850.

34 Ranald Macdonald 1788–1873, Robert Macdonald (d.1863) and Donald Macdonald (d.1837): 'The Macdonald Children'

Oil on canvas 56½ × 44¾in (143.5 × 113.7cm)
Inscribed (later) bottom left: Sir Henry Raeburn, P.S.A. pinx'; and (later) bottom right: Ranald Macdonald/of Clanranald/and two/younger Brothers

Upton House, the Bearsted Collection, The National Trust

PROVENANCE
Sir Cuthbert Quilter; Frank Ernest Hills, 1895; Christie's, 2 July 1920 (39); Davis Brothers, on behalf of 1st Viscount Bearsted, by whom given to the National Trust, 1948

EXHIBITIONS
London, Royal Academy, *Winter Exhibition of Old Masters*, 1895 (17); London, Guildhall Corporation Art Gallery, *Loan Exhibition of Turner and a Selection of Pictures by Some of his Contemporaries*, 1899 (174); Brussels, Royal Museum of Fine Art, *Exhibition of English Painting of the Eighteenth and Nineteenth Centuries*, 1929 (127); London, Royal Academy, *Exhibition of British Art*, 1934 (197); London, Royal Academy, *Exhibition of Scottish Art*, 1939 (97); London, Royal Academy, *European Masters of the Eighteenth Century*, 1954–5 (401); London, Whitechapel Art Gallery, 1955 (17); Edinburgh, National Gallery of Scotland, *Raeburn*, 1956 (18)

LITERATURE
Armstrong, pp.90, 91, 107; Pinnington, p.278; Caw, *Masterpieces*, p.73; Greig, pp.xxxiv, 51; Dibdin, p.139; Irwin and Irwin, p.159; Mackie, no.479

NOTES
1. London, Tate Gallery.
2. Private collection: see Benedict Nicolson, *Joseph Wright of Derby*, London and New York, 1968, vol.2, plate 243.
3. Firle Estate Settlement: see Nicholas Penny (ed.), *Reynolds*, exhibition catalogue, London (Royal Academy of Arts), 1986, no.133.
4. Collection of Her Majesty The Queen: see Oliver Millar, *The Later Georgian Pictures ...*, London, 1969, vol.I, no.712, and vol.II, plate 129.

fig.65 *The Three Youngest Children of George III* by John Singleton Copley
The Royal Collection © Her Majesty The Queen

There is a long British tradition of group portraits of children frolicking in landscape settings or, less frequently, interiors. Their dress is often a down-scaled version of that of their elders, their actions in varying degrees an imitation (and sometimes with childish irony) of the adult world. But usually there are elements that speak purely of play, innocent, solemn or frenetic. Sometimes an adult is present, but that is the exception. It is a tradition that stretches back to the early seventeenth century, but predecessors most relevant to what Raeburn attempted in a number of such portraits are painters like Hogarth, Wright of Derby, Zoffany, Gainsborough, Copley and, inevitably, Reynolds. Hogarth's *The Graham Children*, painted in 1742,[1] is a pre-eminent example of the type, the children engrossed in their own activities, joyous and not entirely innocent. Loosely 'a conversation piece', conversation is hardly the point. Wright of Derby's *Leaper Children*, of about 1785,[2] is a predecessor of the interlinked quality of the present portrait, as is Reynolds's *The Lamb Children*, which must date from about 1783[3] and was probably seen by Raeburn. Although far more elaborate in composition, and decorative in intent, closer in spirit is Copley's *The Three Youngest Children of George III*, exhibited at the Royal Academy in 1785 (fig.65).[4] It has the same sense of suggested sound – the eldest child shakes a tambourine, a feature Raeburn introduced in the much later 'Elphinston Children' (cat.no.51) – and barely controlled movement, with dogs struggling to be part of the action.

In Raeburn's portrait the two older brothers, Ranald and Robert, sit astride shelved rocks, each clasping the other, their smiling, open-mouthed faces in contact. Their outer arms are raised in what is virtually a continuous curve, each snapping his fingers. The meaning of these gestures, and the implied sound is not clear – but are they, perhaps, a

reference to their ethnic origins, a childish parody of Highland dance? In the lower left of the picture is a loosely sketched Highland landscape that may be intended to indicate the family estates (the Small Isles, Arisaig, Moidart and South Uist).

The youngest of the brothers, Donald, completes the diagonal composition formed by the other two and the pile of rocks. Leaning on the far side of the rocks, he turns admiringly towards his older brothers, cheeks round and rosy in a fetching way, at the same time clasping to his breast a spaniel that barks and squirms to be free of his restraint. The diagonal nature of the composition has resulted in two large triangles, top left and bottom right, that have somehow had to be integrated with the rest, and this has not been done all that convincingly. The solution has been an expanse of sky endlessly scuffed with variegated colour and a deep, blackish shadow that fills in the near side of the rocks, too large for pictorial comfort.

All three children wear the fashionable 'skeleton' suits that had become popular in the 1780s – so called because of their close fit and the fact that they had a kind of jointed continuity, the trousers buttoned to the upper garment. The eldest and youngest wear red suits, the middle one yellow, with a wide blue sash wrapped round his midriff. The suits and the open collars with ruffled edges are all painted with a loose vigour.

The sitters were the sons of John Macdonald of Clanranald and Katherine Macqueen, daughter of the judge, Lord Braxfield. There is some doubt about the first name of the eldest son, who is in some records referred to as Reginald. He succeeded his father as 19th Chief of Clanranald in 1793 when he was only five years of age. In 1812 he married Lady Caroline Edgcumbe and in the same year he entered parliament as one of two members for Plympton Earl in Devon. He

sat until 1824. His estates were burdened by debt, perhaps through his own extravagance, and he had started to sell them by 1813. By 1838 all that remained was an islet in Loch Moidart. In 1844 he sought help from Sir Robert Peel on the grounds that his father's trustees had been fraudulent. Peel refused to help.

After the death of his first wife in 1824 he married Anne Cunningham, widow of the 2nd Baron Ashburton. In 1855 he married for the third time, Elizabeth Rebecca Newman. Neither of his brothers married.

35　Ann Fraser, Mrs Alexander Fraser Tytler (d.1835)

Oil on canvas 30¼ × 25in (76.8 × 63.5cm)

The Brooklyn Museum of Art, New York: gift of Mrs Arthur Lehman

PROVENANCE
By descent to Lieut-Colonel Neil Fraser Tytler;
?Howard Young Galleries, New York, 1929;
M. Knoedler & Co.; Arthur Lehman, 1930; given
by Mrs Arthur Lehman to The Brooklyn
Museum, 1953

LITERATURE
Handbook, The Brooklyn Museum, 1967, pp.454–
5; Mackie, no.717

NOTES
1. 'An Account of some extraordinary Structures
on the Tops of Hills in the Highlands, with
Remarks on the Progress of the Arts among the
Ancient Inhabitants of Scotland', *Transactions of
The Royal Society of Edinburgh*, vol.ii, 1790,
pp.3–32.
2. Henry Cockburn, *Memorials of his Time*,
ed. Harry A. Cockburn, Edinburgh and London,
1909, pp.265–6.
3. Secretary and legal adviser to the commander-
in-chief. See David M. Walker, *The Oxford
Companion to Law*, Oxford, 1980, p.670.
4. Mackie, no.716.

Ann Fraser was the eldest daughter and heiress of William Fraser of Balnain, an estate in the valley of the River Enrick in Inverness-shire. She married in 1776 the Edinburgh lawyer, writer and historian, Alexander Tytler. In due course, through this marriage, Tytler became proprietor of Balnain and added the name Fraser to his own. In 1780 he was appointed joint professor of universal history at the University of Edinburgh and from 1786 was sole occupant of the chair. He wrote on a wide variety of subjects (legal matters, history, 'the Progress of the Arts among the Ancient Inhabitants of Scotland',[1] the principles of translation, the benefits of the Union with England, military law, and a life of Lord Kames). Lord Cockburn considered him 'a person of correct taste', but added that there was 'no kindness in insinuating that he was a man of genius, and of public or even social influence, or in describing Woodhouselee [his estate near Edinburgh] as Tusculum'.[2]

Fraser Tytler was appointed judge-advocate[3] of Scotland in 1790 and raised to the bench in 1802. As a judge he took the title Lord Woodhouselee, from the property he had inherited from his father in 1792. He became a lord of justiciary in 1811, two years before his death.

Tytler and Ann Fraser had two daughters and four sons. The youngest of the sons was the historian, Patrick Fraser Tytler (1791–1849). A daughter, also called Ann Fraser Tytler, became a famous children's author.

It is difficult to come close to the personality of Ann Fraser other than through personalities and events that were largely external to herself. Yet Raeburn, by an extraordinary act of involvement and sympathy, has done precisely what even a far more detailed factual account of her life might have failed to do: he has, through a double act of the imagination, looking and making, lit his canvas with the spirit of this woman in such a way that she shines in her singularity, quite undimmed across two centuries.

Ann Fraser's husband was also painted by Raeburn in a far less memorable portrait which is now lost.[4] Both portraits seem to date from the early years of the first decade of the nineteenth century and it would not be idle to speculate that they relate to Woodhouselee's elevation to the bench in 1802.

The present portrait is distinguished by a simplicity, even a severity, of composition which is endlessly enlivened by acts of handling, each mark with its own painterly logic but at the same time utterly responsive to what has been observed. It is salutary, for example, to compare the manner of painting the lace cap in the *Lady in a Lace Cap* (cat.no.2) with that in the present portrait – in the earlier portrait (at least twenty years earlier) there is a laboured, accumulative attention to detail, whereas here each mark has a swift and natural ease that speaks of movement and changing light, which is a measure of the changing and adaptive responsiveness of the artist.

She sits in a simply indicated red chair against a plain, greenish background, the tonal variations very thinly brushed. Her umber dress is flecked with a little light that suggests a silk-like material rather than wool. A dark grey coat of an indoors sort is drawn round her shoulders and envelops both arms, which she holds resolutely against her body. The arms are painted with a freedom that makes the definition of boundaries difficult to resolve and the edge of the coat explodes into what seems to be a fur lining that protrudes from both lapels and the collar. The 'impressionism' of the handling, and it is a breathtakingly extreme example in Raeburn's work, continues in the gleaming, lace-edged collar which seems (in descriptive terms) to break across the square, upper edge of her bodice.

The face is a combination of homely strength and mobile fragility: thickish eyelids with clear grey eyes, intently focused although without highlights; a precise double highlight on the bridge of the nose, that defines its breadth; a faintly mauve shadow cast by the nose on the upper lip; and the lips themselves simply formed, a darkish liquid line of pigment expressing their separation, a pale mark gleaming momentarily on the visible front teeth.

36 Anne Campbell, Mrs Colin Campbell of Park

Oil on canvas 30 × 25in (76.2 × 63.5cm)

Glasgow Museums: Art Gallery and Museum, Kelvingrove

PROVENANCE
G. Maclachlan of Castle Lachlan, 1876; Mrs Atherton, 1890; Miss I. A. H. J. Campbell, by whom bequeathed to Glasgow Art Gallery, 1917

EXHIBITIONS
Edinburgh, Royal Scottish Academy, *Exhibition of the Works of Sir Henry Raeburn*, 1876 (161); Edinburgh, *Loan Exhibition*, 1901 (170); Paisley, Art Institute, 1927; Glasgow, *Empire Exhibition*, 1938 (20); London, Royal Academy, *Exhibition of Scottish Art*, 1939 (121); Edinburgh, National Gallery of Scotland, *Raeburn*, 1956 (39); Glasgow, 1961 (30); Ottawa, *Scottish Exhibition*, 1968

LITERATURE
Henley, no.8; Armstrong, p.107; Pinnington, p.221; Stevenson, p.143; Greig, p .40; Brotchie, p.84; Dibdin, p.147; *Scottish Art Review*, summer, 1946, p.14; Macmillan, 1990, p.160; Mackie, no.109

NOTES
1. Williamstown, Massachusetts, Clark Art Institute.
2. A repetition was sold at Christie's, 16 November 1962 (72). Though it may be from Raeburn's hand it is uninspired by comparison, the pattern on the shawl, for example, clearly (and understandably) having taxed his patience.

Anne Campbell, second daughter of Thomas Campbell of Tomperran in Strathearn, was the wife of Colin Campbell of Park in Renfrewshire, who died in 1793. As this portrait is likely to date from the later years of the first decade of the nineteenth century, the sitter had already been a widow for a number of years when it was painted, hence her ability to wear, with propriety, a bright garment like the shawl along with the usual black materials of her widowhood.

The portrait is one of simple, clear outlines. Despite her considerable age, Mrs Campbell tilts forward with a suppressed watchfulness, her sharp glance hawk-like, though hooded in shadow, her body still, the Indian shawl virtually unruffled by movement. Her black, deep-crowned velvet bonnet, painted with little more than two tones – black for the bonnet and grey for the bows – has a turned-back brim which throws a deep shadow down more than one third of her face, to below the eye sockets. Within this shadow, and it is one of the observational beauties of this portrait, light is reflected up from the illuminated lower area of the face and the double collar of the white fill-in, to glow on the lower edges of the eyelids and under the deep, arching eyebrows. This kind of lighting had, of course, been a major theme for Raeburn in the early 1790s but it may well have proved unpopular with unsophisticated sitters who did not appreciate its originality. Nevertheless, he did revert to it on occasion – most remarkably perhaps in the vast group portrait of the Drummond children (cat.no.37) as well as in the present portrait, which is of about the same date – 1808 or 1809.

The simplicity of the portrait is its other audacious feature. Against a completely plain, greenish-grey background, the creamy white shawl has perhaps eight more or less vertical shadows drawn within it, quite understated, while the sheer repetitiveness of the pine-cone pattern is an aspect of the same simplicity. This pattern is applied with a meticulous care – tiny, reddish-brown horizontal strokes that in one or two places burst into pure vermilion and blue – that in no way conflicts with the broader treatment of the rest of the painting.[2]

Virtually nothing is known of Mrs Campbell's life and personality which might complement the way her intelligence is implied by the portrait. That Raeburn responded to this seems reaffirmed by the quality of the portrait.[1] Her husband, Colin Campbell, had at one time commanded a Custom House cutter, the *Prince of Wales*; later, he headed the Greenock firm, Colin Campbell & Co., which traded with the West Indies. He bought the estate of Park in 1768 and sold it in 1789. He, too, was painted by Raeburn, in the early 1790s.

37 George Drummond 1802–51, his sister Margaret and his foster brother

Oil on canvas 94¼ × 60¼in (239.4 × 153cm)

The Metropolitan Museum of Art, New York: bequest of Mary Stillman Harkness

PROVENANCE

By descent to George Drummond's grandson, George Drummond, of Pitsford Hall, Northampton, 1925; Knoedler, New York; sold to Mr and Mrs Edward S. Harkness, 1927; bequeathed by Mary Stillman Harkness to the Metropolitan Museum, New York, 1950

EXHIBITIONS

Wrexham, *Art Treasures Exhibition of North Wales and the Border Counties*, 1876 (333); London, Grafton Gallery, *Fair Children*, 1895 (146); New York, Knoedler, *Loan Exhibition of Pictures by Raeburn*, 1925 (5): New York, Metropolitan Museum, 1933; Glasgow, *Empire Exhibition*, 1938 (34); New York, The Century Association, *Masterpieces of Art*, 1938 (8); New York, World's Fair, *Loan Exhibition of Masterpieces*, 1939 (291); London, Royal Academy, *Exhibition of Scottish Art*, 1939 (105); London, National Portrait Gallery, 1968; Boston, Museum of Fine Arts, *Masterpieces of Painting in the Metropolitan Museum of Art*, 1970

LITERATURE

Greig, p.43; Dibdin, p.69; Collins Baker, p.164; H. B. Wehle, 'Paintings lent from the Harkness Collection', *Metropolitan Museum of Art Bulletin*, January 1933, p.12; Helen Comstock, 'New York World's Fair Loan Exhibition of Masterpieces', *The Connoisseur*, vol.CIII, June 1939, p.320; Irwin and Irwin, p.159; Mackie, no.219

NOTES

1. See Hector Bolitho and Derek Peel, *The Drummonds of Charing Cross*, London, 1967, pp.115–18, 120, 124, 162–3.
2. New York, The Metropolitan Museum of Art (49. 142).

Both the scale and complexity of this portrait, which in themselves suggest that it had a particular dynastic significance, are in curious contrast to the unformed fragility of its subjects. Despite the potential elements of play, such as the pony and the whip, the portrait has a contrived gravity and seriousness of purpose that distinguish it from Raeburn's other group portraits of children. There is a sense in which, although there is potential for change, the action will never get out of hand in the way that it might, for example, in a portrait like that of the frenetic '*Macdonald Children*' (cat.no.34).

The focus of the portrait, both psychological and formal, is the young George Drummond, perched with an acute sense of his own significance on the squat pony. His face, much of it in shadow and immature, is nevertheless as sentient as any Raeburn ever painted. Born in 1802, he seems little more than six or seven years of age, which means that the portrait must date from about 1808 or 1809. His head with its curious hat, of fur apparently, and bound with a black strap, is placed well to the left of the picture space but is made the centre of attention by the bright light that swarms, mandorla-like, round its dark shape. Although this light is the means of defining his form, it is not, and could not be, the source of the light that picks out the inner forms of his face and body as well as lighting up his two companions. This kind of inconsistency is not unusual in Raeburn, and is of little consequence in a formal sense. At the socio-psychological level, George is also the focus of attention of his sister Margaret and the older boy, who has always been identified as his foster brother, both of whom direct their eyes towards him with a rather necessary kind of admiration.

Contre-jour effects had been of particular interest to Raeburn in the early 1790s, as had been the expressive use of a soft, deep shadow cast across the upper part of the subject's face – witness portraits like the very early *Lady Forbes* (fig.11) or the slightly later *David Hunter of Blackness*

(cat.no.8). It is likely that this did not always appeal to conservative sitters, who found their 'likeness' half obscured in shadow. But the type nevertheless persisted into his mid career: the present portrait and the *Mrs Colin Campbell of Park* (cat.no.36) are examples. What is particularly interesting in the present portrait is the almost heraldic reversal of the shadow on the foster brother's face, which falls, highly unusually, across the lower half.

Apart from George's hat, the three children are dressed in the current fashions of the time, the two boys wearing the more informal 'skeleton' suits that had been in vogue since the 1770s. Their jackets are a dark green, George's open and showing on its right side a long row of eight gleaming brass buttons; their trousers are white, and worn with silk stockings and leather shoes. Margaret's dress is a purer white, freely brushed, with the middle tones contrived from barely touched canvas. Beneath her dress she wears white trousers, a common feature of the time, and in her right hand she dangles what is probably a straw bonnet with a pale blue-grey silk lining, the ties of the same material.

The bloom of light around George's head is echoed less dramatically, although on a larger scale, around all three protagonists, its outline softly indicated in shadows that bind the children together and embed them in a natural world of tree-trunk and creeper, and fresh green boscage.

George Drummond, the focus of this massive portrait, was the son and heir of George Harley Drummond (1783–1855) and Margaret Munro, daughter of a Glasgow merchant engaged in trade with Virginia. The marriage, in the winter of 1801 when George Harley Drummond was only seventeen, seems to have defied a number of social conventions and within three years his wild extravagance had led to his family's excluding him from the family business. This business was the Scottish bank, Drummonds of Charing

Cross in London, founded by Andrew Drummond from Machany in Perthshire in 1717. Harley Drummond was the founder's great-grandson. A list of his property in 1807, perhaps a year or two before the group portrait was painted, included estates in Cheshire and Berkshire, the Adelphi site in London, Stanmore House in Middlesex and Drumtochty Castle in Kincardineshire. The decline in his fortunes – a principal companion in his dissipation was George ('Beau') Brummell – led to the disposal of much of this property, Stanmore House in 1816 and the castellated Gothic Drumtochty, which he had built for £30,000, in 1822. Fortunately, the Adelphi site could not be sold as it was secured to George, born in February 1802. While much of his extravagance was concerned with gambling it may well have included items like the present portrait which in itself is an unusually extravagant statement about family pretensions.

By 1821 Harley Drummond had left his wife Margaret for Emma, wife of a naval officer, who in due course styled herself as his 'widow' and 'Mrs Emma Drummond'. His son George became a partner in the bank in 1826. In 1831 he married Marianne Portman, sister of the future Viscount Portman. Of five children, their only son George James would play a major role in the affairs of the bank over an extended period of time. George, renowned in his later years for his fatness (fig.66), predeceased his dissolute father, dying of heart disease 'suddenly after attending divine service', at his residence in Belgravia in 1851.[1] Nothing is known of the future life of the other named child in the portrait, Margaret. The child traditionally described as a 'foster brother' is also a mystery. If, however, the family was following the old Highland custom of having their children reared in a related family, whose loyalty was by tradition secured by such an arrangement, it may be that he was simply a member of that family and not someone adopted or fostered, in the modern sense. Since such a family would, by the nature of the arrangement, have resided in Scotland, this would explain why Raeburn was chosen for the commission. An alternative explanation of Raeburn's involvement might be, of course, that the Drummond family (disfunctional as it may have been) spent the summer months on their estate at Drumtochty. George Harley Drummond, the children's father, was painted at about the same time by Raeburn, in a full-length equestrian portrait. It is an awkward, rather unsatisfactory painting by comparison with the portrait of his children.[2]

fig.66 *George Drummond*
caricature by George Halse
The Royal Bank of Scotland

38 *Sir Walter Scott 1771 – 1832*

Oil on canvas 72 × 58in (182.9 × 147.3cm)

The Duke of Buccleuch KT, Bowhill

PROVENANCE
Archibald Constable; Walter Francis, 5th Duke of Buccleuch, 1826; thereafter by descent

EXHIBITIONS
Edinburgh, Associated Society of Artists, *Annual Exhibition*, 1809; London, Royal Academy, 1810 (79); Edinburgh, Royal Scottish Academy, *Exhibition of the Works of Sir Henry Raeburn*, 1876 (27); Edinburgh, *Loan Exhibition*, 1901 (153)

LITERATURE
Obituary, p.12; Cunningham, pp.225–6;[8] 'Remarks on the Second Exhibition of Scottish Paintings', *The Scots Magazine*, 1809, pp.674–7, 729–32; John Morrison, 'Random Reminiscences of Sir Walter Scott, of the Ettrick Shepherd and Sir Henry Raeburn', *Tait's Edinburgh Magazine*, January 1844, pp.15–19; Brown, pp.5, 7; Sir W. Stirling Maxwell, D. Laing and J. Drummond, eds, *The Scott Centenary Exhibition. A Descriptive Account of the Portraits, Busts, Published Writings and Manuscripts, of Sir Walter Scott, Bart., etc.*, Edinburgh, 1874, pp.25–7, 61–2, 69–70; Andrew, p.149; Armstrong, pp.76, 79, 111; Stevenson, p.407; Pinnington, p.247; Greig, pp.xxvii, xxviii, xxxix, xlvii, 59; Brotchie, p.71; Sanderson, pp.134, 135, 139, 141; William T. Whitley, *Art in England, 1800–1820*, Cambridge (University Press), 1928, pp.134–5, 170; Irwin and Irwin, p.148; Macmillan, 1986, p.131; Mackie, vol.I, p.60 and no.640

NOTES
1. Henry Cockburn, *Memorials of his Time*, ed. Harry A. Cockburn, Edinburgh and London, 1909, pp.162–3.
2. *The Letters of Sir Walter Scott*, ed. H. J. C. Grierson, vol.II, London, 1932, p.450.
3. J. G. Lockhart, *The Life of Sir Walter Scott, Bart.*, London, 1893, p.394. In this letter Scott refers to the three states his face has gone through: 'my late golden hue', when he had jaundice, 'my present silver complexion (looking much more like a spectre than a man)', and 'my quondam beef-eating physiognomy'. The final appearance may be what he believed he had been given in Constable's portrait, where his face is fresh and rosy. By 'chowder-headed' Scott means a thick-headed person or a block-head.
4. *Ibid.*, p.163.
5. William T. Whitley, *Art in England, 1800–1820*, Cambridge (University Press), 1928, pp.170–1.
6. J. G. Lockhart, *The Life of Sir Walter Scott, Bart.*, London, 1893, p.173. Although Scott apparently disliked the picture he was not attempting to buy it so as to take it out of circulation, as his reference to a possible engraving makes clear. In the event, a mezzotint by Charles Turner was published in 1810.
7. *The Journal of Sir Walter Scott*, ed. W. E. K. Anderson, Oxford, 1972, p.252.
8. Cunningham confuses the present painting and the Abbotsford version.

Although this portrait, commissioned by the publisher Archibald Constable in 1808, hints at Scott as a 'man of destiny', it was painted when much of the work that would establish his reputation was scarcely begun. His novel, *Waverley*, which would give its name to the whole series of historical novels that brought him lasting fame, had been begun in 1805, but set aside unfinished. Apart from some translations from German, his literary inclinations had led him to collect Border ballads, which resulted in the publication of the *Minstrelsy of the Scottish Border* in two volumes in 1802; a third volume came out the following year, all to critical acclaim. One of his own imitations intended for these volumes led in due course to the long poem, *Lay of the Last Minstrel*, which was published in 1805 and proved a brilliant success. Archibald Constable, who had established himself as a major publisher in 1802, when he started the *Edinburgh Review*, had a share in the copyright of both of these publications. In these same years Scott had begun his ultimately disastrous financial relationship with the printer James Ballantyne, whom he had arranged should print all of his books.

Scott's next major work was the poem *Marmion: a Tale of Flodden Field* for which Constable paid a thousand guineas and published at the beginning of 1808. Of the new kind of publishing which Constable represented, Lord Cockburn remarked: 'Abandoning the old timid and grudging system, he [Constable] stood out as the general patron and payer of all promising publications, and confounded not merely his rivals in trade, but his very authors, by his unheard-of prices'.[1] In the same year that he published *Marmion*, as well as Scott's eighteen-volume edition of Dryden, with a life of the English poet, he offered Scott £1,500 for a similar edition of Swift. It was against this background that Constable, with a keen sense of who might succeed, commissioned Scott's portrait.

Scott is seated on two blocks of tumbled ashlar from a broken wall that rises behind him. The perspective of the horizontal joints in this masonry is more carefully calculated than such features normally are in Raeburn's works. This romantic wall, finely jointed but now ruined, is likely to have some special significance but what it is remains unclear. More mysterious still is the stone that lies at an angle in the lower left corner of the picture that seems to bear the outlines of part of an escutcheon, on its side, which contains two five-pointed stars. The darkening sky gleams fitfully, isolating the dark tree-trunk that protrudes from the building like a natural rafter, and flickers above the hills in the distance. By the bend of the river, where the light is caught momentarily in the water, stands a border-keep which echoes the form of the wall before which Scott is seated. Scott identified this building as 'Hermitage Castle which the artist had ingenuity enough to draw from a very wretched sketch of mine'[2] (in his youth he had attempted landscape painting, with little success). Scott, in a dark grey suit and Hessian boots, directs his gaze beyond the artist and thus beyond the viewer in a kind of romantic fixity, echoed in a curious way by his faithful dog Camp who crouches in the lower right corner of the painting, staring in the opposite direction. His relaxed left arm is supported on his raised left knee, his hand marking a place in a small red covered book, perhaps a notebook. In his right hand, poised for action, he holds a silver-mounted pencil. This hand rests on a relaxed right knee, so that there is a kind of counterpoint here of tension and ease. Scott's right foot is hidden by the stone on which his left foot is so firmly placed: this may well be more than a compositional device, for his right foot was deformed as the result of a fever which attacked him when he was only eighteen months old.

It is quite evident that Scott did not much like the portrait. When, many years later, in 1819, a portrait for the Duke of Buccleuch's library at Bowhill was under discussion (see cat.no.64) Scott made it fairly plain that he would much rather sit

to (Sir) William Allan: 'I hesitate a little about Raeburn, unless your Grace is quite determined. He has very much to do; works just now chiefly for cash, poor fellow, as he can have but a few years to make money; and has twice already made a very chowder-headed person of me [the present portrait, and a variation of it: see below]. I should like much (always with your approbation) to try Allan, who is a man of real genius …'[3] The implications of his remarks are clear.

The portrait is described in rather ambivalent terms by Scott's friend and correspondent, John Morritt of Rokeby Park, in a memorandum to the former's biographer, J. G. Lockhart: 'His person at that time [when he was about to publish *Marmion*] may be exactly known from Raeburn's first picture, which had just been executed for his bookseller, Constable, and which was a most faithful likeness of him and his dog Camp. The literal fidelity of the portraiture, how-ever, is its principal merit. The expres-sion is serious and contemplative, very unlike the hilarity and vivacity then habitual to his speaking face, but quite true to what it was in the absence of such excitement. His features struck me at first [they met for the first time in June 1808] as commonplace and heavy, – but they were almost always lighted up by the flashes of the mind within. This required a hand more masterly than Raeburn's …'[4] The sting in the tail of this view of the picture now seems superficial, the result of a socially conditioned notion of the outward signs of genius and a mistaken view of the kind of information a portrait can contain about the sitters' mind – but it may well have coloured Scott's own attitude to the portrait, and to Raeburn. It was also a view he was likely to have read in a criticism published in the *Repository of Arts* in 1810, when the portrait was exhibited at the Royal Academy in London: '… never was a more unpoetical physiognomy delineated on canvas; we might take him for an auctioneer, a travelling dealer or chapman; in short for any character but a bard'.[5]

Nevertheless, when Scott quarrelled with Constable he did everything in his power to acquire ownership of the portrait. The quarrel seems to have been caused by Constable's partner Alexander Hunter, who did not like Scott's Tory politics and believed that the deal with Scott for his edition of Swift was a mistake. So incensed was Scott by Hunter's attitude that he wrote a letter to the firm on 12 January 1809 severing all relations with them. He concluded his irate letter with a reference to the portrait: 'In the present circum-stances, I have only a parting favour to request of your house, which is, that the portrait for which I sat to Raeburn shall be considered as done at my debit, and for myself. It shall be of course forthcoming for the fulfilment of any engagement you may have made about engraving, if such exists.'[6] However, Constable graciously declined to give up the picture and it remained with him until 1826.

In due course the quarrel was repaired and in 1814 Constable brought out *Waverley*, which Scott had decided was worth completing. It was an instant success and was followed in the same year by *Guy Mannering*. There then came in the next ten years the flood of novels which made Scott world-famous.

His extravagant expenditure on build-ing Abbotsford and his deep financial involvement with the affairs of Ballantyne and Constable led ultimately to financial disaster and he would spend the last years of his life attempting, by dint of hard work, to pay off his creditors, much as Raeburn had done. Having failed to persuade Constable to part with the portrait, Scott commissioned another version from Raeburn in 1809, which differs in a number of details: this he managed to save from what he called 'the wreck', and it still remains at Abbotsford. Constable, how-ever, was forced to sell his portrait, which was bought by Scott's friend, the Duke of Buccleuch. Scott saw it hanging at Dalkeith House on 12 December 1826, when he remarked, with feeling: 'One thing I saw there which pleased me much and that was [my] own picture painted twenty years ago by Raeburn for Consta-ble and which was to have been brought to sale among the rest of the wreck; hanging quietly up in the dining room at Dalkeith … I am obliged to the friendship and delicacy which placed the portrait where it now is.'[7]

39 *William Hunt of Pittencrieff 1781 – 1812*

Oil on canvas 77 × 60in (195.6 × 152.4cm)

Private collection

PROVENANCE
By descent

EXHIBITIONS
Edinburgh, Royal Scottish Academy, *Exhibition of the Works of Sir Henry Raeburn*, 1876 (186); University of Edinburgh, *Masterpieces of Scottish Portrait Painting*, 1981 (22)

LITERATURE
Andrew, p.130; Armstrong, p.105; Pinnington, p.235; Greig, p.49; Mackie, vol.I, p.60 and no.412

NOTES
1. I am indebted to Nick Norman for help in identifying the hunting equipment in this portrait.
2. A variant of the portrait, once the property of Hunt's sister, Christian, is in the Chrysler Museum, Norfolk, Virginia. See Denys Sutton, 'Bright as New Sovereigns', *Apollo*, April 1978, p.240.

This is a portrait of wonderful textural and colouristic variety, not always consistent in the way various parts of the picture are fashioned – but much of its strength and beauty lying in these very inconsistencies. It is a hunting picture of such internal force and surface intensity that, in a curious way, it calls to mind the work of Courbet, from a different tradition, and half a century later.

Raeburn's inclination towards natural abstraction is perhaps nowhere more evident than in the area of tree-trunks, branches and foliage behind and above Hunt's figure. Here there is no clear determination of how the tree (or is it trees?) grows, how the branches bifurcate and how the whole mass coheres, but such is the autonomy of the marks, that is, the paint that constitutes the picture's surface – flickering, dashed on, scratched, the deep blacks, the lightning-like zigzags (twigs presumably) – that there can be little doubt that Raeburn was aware that this area was an equivalent for nature, rather than simply a representation. To eyes grown used to twentieth-century abstraction the beauty of an area like this is evident, but it must be a matter of speculation how it was perceived in its time. This abstract richness continues even in the figural and more obviously descriptive areas of the painting and gives it a unique vibrancy.

Compositionally the painting grows from the strong diagonal of Hunt's seated figure, lying on the imaginary line from top right to bottom left. The diagonal is repeated within the skewed parallelogram of his legs and the visual movement is enforced by the tumbling steps of rock on whose ledges his body is lodged. In counterpoint to these movements is the thrust of the man's head, off to his right, and the entry of the crouched hunting dog from the bottom corner of the picture, its nose linking with the loop of the shot belt[1] between Hunt's legs.

These solutions to the picture's complex aims were reached after considerable struggle: despite the many passages of delicious painterliness there is nothing particularly easy or relaxed about the painting. Originally the composition was radically different, with Hunt's right arm thrust out into the area of sky on the left of the picture, the hand grasping the vertical barrel of a gun. Increasing transparency of the paint has made this once more visible, and it is clear that the foliage at the sitter's right elbow, hardly an expected place for it, was Raeburn's quick solution to obliterating an arm that had been pretty firmly established (and hovers once more as a ghost). There is similar evidence that the positions of the legs were also quite drastically altered – the curved calf of his left leg, for example, was originally a number of inches nearer the centre than its present position, a ridge of the original paint still clearly visible where it cuts into his left knee. The dog, possibly a pointer, has also undergone considerable reworking of its chest and forelegs: it remains unclear whether the leg at the bottom edge of the picture is its right leg thrust under what is clearly a left leg or whether it is an earlier left leg that has simply not been painted out.

The treatment of Hunt's head is of great refinement, the flesh painted in small, nuanced, liquid brushstrokes, in a way similar to the head in the portrait of *John Playfair* (cat.no.43); it is likely to be of a similar date – 1811 or 1812, close, that is, to the end of Hunt's short life. As a compositional type, it has a good deal in common with Raeburn's portrait of Scott, painted for the publisher, Constable, in 1808 (cat.no.38). The force of the sitter's eager, youthful glance emerges from dark, shaded eyes, the inner and outer curves of the irises lit by tiny white highlights. The intensity of the head has a kind of focus in its highest keyed area, just above his left eyebrow, while there is a tremulous vibrancy in the finely interlaced, horizontal strokes in the lower part of the face, a fleck of vermilion on the upper lip and a white, lustrous line on the lower one. Beneath his head is an outburst of colour – orange, pink and white – in the cravat, and a froth of light and movement that fills the

gap revealed by his open, yellow waistcoat, a visual foil to the strong greenish grey of his coat and the pale grey of his trousers. The sitter's right hand is painted in the same refined manner as the head; but, and this is the kind of inconsistency that makes Raeburn's stylistic development often problematic, the left hand is painted in a rather summary, 'cubic' manner that looks back to an earlier period.

The lower area of the portrait is rich in content. Hunt's gun, a flintlock fowling-piece, is wedged between the slabs of rock where the dog lies, and a cow-horn powder flask and an upturned hat with gloves protruding lie on the surface of the rock that supports the sitter's sharply fore-shortened left foot. Adjacent to the dog's head is a buckled strap, which appears to be attached to the gun. Hunt's right foot is thrust into a clump of dock or burdock (or some species of xanthium) vigorously painted and scored in a variety of dark grey-blues and russet colours. In the distance is a hazy landscape of water, a wooded islet, low hills – a generalised kingdom of Fife – and a changing sky.

William Hunt was the elder of the two sons of William Hunt of Pittencrieff, an estate on the edge of Dunfermline acquired by the latter in 1800, and Janet Alexander, daughter of a James Alexander of Balrudery. He succeeded his father in 1807, an event which may have set the portrait commission in motion.[2] He died, however, unmarried, only five years later.

40 *Mrs James Campbell 1739–1815*

Oil on canvas 30 × 25in (76.2 × 63.5cm)

R. Patrick Thomas Esq.

PROVENANCE

By descent to Lieut-Colonel A. N. Muirhead; his nephew, Colonel P. M. Thomas

EXHIBITIONS

Edinburgh, *Loan Exhibition*, 1901 (145); Paterson's Gallery, London, 1902; Agnew's, 1908; Paris, *One Hundred Portraits of Women*, 1909 (33); London, *Japanese-British Exhibition*, 1910 (1); Edinburgh, Royal Scottish Academy, *Centenary Exhibition*, 1926 (79); London, Royal Academy, *Exhibition of British Art*, 1934 (284); Glasgow, *Empire Exhibition*, 1938 (22); London, Royal Academy, *Scottish Art*, 1939 (119); Edinburgh, National Gallery of Scotland, *Raeburn*, 1956 (48); Montreal, *British Painting of the Eighteenth Century*, 1957–8 (48); Edinburgh, Talbot Rice Art Centre, and London, Tate Gallery, *Painting in Scotland, the Golden Age*, 1986–7 (108)

LITERATURE

Armstrong, pp.67, 76, 77–8, 92, 98; McKay, p.59; Pinnington, pp.169, 170, 172, 195, 221; Caw, 1908, pp.74–5; Caw, *Masterpieces*, p.79; Greig, pp.xl, xli, xlvii, liv, 40; Cursiter, p.67; Brotchie, p.83; Dibdin, pp.146, 147; Irwin and Irwin, pp.148, 157; Macmillan, 1986, pp.129, 195; Macmillan, 1990, p.160; Mackie, no.114

NOTES

1. Most of the information quoted here is taken from annotations added by Sir James Ferguson, Keeper of the Records of Scotland, to his text in the Raeburn exhibition catalogue of 1956 (Scottish National Portrait Gallery library).

Monolithically simple and four-square, Raeburn's image of the elderly Mrs Campbell uniquely combines his manner at its most audacious with his engagement with an individual whom we assume he knew only briefly but whose face, and what it had come to represent, he maps with delight and deep understanding. It is in the contrast between the subtle intricacies of that map and the bravura abstractions of the materials in which she wraps herself that the portrait's particular power lies.

These intricacies have a quality that is both liquid and feathery and yet add up to something of great solidity. The deepest pool in the wide tonal range is the black of her eyes which, although so deep-set beneath the massive eyebrows that they avoid the light source that would normally have been reflected there, are nevertheless steadily focused. The range extends through the browner darks that define the solid end of the nose to the lesser darks within the creases around her mouth and chin and the simpler, but still minutely varied, areas of brightly lit flesh. Among the subtlest of these modulations are the flecks of light on her right eyelid and beneath the outer corner of her left eye, the unflattering traces of grey on her upper lip and the tiny, horizontal lines of pink that vivify the lower one.

Surmounting this resolute face is the complexity of the thickly brushed mob cap which fills the reserve left by the dark olive background. Her chin lightly rests on a high-necked chemisette which rises through the opening of the white kerchief, the two layers pinned together with a piece of jewellery. Around her shoulders is a bright red Kashmir shawl which hides most of her black silk dress. Her left arm and gloved hand emerge from beneath the tangled fringes of the shawl and there is a casual trace of her right fist at the bottom edge of the painting. It is in these areas that Raeburn cuts fiercely loose with an unexampled vigour, so that the act of painting virtually takes precedence over what is depicted. The sheer audacity of what he achieves here is exemplified by the unbroken diagonal brushstroke, loaded with red, that runs from the dark shadow where the shawl turns behind the sitter's left shoulder down across the white kerchief on her breast, the pigment dispersed at its edge as it cuts into the black dress (where, in turn, it is itself cut across by another, shorter vermilion stroke). This continuous brushstroke which perfectly defines the spatial relationship between the shawl and the kerchief is an astonishing eleven inches or so in length. Ultimately, as in Rembrandt, all these varied acts of painting are subsumed within an essence that is profoundly human.

The portrait appears to have been painted in 1811 when Mrs Campbell would have been about seventy-two. So little is known of her that she can only be defined by facts that speak of her male relatives. Said to have been a cousin of the engineer James Watt, she was born Marion Muirhead, daughter of John Muirhead of Croyleckie, an estate near Killearn in Stirlingshire. She married James Campbell, a merchant in Glasgow (who had been born in Alloa in 1736). They had fifteen children. As James Campbell died in Glasgow in 1800, she has been depicted by Raeburn when a widow, a fact which the bright colour of the shawl might have belied. She herself died at 35 Heriot Row in Edinburgh, the house of her son Colonel John Campbell.[1]

41   *Sir Duncan Campbell of Barcaldine 1786–1842*

Oil on canvas 50⅜ × 40in (128.2 × 101.5cm)

The Fine Arts Museums of San Francisco, Roscoe and Margaret Oakes Collection

PROVENANCE

By descent to the sitter's grandson, Sir Duncan Alexander Dundas Campbell; Christie's, 28–9 August 1926 (144); Knoedler; Edward S. Moore, Lexington, Kentucky; Roscoe and Margaret Oakes, 1955, by whom gifted to The Fine Arts Museums of San Francisco, 1975

EXHIBITIONS

Indianapolis, Herron Museum of Art, *The Romantic Era: Birth and Flowering, 1750–1850*, 1965 (15); Oakland, The Oakland Museum, *Art Treasures in California*, 1969; Auckland, Auckland City Art Gallery, *Rembrandt to Renoir, 300 years of European Masterpieces from The Fine Arts Museums of San Francisco*, 1993 (22)

LITERATURE

Greig, p.40; Helen Comstrock, 'The Connoisseur in America', *The Connoissuer*, no.138, September 1956, p.74; Paul Wescher, 'Neuerwurbungen des de Young Museums in San Francisco', *Kunstchronik*, vol.10, no.11, November 1957, p.311; Irwin and Irwin, pp.160, 430; Joseph R. Goldyne, 'British Art at San Francisco', *Apollo*, vol.cxi, no.217, March 1980, p.126; Catherine Gordon, *British Painting, Hogarth to Turner, An Observer's Guide*, London, 1981, p.48; Macmillan, 1986, p.134; Mackie, no.640b

NOTES

1. Allan Cunningham, *The Lives of the Most Eminent British Painters, Sculptors, and Architects*, London, 1832, vol.v, p.220. Cunningham says that he is quoting an informant who had been painted by Raeburn.
2. Scottish Record Office, Barcaldine Papers, GD 170/2677. The letter is addressed from York Place.
3. See Mackie, no.640b. This is his interpretation of the letter.

The assurance of this portrait is not simply an aspect of the sitter's character, superbly realised, but a reflection of Raeburn's certainty of purpose within the context of his own studio practice on matters of positioning the figure, degree of elevation and control of lighting. Campbell has clearly been placed on quite a high dais of some sort, his eyes perhaps as much as three feet above the level of the artist's. His back is towards the east side of the painting room (always presumed to be on the first floor of the York Place house, but that the ground floor rooms, which have an equally large, north-facing window, were used for this purpose should not be discounted), though skewed at a slight angle, so that the north light illuminates most of the face, but leaves a deep shadow on its left side. The main direction of the light is downwards from the artist's left, that is, from the north, as the greyish shadow on the underside of the sitter's nose indicates, as well as the nearly vertical shadow cast by his right index finger on the sash wrapped round his waist. Presumably the vertical shutters on the east side of the window were arranged so that the east wall was darkened, to provide the deep, slaty black background against which the figure is placed. When Allan Cunningham described Raeburn placing his easel next to the sitter and then, while continuously studying the subject, retreating step by step to 'the other end of his room' before coming rapidly forward again to work on the canvas,[1] the implication might be that he had stepped back as far as the street (south) side of the double cube room. This is unlikely, however, as it would have tended to position him so that he was dazzled by the light from the north-facing window. He is more likely, therefore, to have taken the few steps back that would place him against the west wall of the room; or, just possibly, his retreat may have been diagonal, taking him into the street half of the room, but his eyes shielded from the north light by the section of partition wall that partly divided the room into two. It is difficult, however, to reconcile this with the spread of the light on the face, which must come from the north window, or with the sense of the artist's proximity to his subject. Finally, two aspects of the directional nature of the light are worth remarking on: the first is that, very unusually, the highlights of the eyes are on the *lower* edge of the pupil, a fact that is both evidence of unpremeditated observation and also an important factor in the still, contemplative gaze of the sitter; and, secondly, that the angle of light striking the bright red of the tunic is reflected upwards (by means of tiny markings of pigment) into the shadows on the underside of the chin, the upper lip and the flesh around the nostrils.

Within the almost *di sotto in sù* drawing of Campbell's figure is the painting's other outstanding characteristic: the virtual conflagration of the vermilion tunic, modified very sparingly by broad, smoky shadows on his left side and, rather darker, down the outer contour of his left arm. Textural counters to the boldness of this area are the narrow strips of lemon yellow braiding and the fractured yellow and yellow ochre of the epaulettes and tassels. These threads of gold colour are also picked up on the buckle of his low-slung belt, the fob which hangs from it and in the hat grasped in his left hand. The belt itself gleams audaciously with a single stroke of dry white on top of black, which lights up the texture of the canvas. Boldest of all, in colouristic effect and handling, is the pale alizarin crimson sash which cuts across the vermilion tunic at his waist, the number of swift horizontal strokes virtually countable.

The portrait of Duncan Campbell has generally been dated around 1812 on stylistic grounds, a date which might seem to be supported by the evidence of a letter from Raeburn to the sitter requesting payment, dated 10 November 1812.[2] However, the content of the letter would seem to imply that the portrait is as much as two or three years earlier than this, as Raeburn (who, as far as is known, was

never paid in advance) is likely to have let some considerable time elapse before he wrote reminding the sitter that he was still to be paid.[3] The letter also catches so well the sound of the artist's voice and something of the originality of his personality, that it is worth quoting in full:

Dear Sir,

Painters and poets and these sort of people, you know, are always poor, and as I am no exception to this general description, and have considerable sums to pay about this term, I have taken the liberty to remind you of your portrait, and to say it would be doing me a particular favour if you would send me an order for the

amount: the sum is 50 gns [50 guineas, that is, £52 10s.]

I would not have taken this liberty but that I know it is a trifle to you, and may have escaped you.

I am with esteem, Dear Sir, your most Obedient Servant.

Henry Raeburn

Duncan Campbell was the eldest son of Alexander Campbell of Barcaldine and Glenure, an advocate, and Mary Campbell. When the portrait was painted he held 'double rank' as a lieutenant in the 3rd Regiment of Foot Guards and a captain in the Army. He served at Copenhagen in 1801 and took part in the British

seizure of the island of Walcheren in Zeeland in 1809. In the same year he was with the British and Spanish forces, under Wellesley, who defeated the French at Talavera de la Reina in the Peninsular Wars. These achievements in 1809, in both zones of the war, may have been significant in the genesis of the portrait.

Campbell married Elizabeth, daughter of James Dennistoun of Dennistoun and co-heir of her mother, Margaret Dreghorn, in 1815. In later life he became Deputy Lord-Lieutenant of Argyll, and a magistrate. He was created baronet in 1831.

42   *Major William Clunes (fl.1790—1812)*

Oil on canvas 93 × 59in (236.2 × 150cm)

National Gallery of Scotland, Edinburgh

PROVENANCE
Bequeathed by Lady Siemens to the Royal
Scottish Academy, 1902; transferred to the
National Gallery of Scotland, 1910

EXHIBITIONS
Edinburgh, 32 York Place, *Portraits by the late Sir
Henry Raeburn*, 1824 (55); Edinburgh, National
Gallery of Scotland, *Raeburn*, 1956 (35)

LITERATURE
Armstrong, p.98; Pinnington, p.223; McKay,
pp.49, 63; Greig, p.41; National Gallery of
Scotland, *Shorter Catalogue*, 1978, p.80; Mackie,
no.160

There are three areas of special force in this portrait – the sullen power of the head of Clunes (of whom little is known), the arched profile of the horse's neck and head, pulling darkly to the right in contrast to the brightly lit human face, and the massive, shimmering rear quarters of the horse, which take up a large proportion of the picture's surface. Man and animal are thus given a surprising equality, neither subdued by, nor secondary to, the other. Compositionally, the size and rippling tension of the animal's hindquarters are counterbalanced by the sharp definition of the dark vermilion tunic and crimson sash that Clunes wears. Within these reds are blackish shadows from light cast downwards, and a thin, bluish-grey line that defines the centre edge of the waistcoat.

Clunes and his mount, a bay charger, are linked, not only physically by his left arm which gathers the reins above the saddle but also by the softly broken contour – a kind of *sfumato* – that runs from his face and upturned collar of his coat to the nape of the horse's neck and up and round its profile. Behind them is a fiercely romantic sky, fitfully lit and intermingled with this contour. These soft effects are continued within the features of Clunes's face, the warm flesh of the man expressed by paint so finely nuanced that it seems to lack determinacy, yet in effect the face has a blunt, compelling sentience.

Although a downward light has created the shadows within Clunes's tunic and backlighting has carved out the shoulders of the man and the head of the horse, light also enters from the front, flaring on Clunes's Hessian boots and spurs and the tip of his long, curved sword. The shadow of his legs is also cast inwards, mingling with the charger's legs. This light, which has the effect of warming the dark grey breeches and the black, fur-trimmed coat, is also an important element in the 'swagger' of the portrait by intensifying the vermilion of the tunic at his right hip which marks out the near

arrogance of the turned-back right wrist.

William Clunes is believed to have been a native of Sutherland. He joined the 50th (West Kent) foot regiment in 1790, becoming lieutenant in 1794 and captain in 1797. From 1807 he served in the Peninsula under Sir John Moore. He was promoted major in July 1809 in the 54th (West Norfolk) regiment, the uniform of which he wears in the portrait. His name does not appear in the Army List after 1812. The portrait is therefore presumed to have been painted in the years 1809 to 1812.

43 *Professor John Playfair 1748–1810*

Oil on canvas 50 × 40in (127 × 101.6cm)

National Portrait Gallery, London

PROVENANCE
By descent in the Raeburn family; studio sale, Christie's, 7 May 1877 (18); Duke of Somerset; Christie's, 26 June 1890 (30); Agnew's, on behalf of the National Portrait Gallery, London

EXHIBITIONS
Possibly London, Royal Academy, 1815 (277);[3] possibly Edinburgh Exhibition Society, 1815 (83);[4] Edinburgh, Royal Scottish Academy, *Exhibition of the Works of Sir Henry Raeburn*, 1876 (177)

LITERATURE
Obituary, p.12; Brown, p.9; Andrew, p.145; Armstrong, p.110; Pinnington, p.245; Greig, p.56; Richard Walker, *Regency Portraits*, London (National Portrait Gallery), 1985, vol.I, pp.397–8; Mackie, no.590

NOTES
1. National Library of Scotland, MS 19828, fol.156.
2. See *The University Portraits*, eds D. Talbot Rice [and] Peter McIntyre, Edinburgh (University Press), 1957, pp.171–3.
3. It is not certain which of the two versions discussed was exhibited at the Royal Academy. It is even conceivable that it was a different portrait by Raeburn of Playfair, which belongs to the Marquess of Lansdowne, where the pose is similar, but reversed.
4. Again, it is not certain which was the picture exhibited.

Raeburn, writing on 17 September 1811 to the engineer John Rennie about a copy of Rennie's portrait, remarks: 'I have now finished the copy of your portrait ... I heard of your welfare from your friend Mr Playfair, who says you are as much heard of and as often mentioned as a minister of State. He too is under my hand at present.'[1] Besides giving a fairly precise date for what is presumed to be the present portrait, the letter touches on another factor that is cognate to its status – namely, that a second version of a portrait by Raeburn is quite likely to be from his own hand. That he was able to reactivate his concentration in such a manner, especially as he was a painter to whom direct observation was his lifeblood, is remarkable. It seems reasonable, however, to decide the question of which picture came first – that is, was painted from life – by means of an assessment of quality, quality being the evidence of the degree of response to an actual subject rather than to a two-dimensional image. It is on this basis that the portrait discussed here is given primacy over the well-known painting in the University of Edinburgh.[2] This assumption has to override at least two facts that are both awkward and puzzling: first, that the version in Edinburgh was in the possession of the sitter's daughter, Miss Margaret Playfair, prior to its presentation by her to the University in 1857; and, secondly, that the London version remained with Raeburn until its sale by his descendants in 1877.

Although the portrait has great compositional complexity (the pose is conventional enough, but its surface variety introduces a new dimension) and a powerful sense of personality, the means by which these qualities are obtained are remarkably refined and responsive to the subtlest variations of appearance. The face, particularly, is composed of an almost endless series of tiny variations of tone, minute parallel strokes of creamy pigment on the forehead and a web of marks made up of whites and pinks and deeper tones that follow every declivity of the surface of

the flesh. The nature and function of this interweaving of brushstrokes is no better exemplified than in the tiny diagonal flash of pink that cuts away part of the too large blob of white which had originally stood for the lustre at the tip of the nose. Yet, despite the variations, the head remains totally unified. It is a method that is evident, to perhaps a slightly lesser extent, in the head of *Clunes* (cat.no.42) which is of about the same date – yet hardly used at all in the *Mrs Hamilton of Kames* (cat.no.45), also of a similar date. This wide variation of method within a single year remains puzzling.

These subtleties of handling, which amount to a distinctive *sfumato*, are continued throughout the picture, especially in the contour of Playfair's body, in the bright areas of the crimson drapery gathered behind his head, in the powerful suggestiveness of the hands and even in the lively details of the surface of the globe. Although the function of the portrait must have been broadly similar to that of the *Professor Robison* (cat.no.33) of about ten years earlier, the approach is almost disconcertingly different – there is hardly a trace left of the broad, cubic ('square touch') handling of that picture.

The Edinburgh painting superficially apes these characteristics, but the subtlety has departed. It is more or less similar in disposition, although the globe and pile of books are much diminished – not only in compositional weight but in liveliness: their quiddity has gone. Also (and this appears to be a characteristic of copies generally), the face has been imperceptibly widened. To that extent, therefore, in this case at least, Raeburn was unable to keep his inspiration at the same pitch in the process of copying. The life of what he attempted to observe was now elsewhere.

John Playfair was born at Benvie, near Dundee, where his father, James, was the parish minister. He was educated at the University of St Andrews and graduated there in 1765. Although he aimed at an academic career he was initially unsuccessful. Continuing his studies in divinity, he

was licensed as a minister in 1770, a calling he followed until 1783. He then resigned the living of Liff in order to educate Robert and Ronald Ferguson of Raith, the subjects of Raeburn's portrait '*The Archers*' (cat.no.12), which must have been painted quite soon after Playfair's tutorship ended in 1787.

In the meantime Playfair had been appointed Professor of mathematics in Edinburgh, jointly with Adam Ferguson (see cat.no.26). He held this post until 1805 when he took the chair of natural philosophy in the same university. Playfair was a man of wide interests, ranging through mathematics to meteorology,

astronomy and geology. It was, however, in his exposition of the theories of James Hutton (cat.no.10) that his chief claim to fame lay. His *Illustrations of the Huttonian Theory of the Earth*, published in 1802, played a great part in laying the foundations of the science of modern geology.

44 *Charles Hay, Lord Newton 1747−1811*

Oil on canvas 50 × 40in (127 × 101.6cm)

The Earl of Rosebery, Dalmeny House

PROVENANCE
Sir G. Macpherson Grant sale, Christie's, 12 July
1912 (80); A. Wertheimer; the 5th Earl of
Rosebery; thereafter by descent

EXHIBITIONS
Edinburgh, National Gallery of Scotland, *Ramsay,
Raeburn and Wilkie*, 1951 (46); Edinburgh,
National Gallery of Scotland, *Raeburn*, 1956 (42);
Edinburgh, Talbot Rice Art Centre, and London,
Tate Gallery, *Painting in Scotland, the Golden Age*,
1986–7 (109)

LITERATURE
Brown, p.6; Stevenson, p.411; Greig, p.55; Harris,
pp.5, 7; Irwin and Irwin, p.148; Macmillan, 1986,
pp.106, 131, 195; Macmillan, 1990, pp.156, 160;
Mackie, no.377

NOTES
1. Henry Cockburn, *Memorials of his Time*, ed.
Harry A. Cockburn, Edinburgh and London,
1909, pp.209–10.
2. Scottish National Portrait Gallery, PGL 301.

This portrait is one of Raeburn's greatest achievements. Part of that achievement is the startling agreement between the personality and outward appearance of the man as Raeburn has portrayed him, and how he was perceived and described by his contemporaries. There is a sense, rare in any portrait, that this image contains the unassailable truth about an individual. The other principal aspect is the vigorous continuity and inventiveness of the picture's surface, where solutions to the problems of observing appearance – in, for example, the complex stuff of the legal robes – are worked out in a kind of looking and marking, a questioning and answering, as the brush and loaded pigment ply ceaselessly across the pliant canvas.

When the Whigs came briefly to power in 1806 they took the opportunity of creating Charles Hay a judge with the title of Lord Newton. He had become an advocate as far distant in time as 1768, virtually a different era, when he had been a friend and companion of James Boswell. Henry Cockburn, writing more than a decade after Newton's death, recalls him as a man 'famous for law, paunch, whist, claret and worth … in private life he was chiefly known as *The Mighty*. He was a bulky man with short legs, twinkling eyes, and a large purple visage … Honest, warm-hearted, and considerate, he was always true to his principles and his friends.' Cockburn then goes on to speak of his monumental drinking and how – can we believe it? – it failed to affect his judicial powers: 'His daily and flowing cups raised him far above the evil days of sobriety on which he had fallen, and made him worthy of having quaffed with the Scandinavian heroes. But there was no noise in his libations, no boisterousness, no wrangling, not even disputation … His delight was to sit smiling, quiet, and listening; saying little, but that little always sensible … Newton's potations and bulk made him slumberous both in society and Court … In Court his head generally rested either on his heaving chest, or on his hands crossed on the bench, while,

after getting a grip of the case, his eyes were locked in genuine sleep. Yet, from practice and a remarkably quick ear and intellect, nobody could say anything worth hearing without his instantly raising his huge eyelid, and keeping it open, and directing his powerful knowing eye, like a mortar, at the speaker, till he got what was necessary; after which, when the babbling began, down sunk the eyelid again, till lighted up by the next shot … I never heard this able, kind, and honest man mentioned by anybody but with respect and affection.'[1]

Raeburn, it seems, saw the same man, to the extent that, perhaps reacting unconsciously to his large presence, he has made Newton over life-size. While the eyes, lacking highlights, do not literally twinkle, the heavy upper lids and the sharp white lines of the lower ones suggest the querulous sagacity that Cockburn remembered. This heavy, compact head is tightly encompassed by the whorls of white, greys and dull browns that make up the short wig. Descending from the double chin is a long white band which darkens as it absorbs some of the black of the suit which Newton wears under his robes. Although the total impression of these robes is of strong pinks and reds, the colour is in fact quite subdued – but the action of the brush as it builds up to the highlights on the large ribbons that ripple down each side of the open garment and on the folds of the cloth makes no concession to the idea of finely blended nuances. The 'action' that composes this substantial part of the picture surface is untrammelled, and the abstractions that appeal to modern eyes may well have raised eyebrows in Newton's time – although it is quite likely from the perspectival elevation of the sitter that the picture was intended to be viewed quite high, and from a distance. One of the boldest of these 'abstractions' is the nearly continuous zigzag edge of the right side of the robe which cascades from the uppermost ribbon down to the sitter's lap. But boldest of all, and seemingly the last strokes of the artist, are the darkest

shadows of the robe, particularly on the subject's left breast, which, appropriately, have an element of claret in their deep colouration. They are swept in with an assurance that borders on the foolhardy.

The tension of Newton's figure, still contained within his massive left fist, is released in the magniloquent gesture of the right hand. It is this gesture, so finally articulated in light and shadow, that gathers together the forces at play within the rest of the portrait and explodes them in a wonder of visual eloquence.

The portrait has been dated between Newton's elevation to the bench in 1806 and his death in 1811. However, an excise stamp of 1810 has been noticed on the reverse of the unlined canvas which can only mean that it was painted during that year. Its early history is not recorded.

A head and shoulders version which seems to be solely from Raeburn's hand exists;[2] it was engraved by Charles Turner in 1814. A similar portrait, but in black, everyday dress, is in a private collection. Many early copies and versions are also known or recorded.

45 *Frances Harriet Wynne, Mrs James Hamilton of Kames 1786–1860*

Oil on canvas 93 × 58½in (236.2 × 148.6cm)

National Gallery of Scotland, Edinburgh

PROVENANCE

By descent in the artist's family; studio sale, Christie's, 7 May 1877 (40); purchased privately by Sir William Stirling-Maxwell of Pollok, by whom bequeathed to the National Gallery of Scotland, 1877

EXHIBITIONS

London, Royal Academy, *Exhibition of Scottish Art*, 1939 (122); Edinburgh, National Gallery of Scotland, *Ramsay, Raeburn and Wilkie*, 1951 (59); Edinburgh, National Gallery of Scotland, *Raeburn*, 1956 (52)

LITERATURE

Armstrong, p.104; McKay, pp.58, 63; Pinnington, p.233; Greig, p.47; Mackie, no.365

NOTES

1. Anne Fremantle (ed.), *The Wynne Diaries*, vol. III (1798–1820), London, 1940, p.334.
2. *Ibid.*
3. I am grateful to my colleague Rosalind Marshall for discussing details of the costume with me.
4. National Gallery of Scotland, NG 623.

Elizabeth Wynne, Mrs Thomas Fremantle, one of the sitter's elder sisters, saw this portrait in Raeburn's studio on 1 June 1811. She recorded in her diary: '… call'd to see some of Mr Rayburn's paintings, the portrait he has done of Harriet I do not like, but some of his other Portraits are very finely painted'.[1] Unfortunately she does not express the nature of her dislike, but, since the history of the picture implies that it was not accepted by the sitter's family, it may have concerned the matter of likeness. Since the portrait has a grand sonority of form and colour, and no particularly revolutionary feature, it may seem unlikely that she took exception to any formal or surface quality. But could she, for instance, have been upset by the large and rather odd hiatus in the tree-trunk, just above the sitter's right arm? This seemingly unresolved area may simply represent a romantically decaying cleft in the tree (and if so, the tree is in danger of collapse!) – or it may be unfinished, though if that were the case it would be strange in the context of an otherwise quite highly finished picture. That she might have intended to criticise the rather vague landscape in the background at the left (as others sometimes did of other similar landscapes in Raeburn's portraits) seems less likely, for it actually accords surprisingly closely to her own description of the same date of the valley of the Water of Leith near to Raeburn's house and which she evidently appreciated: '… walked in the evening to St. Bernard's Well, which was very romantic & wild scenery, the walk being by the Side of a stream which runs with rapidity through Rocks, the banks are finely wooded, & it is so perfectly countrified that one could fancy oneself many miles from a Town.'[2]

Whatever may have occasioned Mrs Fremantle's reaction it seems safe to assume that the portrait was painted during that same year of 1811. At that date Mrs Hamilton was about twenty-five, which seems to agree closely with her apparent age in the portrait. This date is also borne out by the high-waisted, full-breasted line of the dress. Harriet Wynne had married her husband, James Hamilton, a Writer to the Signet, on 12 December 1808 but that seems too early if a specific occasion for the portrait is sought.

Her tall, columnar figure leans against a plinth of some indeterminate sort, at the top of which her right hand gathers an end of the large brick-red shawl that has been folded diagonally and wrapped round her body. The shawl, of a type imported from Kashmir and 2½ yards square with two fringed ends, has a narrow patterned border and large figured areas at the corners – an intermingling of silver colours, pinks and greyish green.[3] The red areas of the shawl, especially at the left shoulder and upper arm, and where it is tucked round the hidden left hand, are painted with great vigour and plasticity. Despite criticisms of Raeburn's understanding of anatomy beneath clothes it is, in this case, difficult to imagine a better implication of flesh and bone. The colour at the shoulder area changes very slightly, rather as if a barely perceptible crimson glaze had been washed across it. This slight brightening here may be supposed to be effected by the great effulgence of light behind the figure, although the light that falls on the breasts and the area of white muslin dress immediately below the waist cannot, in the main, derive from that source.

It is presumably because of the obliquity of this lighting that the eyes have no highlights. These are shaded by the dishevelled curls of black hair (the rest pinned on the top of her head) that fall across her forehead. The face is rather smoothly painted, highlights, shadows and mid-shadows blended in a way that looks back to the back-lit portraits of the early 1790s. The reflection of some light back into cast shadows is a notable feature of the contour of the sitter's right cheek and throat and the underside of her chin. In addition, Raeburn seems to have introduced tiny areas of lustre (pure light reflected from a curved surface) at the left cheekbone and on the tip of the nose. That

at the cheekbone and one of two on the tip of the nose have been painted over (although the thick pigment remains) but a third blob still gleams at the end of the nose. (This lustrous effect is continued in the long gold chain across the sitter's right breast.)

It remains puzzling that this way of treating the face is so at variance with the broken, nuanced manner that is used

in the portrait of *Clunes* (cat.no.42), which is of a very similar date. It is an example of the kind of intuitive diversity that makes dating Raeburn's portraits on purely stylistic grounds so difficult.

Harriet Wynne was the fifth daughter of Richard Wynne of Folkingham in Lincolnshire. Her mother was French and she was brought up as a Roman Catholic. James Hamilton was considered by Mrs

Fremantle as 'by no means a desirable match altho' a very good sort of man', but the marriage proved a success. In 1810 they acquired the lands and barony of Kames in Bute. Harriet's sister Justina (1785–1814) married a friend of Hamilton, Alexander Finlay of Glencorse, and was also painted at full-length by Raeburn at about the same date.[4]

46 *Francis MacNab 1734–1816: 'The MacNab'*

Oil on canvas 95 × 60in (241.3 × 152.4cm)

United Distillers

PROVENANCE

Marquess of Breadalbane by 1857; by descent to Lady Elizabeth Pringle; the Hon. Mrs Baillie Hamilton by 1901; Major the Hon. Thomas Breadalbane Morgan-Granville-Gavin; Christie's, 6 July 1917; Sir Thomas Dewar; Messrs John Dewar & Sons Ltd

EXHIBITIONS

Probably London, Royal Academy, 1819 (212); Manchester, *Art Treasures*, 1857 (252); Edinburgh, Royal Scottish Academy, *Exhibition of the Works of Sir Henry Raeburn*, 1876 (135); London, Grafton Galleries, *Scottish Old Masters*, 1895 (4); Edinburgh, *Loan Exhibition*, 1901 (180); Rome, *International Fine Arts Exhibition*, 1911; London, Grafton Galleries, *Exhibition in Aid of the National Art-Collections Fund*, 1911; London, Wembley, *British Empire Exhibition*, 1924 (W.2); Glasgow, *Empire Exhibition*, 1938; Edinburgh, National Gallery of Scotland, *Raeburn*, 1956 (41); Manchester, City Art Galleries, *Art Treasures Centenary Exhibition*, 1957; London, Christie's, *Bi-Centenary Exhibition*, 1967

LITERATURE

Obituary, p.12; Armstrong, pp.73, 76, 79, 108; Pinnington, pp.90, 162, 166, 195, 196, 205, 207, 240; 'Sir Henry Raeburn', *Masters in Art*, 6, 1905, p.40; McKay, pp.45, 52, 54; Greig, pp.xxxi, xxxii, xxxiii, liv, lv, 52; Brotchie, pp.76, 92; Dibdin, pp.136, 137; William T. Whitley, *Art In England 1800–1820*, Cambridge, 1928, pp.301–2; Collins Baker, p.163; Mrs Charles McNab, 'Francis MacNab', *Apollo*, September 1943, p.74; Harris, pp.5, 7; Irwin and Irwin, pp.147, 148, 159; Macmillan, 1986, p.160; Mackie, no.513

NOTES

1. *Autobiography of a Scotch Country Gentleman Rev. John Hamilton Gray*, ed. Mrs J. H. Gray, Edinburgh, 1868, pp.55–7.
2. John Morrison, 'Reminiscences of Sir Walter Scott and Sir Henry Raeburn', *Tait's Edinburgh Magazine*, 11, 1844, p.17.
3. John Telfer Dunbar, *History of Highland Dress*, London, 1979, p.185.
4. Sir James Ferguson's biographical note in *Raeburn*, exhibition catalogue, National Gallery of Scotland, 1956, p.38.
5. British Museum, Department of Prints and Drawings, Whitley Papers, vol.x, fol.1219. This is W. T. Whitley's transcription of an article in an unspecified newspaper of 1819.
6. Henry E. Huntington Library and Art Gallery, San Marino, California, Collins Baker's unsorted Raeburn papers: letter from W. T. Whitley to Frank Rinder, 31 July 1918.

This portrait is included in the group of seven which the young John Hamilton Gray saw in Raeburn's studio in 1813, which he lists as follows: 'Two Highland Chiefs, Glengarry and MacNab'.[1] It is not clear if the painting was finished by that date, but, if not, it can be assumed to have been completed not long after. On the other hand, the picture had conceivably been finished for some time, for there is no evidence that it was ever in the possession of the sitter, or his family. It seems almost certain that it was exhibited by Raeburn at the Royal Academy in 1819 and that it remained in his possession for some time. However, in terms of the sitter's apparent age, a date later than about 1810, when the sitter was aged seventy-six, seems unlikely.

The portrait evoked a famous response from Sir Thomas Lawrence, presumably after seeing it exhibited in London: 'His portrait of the Highlander MacNab, is the best representation of a human being that I ever saw. Mr Raeburn's style is freedom itself'. Although his remarks prior to this statement, that Raeburn 'ought to be richer than I can be, for he can paint three pictures for my one',[2] may contain an implied criticism of Raeburn's unpremeditated method, there seems nothing in his remarks about the MacNab that he did not genuinely mean. While the 'freedom' is what struck Lawrence, MacNab's aged, formidable face is actually composed of very fine brushwork, nervous and continuously angled, so that the facets of its surface have an indeterminacy that is full of life.

There is something fierce, fantastical, even fanatic, about the personality that Raeburn projects, yet profoundly human, as Lawrence perceived, within the excess of his dress and arms as he hovers aggressively above a Highland landscape. There is a dark, shifting quality about this landscape, whose romanticism may be truer than the man's and which may be imagined to ultimately overwhelm him, as he was overwhelmed by debts to the past, and, despite his indomitable stance,

financial embarrassment in the present.

Behind MacNab are stepped rocks of a dullish olive green and a gnarled tree, and he is enveloped in a moving sky that swirls in greenish turmoil at the top right. From behind this darkness light breaks in 'smeared' clouds and, lower in the picture space, filters in a subdued way among the sharp, overlapping angles of the hills. Again, the space darkens in the foreground where there is a pile of squarish boulders, blending with the 'cubism' of the more distant landscape, and a conglomeration of boscage, dark leaves, perhaps, and ferns whose silvery greens contain flecks of pure blue. Although this landscape contains no specific references to Perthshire, where MacNab's debt-burdened estates lay, it has been conceived as a significant element in the meaning of the picture, its atmospheric turbulence an expression of pride that such a land can embody such characters.

MacNab was commissioned as a major in the 1st Battalion (Breadalbane Highlanders), 2nd Royal Perthshire Brigade, usually referred to as the Breadalbane Volunteers, in 1803. The portrait could, therefore, be as early as that date, though that is unlikely. There is, apparently, little that is specifically military about MacNab's uniform, apart from the tall, feathered bonnet.[3] The coat is a dull green, with white braid on the wide lapels, cut high at the waist to reveal a red and green tartan waistcoat, cut on the bias. Across the coat is a broad belt, a warm black in colour, which has a metal end, curiously shaped like a heart. This 'heart' also features on the upper flap of the sporran, formed from a badger's head. There are also broad frogs and buttons at the right cuff of the coat, where MacNab's fist emerges holding a tiny pistol. A reddish plaid hangs at his back and is tucked under a belt at his waist, from where it falls to a tasselled end. A long dirk sheath hangs at the side of the red kilt, another pistol is hooked to the coat, or belt, and the basket hilt of a sword emerges from behind his left hip.

Francis MacNab, 16th chief of the Clan MacNab was the son of Major John MacNab and Jean Buchanan. He is said to have 'behaved in the Age of Reason like an unruly feudal lord, trying to ignore a load of inherited debts and becoming involved in numerous law suits … he considered it not merely incorrect but a positive insult to address the Laird of MacNab by the "contemptible Saxon prefix" of "Mr"'.[4] He was succeeded by a nephew who sold what remained of the estates and emigrated to Canada.

While the details of the commission and the early history of the portrait are not clearly known a newspaper review of the Royal Academy exhibition of 1819 does seem to refer to it: 'The portrait of a Highland Chief by Raeburn is a whole length figure in which the national character and costume are represented with great truth and vigour'.[5] Another review of the same exhibition, this time in the *Literary Gazette*, referring again to number 212, also seems to describe the portrait of MacNab: 'a full length, a capital work; the slightest relief would throw out its massive and broad forms and render it a *chef d'oeuvre* of this able artist'.[6] It seems virtually certain that these references are to the present portrait.

47 *Colonel Alastair Ranaldson Macdonell of Glengarry*
1771 – 1828

Oil on canvas 95 × 59in (241 × 150cm)

National Gallery of Scotland, Edinburgh

PROVENANCE
Mrs H. F. Maclean, the sitter's grand-daughter;
John Cunninghame of Balgowrie, the sitter's
great-grandson, from whom purchased by the
National Gallery of Scotland, 1917

EXHIBITIONS
London, Royal Academy, 1812 (1); Edinburgh,
Royal Scottish Academy, *Exhibition of the Works
of Sir Henry Raeburn*, 1876 (164); London, Royal
Academy, *Old Masters*, 1877 (271); London,
Royal Academy, *Exhibition of British Art*, 1934
(453); Edinburgh, National Gallery of Scotland,
Ramsay, Raeburn and Wilkie, 1951 (56); London,
Royal Academy, 1951–2 (80); Edinburgh,
National Gallery of Scotland, *Raeburn*, 1956 (46);
Madrid, Prado, *British Painting from Hogarth to
Turner*, 1988–9 (39)

LITERATURE
Obituary, p.12; Brown, p.43; Andrew, pp.135–6;
Armstrong, pp.76, 107; Pinnington, p.239;
McKay, pp.45, 49, 51, 54, 63, 65, 66–8; Greig,
pp.xxxii, 51; Brotchie, pp.74, 76, 83; Dibdin,
pp.75, 135, 137; William T. Whitley, *Art in
England 1800–1820*, Cambridge, 1928, p.20;
Sanderson, pp.139, 150, 152, 154; James Greig,
'Masterly Portrait by Raeburn, Fresh Information
About his Art', *Apollo*, June 1930, p.412; Collins
Baker, p.163; Irwin and Irwin, p.159; Macmillan,
1986, pp.132, 196; Macmillan, 1990, p.160;
Mackie, vol.I, p.70 and no.482

NOTES
1. Thomas Hodgett's undated mezzotint of the
portrait is dedicated to Alexander, 4th Duke of
Gordon.
2. Ian Finlay, *Art in Scotland*, Oxford University
Press, 1948, pp.88–9.
3. *The Journal of Sir Walter Scott*, ed. W. E. K.
Anderson, Oxford, 1972, pp.88–9.
4. *Ibid*, p.89.
5. Letter from Maldwin Drummond, in National
Gallery of Scotland accession files, NG 420.
6. *The Journal of Sir Walter Scott*, ed. W. E. K.
Anderson, Oxford, 1972, p.420.

Although Raeburn's portrait of Glengarry is remarkable for its finely detailed observation, ultimately its message concerns artifice and a romantic longing for a nebulous past. That the Highland chieftain stood thus by the window at the north end of Raeburn's painting room in York Place, his figure flooded by bright northern light, is highly likely – and no doubt in due course his amazing costume was fixed to a lay-figure or even worn by a studio helper – but that he and Raeburn were complicit in concocting a statement about Scotland's past, Jacobite as well as Celtic, is also more than likely. It is worth noting that the proscription on the wearing of Highland dress had been lifted as recently as 1782 and, although many portraits containing such costume had been painted since then, given what is known of the sitter's character and beliefs, it is likely that there is an element of reasserted triumphalism in the conception of the portrait, and one that had a London audience in mind. On Raeburn's side, it seems probable that the potential impact of the portrait in London was something that he also considered. The precise circumstances of the commission, if such it was, are not known[1] but the portrait was exhibited at the Royal Academy in 1812 – and was presumably painted shortly before that date. The impact of its exoticism must have been considerable, although there is little indication of that in the somewhat half-hearted praise it received in a notice in *The Morning Post*: 'A fine whole length of a Highland chieftain in his tartan dress is full of character and of considerable novelty. Much of its force, however, is lost from being sunk deeply in shade. A coat of varnish would bring the figure forward, and add infinitely to the effect it is calculated in every respect to produce.'

The element of falsity and spurious posturing, the feeling that this is a portrait of a lion tamed – a Highlander for easy consumption – is expressed with such a wealth of reference by a modern writer, concerned with rediscovering a true Scottish spirit in the years following the Second World War, that it is worth quoting at length:

Take Raeburn's painting of Macdonell of Glengarry. There you have the lion nearly captive – mane grown, but eye still defiant, the spirit still in him but translated into a form which enables any Lowland or London shopkeeper to believe he understands it. Sartorially, if bizarre, the chieftain is magnificent, and his trappings and weapons are as curious and colourful as a reader of Scott's novels could desire. The weapons are, no doubt, the very ones with which, retinue behind him, the chieftain is said to have stalked into King George's presence, declaring, in response to protest 'Macdonell goes nowhere without his arms and his tail [his retinue]'. Poor Macdonell, and his harmless bravado ... Those weapons, as it happens, still exist. They are magnificent. But the gorgeous, clumsy over-elaboration of the pistols would have made them ill weapons to shoot with, and, taken to pieces, they reveal the London proof-mark. The dirk, with its ivory handle and gold mounts with their English hall-marks, is all very well for fancy dress, but its handle gives a man's fingers a poor grip for a tight place. In the days when freedom was still to be won and kept by fighting, the Highlander entrusted the making of his weapons only to his own chosen armourers ...[2]

Writing about a dozen years after the portrait had been painted, Scott, a close contemporary and friend (Macdonell had presented him with a cross-breed hound to take the place of the famous Maida) had taken a similar view, although he felt a good deal of warmth for the man:

This gentleman is a kind of Quixote in our age, having retaind in its full extent the whole feelings of Clanship and Chieftain ship elsewhere so long abandoned. He seems to have lived a century too late and to exist in a state of complete law and order like a Glengarry of old whose will was law to his sept. Kindhearted, generous, friendly, he is beloved by those who know him and his efforts are unceasing to show kindness to those of his clan who are disposed fully to

meet his pretentions. To dispute them is to incur his resentment which has sometimes broken out in acts of violence which have brought him into collision with the law. To me he is a treasure as being full of information as to the history of his own clan and the manners and customs of the highlanders in general. Strong, active and muscular, he follows the chase of the deer for days and nights together sleeping in his plaid when darkness overtakes him in the forest.[3]

Macdonell was the eldest son of Duncan Macdonell of Glengarry (died 1788) and his wife Marjory, a daughter of Sir Ludovick Grant of Dalvey. In 1794–5 he raised a company for the British army, the Glengarry Highland Fencible Infantry, in which he was a Major; it was disbanded in 1801. He married Isabella Forbes, a daughter of Sir William Forbes, a fortunate alliance in Scott's view because, 'yielding to his peculiar ideas',[4] she was able to exercise a restraining influence on him. However, despite his passion for Gaelic culture, he treated his tenants badly, evicting them to make way for sheep. Nevertheless, his estates fell into substantial debt. His death, like his life, was dramatic – the result of injuries received when the canal steamer *Stirling Castle* went aground in Inverscaddle Bay, near the Corran Narrows in Loch Linnhe in the winter of 1828.[5] His butler was drowned in the same incident. Scott was saddened by his death and proposed his memory at the Celtic Society's dinner on 26 January 1828, though well aware that there was an ongoing 'rough dispute' about a piper between Glengarry and the Society. He noted that fewer of the men were wearing tartan than usual, concluding his journal entry with a thought that must have been prompted by Glengarry's life and which the portrait personifies: 'I like to see men think and bear themselves like men.'[6]

Whatever Raeburn's views of the tartanry were, it is a measure of the portrait's success that he fulfilled Glengarry's expectations (we assume) and responded to the romantic spirit of the time, while also coping with the thinking part of Scott's equation, for Glengarry's staunchly directed, rather fleshy face is convincingly full of thought and sensitivity. The portrait as a whole is finely wrought, and atmospherically unified by the deep, soft shadows, which the London critic objected to, from which Glengarry's right side thrusts forward into the downward-slanting light, the motion anchored by the right hand grasping the octagonal gun barrel, just below the tiny loop of paint that describes the sight. Details of this kind enrich the entire picture, from the powder-horn, strap and gun at the top left, the targe studded with brass nails and the crossed, basket-hilted swords at the top right, to the workings of the belt across his breast, the fob at the bottom edge of his waistcoat and the tassels on the sporran, which are made up of little flickers of yellowish paint, golden in effect where they are touched by the light flooding in from the left. The tracing of the pattern of the tartan is a *tour de force* of observation and understanding and must have taxed the artist's patience. This remarkable accumulation of information is unusual for Raeburn at this period – and the date of 1811 or 1812 is supported by Glengarry's apparent age – as is the sense of an actual room, though the plain wall articulated by a wide pilaster is likely to be a fiction rather than a record of Glengarry's ancestral home.

48 *Harriet Charlewood, Duchess of Roxburghe (d.1855)*

Oil on canvas 78⅝ × 60½in (199.5 × 153.7cm)

The Duke of Roxburghe

PROVENANCE
By descent

EXHIBITIONS
Edinburgh, Associated Society of Artists, *Annual Exhibition*, 1812 (186)

LITERATURE
Armstrong, p.106; Pinnington, p.237; Greig, p.50; Dibdin, pp.69, 76; Harris, pp.5–6, 8; Mackie, no.445

This portrait of Harriet Charlewood lacks perhaps some of the 'care and address' which *The Scots Magazine*'s critic noted in the companion portrait of her husband, the *5th Duke of Roxburghe* (cat.no.49). The freely brushed plinth and landscape before which she sits has a looseness of touch which verges on the careless and does not entirely sustain the gentle gravity of the figure. To what extent it is truly a matching companion portrait, created to have a specific visual relationship with the portrait of her husband, is not entirely clear, but both figures face inwards, relate to the picture space in a similar, proprietorial way and engage the artist's gaze – and hence that of the viewer – with the same degree of concentration. In addition, the portraits are precisely the same size, as if created for a specific setting, and were exhibited in the same year, 1812. On balance, it seems that the two paintings were intended to make a single statement.

The sitter's face has a smoothness of finish which does not quite match the refined, exploratory nature of that of her elderly husband, and the coagulations of pigment of the white dress seem, at least to modern eyes, to lack the abstract densities of the costume in the duke's portrait. The crossed hands, however, gathering together the two sides of the terracotta-coloured shawl on her lap, have the same simplified expressiveness of those in the later, full-length portrait of *Lady Montgomery* (cat.no.58).

Yet the critic writing in *The Scots Magazine* of 1812 had no reservations about the quality of this portrait – although he did have a curious reservation about Raeburn's career: 'The picture does the highest honour to Mr Raeburn as a man of genius, and deserves our most unqualified praise. The attitude is extremely easy and natural, and the drapery beautifully disposed. The picture is entirely free from any affectation of light and shadow, and the colours of the background are broke [*sic*] in that masterly manner, in which Raeburn surpasses most of the artists of the present age.' What

seems to appeal is a certain blandness that in an odd way presages a kind of Victorian taste. The writer then concludes, rather inexplicably: 'In looking at such a picture, we regret the small field of action offered to such an artist in our city, and believe that had he commenced his career in the Metropolis, instead of in this place, he would ere now have ranked with any master of the present.'

At some date after the death of the duke in 1823, Harriet, Duchess of Roxburghe, whose son James Henry had succeeded his father in the title, married a Lieut-Colonel Walter Frederick O'Reilly of the 41st Regiment of Foot. She was widowed again in 1844 and died in Brighton in 1855.

Cat.no.48

Cat.no.49

49 *James Innes-Ker, 5th Duke of Roxburghe*
1738 — 1823

Oil on canvas 78⅝ × 60½in (199.5 × 153.7cm)

The Duke of Roxburghe

PROVENANCE
By descent

EXHIBITIONS
Edinburgh, Associated Society of Artists, *Annual Exhibition*, 1812 (188); London, Royal Academy, *Exhibition of Scottish Art*, 1939 (92); Edinburgh, National Gallery of Scotland, *Raeburn*, 1956 (49); London, Royal Academy, *British Portraits*, 1956–7 (403)

LITERATURE
Armstrong, p.106; Pinnington, p.237; Dibdin, p.69; Mackie, no.444

NOTES
1. A reviewer of the exhibition in Edinburgh in 1812 remarked: 'We cannot omit mentioning a trifling circumstance in this picture, the bronze figure supporting the table, as it shows that the artist can execute every part of his pictures with equal care and address.' *The Scots Magazine*, 1812, p.350.

Sir James Innes of Innes, who succeeded to the baronetcy of that ilk in 1764, was, in 1805, one of the claimants to the Roxburghe titles, being the male heir of the first Earl of Roxburghe, through his great-grandmother. The House of Lords finally decided in his favour in 1812 and it is probably more than coincidence that the present portrait was shown at the Associated Society of Artists' annual exhibition in Edinburgh in the same year. Despite the quite homely appearance of the man's face, the massive, grandiloquent nature of the portrait, with its heavy emphasis on status and material wealth, seems a fairly deliberate expression of what had been achieved by a fairly minor Elginshire laird who had been forced to sell the barony of Innes to a cousin (the 2nd Earl of Fife) in 1767.

The calculated grandeur of the portrait, with its strong sense of property, resides in the Baroque, virtually seamless merging of a richly endowed interior with the estate that lies beyond (two trees caught so sharply in light that they might have some special significance) and, in the far distance, probably the triple hill of Melrose, which is visible from the Roxburghe seat of Floors Castle. The swagged red drapery along the top of the picture frames this golden landscape, provides a backdrop for the duke, wraps itself round the massive urn behind him and falls across the elaborate, caryatid-legged table, to the green carpet at his feet. The red of this cloth is picked up in reflection on the underside and base of the urn and also spreads – a typical piece of Raeburn's direct observation – into the fore-edge of the slate table-top. The caryatid and the rest of the underside of the table is a thickly painted concoction, the highlights deftly placed, of browns, yellow ochres and traces of a brighter orange.[1]

Roxburghe's girth and the pent-up energy in his elderly body, sunk in the cushioned red chair, seem a natural extension of the furniture of the room, though also homespun in contrast to the grandeur of the setting. The heavy face is

finely lit from the top left, this light falling in simple planes and creating deep folds of shadow on his thick grey coat. The lower limbs are still heavily muscled, firm within the yellow breeches, whitish stockings and spats of a stronger colour, whose rougher handling suggests a looser relationship to the flesh beneath.

In 1769, Innes, as he then was, had married Mary Wray of a Lincolnshire family, at the lowest point in his fortunes. She subsequently inherited the Langton estate in Berwickshire, when they assumed the additional surname of Norcliffe. However, eight days after his wife's death, childless, in 1807, he dropped this name and married Harriet Charlewood of Windlesham in Surrey. By this time he styled himself Innes-Ker and his pursuit of the Roxburghe dukedom continued. Harriet, far younger, was also painted by Raeburn (cat.no.48) in what seems to be consciously a companion portrait to the present one.

Their only son, James Henry, born in 1816, succeeded as duke on the death of his father at Floors Castle on 19 July 1823 (just a few days after the death of Raeburn himself).

50 *General Francis Dundas c.1755–1824 and Eliza Cumming, Mrs Francis Dundas*

Oil on canvas 40¾ × 56in (sight) (103.5 × 142.2cm)
Inscribed (later) bottom left: *General and Mrs Francis Dundas*

Mrs Althea Dundas-Bekker, Arniston House

General and Mrs Francis Dundas

PROVENANCE
Presumably by descent in the family of Francis
Dundas's elder brother, Robert Dundas, Lord
Arniston

EXHIBITIONS
Edinburgh, Scottish National Portrait Gallery,
Scottish Groups and Conversations, 1956 (19);
London, Royal Academy, *British Portraits*, 1956–
7 (396); Washington DC, National Gallery of Art,
The Treasure Houses of Britain ..., 1986 (524);
Edinburgh, Talbot Rice Art Centre, *Masterpieces
of Scottish Portrait Painting*, 1981 (21)

LITERATURE
Harris, p.8; Mario Praz, *Conversation Pieces. A
Survey of the Informal Goup Portrait in Europe and
America*, Pennsylvania and London, 1971, pp.98,
101; Macmillan, 1986, pp.132, 196; Macmillan,
1990, pp.154, 160; Mackie, no.239

There is perhaps a humorous undertow to this portrait – the fact that Mrs Dundas, with a degree of quiet triumph, her lips faintly parted, is removing her husband's Queen from the chess-board, while he contemplates the situation with a mixture of puzzlement and resignation.[1] The placing of the figures within the composition, he in near profile to the left, she at a three-quarters angle on the right, in a more or less conventional head and shoulders format, so as to accommodate the full width of the chess-board, has of necessity created a considerable void in the centre of the painting that Raeburn has had some difficulty in enlivening. His solution, a not entirely satisfactory one,

has been the introduction of a complex, reddish-brown drapery with bright, zigzag vermilion highlights that seem to spark between the two protagonists – or, as they truly are, antagonists. It is not entirely clear if this drapery fills the entire background: the dark area around Mrs Dundas may simply be a wall while the more ochre-coloured material above her right arm seems to represent a drape thrown across the back of a red sofa in which she sits, off centre. The far end of this sofa is perhaps the red flash of colour in the virtual centre of the picture. However, it is not at all unlikely that Raeburn never fully resolved these problems, being content with the tonal and colouristic abstractions that his brushwork represented.

The firm foundation of the painting is the green, cloth-covered table that sits four-square in the centre, its top fore-shortened to little more than the ivory and vermilion armies of chess pieces that shimmer there. They have an almost joyous, individualised liveliness and sense of potential movement that the rest of the picture builds upon. Dundas, a rather compressed figure, a tense right hand on his right knee and a relaxed arm and hand lying along his edge of the chess-board, is clothed in a warmish chocolate-brown coat from which breaks a cravat of thick white and semi-transparent greys. Above this is a solid, down-turned head which has an even, reddish hue, the features formed by deep shadows cast by the high angle of the light. By contrast, Mrs Dundas's face is evenly lit and more softly handled, her

forehead defined by dark ringlets of hair that break from beneath a dark ochre bandeau. A shawl, with 'lightning flash' highlights that echo those in the background, is held round her ample shoulders and breasts.

The costume and technique indicate a date of about 1812–15. It was in the former of these years that Dundas, who had entered the army in 1775, was promoted to general and the portrait, with its emphasis on the tactics of combat, may coincide with that event, though he does not wear uniform. As a much younger man he had been portrayed twice in uniform, by Daniel Gardner (about 1775) and John Downman (1793).[2]

Dundas was the second son of Robert Dundas, Lord Arniston (see cat.no.5) and Jean Grant. He became lieutenant and then captain in the foot guards in 1778 and saw much service in America, where he

surrendered with Cornwallis at Yorktown in 1781. He served subsequently in Jamaica (from 1787 to 1791) and in the Cape Colony, where he was twice acting governor (from 1798 to 1799 and 1801 to 1803). He was also active on the south coast of England during the various invasion scares of the early years of the nineteenth century. He married Eliza Cumming, daughter of Sir John Cumming, of whom little is known.

NOTES
1. A similar situation is portrayed in a subject picture (or it may be a double portrait) by Raeburn's rival, George Watson, which was exhibited at the British Institution in 1816 (34). This painting, which is superficially livelier, was titled 'A Chess Party. The game is mine, she cries with joy. You can't prevent checkmate' (see Algernon Graves, *The British Institution 1806–1867*, London, 1908, p.568). It seems not unlikely that one influenced the other, but which is not clear.
2. Both portraits are also at Arniston House.

51 *Alexander Elphinston 1801–88, Maria Elphinston (b.1804) and Jane Elphinston (b.1806): 'The Elphinston Children'*

Oil on canvas 78 × 60½in (198.1 × 153.7cm)

Cincinnati Art Museum, Cincinnati

PROVENANCE

John Elphinston; by descent to his grandson John's wife, Emma Elizabeth Elphinston; sold by her between 1895 and 1903; Charles Wertheimer, 1908; Scott & Fowles, New York; Mary M. Emery, 1910, by whom bequeathed to the Cincinnati Art Museum, 1927

EXHIBITIONS

Berlin, Königliche Akademie der Künste, *Aelterer Englischer Kunst*, 1908 (38); New York, Scott & Fowles, *Loan Exhibition*, 1913; Cambridge, Massachusetts, Fogg Art Museum, *Eighteenth-Century English Painting*, 1930 (62); St Louis, Missouri, St Louis Art Museum, *Forty Master-pieces*, 1947 (31); Toronto, Art Gallery, *Canadian National Exhibition of Art*, 1950 (p. 13); Indianapolis, Indiana, John Herron Museum of Art, *The Romantic Era, Birth and Flowering, 1750–1850*, 1965 (14)

LITERATURE

Greig, p.44; John Wilson, 'The Romantics 1790–1830', *The British Portrait 1660–1960*, Woodbridge, 1991, p.276; Mackie, no.258

NOTES

1. National Trust, Polesden Lacey.
2. All of the biographical information that follows is taken from the manuscript of the forthcoming catalogue of British paintings in the Cincinnati Art Museum, compiled by John Hayes. That information was supplied to the Art Museum in 1976 by a descendant of the sitters, C. A. J. Elphinston, in a number of documents preserved in the curatorial files.
3. The opposite assumption is made in the catalogue referred to above.

The British tradition of group portraits of children at play is discussed above (cat.no.34). Raeburn produced a number of such portraits, distinguished by inventiveness and a freshness of response, but marked sometimes by a sentiment that can be cloying. One of the earliest is the triple-figure portrait called *The Paterson Children* (fig.67),[1] which must have been painted about 1790, while the present portrait is one of the latest. It appears to have been painted about 1813, though a

date a year or two earlier is not out of the question, depending on what apparent ages are given to the children – and on the assumption that they are now correctly named.[2]

The subjects of the portrait have been identified as the three eldest surviving children of a civil servant with the East India Company, John Elphinston (1771–1835), and his wife Maria Robertson, who were married in Bombay on 19 March 1799. The children were all born in

Bombay – Alexander on 3 April 1801, Maria on 30 March 1804 and Jane on 17 June 1806. As Alexander seems to be no more than twelve years of age, the picture is likely to have been painted in 1813, or earlier. There is an element of doubt concerning which of the two girls is the elder, but it is assumed here that the seated child is Maria, aged consequently about nine, and that the standing child is Jane, aged about seven.[3] There is nothing in their dress or their actions that helps to differentiate them. Both wear white, short-sleeved Empire-line dresses and ivory-coloured slippers. The dresses are brushed in with great freedom but are not over-generalised, for details like the double hems are noted, as well as the hint of an underskirt on the standing child, the visual opacity of the outer skirt lessened a little above the hem by means of a slight horizontal darkening across the vertical brushstrokes. The underskirt of the seated child is also quite carefully recorded in the triangular, warm grey shadow that opens between her feet.

The children are said to have been sent back to Scotland, to be brought up by an aunt, Mrs J. Mackenzie of Applecross in Wester Ross. It may have been she who made the arrangements for the portrait to be painted, but there is no information on what function it was intended to perform. The setting appears to be elevated ground, above what may be a mountainous land-scape, freely painted and with a very low horizon. While it is never absolutely clear with what degree of calculation Raeburn composed his portraits, it is interesting to note that Alexander's head is placed precisely on the vertical centre of the picture. This seems appropriate for the dominant role he plays in this particular drama and in keeping with the supportive roles of the two sisters. His head is painted with great tenderness, his moist lips expectantly parted, the dark eyes enliven-ed with a tiny flash of red at the bottom of each iris. In a chocolate-brown suit, he appears to stride forward rather than being absolutely static, his gloved right hand grasping what appears to be a dismantled fishing rod, his left gripping the belt that crosses his breast. The other interesting elements of his rather strange accoutrements are a variegated fur beret,

fig.67 *The Paterson Children* by Henry Raeburn
Polesden Lacey, National Trust

and tightly arranged rows of ball-shaped buttons on the upper part of his coat. There is perhaps an inherent contradiction in the logic of the picture – the boy's dress seems one for winter, while his sisters are in the flimsy clothes of high summer.

Her gaze firmly on the artist, Maria cradles a somewhat stiff adult doll on her lap, perhaps taken momentarily from the little basketwork cradle on her left. It appears that she (although perhaps it is her sister) has taken off a red cloak with a yellow lining and cast it on the stepped earth where she sits. Some of the intense red of the cloak turns the yellow lining orange, and is also reflected into the shadows in the lower areas of Maria's dress. The cradle, which seems to have a lined hood with a diced pattern, is half hidden behind a not entirely convincing bank of dark earth, its bottom skirted by dark, bluey green burdock leaves. The remainder of the foreground is mainly a much yellower green, a platform for the upright figure of Jane (her gaze rather less focused than the other two) who thumps her elevated tambourine with the knuckles of her right hand.

The children's individual actions should perhaps imply a narrative but there does not appear to be one. They are charmingly integrated and their presences realised with sentiment but the message of the painting is more concerned with posing than with present, or even imminent, action.

Subsequently, Alexander would marry in India in 1831. His wife has not yet been identified. They had a son John, who also served in the Bombay civil service. In 1863 he married for a second time and he and his wife, Margaret Rachel (whose family name is unknown), had a number of children. Latterly he lived in Hampshire and died in Scotland at a great age. Maria married a Captain Alexander Macdonald of the East India Company in Poona on 23 July 1824. The marriage was of short duration, however, for Captain Macdonald died on 4 September 1825. They had a posthumous daughter, Alexandrina, born in Bombay on 12 February 1826. Shortly after, on 15 November 1826, Maria married, in Bombay, a Captain James Morrison, also of the East India Company. The younger of the two sisters, Jane, married another officer of the East India Company, a Lieutenant Bruce Seton, in Bombay on 17 June 1825, her nineteenth birthday.

52 *Margaret Macdonald, Mrs Robert Scott Moncrieff (d.1824)*

Oil on canvas 29½ × 24½in (74.9 × 62.2cm)

National Gallery of Scotland, Edinburgh

PROVENANCE
Robert Scott Moncrieff Wellwood (died 1854), by whom bequeathed to the Royal Scottish Academy; presented to the National Gallery of Scotland, 1910

EXHIBITIONS
Edinburgh, Royal Scottish Academy, *Exhibition of the Works of Sir Henry Raeburn*, 1876 (59); Royal Academy, *Exhibition of British Art*, 1934 (462); Royal Academy, *Exhibition of Scottish Art*, 1939 (96); Edinburgh, National Gallery of Scotland, *Raeburn*, 1956 (37)

LITERATURE
Brown, p.7; Andrew, p.141; Armstrong, pp.63, 91, 109; Pinnington, pp.171, 173, 196, 242; McKay, pp.58, 60; Caw, *Masterpieces*, pp.69, 79; Caw, 1908, pp.74, 75; Greig, pp.xlvii, 54; Brotchie, p.83; Dibdin, pp.131, 141, 148; Irwin and Irwin, p.158; Macmillan, 1986, p.129; Macmillan, 1990, p.160; Mackie, no.542

Cat.no.53 *Ann Pattison, Mrs William Urquhart*

This is pre-eminently a portrait of sensibility and sexuality. By the second decade of the nineteenth century Raeburn increasingly strained after effects in his female portraits that heightened emotion and made a clear demand on the viewer to be complicit with the sentiment he sought to express. This often involved a stalk-like neck that twisted away from the frontality of the body, the head at the same time being thrown back in near ecstasy and the eyes, themselves often upturned, glistening with a watery passion. The immediate origins of portraits of this type are not obvious, but paintings of Baroque saints and martyrs can hardly have been far from his mind. In so far as such forms have an actual origin they seem to derive ultimately from early Raphael, most notably in pictures like his *St Catherine of Alexandra*. For Raeburn there were clearly varying degrees to which this kind of sentiment might be taken and the present picture stands in a somewhat half-way position between the subdued, nearly classical sentiment of the *Mrs William Urquhart* (cat.no.53) and the exaggerated emotionalism of the portrait of *Lady Gordon Cumming* (fig.26), which Raeburn, curiously, believed to be one of the finest of his female portraits.

It is also curious that a painter so concerned with observation of the actual, and with an expression of his sitter's character, should seem to make a portrait where the subject's appearance and personality are generalised to the point of stereotype. The sense of the portrait being a portrayal of feeling rather than an individual is heightened by the parted lips, a feature that Raeburn could of course, on occasion, use realistically, as in a portrait like the *Mrs Fraser* (cat.no.35). Here the breath of profound emotion that the mouth expels is part of the 'saintliness' of the rest of the head, although this is at variance with the erotic undertow that is also present. It remains a matter of speculation to what extent the turn of the head and the mute, though passionate, stare was a matter of social convention in the same way that the dishevelled cloak (painted in a rough, romantic manner) and overt sexuality of the dress undoubtedly were. How that sexuality was read, or suppressed, by Raeburn and his contemporaries remains a matter of speculation. What is clear is that the picture's generalising qualities have allowed it to become an icon for Raeburn and the Edinburgh society of his times.

The portrait is generally dated about 1814 and there is no reason to question that. An unfortunate part of the heightened romanticism in which Raeburn indulged at this time is a greater use of bitumen. This substance plays an important part in the intense dark of the background but has also permeated, and damaged, many other areas of the picture surface.

Margaret (or Margaritta) Macdonald was the wife of an Edinburgh wine merchant, Robert Scott Moncrieff (died 1854), who added the name Wellwood to his name when he inherited the estate of Garvock in Fife in 1847. He was a friend of Sir Walter Scott and was described as 'exceedingly unassuming in manner, and kind and liberal to all'. The couple were childless and Margaret died in 1824, thirty years before her husband. Raeburn's portrait hung undisturbed in his dining room, through his long widowerhood.

53 *Ann Pattison, Mrs William Urquhart*

Oil on canvas 29 × 24½in (73.7 × 62.2cm)

Glasgow Museums: Art Gallery and Museum, Kelvingrove

PROVENANCE

By descent to the sitter's eldest son, William Urquhart; bequeathed to his wife, Caroline T. Urquhart, by whom given to the Gallery, 1900

EXHIBITIONS

Paisley, Fine Art Institute, 1903–4 (101); Glasgow, 1908 (86); London, Royal Academy, *Exhibition of British Art*, 1934 (473)

LITERATURE

Armstrong, p.113; Pinnington, p.251; Greig, p.62; Brotchie, pp.66, 83; Dibdin, pp.131, 146; Irwin and Irwin, p.158; Mackie, no.724

The format of this portrait bears a remarkable similarity to that of the portrait of *Mrs Scott Moncrieff* (cat.no.52), although the direction of the figure is reversed. Within these general outlines, however, the two paintings differ considerably. Whereas the *Mrs Scott Moncrieff* has a generalised sensuality, to the extent that it has been accorded a kind of iconic status, the portrait of *Mrs Urquhart* has a refined individuality, where the emphasis is on sweetness and youth rather than on breathless, glistening sexuality: in a curious way, given the similarities, Mrs Urquhart is social and domestic, while Mrs Moncrieff seems subject to storms that might sweep away convention. How this accords with the reality of their lives is not known, but it has to be acknowledged that Raeburn saw something of the kind.

Ann Pattison, daughter of the town-clerk of Leith, John Pattison, married the Glasgow merchant William Urquhart towards the end of 1812 or near the beginning of 1813. Since the portrait must date from about this time, it may in some respects be a marriage portrait.

The sitter wears a moderately high-waisted dress with a low, square-shaped décolletage. It is thinly painted, warm grey in colour, with a number of bold, pure white brushstrokes swept across it, the breasts distinctly defined. Over this is worn a dark pelisse, of a faintly pink mauve, trimmed with a material of flickering white. The pelisse is turned back to show its inner lining and pulled on to the shoulders to reveal the shining expanse of frock and breast.

The broad treatment of this area is in distinct contrast to the almost porcelain-like effect of the head. The face is high keyed, except for the smooth pink shadow that forms the jawline and the shadow under the jaw and on the neck, which is made marginally lighter in order to account for the upward reflection of light from the breast. The dark, curled hair is arranged in a series of coils at the temples and on the forehead, the paint itself twisted in fine, hair-like circular movements. This is a remarkable instance in Raeburn of the equivalence of the means to the substance of what is observed.

Cat.no.52 *Margaret Macdonald, Mrs Robert Scott Moncrieff*

54 *John Clerk of Eldin, Lord Eldin 1757–1832*

Oil on canvas 50½ × 40in (128.2 × 101.6cm)
Inscribed (later) top left: JOHN CLERK LORD ELDIN

Scottish National Portrait Gallery, Edinburgh

PROVENANCE
Bequeathed by the sitter to Sir William Gibson
Craig, 1832; by descent; purchased by the Scottish
National Portrait Gallery, 1947

EXHIBITIONS
Edinburgh, 32 York Place, *Portraits by the late Sir
Henry Raeburn*, 1824 (48); International Exhibi-
tion, 1862 (147); Edinburgh, Royal Scottish
Academy, 1863 (68); London, Royal Academy,
Old Masters, 1877; Edinburgh, National Gallery
of Scotland, *Raeburn*, 1956 (51); Edinburgh,
University of Edinburgh, *James Hutton and Some
of His Friends*, 1976

LITERATURE
Brown, pp.6, 110–11; Andrew, p.110; Armstrong,
pp.45, 76, 101; Pinnington, pp.80–1, 196, 208,
228; Stevenson, p.411; Greig, pp.xxx, 41; Dibdin,
p.143; Sanderson, pp.139, 140, 141, 152;
Macmillan, 1986, pp.134, 196; Macmillan, 1990,
p.161; Mackie, no.157b

NOTES
1. Henry Cockburn, *Memorials of his Time*,
ed. Harry A. Cockburn, Edinburgh and London,
1909, p.140.
2. *Ibid.*, p.140.
3. *Ibid.*, p.144.
4. Edinburgh, National Gallery of Scotland.
5. *Catalogue of the Extensive, Genuine, and Highly
Valuable Collection of Pictures, late the property of
The Hon. John Clerk of Eldin*, sold by auction by
Messrs Thomas Winstanley & Sons (of Liver-
pool), at no.16, Picardy Place, Edinburgh, on
Thursday the 14th day of March 1833, and
thirteen following days …, Edinburgh, 1833, p.85
(lot 19).
6. See *A Concise and Accurate Account of the
Accident that occurred at the sale of the late Lord
Eldin's Pictures*, by a sufferer, Edinburgh, 1833.

Raeburn had painted a portrait of Clerk when he was a relatively young man. That portrait (fig.8), which is believed to have been accidentally destroyed, may have been as early as 1783, certainly predating the portrait of *Lord Arniston* (cat.no.5), since it has none of that painting's general-ised power. Although the two portraits of Clerk set out to contextualise the life of the man, the contrast between the pains-taking particularity of the early portrait and the blunt, romantic power of the present portrait demonstrates graphically how Raeburn's vision had developed in the intervening years. A mezzotint engraving of the portrait, by Charles Turner, was published in 1815. The portrait is there-fore likely to date from that, or the previous, year.

The portrait's compelling romanticism, the assertive, engaging, perhaps question-ing, nature of the sitter's glance, as well as the active hands – Cockburn described the man in 1806 as 'positive, crotchety and wild' – are all anchored within a particu-larly firm geometry. Clerk is thrust, almost too far, to the left of the picture space, his left arm a black cantilever linking the dark mass of his body and the bright agitation of the face and stock to the steeply sloping book on the right, which acts as a kind of compositional buttress locked on to by the fingers of the left hand, the hand itself so finely related to the book that there is a sense of its soft inside where all the pressure must be collected, although it is not actually depicted. That the book itself is as much a physical support of a practical sort as a reference to the sitter's library is attested by the fact that it is the back cover that is rather oddly pushed towards the spectator by the half-visible thumb.

Two other elements of the basic geometry of the portrait are the vertical line that divides the plain, almost neo-classical background into fields of virtually two to one, and a less sharply defined horizontal marking the contact between the right forearm and the arm of the chair and the forward edge of the covered table.

This more notional line (although it does much to control the composition of the portrait) is punctuated by the wonderfully lit right hand, which gestures vigorously with the fragile spectacles, the confection of whitish papers, tied with pink ribbon, and the dark figurine of a crouching Venus which sits on the green tablecloth. All of this geometry is awash with light and darkly orchestrated shadow.

That Raeburn provided such a frame-work of support for the man was perhaps his unconscious reaction to the fact that Clerk had a serious disability in one of his legs, which Lord Cockburn graphically describes: 'A contracted limb, which made him pitch when he walked, and only admitted of his standing erect by hanging it in the air, added to the peculiarity of a figure with which so many other ideas of oddity were connected.'[1]

John Clerk was the eldest son of John Clerk of Eldin, amateur geologist, topo-graphical draughtsman and etcher and writer on naval tactics, and Susanna Adam, daughter of the architect William Adam and sister of Robert. As the naval tactician was a younger brother of Sir George Clerk of Penicuik, his son, the future judge, was therefore cousin to Sir John Clerk of Penicuik, subject of Raeburn's famous double portrait with his wife, Rosemary D'Acre (cat.no.13).

Clerk was admitted to the faculty of advocates in 1785 and quickly rose in his profession. He became noted for both his dishevelled appearance and his passionate, adversarial style; much of his vituperative sarcasm, what Cockburn described as his 'crazy fierceness', was directed at the judges before whom he pleaded and who were generally unable to control him. Again, Cockburn describes his appearance: 'Blue eyes, very bushy eyebrows, coarse grizzly hair always in disorder, and firm, projecting features, made his face and head not unlike that of a thorough-bred shaggy terrier.'[2] A staunch Whig, he became solicitor-general during their brief period of ascendancy in 1806. He was, in 1823, appointed a senator of the College Justice,

and took the title Lord Eldin. However, he was not temperamentally suited to being a judge and his mental powers were also failing. He resigned in 1828.

Like his father, he was an accomplished draughtsman (praised by Sandby) and was also involved in Hutton's geological endeavours. He was a passionate collector and Cockburn paints a scene that is only hinted at in Raeburn's portrait; indeed, the disorder is decorously ignored: 'Walls covered with books and pictures, of both of which he had a very large collection; the floor encumbered by little ill-placed tables, each with a piece of old china on it; strange boxes, bits of sculpture, curious screens, and chairs, cats and dogs … and all manner of trash, dead and living, and all in confusion; John himself sitting in the midst of this museum … '[3]

This 'museum', in fact, contained a major collection of books, paintings, prints, drawings, china, bronzes and coins. Following Clerk's death, unmarried, in 1832, the collections were sold at auction over a period of twenty-four days in January and March 1833. The books were sold in auction rooms in Hanover Street but the remaining material was sold at Clerk's own house at 16 Picardy Place. The star of the collection was a large *Adoration of the Kings*, then attributed to Titian, but in fact by Jacopo Bassano.[4] There were many other important paintings by Italian, Dutch and Flemish (including Rubens) masters, as well as a nearly complete set of etchings by Rembrandt. Among the bronzes sold, on the eleventh day, was a 'Crouching Venus, very fine' which may well be the one included in the portrait.[5]

There was enormous interest in the sale in Picardy Place and attempts were made to prevent 'improper intrusion'. These were largely unsuccessful and many hundreds visited the house on the two viewing days. On the third day of the sale the drawing room floor, where the sale was being conducted, gave way and about eighty of those attending fell the sixteen feet to the library below. Despite the many injuries, only one, an Edinburgh banker, Alexander Smith, was fatally injured.[6] The crotchety John Clerk, from afar, might have felt just a little satisfaction had the victim been a judge!

55 *Margaret Maclean Clephane, Marchioness of Northampton (d.1830)*

Oil on canvas 50½ × 40in (128 × 101.6cm)
Inscribed (later) lower left: Margaret,/2ⁿᵈ Marchˢˢ of Northampton,/– by Raeburn –

The Marquess of Northampton

PROVENANCE
By descent[10]

EXHIBITIONS
Edinburgh, *Sixth Exhibition of Paintings*, 1813
(69); Manchester, *Art Treasures Exhibition*, 1857;
London, Tate Gallery, *The Swagger Portrait*,
1992–3 (48)

LITERATURE
The Scots Magazine, April 1813, p.246;
Armstrong, p.99; Pinnington, p.224; Greig, pp.41,
55; Irwin and Irwin, pp.159, 430; Mackie, no.22

NOTES
1. *Autobiography of a Scotch Country Gentleman
Rev. John Hamilton Gray*, ed. Mrs J. H. Gray,
Edinburgh, 1868, p.55.
2. J. G. Lockhart, *The Life of Sir Walter Scott,
Bart.*, London, 1893, p.371.
3. *Ibid.*, p.288.
4. *Familiar Letters of Sir Walter Scott*, Edinburgh,
1894, vol.I, pp.301–2.
5. J. G. Lockhart, *The Life of Sir Walter Scott,
Bart.*, London, 1893, p.301.
6. *Ibid.*, p.314.
7. *Ibid.*, p.371.
8. *Ibid.*, p.383.
9. *Autobiography of a Scotch Country Gentleman
Rev. John Hamilton Gray*, ed. Mrs J. H. Gray,
Edinburgh, 1868, p.56.
10. A second version is known to have been in the
collection of Lord Alwyne Compton, the sitter's
fourth son, in 1901. It was last recorded as being
in the collection of Alwyne Compton Farquharson
of Invercauld and Torloisk in 1973.

As a young boy, sitting to Raeburn for his portrait in 1813, John Hamilton Gray noted seven works in the painter's studio, including one of 'Miss Maclean Clephane, afterwards Marchioness of Northampton playing on the harp'.[1] The portrait is therefore not a true companion, in the sense of being painted as one of a balanced pair, to Raeburn's portrait of her husband which is assumed to have been painted shortly before it was exhibited at the Royal Academy in 1821 (cat.no.61). As with that portrait, however, it is not implausible that Walter Scott played some part in its genesis. Scott was a close friend of the family, a friendship that went back to his father's time. He became, in effect, guardian, or ward, to the three daughters of Mrs Maclean Clephane, widow of Major-General Douglas Maclean Clephane of Torloisk on the Isle of Mull. J. G. Lockhart, his son-in-law and biographer, refers to the mother as being someone 'with whom he [Scott] agreed cordially on all subjects except the authenticity of Ossian'.[2] During a tour of the Western Isles by boat in the summer of 1814 he dined with the four women at Torloisk on Loch Tua and stayed overnight. However, good tourist that he was, he did not accept their entreaties to spend another day or two with them but pressed on – only to be becalmed for the best part of the day on the north side of Mull, clearly visible to the amused ladies at Torloisk. Another factor in his departure, and it is redolent of the times, was his unease at seeming to favour one friend, Mrs Maclean, at the expense of another, Ranald Macdonald, laird of Staffa, who had just taken up residence at his house of Ulva. Scott was all too aware of the traditional enmity that still existed between them.[3]

It was likely that Scott brought about the meeting between Margaret and her future husband, Lord Compton. Compton and a friend had come north in July 1813, with a letter of introduction from Scott's correspondent, John Morritt of Rokeby. Scott pronounced them to be 'very good young men', showed them the sights of Edinburgh and dined with them. He then provided a letter introducing them to Mrs Clephane, feeling obliged to find them accommodation 'in the land of mist and billows'.[4] No doubt the relationship between Compton and Margaret which led to marriage in the summer of 1815 ripened here at Torloisk.

Lockhart, writing of her a number of years after her death, remarks that of Scott's friends, 'he had, I think, none more dear', and in her correspondence it is easy to sense the liveliness of this 'gallant highland lassie' that so appealed to him. On one occasion she writes to him about something 'that speaks to me in the voice of a valued friend – *Waverley*'. At this time, October 1814, Scott's authorship was still to be revealed, but it is clear that his intimate friends had already guessed it, although they pretended otherwise. Margaret plays a lively and witty tune on the pretence: 'The turn of phrases in many places is so peculiarly yours, that I fancy I hear your voice repeating them; and there wants but verse to make all Waverley an enchanting poem … But, why did not the author allow me to be his Gaelic Dragoman? Oh! Mr _____, whoever you are, you might have safely trusted _____ M.M.C.'[5]

Such was Scott's affection, and sense of responsibility, for this lively young woman, that he allowed it to interfere with his excitement at the great event of 1815, the final defeat of Napoleon. He had already expended considerable effort in London during June arranging an adequate marriage settlement with the Marquess of Northampton's lawyer. Now eager to visit the field of Waterloo, to see, as he and Lockhart fondly believed, 'the last shadows of real warfare that his own age would afford', he nevertheless delayed his departure from Edinburgh in order to attend their wedding. Only after the marriage of Margaret and Lord Compton, conducted by Daniel Sandford, Bishop of Edinburgh on 24 July, by special licence, did he depart for the Continent.[6]

It is clear from Lockhart that Scott,

although most closely attached to Mrs Clephane and Margaret, also had great affection for the other daughters and 'delighted especially in their proficiency in the poetry and music of their native isles.'[7] The social situation of family warmth, music and romance that so entranced Scott is essential to the portrait. That Scott, as Margaret's guardian and intimate friend, had some role in its conception seems highly likely.

Although the portrait is therefore in some ways a reflection of a certain social situation, there flows from it, in the implied sound of the plucked strings and the song that issues from the parted lips, a reference to bardic culture and whatever was real behind the Ossianic myth. The roughly fringed garment she wears, a

cross and chain gleaming darkly in the dense shadow under the softly rounded left arm, is painted in a complexity of browns, dull reds and little flames of light that is Rembrandtesque in effect. Emerging from this rich darkness and the unarticulated dark background are the delicately modelled arms and face that imply sound and movement, in part fashion, in part an attempt to suggest a culture lost in another time.

Inevitably Scott saw less of Lady Compton after her marriage but to his delight she and her husband turned up at Abbotsford in November 1818 in the midst of 'a grand jollification' by the Forest Yeomanry, 'with glittering sabres, waving standards, and screaming bag-pipes'. Even in what Scott describes as a

'hurricane', their 'presence gave a great zest to the whole affair … I was glad to see Lord and Lady Compton so very comfortable, and surrounded with so fine a family …'

The harp travelled to Rome, when the couple took up residence there, but Margaret's tremulous delicacy seemed to travel less well, perhaps because of child-bearing. John Gray, who had seen the portrait many years before, considered its subject much changed: 'In the winter of 1824–5 I very often saw and heard Miss Maclean Clephane, then Countess of Compton, playing the harp in Rome, but she did not realise Raeburn's early idea of her; she had then become immensely large, so that she was called, by the Italians, "La Voluminosa".'[9] She died in childbirth, at Rome, in 1830.

56 *Sir Henry Raeburn 1756—1823: self-portrait*

Oil on canvas 35¼ × 27½in (89.5 × 69.9cm)

National Gallery of Scotland, Edinburgh

PROVENANCE

By descent in the Raeburn family; Logan White
Raeburn; Sir William Patrick Andrew, husband of
the painter's eldest granddaughter; studio sale,
Christie's, 7 May 1877 (25); Christie's, 9 July
1887 (142); bought by Agnew; Lord
Tweedmouth; Christie's, 3 June 1905 (34); bought
by Agnew for the National Gallery of Scotland

EXHIBITIONS

Possibly London, Royal Academy, 1816 (221 or
286); Edinburgh, 32 York Place, *Portraits by the
late Sir Henry Raeburn*, 1824 (30); Edinburgh,
1850 (1); London, *International Exhibition*, 1862
(188); Edinburgh, Royal Scottish Academy, 1863
(215); London, South Kensington Museum, *Third
and Concluding Exhibition of National Portraits*,
1868 (130); Edinburgh, Royal Scottish Academy,
Exhibition of the Works of Sir Henry Raeburn, 1876
(212); London, Royal Academy, *Old Masters*,
1877 (53); Edinburgh, *Exhibition of Scottish
National Portraits*, 1884 (219); Glasgow, 1902
(93); London, Royal Academy, *Exhibition of
British Art*, 1934 (424); London, Royal Academy,
Exhibition of Scottish Art, 1939 (89); Edinburgh,
National Gallery of Scotland, *Raeburn*, 1956 (47)

LITERATURE

Cunningham, p.228; Brown, pp.6, 10; Andrew,
p.145; Armstrong, p.110; Pinnington, pp.161,
162, 166, 190, 245; McKay, p.55; Greig, p.57;
Brotchie, pp.8, 75; Dibdin, p.82; Sanderson,
pp.128, 134; William T. Whitley, *Art in England
1800–1820*, Cambridge, 1928, pp.240, 258;
Frederick C. Daniell, 'William Walker and his
Family, 1792–1867', *Print Collectors' Quarterly*,
October 1932, p.327; *Raeburn*, exhibition
catalogue, 1956, p.41; Harris, pp.6, 8; Mackie,
no.597

NOTES

1. Royal Academy Library, cv 226.
2. *Ibid.*, cv 269.
3. Assuming that he would naturally raise his
right hand to his chin, he must only have used a
single mirror, rather than the two required to
correct such reversals.

On his election to the Royal Academy,
Raeburn offered this self-portrait as his
diploma work. Unfortunately, he did not
realise that self-portraits were unacceptable for this purpose. On 10 November
1815 the secretary of the Academy was
instructed to write to Raeburn to inform
him 'that it is not usual to receive as
Deposits the Portraits of Members, and
request that he will send the Council as
early as convenient some other specimen
of his talents'.[1] In due course Raeburn
wrote 'expressing his intention of sending
a picture for his Deposit in lieu of his own
portrait transmitted to the Academy, and
requesting that the latter may appear in
the Exhibition of this year'.[2] It is not clear
if the self-portrait was shown in the
exhibition for 1816. Conceivably it is one
of the two portraits listed in the catalogue
as 'Portrait of a gentleman'. An etched
reproduction by W. Nicholson was
published in 1818.

Raeburn had made enormous efforts to
give his self-portrait the intensity and
high seriousness which he must have
deemed necessary to convey his achievement in Scotland to an audience in London. The quality and style of his work
were already known there, for he had
occasionally exhibited at the Royal
Academy from 1792, and regularly since
1810, so that he was less concerned with
demonstrating the originality and freshness of his manner than with making a
statement that would in some way epito-
mise his status as an artist. In the event,
the degree of thought and calculation that
went into the image, and the difficulties
that he evidently experienced in making
the statement he intended, burdened the
work to such an extent that it remains less
than satisfactory.

The arms, and the gesture of contem-
plation that they were meant to take,
created great difficulties, which must have
been partly psychological and expressive,
but also to a very considerable extent
practical. For a painter whose work
depended so much on observation and a
sure and rapid response with the brush,

the difficulties of posing before the mirror[3]
and then transferring the shapes that he
saw to the adjacent canvas created the
problems, not wholly solved, which are
visible in the strained articulation of the
arms and their altered outlines. In other
words, the evidence of the arms in their
posed position vanished when the same
arms were used in the act of painting. For
the viewer, the difficulty of understanding
where exactly the arms begin, where the
crucial joints are and the exact lie of each
section is compounded by the dark,
bituminous nature of much of the body
area. This deep, romantic intensity,
achieved by a material he did not as a rule
use, seems also to be the result of the same
straining for effect that is witnessed in the
pose.

The angle of the figure also, probably
at some quite late stage in the work's
gestation, failed to satisfy Raeburn. He
appears to have concluded that his body
drooped too much within the upright
borders of the canvas and, in order to give
it sufficient dignity, he removed the canvas
from its original support, rotated it
clockwise through about 10°, and then re-
attached it (fig.68). This, as the compara-
tive illustrations show, gave it a dignity
that it previously lacked. The evidence of
this alteration is clearly visible in the angle
of the 'horizontal' threads of the canvas
and at the corners where the original, and
now angled, edges are still faintly visible.

Raeburn's figure is lit from high on his
right (the viewer's left), so that the
forehead, though slightly foreshortened, is
thrown into emphatic relief, befitting the
mental qualities that the portrait was
intended to convey. This sharp angle of
light also darkens and thickens both the
eyebrows and the upper eyelids, which
adds to the romantic force of the portrait.
At the same time, the subtlety of the cast
shadows that play around the forefinger
and thumb of the raised hand emphasise
the tactile quality of this gesture, which
both steadies and focuses the artist's gaze.

This gesture may owe something to a
self-portrait of a fellow Scot that Raeburn

might well have known, that of John Runciman, painted in Italy in 1767, and later in the possession of his brother Alexander (fig.14). It seems to derive, ultimately, from the brooding figure of *Night* by Michelangelo on the Medici tomb in Florence. All these hints at the workings of the mind, even genius, must reflect how Raeburn perceived himself in terms of the artistic community, as does the fact that he wanted the portrait to represent his work in the Royal Academy's collection. In due course, he deposited an entirely different kind of picture, the '*Boy and Rabbit*' (cat.no.57).

fig.68
Reconstruction
of the initial
composition

57   *Henry Raeburn Inglis: 'Boy and Rabbit'*

Oil on canvas 40 × 31 in (101.6 × 78.8cm)

Royal Academy of Arts, London

PROVENANCE
Presented by the artist to the Royal Academy of
Arts as his diploma picture

EXHIBITIONS
London, Royal Academy, 1816 (31); Manchester,
Art Treasures Exhibition, 1857 (182); London,
International Exhibition, 1862 (162); London,
Royal Academy, *Works of the Old Masters: Works
of Deceased Masters of the British School*, 1873
(226); London, Royal Academy, *Exhibition of
British Art*, 1934 (457); London, Royal Academy,
Exhibition of Scottish Art, 1939 (87); London,
Royal Academy, *The First Hundred Years of the
Royal Academy, 1769–1868*, 1951–2 (270);
Edinburgh, National Gallery of Scotland,
Raeburn, 1956 (45)

LITERATURE
Cunningham, p.232; Armstrong, pp.47, 115;
Pinnington, p.236; McKay, p.55; Greig, pp.xliv,
xlvii, 39; Brotchie, pp.63, 75; Dibdin, pp.43, 82,
145; William T. Whitley, *Art in England, 1800–
1820*, Cambridge, 1928, p.240; Harris, pp.6, 8;
Mackie, no.421

NOTES
1. Royal Academy Library, cv 269.

On being informed by the secretary of the
Royal Academy in November 1815 that
self-portraits were not acceptable as
diploma pieces (see cat.no.56), Raeburn
chose to send the present portrait of his
step-grandchild, Henry Raeburn Inglis.
His decision was recorded in the council's
minutes for 6 April 1816: 'The secretary
read a letter which he had received from
Mr Raeburn R.A. elect expressing his
intention of sending a picture for his
Deposit in lieu of his own portrait transmitted to the Academy, and requesting
that the latter may appear in the Exhibition of this year.' Although it is not certain
that the rejected self-portrait was indeed
shown in 1816, it is highly probable that
the present portrait was shown in that
same year under the title, '*Portrait of a
Boy*'.[1]

Since the proffered self-portrait seemed
to have the clear intention of making
reference to Raeburn's high seriousness, it
is perhaps surprising that a portrait of
such sweet sentiment, and indeed something that, if it were not for its title, might
be read merely as an affecting genre
subject, was chosen as an appropriate
substitute. The intention, however, may
have been to avoid leaving his permanent
mark in London as only a painter of
likenesses of the Scottish middle classes
and to show instead the range of his
imaginative powers. The boy and his
rabbit are brought exceptionally close to
the picture plane and both this proximity
and the literally engaging glance of the
child seem calculated to compel the viewer
to be somehow complicit in the act of
creation. Although there is no record of a
critical reaction to the painting, it is
highly likely – and this is borne out by the
picture's subsequent reputation – that the
Academy's audience were indeed drawn
into this virtuoso performance of colour,
handling and feeling.

The virtuoso handling is most evident
in the series of zigzag highlights and
shadows on the left sleeve of the boy's
shirt and in the frills of the collar – drawn
back into a wide V-shape to reveal, it

seems, the innocent breast of childhood.
The setting is a not very clearly defined
earthen bank where the boy cossets his
white rabbit, which nibbles what seems to
be a dandelion plant. From the plants
around his left foot he plucks a leaf of
another kind, as part of the whole action of
protecting and sustaining. The sky behind
is both bright and dark, the deep blue-
green clouds around the head thinly
brushed with a feathery touch. Light falls
across the dark cap, its wide brim throw-
ing a smooth shadow across the upper
quarter of the face. The face itself is very
softly modelled, the left cheek and jaw
marked by a finely graded shadow and a
line of secondary light. The child's parted
lips, pink like the inside of the right nostril
and the corner of the right eye, gain an
extra poignancy when it is recalled that he
was a deaf mute.

Henry Raeburn Inglis was the son of
Raeburn's elder step-daughter, Ann Leslie,
and James Philip Inglis. The portrait may
have been painted purely for the family's
own collection, before it was given its
ultimate role as a player in the cause of
Raeburn's reputation. In date it seems
rather earlier, perhaps about 1814, than
the occasion with which it was to be
connected.

58 *Helen Graham, Lady Montgomery (d.1828)*

Oil on canvas 93 × 59in (236.2 × 149.9cm)

James Montgomery Esq

PROVENANCE
By descent in the sitter's family

EXHIBITIONS
Edinburgh, Royal Scottish Academy, *Exhibition of the Works of Sir Henry Raeburn*, 1876 (204); London, Royal Academy, *Exhibition of Scottish Art*, 1939 (114)

LITERATURE
Andrew, p.142; Armstrong, p.109; Pinnington, p.243; McKay, p.58; Greig, p.54; Irwin and Irwin, p.158; Mackie, no.551

Although the portrait has been designed to hang high, the sitter's head is in no way remote but seeks engagement with the viewer, lips parted in a slight smile. The elongation of the figure is in some respects deceptive, the head being about one seventh of the length of the body, only fractionally less than the norm. Within a setting that is generally rather dark, Raeburn's prime expressive consideration seems to have been the explicit outline of the woman, from the loose froth of white at her throat, down through the tight and curving contour of her left breast, the material of her dress becoming slacker again at her midriff, pushed forward slightly by her belly and descending in a long slope to her ankle which is bound by the criss-cross pink ribbons of her tiny shoe – the ribbons tensely interwoven with a precision that recalls the skate lacings in the far earlier portrait of the *Revd Robert Walker* (cat.no.19). Pinned to her dress at a number of points beneath her breasts is a gold chain, attached to which is what appears to be a heart-shaped watch-key, a not uncommon adornment of the time. Its shape is conceivably a reference to her recent marriage.

Her right hip is thrust forward by the posture she has adopted and over-hung by her wrist and hand, which gathers the reddish strings of a softly folded, deep-crown hat that hangs at the end of them, its inner lining a concoction of blacks, browns and greys. In contrast to this free abstraction are the remarkably precise cast shadows of the hat strings, and particularly their acorn-like ends, thrown by an oblique light on to the dress. As a counter-balance some of the sitter's weight is thrown on to the plinth (of the same type as those in the portraits of *Lady Raeburn* (cat.no.21) and *Mrs Hamilton of Kames* (cat.no.45)) where her left elbow rests, her left hand, itself simply shaped, gathering the schematised folds of the red Kashmir shawl that she has thrown across it.

Lady Montgomery stands on the raised base of this plinth, its border fringed with russet and green foliage. The area of this base is quickly merged into a middle ground where a sheet of water stretches into the distance, its whitish surface streaked with the reflections of the dull green hills beyond. Above, towers an expanse of sky, fictive source of the light that illuminates her seductive figure. This landscape, which is probably an attempt to suggest a specific place, and the area of sky, take up virtually the entire right half of the picture.

Helen Graham married Sir James Montgomery (1766–1839), as his second wife, in 1816. She was the younger daughter of Thomas Graham, MP for Kinross. Sir James, Lord Advocate from 1804 to 1806 and MP for the county of Peebles from 1800 to 1831, erected Stobo Castle in the years 1805–11 and the landscape in the background of the portrait is probably a reference to this. The steep-sided valley in the distance is not unlike the course of the Weston Burn which runs east towards the castle, where it enters the River Tweed. The portrait is likely to have been painted between the date of the marriage and the end of the decade. The simplification of areas like the left hand, the shawl that falls down the front of the plinth and the bare hills, has something in common with the schematic clarity of the full-length portrait of *John, 2nd Marquess of Bute* (cat.no.60), which was exhibited at the Royal Academy in 1821. The portrait of Bute has a somewhat similar landscape, based on a drawing supplied to the artist.

59 *Margaret Haig, Mrs John Jameson 1753 – 1815*

Oil on canvas 34 × 26½in (86.3 × 67.3cm)

Irish Distillers Group plc

PROVENANCE
John Jameson; William George Jameson; John Jameson and Son Ltd

EXHIBITIONS
Dublin, 1957; Edinburgh, Talbot Rice Art Centre, and London, Tate Gallery, *Painting in Scotland, the Golden Age*, 1986–7 (112)

LITERATURE
Armstrong, p.105; Pinnington, p.236; Greig, p.50; Macmillan, 1986, pp.134, 196; Mackie, no.428

This portrait, which the costume suggests was painted about 1818–20, is quite devoid of the rather over-wrought mannerism which crept into many of Raeburn's female portraits in the second decade of the nineteenth century. The faintly smiling subject has her gaze directed at an imagined situation, or even an object that has provoked the reaction which makes her face so lively. This response is very much *hers*, rather than something willed upon her (even inflicted, as it was in some cases) by the artist. This degree of honesty – this true sentiment – enlivens the whole fabric of the picture, where there is a strong sense of shapes in movement and angled into each other, from the coruscating highlights on the sleeves of the silk dress to the sharp, deep shadows around the arms and on the lower part of the dress. It is this sense of incompletion, of infinitely variable form, this sense of the surface being somewhere mysteriously between actuality and the fiction of art, that gives the portrait its near endless richness.

Mrs Jameson is dressed with a degree of elaboration that suggests a step in time away from purer Empire fashions. Beneath her high-waisted dress she wears a muslin chemise, the V-shaped edge of which is faintly visible in the sea of white on her breast. It surfaces again, briefly, at her left wrist. Tucked beneath the neck of the chemise is a translucent chemisette, the pink of the sitter's throat showing through its single layer, which ends in the double ruff below her chin. The bodice is as remarkable an area of tonal painting as any ever devised by Raeburn, its perfectly judged silvery greys, thin mid-tones and darks a seemingly spontaneous invention to convey the intricacies of an unusual material, perhaps cut ribbon, which seems to simulate free-floating flowers or foliage. Wound round her arms is an orange-red shawl which, although it implies a circular movement, is largely made up of rectilinear forms. This 'splintered' theme continues into the pinkish gloved hand, almost claw-like on the edge of the supporting table. Her other hand contrasts with this

by being gloveless (although she grasps it), and also strangely realistic – with a rare sight of a signet ring on the index finger.

The elaboration of the costume is crowned by the fancy muslin cap on her head, painted with a controlled insouciance of gesture across the greenish background colour. Beneath this are dark brown curls which frame a finely carved face, where the mole on the left cheek is, one assumes, unmodified by flattery. The dark, firm shadows around the eyes and beneath the nose are not unlike those in the late, unfinished portrait of *Sir John Maxwell* (cat.no.63).

Margaret Haig was the eldest daughter of John Haig of Gartlands and Margaret Stein of Kennetpans, both in Clackmannanshire. Her father was founder of a whisky distillery and in 1768, at the age of fifteen, she married John Jameson of Alloa who, in 1780, founded a distillery company in Ireland, subsequently John Jameson and Son. The sitter is believed to have died in 1815 but the portrait seems to be of a rather later date. There is no obvious explanation for this discrepancy.

60   *John Crichton Stuart, 2nd Marquess of Bute 1793—1848*

Oil on canvas 94 × 58¼in (238.8 × 148cm)
Inscribed (later) bottom left: RAEBURN.; and bottom right: JOHN 2ND MARQUIS OF BUTE

Private collection

PROVENANCE
By descent

EXHIBITIONS
London, Royal Academy, 1821 (7)

LITERATURE
Armstrong, p.97; Pinnington, p.221; Greig, p.40;
Dibdin, p.83; Sanderson, pp.139, 148; Irwin and
Irwin, p.163; Mackie, no.689

NOTES
1. Letters quoted are in the Mount Stuart
Archives.
2. Kenneth Garlick, *Sir Thomas Lawrence*,
Oxford, 1989, p.241 (no. 582).

fig.69 *Lord Mounstuart* by Thomas Lawrence
Private collection

This portrait was evidently under way by 22 April 1820 when Lady Bute, writing from Edinburgh, requested the factor at Mount Stuart, Archibald Moore, to send a sketch that would enable Raeburn to give some veracity to the setting: 'I begged Lord Bute to mention to you how much I wish to procure a view of Bute, to serve as a background for a picture which Raeburn is now painting of him … I should like to have the sea, and some appearance of the highland mountains of Arran, to mark the character of the country … it does not signify how rough a sketch you send me.'[1] On 26 May Moore, writing from Rothesay, reported: 'I enclose John Mackinlay's sketch taken at Dunagoyle which I hope will answer the purpose, it is very coarse, but gives the mountains of Arran very correctly – he has introduced Capt. McLeod's Cutter which happened to be passing at the moment …' Whatever the quality of the sketch, Raeburn was able to make sufficient use of it to produce effects which are remarkably like those pertaining on the island. Strictly speaking, only the foreground is the island of Bute – the tiny beach of Dunagoil (the current spelling), a wavelet breaking on its margin and strewn with kelp and shells. Dunagoil lies on the western side of the island, just over a mile from its southern tip and some distance from Mount Stuart which is situated on the eastern side. The sitter has presumably been placed astride this shore so that the dramatic view of Arran could be included, which is not visible from Mount Stuart. Sadly, Raeburn, or the sitter, must have concluded that Captain McLeod's cutter was too whimsical to include.

John Stuart was the son of John, Viscount Mountstuart and Elizabeth Penelope Crichton, heiress of the Earl of Dumfries. At the age of five months, on the death of his father in a riding accident, he was styled Lord Mountstuart; and, on the death of his mother's father in 1803, he inherited the earldom of Dumfries. Two years later he received a royal warrant to use the surname Crichton before that of Stuart.

In 1814 John Crichton Stuart succeeded his paternal grandfather, John Stuart, as the 2nd Marquess of Bute. This inheritance may well have played a significant part in the genesis of the present portrait. His grandfather (who had been created Baron Cardiff in the peerage of Great Britain in 1776) was styled Viscount Mountstuart (a courtesy rank) and as such he became a privy councillor and British envoy at Turin. Significantly, in the present context, during 1783, he held the post of ambassador in Madrid; he held this post once again in 1795 and 1796, by which time he had succeeded his father as Earl of Bute (1792) and been created the 1st Marquess of Bute (1796).

The first marquess's son, Lord Mountstuart (father of the present subject), had travelled in Spain before his untimely death in 1794 and had had himself painted in a wildly romantic full-length portrait by Sir Thomas Lawrence, which was exhibited at the Royal Academy in 1795 (fig.69).[2] Although briefly MP for Cardiff, his career was not particularly distinguished and George III is reported to have been repelled by the pretensions of Lawrence's portrait – that is, of its subject – when he viewed it at the Academy. In silver waistcoat, black Spanish hat and wrapped in a voluminous cloak, Mountstuart towers above a distant landscape of the Sierra de Guadarrama and the Palace of the Escorial. This setting must surely be a reference, not to his own Spanish visit, but to the role of his father as ambassador. And, some twenty-five years later, when Raeburn was commissioned to paint the present portrait of the second marquess, it seems highly likely that this precedent of romance and continuing status was very much in a number of minds, including those of the subject, Lady Bute and, of course, Raeburn. It is perhaps unlikely that Raeburn knew the actual portrait but he could have grasped its qualities through someone's vivid description or from a

sketch of the kind that provided a basis for his landscape.

Although the portrait is spectacularly romantic, it is actually painted in quite an understated way. The intense, brooding quality of the pale face is the result of a carefully calculated darkness around the eyes and one precisely placed dark stroke on the left side of the middle line of the lips. The brilliant vermilion lapels, or inner lining, of the tartan cloak are layed in with more concern for their geometry and the harmony of their relationship to the rich shadows they cast than with the manner of their painting. Equally eschewing bravura handling is the long dark shadow that describes the upper limit of the sitter's left forearm and hand that are wrapped unseen within the cloak; and a less pronounced shadow falls smoothly across the careful intricacies of the tartan on the underside of this same hidden arm. The subject's dark suit is largely unmodified, the only visual excitement provided by the heavy encrustation of the watch-key fob and the thin flickers of pale pigment that mark the horizontal creases of his trousers just below the knees and the heart-shaped upper edges of his boots. Even the highlights that shimmer on these boots are applied with a cool precision.

Geometry, indeed, helps to reinforce the impact of this portrait. While its pretensions may owe something to the portrait by Lawrence already referred to, its abstract, linear rigidity is completely different. The simplicities of construction mentioned above are encompassed within a trapeziform shape, made up by the rigid right arm, the steeply angled stick and the rather freer reversed image of these lines on the other side of the cloak. Within this trapezium falls the long parallelogram of the trunk and legs. It is perhaps slightly paradoxical that rigidities of this sort are such an integral part of an image so picturesquely romantic.

A mezzotint engraving of the portrait by William Ward was published in London in 1822.

61 *Spencer Compton, 2nd Marquess of Northampton 1790 – 1851*

Oil on canvas 50½ × 39½in (128 × 100.5cm)
Inscribed (later) lower left: Spencer,/2nd Marquis of Northampton,/ – by Raeburn. –

The Marquess of Northampton

PROVENANCE
By descent

EXHIBITIONS
London, Royal Academy, 1821 (325); London,
Tate Gallery, *The Swagger Portrait*, 1992–3 (48)

LITERATURE
Armstrong, pp.99, 109; Pinnington, p.223; Greig,
pp.42, 55; Dibdin, p.83; Mackie, no.21

NOTES
1. Haddo House, National Trust for Scotland.
2. London, Guildhall Art Gallery.
3. J. G. Lockhart, *The Life of Sir Walter Scott,
Bart.*, London, 1893, p.345.
4. *The Letters of Sir Walter Scott*, ed. H. J. C.
Grierson, vol.VI, London, 1834, p.306.

From the agitated column of Lord Compton's body emerges a head youthfully sensitive and romantically contemplative. The fire of the romantic spirit is expressed almost wholly in the red lining of the cloak in which the sitter enfolds himself. The form of this red lining is, perhaps deliberately and for expressive reasons, never fully defined – nor are the lower reaches of the brown cloak itself, where, towards the bottom of the picture, it is swallowed in enveloping shadow. The one area where it is defined is in Compton's left arm, wrapped entirely within the cloak, which turns across his breast and fixes itself under the right arm, where the more humdrum black coat of everyday use emerges. Here the upper outline of the left arm is drawn with a sharp assurance that implies the bent wrist and the plunging hand beneath. The isolation – the singularity – of Compton's figure, and again this seems deliberate, is emphasised by the starkly plain background, broken by two vague uprights of cast shadow.

Lord Compton (he did not succeed to the marquessate of Northampton until 1828) and his wife Margaret Maclean Clephane (see cat.no.55) were much in the company of Walter Scott, both in London and Scotland, and the portrait's romanticism may owe something to the latter's involvement, although the circumstances of its genesis, as well as those of its 'companion', are not known. It was exhibited at the Royal Academy in 1821 and can be assumed, therefore, to have been painted about 1820, when the sitter was thirty years of age. In the last decade of Raeburn's career, when he became a full Academician and exhibited regularly there, but felt frustrated by his inability to see his pictures hung alongside those of his English rivals, a highly strung mannerism infused many of his works, mostly, it seems, due to the influence of Sir Thomas Lawrence. It is never specific, and never entirely pervasive, for despite what the 'swagger' of the present portrait may owe to Lawrence, the head, for example, is painted with a simplicity of planes which owes nothing to the English painter.

How Lawrence's influence reached Raeburn remains unclear. Had he seen, for example, Lawrence's portrait of the youthful Lord Aberdeen, which was shown at the Academy in 1808 (and Raeburn was certainly in London in 1810)? Its concentrated, 'Byronic' essence, the figure darkly cloaked against a red background, could easily have provided a precedent for Raeburn's portrait.[1] Perhaps even closer is the towering figure of *John Philip Kemble as Coriolanus*, the cloaked body in similar torsion, the arms linked in the same way, although a hand escapes from the folds. This portrait – or 'half-history picture', to use Lawrence's term – made a great impact when it was exhibited at the Royal Academy in 1798[2] and may by some means have helped to generate the idea that is embodied in Raeburn's portrait. It is also interesting to note that Scott, writing to the sitter's mother-in-law, Mrs Maclean Clephane, on 23 March 1817, records his reaction to Kemble's farewell performance in Edinburgh (an event for which he had composed some lines): 'He played Coriolanus last night … fully as well as I ever saw him; and you know what a complete model he is of the Roman'.[3] Did this notion and Scott's view of 'the patrician pride of Coriolanus' somehow find their way into the conception of the portrait, which Raeburn may well have begun shortly after?

Lord Compton succeeded the assassinated Spencer Perceval as MP for Northampton in 1812 and served until 1820, when, mainly for economic reasons, he and his wife took up residence in Italy. Politically he was a marked independent, so much so that Lord Castlereagh accused him of 'turning his back on himself'. He favoured direct as opposed to indirect taxation, supported Wilberforce in his campaign to abolish slavery and worked with Sir James Mackintosh on criminal law reform. In 1815 he married Margaret Maclean Clephane, daughter of Major-General Douglas Maclean Clephane of

Spencer,
2ⁿᵈ Marquis of Northampton,
— by Raeburn —

Torloisk on Mull. On her death in Rome fifteen years later he returned to England. Keenly interested in literature, the fine arts and science, he was an early president of the Geological Society, presided at the meeting of the British Association in Bristol in 1836 and became president of the Royal Society in 1838. He wrote poetry and published the work of others, as well as printing a posthumous, though unpublished, edition of his wife's 'Byronic' poem *Irene* in 1833. Scott, while holding him in high regard, confessed to finding him a little tiresome, due to 'a sort of minuteness in his mode of reasoning … He is born to be a splitter of hairs in argument and a gatherer of pebbles in science'.[4] It is a view amusingly at odds with Raeburn's romantic image of the man.

62   *Major James Lee Harvey (fl. c.1780—1848)*

Oil on canvas 93¾ × 60¼in (238 × 153cm)

Musée du Louvre, Département des Peintures, Paris

PROVENANCE
James Widdrington Shand-Harvey;[7] Christie's, 1905; Agnew's, 1906; Camille Groult, about 1906; acquired by the Société des Amis du Louvre, 1995, and given in gift to the Louvre

EXHIBITIONS
Edinburgh, 32 York Place, *Portraits by the late Sir Henry Raeburn*, 1824 (24)[8]

LITERATURE
Armstrong, p.104; Pinnington, p.233; Greig, p.48; Mackie, no.371

NOTES
1. Olivier Meslay, 'Le Portrait du Major James Lee Harvey en Uniforme de Gordon Highlander par Sir Henry Raeburn 1756—1823', *Revue du Louvre*, 4, 1995, pp.16—17.
2. Sir Bernard Burke, *Landed Gentry*, London, 1863, p.661. Burke calls the Hamilton property in Donegal 'Ballymodonell': this should be Ballybodonnell (see above).
3. I am grateful to A. V. B. Norman, formerly Master of the Royal Armouries, for help with the nomenclature of the uniform.
4. Her Majesty The Queen. See Michael Levey, *Sir Thomas Lawrence 1769—1830*, exhibition catalogue, National Portrait Gallery, London, 1979—80, no.37.
5. Formerly in the Metropolitan Museum of Art, New York; with Colnaghi's, London, in the 1980s.
6. Baring Brothers & Company Ltd. See Michael Levey, *Sir Thomas Lawrence 1769—1830*, exhibition catalogue, National Portrait Gallery, London, no.39.
7. He was the eldest son of Sir Charles Farquhar Shand and Margaret Lee Harvey, the sitter's second daughter. His wife may well have been a kinswoman, as the father of Thomas Lee (see above), William Lee of Dublin, married an Elizabeth Widdrington.
8. Number 24 was initially a portrait of 'S. H. Stewart, Esq. of Physgill, with a Horse'. However, the catalogue adds: 'This Portrait will be replaced in two or three weeks, by that of Major Harvey of Castle-Semple.'

James Lee (the subject's original name) was the eldest son of Thomas Lee (of a Dublin family) by his second wife, Catherine Hamilton from Ballybodonnell in County Donegal. His date of birth is not known but is likely to have been about 1780; his subsequent military career, in the 92nd (Gordon Highlanders) Regiment of Foot, took him to Egypt in 1801; he later served at Fuentes de Oñoro (1811), Victoria and Nive (1813), and Orthez and Toulouse (1814).[1] In 1814 he retired from active service on half-pay and in 1830 he was given the rank of lieutenant-colonel.

In 1816 he married Margaret Harvey, daughter and heiress of John Harvey of Castlesemple in the parish of Lochwinnoch in Renfrewshire in Scotland. John Harvey, who had bought the estate of Castlesemple in 1813, also owned property in Grenada. When he died in 1820 his son-in-law took his surname. The portrait must date from about this time and may in some degree celebrate James Lee Harvey's new status. If so, it is possible that the landscape background, which has no war-like connotation, was intended as some kind of representation of the picturesque land around Castlesemple, the river winding past on the left a suggestion of the Black Cart Water which flows from the north-east end of Lochwinnoch, where Castlesemple stands.

Lee Harvey also owned the property of Mouswald in Dumfriesshire and what are described as the 'Upper and Lower Conference Estates' on the island of Grenada.[2] He and Margaret Harvey had three sons and two daughters, their second son James Octavius being in possession of Castlesemple in the 1880s.

The portrait is painted from a particularly low viewpoint, the sitter's feet probably placed some three feet above floor level, the centre of his face being therefore as much as eight and a half feet from the floor so that his gaze is directed well above the head of the artist. Such an elevation would seem necessary for the actual foreshortening of the torso and head, and to account for the areas of flesh

visible under the eyebrows and the tip of the nose and for the consequent length of shadow at these points. This would suggest, of course, that the portrait, like the early portrait of *William Forbes of Callendar* (cat.no.31), was destined to be hung very high at its ultimate location.

The subject wears a closed double-breasted jacket faced with yellow, with silver lace on the collar and cuffs, enriched with a black line. The silver buttons on the coat are in pairs and he has a pair of silver epaulettes. Crossing his jacket diagonally is a sash, of a marginally more crimson colour, under which hangs the ribbon and gold medal of the Order of the Crescent of the Ottoman Empire. Over his left shoulder, under the epaulette and round his waist, is a plaid of Gordon regimental tartan. In his left hand he holds a feathered bonnet with a white, red and dark green chequered band and a plume of red and white hackle. In his right hand (like the left, gloved in white kid) he holds a stirrup-hilted sabre, its knuckle-guard wrapped round with a gold and crimson sword-knot. The steel-mounted scabbard hangs on slings at his left side. He wears white leather breeches, black Hessian boots with black tassels and steel spurs with chain links.[3]

Although the surface of the portrait is handled with all the verve that one has come to expect of Raeburn at his most direct in terms of observation and response to appearances — witness the agitated froth of white, black and yellow at Harvey's throat, the delicious details of silver buttons and gold medal on his tunic, or, most remarkable of all, the highlight running along the blunt edge of the sword and the perfectly pitched red of the reflection of his sleeve on to the blade — the painting has a surprisingly high degree of finish. It has less of the 'natural abstraction' noted in some of his other portraits, such as the *William Hunt of Pittencrieff* for example (cat.no.39): the only area not wholly defined in terms of natural appearances is Harvey's vertical shadow and whatever it is that it is cast on

– neither wholly rock nor tree-trunk. This relative clarity of appearances, this kind of realism which the commission may have demanded, seems to owe a good deal to Lawrence who must have been much in Raeburn's mind in his final years. The most obvious parallel to what Raeburn was attempting here is Lawrence's full-length of *The Archduke Charles of Austria* which he began in Vienna in 1819 and which remained in his studio at his death in 1830 (fig.70);[4] however, Lawrence's source seems to have been Valentine Green's engraving of 1781 of Trumbull's portrait of George Washington and this may well have also provided Raeburn with a starting point. Raeburn's awareness of Lawrence, by some means, in this particular context, is reinforced by the Lawrentian echoes in his 'companion' portrait of Mrs Lee Harvey and her daughter (fig.71):[5] Lawrence's portrait, *Mrs Henry Baring with two of her children*,[6] which was exhibited at the Royal Academy in 1821 (but begun a number of years earlier), might easily be construed as some kind of prototype.

fig.70 *The Archduke Charles of Austria* by Thomas Lawrence
The Royal Collection © Her Majesty The Queen

fig.71 *Margaret Lee Harvey with her Child* by Henry Raeburn
Private collection

63 *Sir John Maxwell of Pollok 1791–1865*

Oil on canvas 29⅞ × 25in (75.9 × 63.5cm)

Private collection

PROVENANCE

By descent in the Raeburn family; purchased by
Sir William Stirling-Maxwell, 1877; thereafter by
descent

EXHIBITIONS

Glasgow, 1911 (227); Edinburgh, National
Gallery of Scotland, 1922; Edinburgh, National
Trust for Scotland, *Raeburns and Eighteenth-
Century Silver*, 1951 (46); Edinburgh, National
Gallery of Scotland, *Raeburn*, 1956 (33)

LITERATURE

Brown, p.9; Armstrong, p.108; Pinnington, p.241;
Greig, p.53; Mackie, no.525

NOTES

1. Sir James L. Caw, *Catalogue of Pictures at
Pollok House*, Glasgow, 1936, p.96.
2. National Library of Scotland, MS 3553, fol.12.

Although there is no record of when this portrait was begun, it is likely to have been close to the end of the artist's life. The subject's mother, Hannah Anne Gardiner, Lady Maxwell, writing to her niece, Hannah Stirling, remarks: 'My son was begun by him [Raeburn]; indeed the head was nearly finished when that eminent artist was removed from this world.'[1] According to the paper label glued to the front of the canvas at the bottom left corner, the picture was 'Painted by Sir Henry Raeburn in 1822'. This label, which the passing of time has fortified as an integral part of a work that has become an icon of the ending of the painter's career, his powers still undimmed, is signed by the pioneer historian of Spanish painting, Sir William Stirling-Maxwell, and was probably attached by him when he bought the painting from Raeburn's descendants in 1877. Stirling-Maxwell was the nephew of the sitter.

The painting bears evidence of having been stacked against others, still wet, in the artist's studio: two vertical lines of thick varnish on the sitter's throat and smudges of the same substance to the left of the neck. These are tiny incidents on the painting's surface that send an enduring signal, however weak, of the daily practices in Raeburn's rooms in York Place. A similar charge is borne by the head, which has been taken well towards completion, and by its smoky, umber 'anti-halo' – an area of potency implying what is still to come, but which was never realised. This thin umber has, in fact, been used as the laying-in colour throughout the canvas, the nearest Raeburn came to drawing. By the mere chance of time, which caused Raeburn to set the painting aside, we have become, in a curious way, party to the act of his creative process.

The process which can be discerned elsewhere, but never more clearly than in this painting, is one of quite crude, almost peremptory beginnings which are then modified and refined. The thick, twisted highlight of the forehead, where there are already hints of the shadows cast by the strands of Maxwell's hair, probably lacks a final glaze which would have reduced its rawness. This highlight continues down the ridge of the nose to the quite large blob of white on the tip (which may also have been ultimately reduced in brilliance), and gleams briefly, and horizontally, on the lower lip. On the left side of the sitter's face, three zones of the thickish pink of that area, descending in virtual steps towards the dark jawline, would no doubt have been modulated so as to be less distinctly separated.

In the area of the deeply shaded eyes, the lower rims of the upper eyelids are unduly thick (a characteristic of the late, Romantic works) and purplish brown in colour, something which would probably in due course also have been modified. The eyeballs themselves are already highly finished, their mirrored liquidity emphasised by the flecks of white carrying from the dark pupil into the greyish iris, especially in his left eye, and the prominence given to the lacrimal caruncles at their inner edges. Whatever remained to be completed here, it seems certain that the gaze would have remained directed, not at Raeburn himself, but at something beyond, a sense of

momentary concentration reinforced by the sitter's slightly parted lips.

This sense of time, of destiny even, may represent a tribute to Maxwell, and it may be that the portrait was intended for Raeburn's own collection as a memorial of his esteem for the man. Raeburn had been knighted in 1822 during George IV's visit to Edinburgh and Maxwell, a noted Whig, had played a major role in the honour being offered to the artist. Raeburn wrote to him on 1 September knowing that Maxwell had himself written to the home secretary, Robert Peel, but for a purpose the former would not reveal: 'I do believe that the honour which was confirmed upon me by his Majesty on the day of his departure is in a great measure owing either to you or to Lord Melville or perhaps to both …' It is redolent of a simpler time that Raeburn, as the arrangements for the conferral of his knighthood were being made, had found himself in Peel's company and failed to recognise him. He went on to Maxwell: 'Now my Dear Sir when you come to thank Mr Peel for his attention to your letter (if such was the subject of it and of which I have now no doubt) will you have the goodness to say that when I saw him I was not aware that I was talking to Mr Peel himself and therefore neglected to express as I otherwise would have done the great obligation I feel myself under to him and which I shall ever remember.'[2]

Maxwell represented Renfrewshire in parliament from 1818 to 1830, and Lanarkshire from 1833 to 1837. He was enlightened and generous and is particularly remembered for championing the cause of the distressed handloom weavers of the west of Scotland. He married Lady Matilda Bruce, daughter of the Earl of Elgin, in 1839. They failed to have a son and the baronetcy, to which he had succeeded in 1844, passed in 1865 to his sister's son, William Stirling of Keir, who took the surname Stirling-Maxwell.

64 *Sir Walter Scott 1771–1832*

Oil on canvas 30 × 25in (76.2 × 63.5cm)

Scottish National Portrait Gallery, Edinburgh

PROVENANCE

The artist's son Henry, thence by descent; studio sale, Christie's, 7 May 1877; Gladwell, to James Duncan of Benmore; Goupil; D. Croal Thomson; Baroness Burdett Coutts, by whom bequeathed to her husband; Knoedler; J. Horace Harding; Knoedler; purchased by the Scottish National Portrait Gallery, 1935

EXHIBITIONS

Edinburgh, 32 York Place, *Portraits by the late Sir Henry Raeburn* 1824 (1); Edinburgh, *Scott Centenary Exhibition*, 1871 (59); Edinburgh, Royal Scottish Academy, *Exhibition of the Works of Sir Henry Raeburn*, 1876 (27); London, New Gallery, *Guelph Exhibition*, 1891 (215); Edinburgh, *Scott Centenary Exhibition*, 1932 (30); London, Royal Academy, *Exhibition of Scottish Art*, 1939 (91)

LITERATURE

Harris, p.8; Mackie, no.640

Writing in his journal on 16 June 1826, about a gift of two engravings of the present portrait,[1] and looking back to a time only about three years distant, Scott refers to 'Sir Henry Raeburn's portrait of me which, poor fellow, was the last he ever painted and certainly not his worst'.[2] The 'poor fellow' is no doubt a sign of sympathy for a fellow toiler whose company he had been in shortly before his sudden death, from someone whose own health, as he was all too aware, was in fairly rapid decline. Nevertheless, he was driven, as Raeburn had been, to clear his debts, so that he might yet enjoy 'the young woods' which he saw burgeoning around Abbotsford in this lovely summer. To accomplish this there still remained only one way: '*I must work*'.[3]

'Not his worst' is faint praise for a portrait Scott was certainly pleased with. Conscious of his own achievement, but in no overbearing sense, Scott must have been aware that the portrait went a little beyond being a mere likeness and somehow summed up the great endeavour of his life – that it was in its sympathetic solemnity a kind of apotheosis. Making another entry in his journal in the winter of the same year, this time about the portrait of himself that Raeburn had painted for his publisher Constable in 1808 (cat.no.38), and which he was pleased to see now hanging in the Duke of Buccleuch's Dalkeith House, having been saved from 'the rest of the wreck' (the sale resulting from his bankruptcy), he remarks: 'I do not care much about these things yet it would have been annoying to have been knocked down to the last bidder even in effigy …'[4] It is a remark which, while denying one thing, unconsciously asserts the opposite – that he was indeed conscious of such things and aware that these images would follow him into a distant future and would become a vital component of his reputation.

It is clear from Scott's correspondence that a portrait had been planned for some time. From the fact that the portrait had not been commissioned by Scott himself, or by a third party, but that it was intended for Raeburn's own collection, there emerges at least a hint – and this is borne out by a remark made by the painter's son Henry – that the portrait was planned to be a definitive statement about Scott's fame. In a letter written on 17 July 1823 to Lord Montagu of Ditton Park, Windsor, brother of the late Duke of Buccleuch, in which he describes the circumstances of Raeburn's recent death, Scott says that he 'had agreed long since to sit to him on his own account …';[5] and in a letter of rather more than a week later to the younger Henry Raeburn he refers to 'an old promise [to his father] that I would sit for a picture for himself'.[6] The correspondence with Lord Montagu and Henry Raeburn, however, is not primarily about the present portrait but about one that had been commissioned at the same time, with Scott's agreement, for Lord Montagu himself and which was said to be 'in all respects … quite the same only the dress is different to show that both were originals'.[7] Evidently, at the time of Raeburn's death, the portrait from his own collection was complete while that intended for Lord Montagu was not, and Scott felt under some pressure to try and ensure that Montagu received the finished picture. This, the correspondence makes clear, he was unable to effect.

The excursion to Fife, which seems to have occasioned Raeburn's final illness, and which Scott describes to Lord Montagu, gave the painter a new familiarity with the writer's appearance. Scott quotes him as saying: '… now I am better acquainted with your face than ever I was (having been three or four days in company) I will finish Lord Montagu's picture & my own …' Scott continues: 'I went accordingly and sate to him for nearly three hours when he finished his own head in a most masterly manner and did a great deal to that designd to your Lordship [Lord Montagu] but chiefly to the drapery. I upbraided him in jest with having taken best care of himself & he allowd he had but agreed whenever the paint on your copy was dry I should have a finishing sitting. All this being the case I think your Lordship should have the finishd picture which is really considered as the best likeness which ever has been made of so indifferent an original ...'[8]

The 'finishing sitting' for Lord Montagu's picture did not, of course, take place. Beneath Scott's evident pleasure in the finished picture lay, it appears, a nagging worry that his friend Raeburn had been rather too single minded in pursuing his own interest. He therefore wrote – probably prompted by Lord Montagu – to the painter's son on 28 July to enquire if there was any possibility that the finished picture could be transferred to Montagu's ownership. He repeated, more or less, the sequence of events he had given Montagu: 'After we returnd from Fife I had one long sitting which I meant indeed chiefly for Lord Montagus picture as I wishd it to be finishd against he come down but your father said in his goodnatured way that he would look after his own interest first and finishd accordingly the head which he meant to keep for himself and only touchd the drapery of that intended for Lord Montagu which is therefore left in an unfinishd state.'[9]

Unfortunately, from Scott's point of view, Henry Raeburn was adamant: although he knew it was difficult to say which of the heads was the best (which tends to imply that someone had subsequently completed the 'Montagu' version) he could not contemplate parting with his picture because his 'Father, from the time he first laid a Brush on it, called that particular one his own. ... I shall ever value it, as being one of my beloved & ever to be lamented Fathers last & greatest efforts, and on account of it being the absolute Portrait of the greatest man alive.'[10]

No doubt Scott smiled ruefully at the last part of the sentence, but probably also with a little pleasure. His use of the word 'masterly' when he had written to Lord Montagu earlier in July was certainly justified. The portrait is strikingly assured and sympathetic and, although it shows some of the mannerisms of Raeburn's latest style, it is painted with vigour and subtlety. The handling of the paint on the face has an almost contorted quality, the brushstrokes turned and twisted against themselves, with particularly heavy impasto on the forehead. On the other hand, the area of the hair is thinly painted, in effect rather wispish with some of the ground left visible. Perhaps the most 'masterly' area of the picture is the area of the deeply folded, pale yellow waistcoat with looped chain, with the lower edges of the standing white collar deftly defined by single strokes of the black cravat. As a performance, all of this shows Raeburn painting with an undimmed eye at the very end of his career.

The degree of mannerism is of course part of that quality of idealisation that is essential to the portrait, Scott's pale blue eyes turned upwards and towards the vision of his own star quality. Scott, in fact, was not a particularly prepossessing-looking man as his numerous portraits show: his oddest feature, attested by his death mask, was a preternaturally high dome on his forehead and this Raeburn has played down by elevating his sitter and slightly foreshortening the head. Another painter, C. R. Leslie, met Scott in London in 1820 and has left a verbal description of the man, which it is interesting to compare with Raeburn's image: 'His face is perfectly Scotch, and though some people think it heavy, it struck me as a very agreeable one. He never could have been handsome. His forehead is very high, his nose short, his upper lip long, and the lower part of his face rather fleshy. His complexion is fresh and clear, his eyes very blue, shrewd, and penetrating. I should say the predominant expression of his face is that of strong sense. His hair, which has always been very light (as well as his eyebrows and eyelashes) is now of a silvery whiteness, which makes him look somewhat older than he really is ...'[11]

NOTES

1. By William Walker: published 1826. The present portrait has pin-pricked holes at one-inch intervals round all four sides, which may mean that a grid of threads was fixed across its surface so that it could be redrawn on a reduced scale by the engraver or a copyist.
2. *The Journal of Sir Walter Scott*, ed. W. E. K. Anderson, Oxford, 1972, p.159.
3. *Ibid.*, p.159 (Sunday, 18 June 1826).
4. *Ibid.*, p.252 (Tuesday, 12 December 1826).
5. *Letters of Sir Walter Scott*, ed. H. J. C. Grierson, vol.VIII, London, 1935, p.45.
6. *Ibid.*, p.63 (28 July 1823).
7. *Ibid.*, p.46 (21 July 1823). The surveyor, topographical draughtsman and painter, John Morrison (1778–1853), writing much later, narrates the events surrounding the making of the two portraits, not greatly different but probably giving himself a much bigger role in the matter than he perhaps played (see John Morrison, 'Reminiscences of Sir Walter Scott,' *Tait's Edinburgh Magazine*, vol xi, 1844, pp.16–17).
8. *Ibid.*, pp.45–6 (21 July 1823).
9. *Ibid.*, p.63 (28 July 1823).
10. *Ibid.*, p.63, n. 1 (2 August 1823). The 'Montagu' version arose from a request by the 4th Duke of Buccleuch to Scott in a letter of 15 April 1819 to have his portrait done by Raeburn, as previously promised, for the new library at Bowhill. Scott demurred: 'I hesitate a little about Raeburn unless your Grace is quite determined. He has very much to do works now chiefly for cash poor fellow as he can have but a few years to make money and has twice done a very chowder headed person of me.' (*Letters of Sir Walter Scott*, ed. H. J. C. Grierson, vol.v, London, 1933, p.349). However, the Duke died on 20 April and the matter seemed to end – but only until May 1822 when Scott agreed to the commission being revived for the late Duke's brother, Lord Montagu (*Letters of Sir Walter Scott*, ed. H. J. C. Grierson, vol.VII, London, 1934, p.172). Montagu's portrait passed to his son-in-law Lord Home. It was sold in 1919 and had entered the collection of Sir Robert Usher of Wells by 1923. In general form it follows the Edinburgh painting closely, though as Scott remarked, the costume is different (or very possibly changed at some stage) – the green coat is virtually black, crosses the breast so that no chain is visible and has a fur collar. Although Scott referred to its requiring 'one long sitting to bring it to the same perfection' (as the one done for Raeburn's own collection), it is not known how its present completed form was reached. There is a suggestion in Scott's letter to Montagu of 4 August 1823 that John Syme who 'was used to finish the draping of Raeburn's portraits' might be asked to complete it. Syme is also mentioned in Scott's letter of the following day to Henry Raeburn junior, as having requested to be allowed to make a copy of the latter's portrait (*Letters of Sir Walter Scott*, ed. H. J. C. Grierson, vol.IX, London, 1935, pp.68–9). It is not known if Raeburn agreed. He did, however, agree to a copy being made by an artist called Watson (probably the future John Watson Gordon). This was under way in January 1825 and was for a cousin of Scott, Hugh Scott, who lived at Draycott, near Derby. Raeburn had stipulated that 'this copy should not be again copied' (*Letters of Sir Walter Scott*, ed. H. J. C. Grierson, vol.VII, London, 1935, p.493).
11. Charles Robert Leslie, *Autobiographical Recollections*, ed. Tom Taylor, 1860, vol.II, p.84.

65   *Sir Francis Legatt Chantrey 1781–1842*

Pencil drawing 8½ × 11⅝in (21.4 × 29.3cm)
Inscribed bottom right: F. Chantrey R.A./Sketched by H. Raeburn/in Princes St
Edinborough/1818 wc

Scottish National Portrait Gallery, Edinburgh

PROVENANCE
Wilkie Collins; C. Fairfax Murray; given by him
to the Scottish National Portrait Gallery, 1902

EXHIBITIONS
Sheffield, Graves Art Gallery, *Art Exhibition*
(Festival of Britain), 1951 (28); Edinburgh, Royal
Scottish Academy, *Light from the Dark Room*,
1995

LITERATURE
Armstrong, opp.p.110; Greig, p.57; Alison
Morrison-Low and Allen Simpson, 'A New
Dimension: a context for Photography before
1860', *Light from the Dark Room*, exhibition
catalogue, Edinburgh, 1995, p.25

NOTES
1. National Library of Scotland, Miscellaneous
artists' letters, MS9994: letter from Raeburn to
Chantrey, dated 26 January 1814. The portrait
was at Christie's, 12 April 1991 (22).
2. John H. Hammond and Jill Austin, *The Camera
Lucida in Art and Science*, Bristol, 1987, p.84.

This is the only known drawing by
Raeburn. Although the inscription does
not say so, it was clearly done with the aid
of a camera lucida, probably with no more
than a playful intent. It is something of a
curiosity, but perhaps a little more. On its
reverse is a drawing of Raeburn, done by
Chantrey, which is technically a more
accomplished affair (fig.72). It is similarly
inscribed, the two inscriptions apparently
being in the hand of the novelist, Wilkie
Collins. How the sheet came into his
possession is not known.

Chantrey and Raeburn had known each
other since at least 1814, when Raeburn
painted the sculptor's portrait, which did
not entirely satisfy him.[1] It is known that
Chantrey made considerable use of the
camera lucida, invented in 1806, in
planning his sculptures and Raeburn must
have been intrigued by its mechanics, if
not its usefulness. Chantrey was acquainted with the inventor of the instrument, William Hyde Wollaston, and
became adept in its use. Although the
small instrument was easily portable, the
reference to Princes Street in the inscription may mean that Chantrey demonstrated its properties to his friend on the
premises of an instrument maker.
Raeburn's lines are tentative and rather
straight, and he tried a number of times.
One of the major problems in the instrument's use was the difficulty of keeping the
eye in exactly the same place as the
outlines were drawn.

As an early commentator on the
camera lucida (the name seems to have
been chosen as the simple opposite of
camera obscura, which involved a dark
box) stated, the device had 'no means of
supplying taste … neither will it enable
people, who are totally ignorant of the use
of the pencil … to make good drawings'.
Thus, although Raeburn's difficulties with
it are evident, the lines he made have his
own peculiar liveliness.

fig.72   verso of cat.no.65 showing Chantrey's
drawing of Raeburn

F. Chantrey R.A.
Sketched by H. Raeburn
in Princes St. Edinborough
1818 W.C.

Thomas Campbell 1790–1858

66 *Sir Henry Raeburn 1756–1823*

Marble bust, height 25⅜in (64.4cm)
Carved signature and date at the back: THO.ˢ CAMPBELL ROMA. 1822.

Scottish National Portrait Gallery, Edinburgh

PROVENANCE
William Raeburn Andrew, the sitter's great-
grandson; Charlotte Raeburn, 1886; Henry J.
Brown, The Raeburn Gallery, London; purchased
from him by the Scottish National Portrait
Gallery, 1926

EXHIBITIONS
Edinburgh, National Gallery of Scotland, 1886

LITERATURE
Greig, p.57; Rupert Gunnis, *Dictionary of British
Sculptors 1660–1851*, London, 1953, pp.76–7
(bust wrongly dated 1827); Robin Lee Woodward,
'Nineteenth Century Scottish Sculpture', unpublished Ph.D. thesis, University of Edinburgh,
1977, vol.3, pp.41–5

NOTES
1. Royal Academy of Arts, Library, Law. 2.288.
2. Scottish Record Office, Letterbook of the
Board of Trustees, NG1/3/23. Campbell's address
in Rome was 12 Piazza Mignanelli.

Although this portrait bust was not made directly from life, Campbell is likely to have been quite familiar with Raeburn's appearance. Campbell, from Edinburgh, studied at the Royal Academy Schools in London from 1815. With the aid of financial assistance from his first patron, Gilbert Innes of Stow, he was enabled to travel to Rome in 1818 where he established a highly successful studio. On 18 June, prior to his departure from Edinburgh, Raeburn gave him a letter of introduction to Sir Thomas Lawrence.[1] Whether or not a meeting took place is unknown, but it is highly probable.

Campbell is quite likely, therefore, to have felt under an obligation to Raeburn and the bust may have been the result. Apart from what he remembered of Raeburn's appearance, two sources could have been available to him: the *Self-portrait* (cat.no.56) which was exhibited at the Royal Academy in 1816, and which he must have seen, and an etched copy of it of 1818, by William Nicholson (fig.73). Neither, however, is particularly close to the finished marble. It is not impossible that Campbell took some sort of modello of his famous countryman with him when he set off for Rome.

If the bust was not done to repay Campbell's debt to Raeburn for introducing him to Lawrence, it is possible that Raeburn encouraged the sculptor to produce it as a means of furthering his career – it is Campbell's earliest recorded portrait, done the year before a bronze bust of his next major patron, the Duke of Devonshire. A further possibility is that it was commissioned by the trustees of the Board of Manufactures, because of Raeburn's fame (he had been knighted in the summer of 1822), although it eventually became the property of Raeburn's descendants. A letter from the secretary of the Board of 16 February 1824 to Campbell in Rome shows that the bust must have reached Edinburgh before Raeburn's death in July 1823, as it records his reaction to it: 'I was much gratified by seeing the Bust you did in

marble of our renowned townsman Sir Henry Raeburn, now unhappily no more. It does you great credit, and Sir Henry himself was much pleased with it.'[2]

fig.73   Etching by William Nicholson after *Self-portrait* by Henry Raeburn (cat.no.56)

Documentation

DAVID MACKIE

The following abbreviations are used:

SRO   *Scottish Record Office*

NLS   *National Library of Scotland*

SNPG *Scottish National Portrait Gallery*

1743

Ann, daughter of Revd John Hay, minister of Peebles, marries Peter Edgar of Bridgelands

Hew Scott, *Fasti Ecclesiae Scoticanae, the Succession of Ministers in the Parish Churches of Scotland, from 1560 to the Present Time*, Edinburgh, 1915–28, vol.1, p.287

1744

3 September
Birth of Ann Edgar, future Lady Raeburn (d.1832).

10 September
Ann Edgar baptised at Cramond Parish Church. Her father, Peter Edgar of Bridgelands, described as factor to Earl of Selkirk.

Grampian Club, *Genealogical Collections Concerning the Scottish House of Edgar*, London, 1873, p.33

1746

6 February
Robert Raeburn, Raeburn's father, arrested for participation in 1745 Rising.

NLS, MS17515, fol.49

1748

12 February
George II grants in liferent to Peter Edgar 'lately factor to the Countess of Ruglen' lands of Bridgelands.

Grampian Club, *Genealogical Collections Concerning the Scottish House of Edgar*, London, 1873, p.57

1752

15 April
Robert Raeburn in legal difficulties over bill for £7 12s 6d.

SRO, RD4.178, fol.430

Between late 1752 and early 1753 Robert Raeburn builds house in Stockbridge, also used as boiling-house. See 12 June 1760.

1753

22 March
Marriage contract drawn up between George Leslie, Ann Edgar's father-in-law, and his first wife, Elizabeth Bowles. Binds himself to lay out £8,000. Registered 9 September 1772.

In late 1753 or early 1754 Robert Raeburn builds extension to house in Stockbridge. See 12 June 1760.

1754

5 April
Governors of Heriot's Hospital grant feu charter to Robert Raeburn.

SRO, RD5.434, fols.353–64

September
Robert Raeburn begins four years as treasurer of Incorporation of Weavers of Easter and Wester Portsburgh. See 12 June 1760.

6 November
Robert Raeburn in legal difficulties over bill for £2 15s.

SRO, RD2.176

1755

Robert builds 114-feet boiling-house on land in Stockbridge. See 12 June 1760.

1756

4 March
Birth of Raeburn.

General Register Office (Scotland), St Cuthbert's British Register, OPR 685.5

7 March
Raeburn baptised at St Cuthbert's Parish Church, Edinburgh. Father described as yarn-boiler.

Ibid.

1757

21 April
Robert Raeburn acquires land in Stockbridge from Governors of Heriot's Hospital.

SRO, RD4.183.1

In 1757 Robert Raeburn builds additional house on land in Stockbridge. See 12 June 1760.

1758

5 June
Charter granted by Governors of Heriot's Hospital to Robert Raeburn concerning property in Barony of Broughton.

SRO, RD5.434, fols.353–64

September
Robert Raeburn made deacon of Incorporation of Weavers of Easter and Wester Portsburgh. See 12 June 1760.

1759

10 April
Robert Raeburn involved in litigation over bill for £13 10s.

SRO, RD4.186

In 1759 Robert Raeburn made Convener of all Incorporated Trades at Portsburgh. See 12 June 1760.

1760

12 June
Summary of legal case against Robert Raeburn, accused of owing £46 7s 3½d plus £15 10s interest to Alexander Newlands by 25 July 1757 and of fraudulently attaching Newland's signature to relevant bills in attempt to clear debts. Testimony of character witnesses given. Christian Crawfurd states that she worked as washerwoman for Robert Raeburn for nine or ten years. Newland's lawyers deem reference unacceptable due to rumours that she had several illegitimate children by Robert Raeburn. Crawfurd acknowledges rumours but denies that Robert Raeburn is father of her children.

Records state that Robert Raeburn acted as agent for David Doig, Deacon of Weavers of Edinburgh. Robert Raeburn found guilty on 18 January 1760 and briefly imprisoned.

State of the Process, Alexander Newlands, Merchant in Edinburgh, Charger; Against Robert Raeburn, Weaver in Edinburgh, Suspender, Edinburgh, 12 June 1760. See also SRO, CS21, box 813. February–March 1761

1765

15 April
Raeburn, now orphaned, enters George Heriot's Hospital 'upon Sandilands presentation'.

Heriot's Muniments, *Register of the Boys Educated in George Heriot's Hospital*, fol.63

1771

21 October
Arrangement between George Heriot's Hospital and Raeburn's future master recorded.

Ibid.

1772

2 January
Disposition registered between James Leslie, first husband of Ann Edgar, and his father, George Leslie.

SRO, RD4.211, fols.12–19

27 June
Abstract of Raeburn's indenture to James Gilliland, goldsmith, recorded.

SRO, *Goldsmiths of Edinburgh Apprentice Book, 1694–1786*, GD1.482.13

9 September
Marriage contract registered between George Leslie and his first wife, Elizabeth Bowles, mother of James Leslie.

SRO, RD4.212.1, fols.938–41

16 September
Marriage contract drawn up between Ann Edgar and her first husband, James Leslie. Registered 27 January 1778.

SRO, RD2.223, fol.184

27 October
Two contracts registered between George Leslie and his son, James.

SRO, RD2.212, fols.659–67

1777

17 September
James Leslie purchases Deanhaugh House from James McDowall of Canonmills.

SRO, RS27.822, fol.126r

1778

6 February
Will drawn up by George Leslie. Registered 4 July 1780.

SRO, CC8.8.125.1, fols.229v–243r

15 May
Death of Charles Darwin (b.3 September 1758), medical student at University of Edinburgh. In Gilliland's workshop Raeburn makes memorial trinket to commemorate Darwin's life for Andrew Duncan, sitter to Raeburn (Royal College of Physicians, Edinburgh).

Andrew Duncan, *Tribute of Regard to the Memory of Sir Henry Raeburn*, Edinburgh, 1824, pp.10–12

1779

23 December
Death of George Leslie. See 4 July 1780.

1780

4 July
George Leslie's will registered. He makes provision for his second wife, his daughter and his daughter-in-law Ann Leslie. £1500 pounds to be divided between grandchildren by Ann Leslie, including any child born after James Leslie's death. Property listed in both Edinburgh and Paris.

SRO, CC8.8.125.1, fols.229v–243r

1781

9 January
Death of Peter Edgar of Bridgelands (b.1706/7), father of Ann.

The Scots Magazine, 1781, vol.43, p.54

18 May
Birth of Peter Raeburn, Raeburn's first son (d.1798). See 25 May 1780.

25 May
Peter Raeburn baptised at Cuthbert's Parish Church, Edinburgh.

Grampian Club, *Genealogical Collections Concerning the Scottish House of Edgar*, London, 1873, p.32

In 1781 Raeburn formed a private drawing class with a number of other young artists, borrowing casts and taking some instruction from Alexander Runciman.

William Dunlap, *History of the Rise and Progress of the Arts of Design in the U.S.A.*, 2 vols., New York, 1834.

1783

24 October
Birth of Henry Raeburn Jr (d.1863), Raeburn's younger son.

10 November
Henry Raeburn Jr baptised at St Cuthbert's Parish Church, Edinburgh.

Grampian Club, *Genealogical Collections Concerning the Scottish House of Edgar*, London, 1873, p.32

1784

14 May
Raeburn registers factory giving control of his affairs to his wife when he is abroad. Gives her power to 'uplift and receive' £60 annually from her late father-in-law's estate.

SRO, RD4.235, fols.725–6

9 July
Sir James Hunter Blair receives letter from Raeburn's neighbour, Walter Ross, requesting letter of credit for Raeburn in Rome.

Private Muniments, Scotland

1785

7 July
Deed recorded concerning purchase of Deanhaugh House by James Leslie in 1777.

SRO, RS27.822, fol.126r

December
Lost letter from Gavin Hamilton (1723–98) stating that 'young Raeburn would soon be leaving Italy' and 'he might stay a while in Paris'.

Paul Mellon Centre for Studies in British Art, London, Ford Archive

1786

26 January
James Byres sends to George John Spencer, 2nd Earl Spencer, miniature by Raeburn after his portrait (cat.no.4).

Althorp Muniments

29 March
Letter from Colin Morrison, painter and sculptor (1732–1810), in Rome to unidentified correspondent in Scotland saying, 'Mr Ryburn (*sic*), an ingenious artist and who has passed some time here, does me the favour of bringing these few lines' (suggests Raeburn's imminent departure).

NLS, MS14835, fol.67

14 June
Letter from James Byres to Lord Spencer to confirm safe arrival in Paris of miniature (cat.no.4).

Althorp Muniments

1788

September
Portrait of George Hill (1750–1819) (location unknown) sent out from Raeburn's studio.

Quotation from lost letter, National Gallery of Scotland, Library, Raeburn Sitters' File

2 October
Raeburn receives 16 guineas for *Sir William Forbes of Craigievar (1755–1816)* and *Lady Forbes (d.1799)* (National Trust for Scotland, Craigievar).

National Trust for Scotland, Craigievar Muniments

In 1788 Raeburn established in first studio, '18 George Street, south side'.

Edinburgh Directory, 1788

1789

6 March
William Raeburn, Raeburn's brother, draws up feu contract with Walter Ross and spouse, Margaret Moubray.

SRO, RD5.434, fol.355

William Raeburn and Raeburn signatories to feu contract for site of St Bernard's Well.

Dibdin, p.117

1790

20 April
James Liddle, framemaker, Edinburgh, paid £6 6s by John Anderson for two frames 'for paintings by Mr Raeburn'.

Perth Art Gallery and Museum, Perth, Scotland, curatorial files

June
Sittings begin for *Robert Colt of Auldhame (1756–97) and his Wife, Lady Grace* (Carnegie Museum of Art, Pittsburgh).

7 July
Sittings begin for *David Anderson of St Germains (1750–1825)* (National Gallery of Art, Washington DC). Portrait a gift for Warren Hastings (1732–1818).

British Library, ADD MS455.418, fol.375

Raeburn paid 60 guineas for *Sir John and Lady Clerk of Penicuik* (cat.no.13).

Caw, 1908, p.77

1791

4 March
Raeburn leases land to Mathew Craw, goldsmith in Edinburgh. See 12 October 1807.

SRO, RD2.302, fols.63–70

23 April
Council of Royal Company of Archers decides to commission portraits of Sir James Pringle and Dr Nathaniel Spens (cat.no.17) from David Martin and Raeburn.

National Register of Archives, Scotland, no.0180, Scroll Book of the Royal Company of Archers

9 September
Raeburn intimates to Sheriff Clerk of Mid-lothian intention to enclose land in parish of St Cuthbert's.

30 November
Raeburn paid 15 guineas for portrait of Mrs Bruce (location unknown). See 24 April 1792.
SRO, GD152.216.11

In 1791 Raeburn elected member of Royal Company of Archers.
Ian Hay, *The Royal Company of Archers, 1676–1951*, Edinburgh, 1951, p.284

1792

31 March
Dr William Robertson (1721–93) commissioned (cat.no.22).

24 April
Note from Raeburn concerning *Mrs Bruce* (location unknown) to sitter's daughter, saying portrait has been dispatched and if frame required, Mr Liddle, framemaker, will call.
SRO, GD152.104.21.1

Review by Caleb Whiteford of *Sir John and Lady Clerk of Penicuik* (cat.no.13).
Morning Chronicle

19 September
Raeburn successfully petitions to become member of Cape Club.
NLS, MS2041, fol.433

Raeburn erects monument on east wall of St Cuthbert's Churchyard, Edinburgh.
W. P. Anderson, *Silences That Speak*, Edinburgh, 1931, pp.65–6

1793

18 May
Letter from Raeburn to Kenneth Murchison, discussing completion and dispatch of portrait of Murchison's wife (location unknown) and alterations undertaken to unidentified painting by Batoni.
Greig, p.xxxiv

May
Raeburn paid by Honourable Company of Edinburgh Golfers for *James Balfour* (location unknown).
Company Muniments

1794

10 January
Raeburn receives 40 guineas in connection with portraits of *Eleanor Urquhart of Craigston* (National Gallery of Art, Washington DC), *Mr Urquhart of Craigston* and *Mrs Urquhart of Craigston* (both private collection, Scotland).
National Gallery of Art, Washington DC, curatorial file, transcript of receipt

10 June
Letter to Raeburn from Sir James Campbell of Inverneil discussing two versions of his and his wife's portraits and their dispatch (*Sir James Campbell of Inverneil (1737–1805)* and *Lady Lilias Campbell (d.1805)*, location unknown).
SNPG, Library

11 June
John Beugo (1759–1841), engraver, receives 'twelve pounds sterling in part payment of 150 guineas agreed upon by the Royal Company and me for engraving Mr Raeburn's picture of Dr Spens' (cat.no.17).
National Register of Archives, Scotland, no.0180, box K, no.360

22 August
Raeburn receives 30 guineas for *Professor John Bruce (1745–1826)* (Scottish National Portrait Gallery).
SRO, GD152.104.21, fol.2

19 November
Letter from Raeburn to Hugh Innes of Balmacara, patron, discussing completion of *Robert Cunninghame Graham of Gartmore (d.1797)* (Scottish National Portrait Gallery).
NLS, Acc.9499

1795

2 February
Raeburn receives 30 guineas for *Mrs Austin of Kilspindie (d.1793)* (Colby College, Waterville, Maine).
SNPG, Library, Greig Archive, transcript of receipt

3 March
Raeburn receives 18 guineas for portrait of Lord Advocate, *Robert Dundas of Arniston, Chief Baron (1758–1819)* (Mrs A. Dundas-Bekker, Arniston House, Gorebridge).
George W. Omond, *The Arniston Memoirs*, Edinburgh, 1887, p.50

26 December
Raeburn opens cash account at Bank of Scotland, running until 20 August 1802 (highest borrowing £617).
Bank of Scotland, Archives Department, Cash Account Progressive Ledgers BS 1.106.41, fol.158; 42, fol.235; 43, fol.276; 45, fol.46

In 1795 Raeburn gets cash credit bond with assignation of nine shares of old stock and proportion of new stock in security from Bank of Scotland.
Charles A. Malcolm, *The Bank of Scotland 1695–1945*, Edinburgh, 1945, p.227

1796

27 April
Letter from Raeburn to Alexander Nairn of Royal Company of Archers saying that £52 10s is outstanding from 4 October 1793 for *Dr Nathaniel Spens* (cat.no.17).
National Register of Archives, Scotland, no.0180, box N467

16 May
Letter from Charles, 8th Earl of Haddington, to Revd Alexander Carlyle reminding him of promise to sit for portrait to Raeburn. Painting intended for Earl's new library.
NLS, MS23764, fol.132

19 May–9 June
Sittings for *Revd Alexander Carlyle (1722–1805)* (Scottish National Portrait Gallery).
NLS, MS23781, fols.4–5

7 December
Board of Trustees' Academy reject proposal by Raeburn and Alexander Keith of Ravelston that candidates for post of drawing master undergo trials 'shut up in a room … to prevent their receiving any private assistance'.
SRO, NG1.1.29, fols.205–7

1797

26 May
Raeburn feus land to Elizabeth Wright, widow of James Cleland.
SRO, RD2.310, fols.738–55

Caw quotes lost letter from Raeburn of 1797 in which he suggests a price of 30 guineas for a portrait of a Mr David Anderson, saying 'he has no consideration for his present prices'.
Caw, 1908, p.97

George Watson's Hospital commissions *Baillie William Galloway (1716–1801)* (Company of Merchants of the City of Edinburgh).
SRO, Company of Merchants of the City of Edinburgh Records

1798

6 February
Death of Raeburn's eldest son, Peter (b.1781). Buried in St Cuthbert's Churchyard, Edinburgh.
W. P. Andrew, *Silences that Speak*, Edinburgh, 1931, pp.65–6

8 February
Masters and Assistant Masters of Trinity House, Leith, agree to commission portrait of Admiral Duncan 'if it would be agreeable to him' (*Admiral Viscount Adam Duncan of Camperdown (1731–1804)*, Trinity House, Leith).
SRO, GD226.1.8, fol.47

31 March
University of Edinburgh commissions *Thomas Elder of Forneth (1737–99)* (University of Edinburgh).
Brown, pp.97–9

5 April
Advert in *Edinburgh Evening Courant* proposes publication of line engraving by Paton after portrait of Admiral Duncan. Not carried out. See also 2 August 1798.
Edinburgh Evening Courant

19 May
Raeburn receives 60 guineas for *William Forbes of Callendar (1743–1815)* (cat.no.31).
SNPG, Library, Accession file (photocopy)

22 May
James Liddle, framemaker in Edinburgh, paid for frame of *William Forbes of Callendar*.
Ibid.

17 July
Raeburn begins action against John Bookless, accountant in Edinburgh. Final date on inventory of process 10 February 1809.
SRO, CS229.R.6.38

20 July
Letter from Robert Buchan to William Forbes of Callendar expressing Raeburn's views on hanging of Forbes's portrait (cat.no.31).
Private Muniments, Scotland

21 July
Announcement in *Edinburgh Evening Courant* that line engraving by Birrell after *Revd John Home* will shortly be published from version in collection of Professor Ferguson.
Edinburgh Evening Courant

2 August
Proposal of 5 April repeated in *Edinburgh Evening Courant*.
Edinburgh Evening Courant

15 August
Raeburn paid £73 10s for full-length portrait of Admiral Duncan.
SRO, GD226.4.9

31 August
James Liddle, framemaker, paid £18 8s for frame of portrait of Admiral Duncan.
SRO, GD226.4.9

5 September
Raeburn acquires land in Stockbridge. See 24 February 1808.

29 September

Raeburn receives 18 guineas for *Baillie William Galloway (1716–1801)* (Company of Merchants of the City of Edinburgh).

SRO, Company of Merchants of the City of Edinburgh Records

10 October

Raeburn receives 75 guineas from Admiral Elliot for *Agnes Murray Elliot, Lady Carnegie (1763–1860)* (Earl of Southesk).

Cathcart Muniments. See *Raeburn*, exhibition catalogue, Edinburgh, 1956, p.25

1799

24 April

Letter from Professor Alexander Monro (1733–1817), sitter (location unknown), in London to Professor Joseph Black (1728–99) concerning publication of engraving after 'the very strong likeness which Mr Raeburn some time ago painted of you' (University of Glasgow, and part replica, location unknown). Letter says engraver, J. Heath, will 'publish your portrait at his own risk'.

University of Edinburgh, Library, La 874.iv, fols.47–8

8 July

Death of John Edgar. Entire property left to his sister, Ann Edgar. See 8 February 1800.

4 December

Letter from John Brown of Lanfine to Raeburn concerning his own and late Mrs Brown's portraits (locations unknown). Raeburn paid £85 4s 7d.

NLS, MS2224, fol.5

10 December

Letter from John Brown of Lanfine to Raeburn requesting small picture of game.

NLS, MS2224, fol.6

23 December

Further letter from John Brown of Lanfine detailing required picture.

NLS, MS2224, fol.7

1800

8 January

Raeburn listed as principal creditor (over £5) in bankruptcy of James Wright, tailor, formerly of Frederick Street, Edinburgh, imprisoned for debts of £134 2s 11d.

SRO, CS25.774.25

8 February

Raeburn's wife inherits property of her brother, John Edgar (d.8 July 1799).

SRO, CC8.8.131.2

3 March

Letter from Raeburn in York Place, Edinburgh, to Harry Guthrie, concerning *Robert Colt of Auldhame (1756–97) and his Wife, Lady Grace* (Carnegie Museum of Art, Pittsburgh, Pennsylvania), saying that 'The pictures were begun in June 1790' and that Lady Grace's portrait was left unfinished. Raeburn suggests fee of 45 guineas plus interest, but declines interest.

Carnegie Museum of Art, Archive

28 March

Raeburn receives £30 in part payment for *Dr Nathaniel Spens* (cat.no.17). £22 10s still outstanding.

National Register of Archives, Scotland, no.0180, box N467, Raeburn to Alexander Nairn, 27 April 1796

30 June

William Macdonald of St Martins (1732–1814) retires as principal secretary of Royal Highland and Agricultural Society of Scotland. He is 'requested to sit for his picture to Mr Raeburn' (Royal Highland and Agricultural Society of Scotland, Edinburgh).

Alexander Ramsay, *History of the Agricultural Society of Scotland*, Edinburgh, 1879, pp.512–15

1801

20 April

Instrument of sasine concerning York Place.

SRO, RD27.482, fols.27v–35r

23 September

Joseph Farington (1747–1821) visits Edinburgh and calls at Raeburn's studio in York Place. In Raeburn's absence he is shown paintings by servant. Remarks on their 'great inequality'.

The Diary of Joseph Farington, ed. Kenneth Garlick and Angus Macintyre, vol.V, New Haven and London, 1979, p.1631

26 September

Letter from Raeburn to John Brown of Lanfine saying he has found suitable painting. See December 1799.

NLS, MS2224, fol.8

16 November

Raeburn receives 80 guineas from James Dundas for portrait copied after miniature by Engleheart of Lieut-Col. Charles Erskine of Cardross (1768–1801) (both private collection, Scotland).

Private Muniments, Scotland

21 November

John Brown of Lanfine pays Alexander Thomson, framemaker, 18s for frame and box for painting acquired for him by Raeburn.

NLS, MS2224, fol.9

25 November

Raeburn pays Lachlan McLean 2s 6d for cleaning and varnishing painting for John Brown of Lanfine.

NLS, MS2224, fol.10

1802

18 February

Raeburn paid £3 2s 6d for painting purchased for John Brown of Lanfine in September 1801.

NLS, MS2224, fol.11

February

Raeburn judges drawings for Trustees' Academy.

SRO, NG1.3.18

12 March

Sasine of Raeburn's studio in York Place recorded.

SRO, RS27.482, fols.27v–35r

7 July

Directors of Bank of Scotland request that Henry Dundas, 1st Viscount Melville, 'sit for his picture to some eminent artist either in Edinburgh or London'. Sitter selects Raeburn.

Bank of Scotland, Archives Department, Minutes of Court of Directors

20 August

Raeburn deposits £439 8s 11d in cash account at Bank of Scotland and clears borrowing. Account, opened on 26 December 1795, closed.

Bank of Scotland, Archives Department, Cash Account Progressive Ledgers BS 1.106.45, fol.46

28 September

Letter from Henry Mackenzie (1745–1831) to son concerning his portrait (location unknown) which appears to have displeased patrons, Cadell and Strahan, publishers in London. Suggests portrait be returned by publishers for another sitting because Raeburn 'was rather hurried in its execution'. Cost was Raeburn's 'customary one of 15 guineas'.

NLS, MS6364, fols.35–6

1803

14 November

Letter from Raeburn to Cadell and Davies, publishers in London, informing them he has finished copy (location unknown) of Alexander Nasmyth's portrait of Robert Burns. Order transmitted to Raeburn via a Mr Cunningham who thinks copy 'very like him'.

Greig, p.xxvi

1 December

Further letter from Raeburn to Cadell and Davies concerning transport to London of copy after Nasmyth's portrait of Burns. Cost of portrait 20 guineas.

Greig, p.xxvi

Bartolozzi's engraving after Raeburn's *Revd Hugh Blair in Robes (1718–1800)* (location unknown but see cat.no.25) advertised in *Monthly Magazine*. Favourable mention made of *Sir John and Lady Clerk of Penicuik* (cat.no.13) and engraving praised.

Whitley Papers, British Museum, Department of Prints and Drawings, vol.x, fol.1225

William Macdonald of St Martins (1732–1814) (Royal Highland and Agricultural Society of Scotland, Edinburgh), commissioned in 1800, bears inscription dating it to 1803.

1804

22 February

Reply from Raeburn to lost letter from Cadell and Davies, publishers in London, concerning copy after Nasmyth's portrait of Burns.

Greig, p.xxvi

Raeburn commissioned to produce version of *William Law of Elvingston (1714–1806)* for Town House, Haddington. See 30 October 1810.

1805

13 June

Firm of Henry Raeburn and Company involved in litigation against Arnott.

SRO, CS238.R.6.36

25 June

Letter from Raeburn to James Moray of Abercairney, son of Colonel Charles Moray of Abercairney (1746–1810), both sitters to Raeburn (private collection, Scotland, and other versions), concerning copy of colonel's portrait. Copy finished and frame chosen by Mrs Moray.

SRO, GD24.1.627, fol.39

21 December

Entry in Jessy Harden's journal: 'Raeburn still improves. He has done my father's picture great justice' (*Robert Allan of Kirkliston (1740–1818)*, Laing Art Gallery, Newcastle-upon-Tyne).

NLS, MS8848, fols.15–16

23 December
Letter from Raeburn to Mrs Moray-Stirling acknowledging payment of £42 and saying copy of *Charles Moray of Abercairney (1746–1810)* (location unknown), intended for Sir William Erskine, still in Raeburn's possession.
SRO, GD24.1.627, fol.40

In 1805 firm of Henry Raeburn and Company brings action against Crawford.
SRO, CS238.R.6.26

In 1805 Raeburn appointed member of board of directors of newly founded Caledonian Insurance Company.
Caledonian Jottings, 4, Edinburgh, 1900–2, p.8

1806

6 March
Alexander Thomson, gilder in Edinburgh, paid £10 15s 2d for 'three three-quarter length picture frames and two packing boxes' ordered from Robert Hay of Drumelzier. See 7 March 1806.

7 March
Raeburn receives 60 guineas for three portraits done for Robert Hay of Drumelzier: *James Erskine of Cardross (1732–1802)* (location unknown), *Lady Christian Erskine of Cardross (d.1816)* (location unknown) and Hay's own portrait, *Robert Hay of Drumelzier and Duns Castle (1731–1807)* (Boston Museum of Fine Arts).
SNPG, Library

5 May
Sittings for *Robert Allan Harden as a Child* (private collection, England). Mother records in diary: 'Mr R. offered to do it but who it is for I can't tell'. Her son 'got his little Phiz finished, to my astonishment he has really got it very like but one still minute he hardly got him to rest'.
NLS, MS8849, fols.18–19

22 September
Raeburn acquires property in Leith, later premises of Henry Raeburn and Company. See 24 February 1808.

Raeburn resigns from board of directors of Caledonian Insurance Company.
Dibdin, pp.22, 61

Raeburn, along with William Inglis of Middleton (d.1830), sitter (Grand Lodge of Scotland, Freemasons' Hall, Edinburgh), made guardian of Henry David Inglis Jr.
R. S. Lindsay, *A History of the Mason Lodge of Holyrood House etc.*, Edinburgh, 1935, vol.2, pp.269–73

Raeburn paid 90 guineas by Bank of Scotland for *Henry Dundas, 1st Viscount Melville (1742–1811)* (Bank of Scotland, Edinburgh).
Charles A. Malcolm, *The Bank of Scotland, 1695–1945*, Edinburgh, 1945, pp.230–1

1807

29 January
Raeburn registers feu contract with Broomfield and Robertson, builders in Edinburgh.
SRO, RD2.229, fols.201–9

4 February
Masters of Trinity House, Leith, pay £3 3s to unknown framemaker for frame of *George Smith* (Corporation of Masters and Assistants of Trinity House of Leith).
SRO, GD226.4.9

7 February
Raeburn receives £21 from Masters of Trinity House, Leith, for *George Smith*.
SRO, GD226.4.9; Trinity House Muniments, Leith

12 October
Raeburn feus land to Mathew Craw, goldsmith in Edinburgh.
SRO, RD2.302, fols.63–70

27 October
Firm of Henry Raeburn and Company rumoured to be insolvent. See 15 September 1808.

1808

4 January
Raeburn borrows £2,550 from 'George Dempster of Dunnichen and others, co-trustees with him appointed by the deceased George Willison … late portrait painter in India … which he binds himself to repay by Whitsunday next'.
SRO, RD4.285, fols.86–98

11 January
Letter from Raeburn to lawyer, John Ross (d.1817), instructing him to apply to court of session 'for a sequestration of my whole means and estate heritable and moveable'.
SRO, West Register House, CS29.10, December 1808, box 1867, hereafter termed Bankruptcy Papers

12 January
Public announcement of Raeburn's bankruptcy.
Edinburgh Gazette

13 January
Raeburn petitions for sequestration because his affairs, 'owing to some unexpected misfortunes, have lately fallen into disorder'.

Undated condescendence for Henry Raeburn, portrait painter and underwriter in Edinburgh, states that 'the petitioner for several years carried on the business of an underwriter in Edinburgh'. Instance of Raeburn's activities in this field cited as having been before Lord Newton, sitter (cat.no.44), on 1 December 1807.
Bankruptcy Papers

Beginning of sequestration of Henry Raeburn and Company, merchants in Leith and 'the whole real and personal estates' of Henry Raeburn Jr and James Philip Inglis, 'the individual partners of said company'. William Scott Moncrieff appointed trustee on sequestrated estates.
SRO, RD4.283, fols.905–8

16 January
Adam Rolland of Gask (1734–1819), sitter (Bank of Scotland, Head Office, Edinburgh; Art Institute of Chicago; and two other portraits, locations unknown), appointed interim factor on Raeburn's estate.
Bankruptcy Papers

Adam Rolland of Gask appointed 'to act as an interim factor or trustee on the sequestrated estates of Henry Raeburn and Company, merchants in Leith, and the individual partners of that concern, in so far as respects the vessel Ann of London, part of said sequestrated property'.
Minute Book of the Court of Session, 1808, p.30

Henry Raeburn and Company, merchants in Leith, vendition to Adam Rolland of Gask.
SRO, RD4.233, fols.107–9

22 January
First meeting of Raeburn's creditors. Interim factor authorised to apply to court of session for personal protection for Raeburn. Recommends weekly allowance be made to him and his family. Some creditors come forward including Bank of Scotland with bills amounting to £9,000 and Daniel Vere of Stonebyres, Raeburn's son-in-law, with bill for £400 dating from 2 February 1804.
Bankruptcy Papers

27 January
Petition made to court of session: 'May it therefore please your lordships to grant a personal protection to the said Henry Raeburn from the diligence of his creditors for the space of six months from this date'. Petition granted, also personal protections for partners in Henry Raeburn and Company, Henry Raeburn Jr and James Philip Inglis.
Bankruptcy Papers

12 February
Meeting of Raeburn's creditors. William Scott Moncrieff, accountant, appointed trustee. Some new creditors come forward.
Bankruptcy Papers

16 February
Letter from Alexander Cunningham to John Morrison, then at Auchincruive House, Ayr, saying that Raeburn has 'realised almost £17,000 which is all gone. He has offered a small composition, which he is in hopes will be accepted. He quits this to try his fate in London, which I trust in God will be successful. While I write this I feel the tears start.' See also 1 April 1808.
Glasgow Herald, 28 November 1908

23 February
Robert Burn and James Gillespie, architects, value Raeburn's land in Stockbridge. See 5 December 1808.
Bankruptcy Papers

24 February
Petition presented to court of session by William Scott Moncrieff for confirmation as trustee. In it Raeburn 'is professed of the following heritable subjects': studio property in York Place; range of dwelling houses with bleaching green in Deanhaugh; 'two acres or thereby leading from Canonmills to the Dean … But excepting always a feu right and disposition of the property … granted by James McDowall of Canonmills the author of the said Henry Raeburn in favour of James Leslie sometime residing at Deanhaugh, dated the 17th of September 1777 … In which subjects he stands infeft, conform to his instruments of sasine, dated the 11th and recorded in the Particular Register of Sasines for Edinburgh etc. the 12th day of June 1794.'; piece of ground lying to north of previously described property consisting of about one acre; acre and a half of ground 'part of the field of St Bernards still unfeued'; further half acre of land in Barony of Dean 'with the whole houses built thereupon, yard, well and other thereto belonging'; some nine acres to which 'the said Henry Raeburn has right by articles and enactment of roup, and sale thereof entered into by the trustees of the said Mrs Margaret Moubray, alias Ross, dated the 5th of September 1798'; 'the lease or Subtack, during the years yet to run thereof of the lands of Cuddyhaugh'; property 'lying in the south east corner of the Citadel of Leith, with the offices thereto belonging' acquired by Raeburn 'by missive of sale dated the 22nd day of September 1806' out of which firm of Henry Raeburn and Company, Leith, has operated.

Petition granted and William Scott Moncrieff made trustee.
Bankruptcy Papers

17 and 31 March
Examination of bankrupt takes place. Detailed records do not survive.
Bankruptcy Papers

1 April

First meeting of Raeburn's creditors: Patrick White of Leith presents promissory note for £400 dated 7 November 1807 granted by Raeburn and his son-in-law, Daniel Vere of Stonebyres; James Anthony Taylor produces promissory note for £280 dated 27 November 1805 by Raeburn and Henry Raeburn and Company and another for £136 dated 5 June 1805 by Raeburn and Henry Raeburn and Company dated 27 November 1807 granted by Raeburn and Henry Raeburn and Company; Gilbert Innes of Stow produces bill for £240 dated 22 December 1807 drawn by Henry Raeburn and Company on Henry Raeburn 'payable at three months after that date'; British Linen Company produces bill dated 7 October 1807 drawn by Henry Raeburn and Company 'on and accepted by Henry Raeburn for the sum of £500' and payable three months after.

Trustee shows creditors letter from Raeburn 'offering a composition of four shillings in the pound' and saying 'It would have given me the greatest pleasure to have been able to have paid the last shilling I owe in the world, and it is with infinite regret I now find that after all my means are collected it will afford so small a sum to my creditors'. Composition 'payable six months after it shall have been approved by the Court of Session'.

Raeburn gives as sureties John Taylor (d.1810), Thomas Hutchinson, merchant, Alexander Cunningham (see 16 February 1808) and John Buchan (1742–1822).

Meeting directs 'the trustee to advertise the property of St Bernards to be let, at the rent and under the conditions to be afterwards settled'.

Further meeting planned for 27 April to 'decide upon the offer of the above composition'. Minutes bear date 22 June 1808.
Bankruptcy Papers

Public announcements made to Raeburn's creditors of offer of composition. Meeting proposed for 27 April.
Edinburgh Gazette, 1 and 19 April 1808

27 April

Second meeting of Raeburn's creditors. New creditors come forward: John Somerville acting for William Sibbald produces missive letter from Raeburn dated 21 May 1807 'acknowledging receipt of nine hundred pounds and obligation to grant bonds along with Daniel Vere Esquire of Stonebyres'; John Taylor produces account for £108 6s 2d to Broomfield and Robertson; John Buchan produces bill dated 29 May 1800 drawn by late Henry David Inglis, sitter to Raeburn (location unknown) 'upon and accepted by the said Henry Raeburn' for £100; William Forbes produces promissory note for £700 dated 22 May 1807 by Raeburn and Daniel Vere of Stonebyres.

Creditors accept Raeburn's offer of composition.
Bankruptcy Papers

21 June

William Scott Moncrieff presents report stating that claims lodged against Raeburn total £33,006 6s 11½d and as Raeburn 'has the consent of more than nine tenths of his creditors both in number and value', composition can be accepted.
Bankruptcy Papers

22 June

Raeburn petitions court of session 'for discharge on a composition'. Creditors request all steps be taken 'recalling the sequestration, and discharging' Raeburn. Document carries signatures of Daniel Vere and William Scott Moncrieff. If forced sale of Raeburn's property goes ahead it is estimated that £5,188 7s 6d will be available for distribution among creditors, equivalent to 2s 9¼d in the pound. Raeburn's composition to yield 4s in the pound.
Bankruptcy Papers

23 June

Raeburn's application for acceptance of composition recorded.
Court of Session Minute Book, 1808, p.373

24 June

Public announcement made of acceptance by creditors of composition. Trustee has requested to court of session that Raeburn be 'discharged of all debts contracted previous to 14th January last … with the exception of the said composition'.
Edinburgh Gazette

2 July

Certain creditors object to acceptance of composition, claiming that Raeburn's property in Stockbridge 'has been very much under-valued'. Value of £6,000 placed on it but said to be worth nearly twice this. Robert Brunton, objector, has debt consisting of bill dated 27 October 1807 for £477 4s 6d drawn by Brunton upon and accepted by Henry Raeburn and Company and endorsed by Raeburn; bill dated 28 October 1807 for £338 2s 2d drawn by Brunton upon and accepted by Henry Raeburn and Company; bill dated 21 October 1807 for £338 6s 11d by Brunton upon and accepted by Henry Raeburn and Company; and 'letter of guarantee by Mr Henry Raeburn, obliging himself to see the two last bills retired'. Further debt recorded of Alexander George Mylne of London, totalling £4,968 0s 2d 'in consequence of a real lien which he held over the ship *Isabella Simpson*, belonging to Mr Raeburn'.
Bankruptcy Papers

Undated minute in process concerning claim that Stockbridge property is undervalued records that 'Mr Brunton was willing to pay nine thousand pounds for that property instead of six thousand, the sum at which it was valued'.
Bankruptcy Papers

6 July

William Scott Moncrieff obliged to present additional report, 'Interests having been lodged'. Claims now total £36,427 17s 3½d.
Bankruptcy Papers

8 July

Sequestration declared at an end and 'the petitioner, Henry Raeburn, upon payment of said composition freed and discharged of all debts contracted by him prior to the fourteenth day of January last'. Legal action continues because of actions of Sceales and Brunton.
Bankruptcy Papers

Letter from Bank of Scotland to Raeburn saying 'Mr Alexander Macfarlane, for whose cash account you are bound, having not complied with the demand made on him for payment of the Balance due on it at Whitsunday, I am now ordered to insist for it at Martinmas, and if not then paid to use diligence.'
Bank of Scotland, Archives Department, Edinburgh, BS 1.146.4

9 July

Sceales and Brunton 'object to the prayer of Mr Raeburn's petition, because his offer has not been consented to by nine tenths of the creditors, as required by law'.
Bankruptcy Papers

August

Letter from Sir Walter Scott to J. C. Schetky saying he had sat to Raeburn 'last spring' (cat.no.38).
William T. Whitley, *Art in England, 1800–1820*, Cambridge, 1928, p.134

15 September

Sceales and Brunton make additional petition to courts. They state that one complexity in case is that most creditors 'are either personal friends or near relations of Mr Raeburn'. These men 'are certainly conferring a great favour upon the bankrupt'. Sceales and Brunton request that 'a new valuation of the bankrupt's estates be taken'. Account given of circumstances relating to Brunton's bill on Henry Raeburn and Company of 27 October 1807. Brunton took bill to banking firm of Sir William Forbes to get it discounted but was told of rumours regarding solvency of firm. Brunton told Raeburn of rumours. 'To this Mr Raeburn senior replied with much indignation, that such suspicions were utterly groundless, that the credit of his son's house was undoubted; that he knew the situation of their affairs, and that he would himself willingly guarantee the payment of every shilling of their debts.' Raeburn then endorses bill. Sceales and Brunton request that the court 'refuse the desire of Mr Raeburn's petition'.
Bankruptcy Papers

15 November

Courts consider petition of Sceales and Brunton and 'having heard and considered this petition appoint the same to be seen and answered'.
Bankruptcy Papers

5 December

Raeburn answers Sceales and Brunton. Presents letter from Robert Burn and James Gillespie, architects, of 23 February 1808, valuing his land in Stockbridge at or near £6,000. Regarding offer of composition and security he has raised to allow this, Raeburn says that against this security 'he will most gladly task the remaining years of his life. In the profession to which he has already devoted the best of his days, he cannot promise himself a long period of successful exertion, for it is one which the trembling hand of age is unfit to execute long before the faculties decay, but while he does possess any remains of professional skill, his gains may enable him to save his surities from loss and those gains he is willing to anticipate, while they are generous enough to run the risk.' Respondents conclude 'in full confidence that your Lordships will adhere to the former judgment'.
Bankruptcy Papers

10 December

Court considers additional petition of Sceales and Brunton and refuses 'the prayer of both'. Sequestration declared at an end.
Bankruptcy Papers

27 December

Registration of Raeburn's bond of caution for composition, dated 13 May 1808
SRO, RD 4.284, fols.1065–7

29 December

David Hatton paid for frame for *William Law of Elvingston (1714–1806)* (East Lothian Council). Raeburn paid in 1810.
SRO, GD 302.12.11

1809

11 May
Raeburn requests permission from directors of Bank of Scotland to copy *Henry Dundas, 1st Viscount Melville* in Bank's collection.

15 May
Directors of Bank of Scotland grant permission, and request 'sending your Receipt for the Picture, obliging yourself to return it on demand, and giving … notice before taking it away'.
Bank of Scotland, Archives Department, Edinburgh, BS1.146.5

22 July
Advertisement in *Caledonian Mercury* for publication of Dawe and Hodgett's mezzotint after *Revd Andrew Hunter of Barjarg (1744–1809)* (private collection, Scotland), published in 1810. Portrait 'will be exhibited for a few days only, and subscriptions received at John Marnoch's looking-glass manufactory, no.12 Princes' Street'.
Caledonian Mercury

24 August
Letter from Raeburn to London publishers Cadell and Davies offering eight portraits for engraving. Gives brief biographies and details of ownership: *Robert Blair of Avontoun as Lord President (1741–1811)* (version uncertain), *James Byres of Tonley (1734–1817)* (Baltimore Museum of Art, Maryland), *John Clerk of Eldin (1728–1812)* (Currier Gallery of Art, Manchester, New Hampshire), *Sir William Forbes of Pitsligo (1739–1806)* (version uncertain), *Dr James Hamilton (1749–1835)* (version uncertain), *Henry Mackenzie (1745–1831)* (two portraits, the earlier untraced, the later in numerous versions), *Sir Walter Scott (1771–1832)* (cat.no.38), and *Professor Dugald Stewart (1753–1828)* (Scottish National Portrait Gallery).
Greig, p.xxxix

1 September
Raeburn returns portrait of Viscount Melville to Bank of Scotland.

14 September
Letter from Bank of Scotland to Raeburn concerning portrait of Viscount Melville, informing him that as 'it appears to be slightly injured in the lower part of the canvas, I am directed to beg the favour of your calling at the Bank any morning before 12 o'clock to look at it'.
Bank of Scotland, Archives Department, Edinburgh, BS1.146.7

September
The Scots Magazine publishes review of second exhibition of Associated Society of Artists which was held in Raeburn's studio. Three portraits identified and Raeburn highly praised.
The Scots Magazine, September 1809, pp.674–7, 729–32

28 October
Surviving trustees of George Willison hold bond and disposition in security of this date over some of Raeburn's land in Stockbridge.
SRO, RD5.111, fols.356–66

October
Raeburn purchases St Bernard's House in Stockbridge, Edinburgh.
Caw, *Masterpieces*, p.52

November
Raeburn paid 50 guineas for *Charles Hope of Granton (1763–1851) as Lord President* (Marquis of Linlithgow, Hopetoun House, South Queensferry, Scotland).
Hopetoun House Muniments

1810

2 March
Sir David Wilkie notes in diary that Raeburn is coming to London to live in John Hoppner's house.
Allan Cunningham, *The Life of Sir David Wilkie*, 3 vols., London, 1843, vol.1, p.280

24 April
Letter from Andrew Robertson (1777–1845), miniaturist, in London, to John Ewen, saying Raeburn intends settling in city. Robertson believes Raeburn 'would be a great acquisition in London, both for the strength of his art, and his respectability as a man'.
Emily Robertson (ed.), *Letters and Papers of Andrew Robertson*, London, 1895, p.168

12 May
Sir David Wilkie notes in diary that Raeburn called on him and is considering establishing himself in London. At Raeburn's request Wilkie takes him to see Sir William Beechey (1753–1839), who invites them to dine next day.
Cunningham, *op. cit.*, vol.1, p.296

13 May
Sir David Wilkie notes that he visited Raeburn. Together they called on a number of London artists who were not at home.
Cunningham, *op. cit.*, vol.1, p.296

21 May
Sir David Wilkie notes that Raeburn called on him and they visited Thomas Stothard (1755–1834).
Cunningham, *op. cit.*, vol.1, p.297

4 June
Sir David Wilkie notes that he goes to Crown and Anchor with Raeburn to meet members of Royal Academy. Raeburn introduced to John Flaxman (1755–1826). Sir William Beechey invites Raeburn to sit near president, Benjamin West (1738–1820), 'where his health was proposed by Flaxman; great attention was paid to him'.
Cunningham, *op. cit.*, vol.1, p.299

9 June
Letter from Raeburn at address in Cecil St, London, to unknown correspondent.
Maggs Brothers catalogue, 1925, no.579

3 July
Letter from Raeburn to Robert Sym, sitter (Rhode Island School of Design, Providence), saying that *William Craig, Lord Craig (1745–1813)* (Faculty of Advocates, Edinburgh) is finished and will be sent out in a few days.
NLS, MS9994, fol.94

30 October
Letter from Raeburn to Henry Davidson, Haddington, enclosing receipt in payment for version of *William Law of Elvingston (1714–1806)* (East Lothian Council). Raeburn charges six years' interest on delayed payment.
SRO, GD302.12.13

5 December
Raeburn registers feu contract with Elizabeth Wright, widow of James Cleland, drawn up 26 May 1797.
SRO, RD2.310, fols.738–55

6 December
Death of William Raeburn, Raeburn's elder brother.
Edinburgh Evening Courant, 13 December 1810

8 December
Letter from Raeburn to authority on Scottish bankruptcy law, George Joseph Bell (1770–1843), sitter (two versions: private collection, Washington DC; Faculty of Advocates, Edinburgh), informing him he had overpaid for his wife's portrait, *Mrs Barbara Bell* (location unknown). Raeburn accepts payment with reluctance, because of obligations to Bell.
Greig, p.xl

1811

21 February
Raeburn and sister, Ann, Mrs Robert Wemyss, raise petition to appoint factor on estate of their late brother William. Granted 5 March 1811.
SRO, CS235.R.20.6

May
Raeburn produces copy of *Robert Blair of Avontoun (1741–1811) as Lord President* for Society of Writers to His Majesty's Signet.
Armstrong, p.96

June
A diary entry indicates that *Mrs James Hamilton of Kames (d.1860)* (cat.no.45) was completed by this time.
Anne Fremantle (ed.), *The Wynne Diaries*, vol.III (1798–1820), London, 1940, p.334

7 September
Letter from Raeburn to John Rennie (1761–1821), engineer, then in London, concerning one of numerous versions of his portrait. Raeburn has produced copy and asks for address to which it should be sent. The patron not named. In same letter Raeburn says that Professor John Playfair (1748–1810) (cat.no.43) 'is under my hand at present'.
NLS, MS19828, fol.156

10 September
Raeburn receives 25 guineas from Sir William Gordon-Cumming for *Sir Alexander Penrose Gordon-Cumming* (private collection, Scotland).
SNPG, Library

14 September
Feu contract drawn up between Raeburn and son Henry Raeburn Jr. Raeburn feuing land at £40 per acre.
SRO, RD5.111, fols.356–66

7 October
Raeburn receives 25 guineas from Sir William Gordon-Cumming in payment for *Lady Gordon-Cumming (d.1830)* (private collection, Scotland).
NLS, MS175.162

4 November
Letter from Raeburn to Colonel F. William Grant MP (1778–1853) recording dispatch from studio of three portraits: *Lady Innes*, *Sir James Grant (1738–1811)* and *Mr Mackenzie*. Portraits untraced.
SRO, GD248.965, fol.1

Charles Hay, Lord Newton (1747–1811) (cat.no.44) carries excise stamp on canvas dating it to 1811.

In 1811 York Place renumbered: Raeburn's studio changes from no.16 to no.34.
Dibdin, p.58

Caleb Whiteford sale, London, 1811, includes version of *Revd John Home (1722–1808)* (location unknown).

1812

2 April
Raeburn resigns from Associated Society of Artists due to disagreement over hanging of his and George Watson's (1767–1837) portraits. Raeburn says 'he cannot prevail upon himself to act a second part in the eye of the public to any man in his own line'.
Royal Scottish Academy, Library, uncatalogued papers

16 April
Missive of feu drawn up between William Cockburn and Henry Raeburn Jr concerning building land in Hermitage Place, Edinburgh.
SRO, RD5.121, fols.200–2

28 April
Missive of feu drawn up between William Whitlaw and Henry Raeburn Jr regarding building land in Raeburn Place, Hermitage Place and Dean Street, Edinburgh.
SRO, RD5.121, fols.202–6

1 May
Raeburn sells property in Citadel of Leith, formerly premises of Henry Raeburn and Company.
SRO, RD5.11, fols.408–15

23 May
The Scots Magazine reviews exhibition of Associated Society of Artists. Raeburn highly praised, 'a man who would have done honour to any age'. Portraits unidentified except for *Lady Innes-Ker, Sir James Innes-Ker* (cat.nos. 48 and 49) and *The Earl of Rosebery* (private collection, Scotland) which, according to reviewer, show Raeburn's 'powers of colouring and effect'.
The Scots Magazine, 23 May 1812, pp.246–9, 346–56

22 June
Raeburn adds name to candidate list for associate membership of Royal Academy.

24 August
Raeburn conveys to son superiority of piece of land in Stockbridge having previously conveyed property.
SRO, RD5.111, fols.366–77

27 August
Henry Raeburn Jr draws up procuratory of resignation concerning some property in Stockbridge.
SRO, RD5.111, fols.377–84

28 August
Raeburn sends account to Thomas Buchanan for his own portrait (private collection, Scotland) and for copy of brother's portrait (location unknown), price 20 guineas each.
Captain Neil Baillie-Hamilton of Cambusmore Muniments

8 September
Letter from Raeburn to John Richardson regarding *Alexander Douglas, 10th Duke of Hamilton (1767–1852)* (private collection, England). Says horse complete and Raeburn awaits duke. Discussion of Marchioness sitting to Raeburn but he mentions 'rule to which I have invariably adhered, never to leave my own house without a reasonable consideration for loss of time'.
'Letters from Dr Gregory and Sir Henry Raeburn as to Their Fees for Their Respective Services as Physician and Portrait Painter', *Book of the Old Edinburgh Club*, vol.21, 1962, p.173

2 November
Raeburn elected Associate Royal Academician.
The Scots Magazine, vol.lxxiv, 1812, p.349

10 November
Letter from Raeburn to Sir Duncan Campbell of Barcaldine (cat.no.41) requesting payment for portrait.
SRO, GD170.2677

11 December
Letter from Lord Frederick Campbell (1729–1816) to George Home of Wedderburn concerning Campbell's portrait (Scottish Record Office, Edinburgh), saying, 'if Raeburn's painting is worthy of your collection, it is from this instant yours'. Painting declined.
SNPG, Library, Greig Archive

In 1812 pre-nuptual agreement drawn up and Henry Raeburn Jr marries Charlotte White of Howden.
SRO, RDS.1139, fols.105–91

Imprecisely dated review of Royal Academy exhibition of 1812 published in *Morning Post*. Identifies portrait of anonymous man exhibited by Raeburn as no.357: 'We believe of Mr Skirving, the Raeburn in crayons'. Portrait lavishly praised: 'here criticism is changed to eulogy'.
SNPG, Library, Greig Archive

1813

25 January
Letter from directors of Bank of Scotland to Henry Raeburn Jr concerning request to have 'Cash Account with the bank to the extent of £1,000'. Offers personal security of Raeburn's father and of John Ross, father's lawyer. 'The Directors have agreed to grant a Credit to the extent of six hundred pounds on the personal security offered.'
Bank of Scotland, Archives Department, BS1.146.7

13 February
Sir David Wilkie notes in diary that he has corresponded with Raeburn, 'urging him to put forward all his strength at the next exhibition'.
Armstrong, p.75

28 March
Letter from William Fraser Tytler to publishers, Cadell and Davies, concerning Picart's engraving after *Alexander Fraser Tytler, Lord Woodhouselee (1747–1813)* (several versions, one in Montreal Museum of Fine Arts called Alexander Selkrig). Tytler has shown copy of engraving to Raeburn who has corrected it.
University of Edinburgh, Library, La.ii.602

2 April
Henry Raeburn Jr feus land to Thomas Mair, builder in Edinburgh.
SRO, RD5.29, fols.122–31

April
Review published of sixth exhibition of Associated Society of Artists. Raeburn favourably received but no portraits named. No.69 can be identified as *The Marchioness of Northampton (d.1830)* (cat.no.55) and no.191 is equestrian portrait.
The Scots Magzine, April 1813, pp.246–8

27 November
Letter from A. Dirom to Lieut-Gen. Alexander Dirom of Mount Annan (1757–1830), sitter (location unknown), recounting visit to Raeburn's studio to see *Colonel John Pasley Dirom (1794–1858)* (location unknown).
Private Muniments, England

In 1813 young John Hamilton Gray (later Revd) sat to Raeburn (Aberdeen Art Gallery, Scotland) and recorded group of portraits in studio: *The Marchioness of Northampton, Francis MacNab, Macdonell of Glengarry* (cat.nos.55, 46 and 47), *John Francis Erskine, later 7th Earl of Mar (1741–*

1825), William Forbes (1802–26) (location unknown), *Francis, Lord Elcho, later 8th Earl of Wemyss (1795–1882) with his brother the Hon. Walter Charteris (1797–1818)* (private collection, Scotland) and *Lady Maxwell of Springkell (d.1856)* (location unknown).
Mrs J. H. Gray (ed.), *Autobiography of a Scotch Country Gentleman Revd John Hamilton Gray*, Edinburgh, 1868, pp.55–7

1814

26 January
Letter from Raeburn to Sir Francis Chantrey (1781–1841), sculptor, concerning plaster bust of Mrs Maconochie by Chantrey. Raeburn has been working on Chantrey's portrait (two versions, location unknown) but expresses dissatisfaction: 'I would send it to you if I thought you would not show it to anybody … for I am much disappointed with it.'
NLS, MS9994, fols.96–7

7 February
Correspondence concerning copies made by Raeburn after portrait believed to depict George Buchanan by Titian. Painting in fact by François Quesnel (1533 or 1543/4–1619) and represents Pierre Jeannin, minister of finance to Henry IV of France. Raeburn produces copies for Hector Macdonald Buchanan (location unknown) and Buchanan Society of Glasgow (Glasgow Museums and Art Galleries).
Greig, pp.xli–xliii

12 May
Letter from Raeburn to George Home of Paxton concerning Home's copy of *Robert Blair of Avontoun (1741–1811)* requesting instructions on framing and dispatch.
Greig, p.xliv

18 October
Letter from Lord Buchan is read to Buchanan Society, Glasgow, and recorded in minutes. It permits Society to have copy made of Buchan's putative portrait of George Buchanan. Offer accepted.
Greig, p.xlii

2 December
Letter from Raeburn to Archibald Buchanan of Buchanan Society, Glasgow, saying that copy of George Buchanan portrait finished.
Greig, p.xliii

13 December
Raeburn dispatches Buchan portrait to Buchanan Society, Glasgow, and requests that 25 guineas 'be paid into the office of the Royal Bank at Glasgow on my account'.
Greig, p.xliii

18 December
Start of extensive correspondence concerning family dispute over ownership of *William Murray of Polmaise (d.1814)*. Eventually Raeburn makes copy (location unknown).
Stirling Council Archive, Stirling, GD189.2.580, fols.1–2

24 December
Letter from Raeburn to Buchanan Society, Glasgow, acknowledging payment.
Greig, p.xliii

Unidentified and imprecisely dated review of Royal Academy exhibition praises unidentified portrait of man, number 35, saying that 'whatever has yet been done and deemed the greatest masterpieces in portrait painting are at least equalled if not eclipsed' by Raeburn.
Whitley Notebooks, British Museum, Department of Prints and Drawings, vol.x, fol.1226

In 1814 letter from Raeburn to unknown correspondent expressing his desire to become member of Royal Academy: 'If they choose to elect me without solicitation, it will be the more honourable to me, and I will think the more of it'.

Cunningham, *op. cit.*, vol.1, p.231

1815

4 January

Letter from George Home of Paxton to Alexander Maconachie-Wellwood, 2nd Lord Meadowbank (1777–1861), sitter (Metropolitan Museum of Art, New York), saying he has received copy of *Master William Blair of Avontoun (1799/1803–1873)* (Henry E. Huntington Library and Gallery, San Marino, California). He says, 'No person of taste who sees it but will ask by whom it is done.'

SNPG, Library, Greig Archive

9 January

Raeburn receives 25 guineas for *James Bruce of Bankton, Midcalder* (Fogg Art Museum, Harvard University, Cambridge, Mass.).

SNPG, Library, Greig Archive

10 February

Raeburn elected member of Royal Academy 'in the room of Henry Fresham Esq deceased'.

Royal Academy, Library, GAIII, fols.183–4

March

Caw quotes letter from Raeburn to unidentified correspondent saying that correspondent's portrait of *William Baillie, Lord Polkemmet (d.1816)* (location unknown) 'was done in March 1815, price 30 guineas'.

Caw, 1908, p.78, note 1

May

The Scots Magazine reviews Annual Exhibition of Edinburgh Exhibition Society. Raeburn treated with sarcasm. Unidentified portrait of lady (no.23) criticised on grounds of colour; *General Sir David Baird (1757–1829)* (two versions: private collection, Scotland; Crieff Hydro Hotel, Crieff, Scotland) criticised on grounds of draughtsmanship, particularly of horse; *James Joseph Hope-Vere of Blackwood and Craigie Hall (1785–1872)* [mistitled 'Hope-Weir'] (Ringling Museum of Art, Sarasota, Florida) condemned for both colour and drawing (sitter's legs 'appear of unequal length, but not knowing the original, this passage may perhaps be perfectly correct'). Of *Rt Hon David Boyle, Lord Justice Clerk (1772–1853)* (private collection, Scotland) reviewer says: 'the under part of his dress … is absolutely a deception in art' and the judge 'appears undersize'.

Two works exhibited by Raeburn in London also discussed: *Thomas Robert Hay Drummond, 11th Earl of Kinnoull (1785–1866)* (North Carolina Museum of Art, Raleigh) and *James Duff, 4th Earl of Fife (1776–1857)* (location unknown). Anonymous reviewer says: 'their black and dingy hue was rendered the more offensive by Sir T. Lawrence's magnificent portrait of the Regent'. Stern criticism follows under guise of quoting London admirers of Raeburn, 'who would not allow any charge of bad taste to lie against him'. They are said to attribute Raeburn's faults in colouring to 'some growing defect of vision'.

The Scots Magazine, 1815, pp.327–9, 441–5

1 August

Raeburn paid 60 guineas for two portraits of late *Honourable William Frederick Mackenzie (1791–1814)* (one version collection Mr Mic Mead, USA).

National Trust for Scotland, Castle Fraser, Muniment Room

10 November

Council of Royal Academy informs Raeburn that it cannot 'receive as deposits portraits of members'. Invites him to send another work as diploma picture in place of self-portrait (cat.no.56).

Royal Academy, Library, CV226

November

Letter from James Watt (1736–1819) to unknown correspondent saying he has sat to Raeburn (Henry E. Huntingdon Library and Gallery, San Marino, California) and commenting: 'it does not come up to my ideas of my own face'. Another letter says: 'My Edinburgh picture is come home and is thought like, only it frowns too much'.

James L. Caw, *Scottish Portraits with an Historical and Critical Introduction and Notes, … etc*, 2 vols, Edinburgh, 1903, vol.2, pp.74–6

23 December

Part of process concerning action brought by Raeburn against neighbour for erecting steam engine.

SRO, CS239.R.47.16

29 December

Letter from Raeburn to William Trotter, furnituremaker, saying: 'Have the goodness not to send me my account for I know it perfectly and am ashamed of it'.

University of Edinburgh, Library, La.ii.133.3

1816

2 March

Reference in deed to sasine of Henry Raeburn Jr and William Bryce, architect in Edinburgh, regarding property in area of St Bernard's, Edinburgh.

SRO, RS27.774, fols.31r–36v

7 March

Raeburn's brother, 'Charles Raeburn, Mariner at South Shields, presently residing in Edinburgh' and their sister Ann, widow of Robert Wemyss, draw up disposition concerning property in Broughton and other areas of Edinburgh. Charles cannot sign document 'by reason of a tremor in his hand'.

SRO, RD5.434, fols.353–64

19 March

Letter from William Say, engraver, to T. Macdonald, framemaker and publisher, London, asking for final payment for plate after *Niel Gow* (cat.no.27).

SNPG, Library, Greig Archive

6 April

Letter from Raeburn to council of Royal Academy saying he will send replacement diploma work.

Royal Academy, Library, CV269

25 April

Henry Raeburn Jr mentioned in sasine concerning tenement in Dean Street, Edinburgh.

SRO, RS27.779, fols.19v–27r

3 May

Raeburn paid 30 guineas for one of many versions of *Henry Mackenzie (1745–1831)*, this example being for Lady Hood Mackenzie (location unknown).

Maggs Brothers catalogue, *Autograph Letters and Historic Documents*, 1961, p.3

17 July

Letter from Raeburn to unknown correspondent, possibly John Taylor, saying he has sent out from studio portrait of young boy.

Greig, p.xlvii

10 October

Letter from Raeburn to Major Buchanan of Cambusmore thanking him for gift of game and saying that unidentified portrait intended for Buchanan, presumably *Captain James Edmonstone Buchanan (d.1809)*, has been collected by carriers, and that framemaker's name not known.

Captain Neil Baillie-Hamilton of Cambusmore Muniments

4 November

St Luke's Masonic Lodge, Edinburgh, invites Grand Master, William Inglis of Middleton (d.1830), 'to sit to Mr Raeburn, the first artist of his time'. Portrait (Freemasons' Hall, Edinburgh) paid for by subscription.

R. S. Lindsay, *A History of the Mason Lodge of Holyrood*, Edinburgh, 1935, pp.312–13

1817

7 February

Sittings for *John Hope, 4th Earl of Hopetoun (1756–1823)* (West Lothian Council, County Buildings, Linlithgow).

SRO, GD26.13.297, fols.1–13

7 March

Raeburn paid 30 guineas plus £6 1s for frame and case for *Charles Mackenzie Fraser of Castle Fraser MP (1792–1871)*.

National Trust for Scotland, Castle Fraser, Muniment Room

8 March

Letter from Sir David Wilkie to Lord Leven concerning choice of artist for Earl of Hopetoun's portrait for Cupar in Fife. He says: 'If Mr Raeburn is to be passed over … it must be for one of first rate excellence'.

SRO, GD26.13.297, fols.1–13

13 March

Noblemen and gentlemen freeholders of Fife 'unanimously agree to employ Mr Raeburn to execute' portrait of Earl of Hopetoun (Fife Council, County Buildings, Cupar).

SRO, GD26.13.297, fols.1–13

25 March

Speculative Society, University of Edinburgh, commissions version of *Francis Horner (1778–1817)*, hung in 1820.

Henley, no.9

17 May

Lady Holland receives letter from correspondent identified only as 'Wishaw' concerning version of portrait of Francis Horner (lost) that she has commissioned from Raeburn. Letter informs her 'that Raeburn is bestowing great pains upon it'.

Earl of Ilchester, *The Home of the Hollands*, London, 1937, pp.318–19

5 July

Raeburn proposed as honorary member of American Academy of the Fine Arts. See also 1819.

Mabel C. Weeks, 'Works by Raeburn in America', *Connoisseur* 97, 1936, pp.275–7

29 August

Council of Royal Academy accepts Raeburn's request by letter that procedure of election be done by proxy so that Raeburn may 'be spared the necessity of coming from Edinburgh for that purpose'.

Royal Academy, Library, CV413

9 October

Sasine registered by Caledonian Insurance Company concerning property in Stockbridge and mentioning Raeburn, son and daughter-in-law.

SRO, RS27.914, fols.3r–10r

3 November
Council of Royal Academy reads letter from Raeburn accompanying signed copy of obligation. Benjamin West, president, inserts Raeburn's name in roll of Royal Academicians.
Royal Academy, Library, GAiii.246

28 November
Letter from Raeburn to George Home of Paxton saying that his portrait of *Admiral Sir David Milne* 'still wants a good deal of being finished'. Raeburn intends sending it to Royal Academy but he has been unable to finish it because 'I have really been oppressed with business'.
SRO, GD267.12.6; 16.7

30 November
Journal of income and expenditure for 1817–28 relating to estate of Alexander Campbell of Hallyards (1768–1817) records 'paid Raeburn for portrait £63' (location unknown, many part replicas).
Mitchell Library, Glasgow, MS79.4

In 1817(?) Raeburn elected member of Imperial Academy of Florence.
Dibdin, p.82

Imprecisely dated review of 1817 from *Literary Gazette* praises Raeburn's unidentified portrait of lady exhibited at Royal Academy (no.84). Portrait recognisable as *Lady Eliza Mary Gordon-Cumming (d.1842)* (location unknown). Reviewer identified by Whitley as William Carey.
Whitley Notebooks, British Museum, Department of Prints and Drawings, vol.x, fol.1226

1818

9 and 10 January
Feu dispositions concerning James Dickinson, slater in Edinburgh, and house in Ann Street feature in petition made to Court of Session of May 1826 by Henry Raeburn Jr.
SRO, CS233.R.6.1

27 February
Raeburn draws up discharge and renunciation concerning James Leslie's burden of £200 resulting from his purchase of Deanhaugh House. Registered 3 March. Deed indicates that third child was born to Raeburn's wife, Ann Edgar, from her marriage to James Leslie. This boy, also called James, died before turning twenty-one but was heir to his father.
SRO, RS27.822, fols.125v–130v

3 March
Sasine registered by James Dickinson, slater in Edinburgh, concerning property in Stockbridge and mentioning Raeburn.
SRO, RS27.822, fols.119v–125v

4 March
Sasine registered by George Sharp and James Lamb concerning property in Ann Street and referring to Raeburn and trustees of deceased George Willison, portrait painter.
SRO, RS27.822, fols.147r–156v

17 March
Letter from Raeburn to George Home of Paxton informing him that *Admiral Sir David Milne* (Paxton House Trust, Paxton House, Scotland) was finished and dispatched by boat for London where it will be included in Royal Academy exhibition. Cost of full-length is 140 guineas, and frame and case 'will not be much under 30 guineas'. Raeburn insures them for this figure because he thinks 'that it is not necessary to risk the loss of money'.
Greig, p.xlv

20 March
Reply from Raeburn to lost letter of Home of Paxton apologising for using wrong name: 'I know your name perfectly, and am quite ashamed of having written John'. Home wants print after *Admiral Sir David Milne* (not engraved). Raeburn asks for intended size and type of engraving.
Greig, p.xlv

20 April
Letter from Raeburn to John Gordon of Aikenhead who has paid £147 for portraits of his wife and himself. Raeburn says: 'To say that the Gentlemen of Glasgow pay like princes would be doing them the highest injustice, for they pay better than any of your great folks that ever I had anything to do with.'
Christie's, 21 November 1986 (95)

18 June
Letter of introduction from Raeburn for young Scottish sculptor, Thomas Campbell (1790–1858), to Sir Thomas Lawrence saying: 'I am sure any advice you may give him will not be thrown away'. See also 1822.
Royal Academy, Library, Law.2.288

11 November
Raeburn involved in litigation with Peter McDowall, accountant in Edinburgh, over account for feu duty of £45 16s 7d.
SRO, CS228.R.8.59

19 December
Raeburn receives £40 10s from Henry Monteith Esq representing 'the balance due on his own and his son's portrait' (location unknown).
SNPG, Library, Greig Archive

December
Letter from Raeburn to Sir William Gordon Cumming saying that Sir Michael Shaw-Stewart has requested that he exhibit portrait in exhibition at Greenock. Raeburn requests permission to exhibit *Lady Gordon Cumming* (location unknown) 'which is by much the best and handsomest female picture I have yet painted'.
SNPG, Library, Greig Archive

Raeburn's sole surviving graphic work, *camera lucida* drawing of Sir Francis Chantrey (cat.no.65), bears inscription identifying sitter and dating it to 1818.

1819

15 February
Letter from 4th Duke of Buccleuch to Walter Scott reminding him of promise to sit to Raeburn. Duke cautions Scott: 'I will not take a half-finished picture off his hands. Many of his works are shamefully finished.'
H. J. C. Grierson (ed.), *Letters of Sir Walter Scott*, vol.5, London, 1933, pp.307–8

16 March
Letter from Raeburn to William Walker, engraver, asking him to call to discuss Lord Huntly's portrait and another commission.
University of Edinburgh, Library, La.iv.26

31 March
Raeburn mentioned in sasine on property in Ann Street.
SRO, RS27.851, fols.165v–172v

15 April
Reply from Walter Scott to Duke of Buccleuch's letter of 15 February expressing reluctance to sit to Raeburn. With Duke's death on 20 April, commission languishes until 22 March 1822 (see cat.no.64).

31 July
Letter from Raeburn to William Walker concerning two engravings. Only one identified: Walker's stipple after *Revd Andrew Mitchel Thomson (1778–1831)*. Raeburn asks how many subscribers are required for print, or fee Walker would charge.
NLS, Acc.8381

10 August
Letter from Raeburn to Alexander Robertson, Secretary to American Academy of Fine Arts, thanking him for election to honorary membership. Sends Academy one of two versions of *Peter Van Brugh Livingston (1793?–1868)* (Wadsworth Athenaeum, Hartford, Connecticut).
Mabel C. Weaks, 'Works by Raeburn in America', *Connoisseur* 97, 1936, pp.275–7

12 September
Letter from Raeburn to Sir David Wilkie asking him to write because he knows almost as little about London painters as if he 'were living at the Cape of Good Hope'.
Greig, p.xlvi

1 October
Unidentified newspaper article discusses foundation of Institution for the Encouragement of the Fine Arts in Scotland. Praises Raeburn at length and mentions *The Marquis of Huntly*, saying it is a 'fine likeness'.
Whitley Notebooks, British Museum, Department of Prints and Drawings, vol.x, fol.1227

Institution for the Encouragement of the Fine Arts in Scotland founded in 1819. Raeburn only artist allowed full membership.
Dibdin, pp.88–9

Imprecisely dated review of Royal Academy exhibition in *Examiner* praises Raeburn's *Archibald William Montgomerie, 13th Earl of Eglinton, as a Child (1812–61)* (National Trust, Upton House, Warwickshire) saying it has 'a charming infantile grace'.
Whitley Notebooks, British Museum, Department of Prints and Drawings, vol.x, fol.1227

In 1819 Raeburn receives commission from Lord De Tabley (1762–1867). Raeburn selects Musidora from Thomson's *Seasons* as subject, but dies before completing work.
William Carey, *Some Memoirs of the Fine Arts*, London, 1826, p.28

In 1819 Raeburn produces copy of *William Dickie* for Caledonian Insurance Company.
Armstrong, p.99

In 1819 sittings take place for *Professor Dugald Stewart (1753–1828)* (location unknown) and continue until shortly before Raeburn's death.
Letter of 6 May 1825 from sitter's widow, SNPG, Library

1820

20 January
Raeburn elected fellow of Royal Society of Edinburgh. His three sponsors had been sitters: *Lord Chief Commissioner William Adam of Blairadam (1751–1839)* (private collection, Scotland), *Sir David Brewster (1781–1839)* (location unknown) and *Sir George Steuart Mackenzie of Coul (1780–1848)* (Lane Fine Art, London).
Dibdin, p.82

7 April
Letter from Raeburn to Alexander Forbes mentioning land and houses in Danube Street and St Bernard's Crescent. Payment required nine years hence.
SRO, RD5.419, fols.25–8

22 April
Letter from Lady Bute to factor of Bute estates requesting sketch of 'the highland mountains or Arran' to assist Raeburn in portrait *John Crichton Stuart, 2nd Marquess of Bute (1793–1848)* (cat.no.60).
Private Muniments

18 December
Governors of Royal Infirmary give permission for Raeburn to copy *John Hope, 2nd Earl Hopetoun (1704–81)* by Allan Ramsay for 4th Earl of Hopetoun (Marquis of Linlithgow, Hopetoun House, South Queensferry).
SNPG, Library, Photographic Survey List of portraits at Hopetoun House

In late 1820 William and Charles Thorold Wood and their two siblings sit for two double portraits (one, private collection, England; location of other unknown).
Private Muniments

Raeburn involved in litigation with Peter McDowall, accountant in Edinburgh.
SRO, CS228.R.8.58

Unidentified and undated newspaper cutting, review of Royal Academy exhibition of 1820, discusses *George, 5th Duke of Gordon (1770–1836)* (private collection, Scotland), saying that portrait is distinguished by 'a flowing decisive pencil' but that all Raeburn's works 'have the same sky'.
Whitley Notebooks, British Museum, Department of Prints and Drawings, vol.x, fol.1219

Raeburn produces copy of portrait of Edmund Spenser (*c.*1552–99), author of *The Faerie Queene*, for Earl Spencer.
Kenneth Garlick, 'Catalogue of the Pictures at Althorp', *Walpole Society*, vol.45 (1974–6), 1976, p.65

In late 1820 Haydon visits Edinburgh. Comments on passers-by in Princes Street: 'First you would see limping Sir Walter … then tripped Jeffrey … you next met Wilson … or Raeburn, as if all had agreed to make their appearance at once. It was a striking scene, – foreigners were impressed like myself.' He dines at Andrew Geddes's with Raeburn and George Thomson (1757–1851). Describes Raeburn as 'a glorious fellow, and more boisterous than any'.
Tom Taylor (ed.), *Life of Benjamin Robert Haydon, Historical Painter*, 3 vols, London, 1853, vol.1, p.383

1821

1 March
Letter from Raeburn to William Walker, engraver, concerning print after *John Hope, 4th Earl of Hopetoun (1765–1823)* (County Hall, Cupar, Fife). Requests return of picture for exhibition in Edinburgh. Raeburn sends, with letter, *Revd Archibald Allison (1757–1839)* (location unknown).
NLS, MS9819, fols.217–18

9 April
Raeburn draws up feu charter to son Henry.
SRO, RD5.284, fols.289–93

10 May
Raeburn draws up feu charter to Andrew Douglas.
SRO, RD5.217, fols.136–45

22 May
Further letter from Raeburn to William Walker concerning Hopetoun engraving, apologising for having interrupted work on print but portrait 'has now received its last touch' and is varnished.
NLS, MS9819, fols.219–20

1 June
Morning Herald's review of Royal Academy exhibition praises Raeburn's portrait of unidentified lady (no.21) saying it 'is nearly free from that disagreeable greenness which so commonly pervades the work of this artist'.
Whitley Notebooks, British Museum, Department of Prints and Drawings, vol.x, fol.1219

10 August
Letter from Sir Walter Scott to Raeburn saying that it is Lady Montagu's wish to have a portrait of her father Lord Douglas, by Raeburn's 'admirable pencil'. As Douglas never leaves Bothwell Castle Raeburn will have to visit. Portrait exhibited at Royal Academy in 1822.
Sotheby's, Autograph Letters and Historical Documents, 15 June 1926 (396)

22 August
Letter from Raeburn to John Flaxman (1755–1826), sculptor, then at Macgregor Hotel, Edinburgh, saying he will call on him today.
Henry E. Huntington Library and Gallery, San Marino, California, 145982–V.3, p.115

20 October
Letter from Raeburn to Robert Thomson Jr of Camphill, Glasgow, saying: 'I have received the £120 which you remitted through the Royal Bank in payment of your sisters' portraits, frames, etc'.
Whitley Notebooks, British Museum, Department of Prints and Drawings, vol.x, fol.1220

November
Raeburn elected honorary member of Academy of Arts of South Carolina. Cunningham transcribes letter (lost): 'Your character and talents have been our admiration for many years', and should the artist accept he will 'confer a favour' on Academy.
Cunningham, *op. cit.*, pp.278–9

6 December
Letter from Raeburn to Hamilton Douglas Boswell concerning the dispatch of copy for County Hall at Ayr of John Singleton Copley's *Hugh Montgomerie, 12th Earl of Eglinton (1726–96)*, 'by the desire of Mr Boswell of Auchinleck'. Price of copy, full-length, 200 guineas.
NLS, MS3836, fols.98–9

29 December
Raeburn draws up feu charter to son Henry concerning land in Stockbridge.
SRO, RD5.284, fols.289–97

1822

17 January
Raeburn paid 50 guineas by Major Buchanan of Cambusmore for copy of Blanchet's portrait of Young Pretender.
Captain Neil Baillie-Hamilton of Cambusmore Muniments

23 January
Raeburn draws up feu charter to Andrew Douglas.
SRO, RD5.251, fols.136–45

22 March
Sir Walter Scott had been asked to sit to Raeburn by 4th Duke of Buccleuch in letter of 15 February 1819 but on Duke's death nothing was done. Now Duke's brother, Lord Montagu, asks Scott if he will agree to commission being transferred to himself.
H. J. C. Grierson (ed.), *Letters of Sir Walter Scott*, vol.VII, London, 1934, pp.97–8

John Morrison approaches Sir Walter Scott on Raeburn's behalf saying: 'I will undertake … to prevail with him to sit'.
John Morrison, 'Random Reminiscences of Sir Walter Scott etc', *Tait's Edinburgh Magazine* n.s. 11 (January 1844), pp.15–19

19 April
Raeburn informed he can collect payment of 80 guineas for *Alexander Scrymgeour-Wedderburn, de jure 7th Earl of Dundee* (private collection, Scotland). Raeburn's receipt dated 24 April.
Private Muniments

20 April
Review by William Hazlitt of Edinburgh Institution's annual exhibition in *The Scotsman* criticising Raeburn's *Hugh William Williams (1773–1829)* (National Portrait Gallery, London).
William Hazlitt, *Works*, vol.18, pp.169–70

8 May
Letter from Sir Walter Scott to Raeburn concerning Raeburn's offer of gift of old building material. Scott says: 'I can but offer you in return the opportunity of making a good picture out of features which never [theless] have undergone a good deal of tear and wear but such a cook as you is independent of the quality of the materials'.
H. J. C. Grierson (ed.), *Letters of Sir Walter Scott*, vol.VII, London, 1934, p.157

24 May
Letter from Sir Walter Scott to Lord Montagu saying that he is ready to sit to Raeburn 'whenever your Lordship shall give him directions'.
Ibid., p.172

5 June
Minute of agreement drawn up between Raeburn and son Henry, and proprietors of Stockbridge Mills. See also 14 November 1822.
SRO, RD5.666, fols.338–43

3 July
James Dundas instructed by C. F. Stuart in undated docket to pay Raeburn 100 guineas for two portraits, *The Hon. Charles Francis Stuart (1780–1858)* and *Lieutenant General the Honourable William Stuart (1778–1837)* (locations unknown). Raeburn's receipt dated 3 July.
SNPG, Library, Greig Archive

5 August
Session of South Leith Parish Church mentions completion of *Revd Dr Robert Dickson (1758–1824)* (South Leith Parish Church, Leith).
South Leith Parish Church Muniments, Session Records

6 August
Letter from Sir Walter Scott to Raeburn saying he has appointment today with Colonel Shipman. Suggests he will 'perhaps bring him with me' to sitting.
NLS, MS9609, fols.28–9

22 August
Dinner held at Raeburn's home for some of the artists visiting Edinburgh in retinue of George IV. Guests include John Thomson of Duddingston, Alexander Nasmyth, J. M. W. Turner, Hugh William Williams and Charles Robert Cockerell.
C. R. Cockerell, *Diary*, Royal Institute of British Architects, Library, London, COC.9.3, vol.2, 1822

29 August
Transcript by Allan Cunningham of part of letter (now lost) from Robert Peel to Raeburn: 'it is his Majesty's intention to confer on you the honour of knighthood, as a mark of his approbation of your distinguished merit as a painter'.
Cunningham, *op. cit.*, p.282

Reply by Raeburn to letter of Robert Peel informing him that he is to be knighted.
British Library, Manuscript Collection, Peel Papers, 40350, fol.190

1 September
Letter from Raeburn to Henry Dundas, Viscount Melville, saying he believes Melville is responsible for his knighthood: 'it is very probable that Mr Peel never heard of my name till he came here'. Raeburn had unknowingly met Robert Peel, for he continues, 'it was not till afterwards that I learned that this Gentleman was the Secretary of State himself'.
NLS, Acc.2618, 1185, fols.213–14

Letter from Raeburn to John Maxwell MP (cat.no.63) concerning knighthood: 'I do believe that the honour which was conferred upon me by his Majesty ... is in a great measure owing either to you or to Lord Melville or perhaps to both'.
NLS, MS3553, fol.12

7 September
Reply from Raeburn to lost letter from Sir William Beechey (1753–1839) congratulating him on knighthood.
Greig, p.l

15 September
Letter from Sir David Wilkie to sister saying that he had been invited to dine with Raeburn and his family on day after Raeburn knighted, recording that 'Lady Raeburn would not allow herself to be called My Lady on any account'.
Andrews, pp.76–7

5 October
Public dinner in celebration of Raeburn's knighthood. Alexander Nasmyth presides and gives main toast.
Cunningham, *op. cit.*, p.282

10 October
Letter from Raeburn to John Morrison, at Annan, saying he has ordered painting materials for him from Middleton of St Martin's Lane 'the gent with whom I deal'.
Greig, p.xxxvii

14 November
Minute of agreement drawn up between Raeburn and son Henry, and proprietors of Stockbridge Mills, registered 12 November 1824. See also 5 June 1822.
SRO, RD5.278, fols.399–403

18 December
Letter from Sir Thomas Lawrence to Sir David Wilkie thanking him for conveying Raeburn's subscription to Canova Monument.
Royal Academy, Library, Lawrence Papers, Law.4.80

24 December
Letter from Raeburn to James Skene of Rubislaw, official of Institution for the Encouragement of the Fine Arts in Scotland. Raeburn has recently been approached by local artists who wish to establish new society. He outlines causes of failure of earlier exhibition societies. Artists stress they feel no antagonism towards Institution but offer four reasons why separate society should be formed: facilities of Institution not readily available to outsiders; every request to Institution 'necessarily implied a power of control'; trivial day-to-day affairs relating to artists' needs are not things 'the Institution would condescend to be troubled with'; and 'there was something degrading in the idea which had gone abroad that they [the artists] were unfit to conduct their own affairs'. Raeburn says: 'there were several of these arguments which I thought unanswerable'. Expresses his neutrality, affirming he has 'nothing to gain by the measure' and concluding: 'I am anxious to be concerned in nothing but what shall be considered just and reasonable'.
Greig, pp.xlviii–xlix

Efforts are made in 1825 by Alexander Nasmyth to obtain a copy of Raeburn's letter for the Associated Artists. On 8 November 1825 Skene writes to Nasmyth saying that he feels it necessary to obtain permission of Raeburn's son before supplying this. On 14 November 1825 artist's son agrees to lend letter for 'three or four days at furthest' with proviso 'that the letter shall on no account be published or printed'.
Royal Scottish Academy, Library, uncatalogued

In 1822 Society of Writers to His Majesty's Signet pays Raeburn 100 guineas for *Professor David Hume (1756–1838)* (Signet Library, Edinburgh).
Caw, 1908, p.78

Thomas Campbell's sculpted bust of Raeburn bears signature 'ROMA. 1822' (cat.no.66).

John Morrison records conversation between Raeburn and Sir Walter Scott when Scott was sitting for his portrait. Raeburn says: 'I am at present painting an admiral, and had some thought of asking my friend, the minister of Duddingston, to paint me a sea, but on second thoughts I am afraid Mr Thomson's sea might put my part of the picture to the blush.'
John Morrison, 'Random Reminiscences of Sir Walter Scott, of the Ettrick Shepherd and Sir Henry Raeburn no.II', *Tait's Edinburgh Magazine* n.s. 11 (January 1844), p.17

1823

24 January
Raeburn paid 39 guineas by Hector Macdonald Buchanan for copy of his father's portrait (location unknown).
SRO, GD47.719

12 March
Reply from Raeburn to letter from Sir David Wilkie, referring to Raeburn's criticisms of Jacques-Louis David (1748–1825). Raeburn says they 'might be transferred to the whole of the French school ... There is some chance of the artists here being associated either by themselves or perhaps in conjunction with the Institution.'
NLS, MS9835, fols.162–3

10 May
Letter from Robert Peel to Raeburn from Whitehall saying that 'out of respect for your character and professional merits' he has been appointed King's Limner.
British Library, Manuscript Collection, 40356, fol.76

14 May
Reply from Raeburn to Robert Peel thanking him for appointment as King's Limner.
British Library, Manuscript Collection, 40356, fol.106

19 May
Review in *Morning Chronicle* of Royal Academy exhibition mentions *Portrait of a Gentleman* (no.142): 'We think in general his works here are better than usual, he has almost abandoned the green and yellow skies'.
Whitley Notebooks, British Museum, Department of Prints and Drawings, vol.x, fol.1221

7 June
Raeburn meets Professor Andrew Duncan, who had previously sat to the artist (Royal College of Physicians, Edinburgh), and they play their last game of golf together. At meal afterwards Raeburn commissioned to paint portrait of Mr John Taylor of the Exchequer but Raeburn dies a month later.
Andrew Duncan, *Tribute of Regard to the Memory of Sir Henry Raeburn*, Edinburgh, 1824, p.19

18 June
Raeburn pays £9 3s 6d to unknown creditor as directed, 'By letter from Mr Spotswood'.
NLS, MS3553, fol.5

8 July
Letter from Andrew Wilson to Andrew Geddes, then in London, informing him of Raeburn's death 'this morning at four o'clock'. He continues: 'yesterday morning when I called the answer was Sir Hy. is just in life and no hope.' Raeburn had been attended by Dr Saunders.
University of Edinburgh, Library, La.iv.26, Geddes bundle, no.7

10 July
Letter from Sir Walter Scott to Raeburn family expressing regret that he cannot attend funeral.
NLS, MS2223, fol.47; Grierson, *op. cit.*, vol.VIII, p.35

13 July
Beginning of extensive correspondence (until spring 1824) concerning portrait of *Mrs Macdonald of Staffa* (Perth Museum and Art Gallery, Perth, Scotland). First letter suggests portrait 'finished' by John Syme. Painting was commissioned by Sir Henry Steuart of Allanton, whose portrait by Raeburn is unlocated. Much of the correspondence concerns payment and delivery.
SRO, GD214.743–214.745.7

14 July
At meeting of Royal Academy's General Assembly Sir Thomas Lawrence, president, announces 'the deaths of Joseph Nollekens Esq and of Sir Henry Raeburn Knt., Royal Academicians'.
Royal Academy, Library, GAIII, fol.390–1

July
John Morrison records that on Raeburn's return from trip to Fife he started work once more on *Mrs Anne Penelope Dennistoun* 'but was unable to proceed. He walked home, and, with considerable headache, went to bed, from whence he never arose'. Portrait 'finished' by another hand (Rory Campbell Gibson Gallery, Oban, Scotland).
John Morrison, 'Random Reminiscences of Sir Walter Scott, of the Ettrick Shepherd and Sir Henry Raeburn no.III', *Tait's Edinburgh Magazine*, n.s. 10 (December 1843), p.782

Unidentified newspaper publishes extended discussion of Raeburn. Anonymous writer says in his paintings 'the light has been contrived in his painting room with the greatest artifice, to fall so as to suit his particular taste'.
Victoria and Albert Museum, National Art Library, Press Cuttings from English Newspapers, vol.5, p.1384

7 August
Reply by Henry Raeburn Jr to letter from George Combe (1788–1858), educationalist and student of phrenology. Letter indicates that cast of Raeburn's head was taken after his death. Combe wishes to study cast but Raeburn's son says: 'I do confess I feel a most insurmountable repugnance to have it made public'.
NLS, MS7211, fols.25–6

7 September
Letter from Henry Raeburn Jr to Sir David Wilkie saying that he could 'furnish from thirty to forty full lengths' for proposed exhibition.
NLS, MS9835, fol.175

9 October
Letter from H. D. Dickie, accountant, to Philip Yorke, 3rd Earl of Hardwicke, requesting payment of 100 guineas for his portrait (Baltimore Museum of Art, Maryland). Dickie states that 'Mr Raeburn has put into my hands the books of the late Sir Henry Raeburn'.
British Library, Manuscript Collection, 35.653, fol.44

November

The European Magazine gives account of Raeburn, praising his modesty, his kindness to young painters and 'his inexhaustible store of anecdote', further stating that his 'practice was said to have been worth about £3,000 per annum'.

'Character of the late Sir Henry Raeburn, R.A.', *The European Magazine*, vol.84, pp.435–7

6 December

Letter from Henry Raeburn Jr to Sir Walter Scott saying that Hugh Murray has written Raeburn's obituary. Henry Raeburn Jr expresses his gratitude to Scott for making 'the very valuable corrections and additions'.

NLS, MS3897, fol.171

1824

15 March

Letter from Henry Raeburn Jr to William Carey, London, regarding his father's obituary. He expresses himself as 'very well pleased with it, except in so far as it respects my father's professional character'. Hopes Carey will remodel these sections.

Whitley Notebooks, British Museum, Department of Prints and Drawings, vol.x, fol.1330

28 April

Henry Raeburn Jr and Raeburn's step-son-in-law, Daniel Vere of Stonebyres, draw up discharge to Samuel Richard.

SRO, RD5.280, fols.451–61

9 June

'Inventory of the Personal Estate of Sir Henry Raeburn Knight deceased' presented to Edinburgh Commissary Court, listing 'Cash in the house £10, Balance in the hands of British Linen Company £16 16s 3d'; payment of £2,526 18s was made prior to this date for portraits left in studio, some of them 'finished' by John Syme (1795–1861); sum of £1,000 thought to be recoverable from works remaining in studio; feu duty arrears total £24 8s 9½d and Raeburn's 'household furniture, bed and table linen, plate, books, liquors etc' valued at £807 11s 2d, giving estate total value of £4,385 14s 2½d.

SRO, SC70.1.31, fols.246–7

30 June

Lord Hardwicke's portrait dispatched by Raeburn's lawyer with account for frame, case and carriage totalling £73 12s 6d.

Greig, p.li

1 July

In efforts to raise funds for father's estate, Henry Raeburn Jr brings action against Alexander Monro of Princes Street, Edinburgh, who had in about 1809 employed Raeburn 'to copy from a miniature … the portrait of a lady in whom the defender [Monro] had taken considerable interest when in India'. Claimed that Monro never paid for copy which accordingly remains in Raeburn family's hands. Monro replies that portrait was neither delivered nor account sent. Painting untraced.

SRO, CS232.R.17.5

17 July

Article on Raeburn published.

London Literary Gazette, p.619

Exhibition of fifty-eight named portraits held in Raeburn's former studio. Extra charge for evening admission 'when gallery is brightly lighted up with oil gas'.

Catalogue of Portraits by the Late Sir Henry Raeburn R.A., Edinburgh, 1824

Obituary of Sir Henry Raeburn published.

'Sir Henry Raeburn', *The Annual Biography for 1823*, London, 1824

Frequently Cited Sources

Andrew — Andrew, William Raeburn, *Life of Sir Henry Raeburn, R.A.*, London, 1886

Armstrong — Armstrong, Sir Walter, *Sir Henry Raeburn*, with an Introduction by R. A. M. Stevenson and a Biographical and Descriptive Catalogue by J. L. Caw, London, 1901

Brotchie — Brotchie, T. C. F., *Henry Raeburn 1756–1823*, London, 1924

Brown — Brown, John, *Portraits by Sir Henry Raeburn. Photographs by Thomas Annan, with Biographical Sketches*, Edinburgh, 1873

Caw, *Masterpieces* — Caw, James L., *Raeburn, Masterpieces in Colour*, London [1909]

Caw, 1908 — Caw, James L., *Scottish Painting Past and Present 1620-1908*, Edinburgh, 1908, reprinted 1975

Collins Baker — Collins Baker, C. H., *British Painting*, London, 1933

Cunningham — Cunningham, Allan, 'Raeburn', *Lives of the Most Eminent British Painters, Sculptors and Architects*, 6 vols, London, 1829–33

Cursiter — Cursiter, Stanley, *Scottish Art to the Close of the Nineteenth Century*, London, 1949

Dibdin — Dibdin, E. Rimbault, *Raeburn*, London, 1925

Duncan — Duncan, Andrew, *A Tribute of Regard to the Memory of Sir Henry Raeburn*, Edinburgh, 1824

Greig — Greig, James, *Sir Henry Raeburn, R.A. His Life and Works with a Catalogue of his Pictures*, London, 1911

Harris — Harris, Rose, *Raeburn*, 'The Masters' series, 46, London, 1966

Henley — Henley, William Ernest, *Sir Henry Raeburn, A Selection from his Portraits Reproduced in Photogravure by T. and R. Annan with Introduction and Notes*, Edinburgh, 1890

Irwin — Irwin, Francina, 'Early Raeburn Reconsidered', *Burlington Magazine*, vol. cxc, April, 1973

Irwin and Irwin — Irwin, David and Irwin, Francina, *Scottish Painters at Home and Abroad 1700-1900*, London, 1975

McKay — McKay, William D., *The Scottish School of Painting*, London, 1906

Mackie — Mackie, David, 'Raeburn, Life and Art', unpublished Ph.D. thesis, University of Edinburgh, 1994, 6 vols

Macmillan, 1986 — Macmillan, Duncan, *Painting in Scotland, The Golden Age*, Oxford, 1986

Macmillan, 1990 — Macmillan, Duncan, *Scottish Art 1460-1990*, Edinburgh, 1990

Obituary — [Murray, Hugh and Scott, Sir Walter], 'Sir Henry Raeburn', *The Annual Biography for 1823*, London, 1824

O'Donoghue — O'Donoghue, Freeman and Hake, Henry, M., *Catalogue of Engraved British Portraits Preserved in the Department of Prints and Drawings in the British Museum*, 6 vols., London, 1908–25

Pinnington — Pinnington, Edward, *Sir Henry Raeburn R.A.*, London, 1904

Sanderson — Sanderson, Kenneth, 'Engravings after Raeburn', *Print Collectors' Quarterly*, 1925

Chaloner Smith — Smith, John Chaloner, *British Mezzotinto Portraits; Being a Descriptive Catalogue of These Engravings from the Introduction of the Art to the early part of the present Century*, 6 vols, London, 1878–84

Stevenson — Stevenson, Robert Louis, *The Works of Robert Louis Stevenson*, ed. Edmund Gosse, vol. 2. *Virginibus Puerisque*, 'Some Portraits by Raeburn', London, 1906

Index of Sitters

References are to Catalogue Numbers

Allen, James 20

Allen, John Lee 20

Arniston, Robert Dundas, Lord 5

Birrell, Captain David 15

Blair, Revd Hugh 25

Bute, John Crichton Stuart,
   2nd Marquess of 60

Campbell of Park, Anne Campbell,
   Mrs Colin 36

Campbell of Barcaldine, Sir Duncan 41

Campbell, Marion Muirhead,
   Mrs James 40

Chantrey, Sir Francis Legatt 65

Clerk of Penicuik, Sir John 13

Clerk of Penicuik,
   Rosemary D'Acre, Lady 13

Clunes, Major William 42

Deuchar, David 1

Drummond, George 37

Drummond, Margaret 37

Dundas, Eliza Cumming, Mrs Francis 50

Dundas, General Francis 50

Eldin, John Clerk, Lord 54

Elphinston, Alexander 51

Elphinston, Jane 51

Elphinston, Maria 51

Ferguson, Professor Adam 26

Ferguson of Raith, Robert 11, 12

Ferguson, General Sir Ronald 12

Ferguson of Kilrie, William 18

Forbes of Callendar, William 31

Glendonwyn of Parton, William 14

Gow, Niel 27

Gregory, Isabella Macleod, Mrs James 30

Hamilton of Kames, Francis Harriet
   Wynne, Mrs James 45

Harvey, Major James Lee 62

Hunt of Pittencrieff, William 39

Hunter of Blackness, David 8

Hutton, James 10

Inglis, Rear-Admiral Charles 7

Inglis, Henry Raeburn 57

Inglis, Sir Patrick 32

Jameson, Margaret Haig, Mrs John 59

Johnstone, Betty 23

Johnstone of Alva, John 23

Lady in a Lace Cap 2

Lothian, William Kerr, 6th Marquis of 9

Lyon, Lieut-Colonel George 6

Macdonald, Donald 34

Macdonald, Ranald (Reginald) 34

Macdonald, Robert 34

Macdonell of Glengarry,
   Colonel Alastair Ranaldson 47

Mackenzie of Coul,
   Katherine Ramsay, Lady 24

MacNab, Francis 46

Maxwell of Pollok, Sir John 63

Moir, Patrick 3

Moncrieff, Margaret Macdonald,
   Mrs Robert Scott 52

Montgomery, Helen Graham, Lady 58

Newton, Charles Hay, Lord 44

Northampton, Spencer Compton,
   2nd Marquess of 61

Northampton, Margaret Maclean
   Clephane, Marchioness of 55

Playfair, Professor John 43

Raeburn, Ann Edgar, Lady 21

Raeburn, Sir Henry 16, 56, 66

Robertson, Dr William 22

Robison, Professor John 33

Roxburghe, Harriet Charlewood,
   Duchess of 48

Roxburghe, James Innes-Ker,
   5th Duke of 49

Scott, Sir Walter 38, 64

Sinclair of Ulbster, Sir George 29

Sinclair of Ulbster, Sir John 28

Spencer, George John Spencer,
   2nd Earl 4

Spens, Dr Nathaniel 17

Tytler, Ann Fraser, Mrs Alexander
   Fraser 35

Urquhart, Ann Pattison, Mrs William 53

Walker, Revd Robert 19

Wedderburn, Miss 23

Index of Lenders

References are to Catalogue Numbers

Althorp Park, Northampton 4

His Grace the Duke of Buccleuch and Queensberry ᴋᴛ 38

Cambridge, The Syndics of the Fitzwilliam Museum 14

Chapel Hill ɴᴄ, University of North Carolina at Chapel Hill 15

Cincinnati, Cincinnati Art Museum 51

Dublin, National Gallery of Ireland 13

Mrs Althea Dundas-Bekker 5, 50

Edinburgh, Kirk of the Canongate 25

Edinburgh, National Gallery of Scotland 1, 2, 6, 8, 19, 28, 42, 45, 47, 52, 56

Edinburgh, Scottish National Portrait Gallery 7, 10, 16, 27, 54, 64, 65, 66

Edinburgh, University of Edinburgh 22, 26, 33

English Heritage, the Iveagh Bequest, Kenwood 29

Captain W. F. E. Forbes (on loan to the Scottish National Portrait Gallery) 31

Fyvie Castle, the Forbes-Leith Collection, National Trust for Scotland 30

Glasgow, Art Gallery and Museum, Kelvingrove 36, 53

Irish Distillers Group plc 59

London, National Portrait Gallery 43

London, The Royal Academy of Arts 57

The Most Honourable the Marquis of Lothian 9

Minneapolis, The Minneapolis Institute of Arts 32

James Montgomery Esq 58

The Most Honourable the Marquess of Northampton 55, 61

New York, The Brooklyn Museum of Art 35

New York, The Metropolitan Museum of Art 37

Paris, Musée du Louvre, Département des Peintures 62

Queen's Bodyguard for Scotland (Royal Company of Archers) 17

Professor Philip Rieff 24

The Right Honourable the Earl of Rosebery 44

His Grace the Duke of Roxburghe 48, 49

San Francisco, Fine Arts Museums of San Francisco 41

R. Patrick Thomas Esq 40

United Distillers 46

Upton House, the Bearsted Collection, The National Trust 34

Washington ᴅᴄ, National Gallery of Art 23

Lenders who prefer to remain anonymous
3, 11, 12, 18, 20, 21, 39, 60, 63